THE AGE OF THE
Common Millionaire

P9-DTR-808

Recent Books by Robert Heller

THE SUPERMARKETERS
THE SUPERMANAGERS
THE POCKET MANAGER
THE NAKED MANAGER

THE AGE OF THE
Common
Millionaire
ROBERT HELLER

T·T

TRUMAN TALLEY BOOKS
E. P. DUTTON
NEW YORK

Copyright © 1988 by Heller Arts Ltd.
All rights reserved. Printed in the U.S.A.

No part of this publication may be reproduced or transmitted in any form or by
any means, electronic or mechanical, including photocopy, recording, or any
information storage and retrieval system now known or to be invented, without
permission in writing from the publisher, except by a reviewer who wishes to quote
brief passages in connection with a review written for inclusion in a magazine,
newspaper, or broadcast.

Published in the United States by Truman Talley Books • E. P. Dutton,
a division of NAL Penguin Inc.,
2 Park Avenue, New York, N.Y. 10016.

Published simultaneously in Canada by
Fitzhenry and Whiteside, Limited, Toronto.

Library of Congress Cataloging-in-Publication Data
Heller, Robert, 1932–
The age of the common millionaire.

"Truman Talley Books."
Includes index.
1. Millionaires. I. Title.
HC79.W4H45   1987   305.5′234   87-19973
ISBN 0-525-24588-X

DESIGNED BY EARL TIDWELL

1 3 5 7 9 10 8 6 4 2

First Edition

Portions of this book appeared in slightly different form in *The Common Millionaire*
(1974) by Robert Heller.

Grateful acknowledgment is made for permission to reprint excerpts from "Men"
in *The Portable Dorothy Parker.* Copyright 1926, renewed © 1954 by Dorothy
Parker. Reprinted by permission of Viking Penguin Inc.

To my children

CONTENTS

CONTENTS

Book III: THE CORPORATE FORTUNE HUNTERS

Book IV: THE PAPER MILLIONAIRES

Book V: THE MONEY MAGICIANS

Book VI: FORTUNE STILL FAVORS THE RICH

THE AGE OF THE
Common
Millionaire

Introduction
THE RICH
ARE
DIFFERENT

Making a million is easier than it used to be; and it never was very hard—which is why the trick has been managed down the ages by so many entrants extracted from the ranks of the untalented, the uninspired, and the forgettable. In this age, moreover, thanks to the workings of inflation, the points total for winning players, while seemingly the same, is far lower. It's as if, in the game of financial football, the target for a successful field goal had been stretched to the full width of the stadium so wide that even wholesale destruction of equity values in the Blackest October of 1987 merely modified the score.

To match a million in the dollars of 1914, when a world war ended the golden age of plutocracy, would require $11 million today. A million dollars in 1928, before a cataclysmic depression robbed some silver age plutocrats of their riches, is the equivalent nowadays of $6.5 million. A million dollars in 1948, when the rebuilders of the postwar economy began to reap their rewards (and the economic winners of the war to spend theirs), equaled $2.2 million in the currency of the early

1

1970s—a time stop that was already deep in a new era: the Age of the Common Millionaire.

The millionaire had become common in numbers, common in the source of wealth, common (in the usage of bygone snobberies) in social origin, common in the continued narrowing of the gap between his fortune and that of the normally affluent middle class. By 1986, after the worst general inflation in the history of the West, the million bucks of 1973 required, to match its purchasing power, no less than $2.5 million. The oil price explosion of the earlier year doubly expanded the supply of new millionaires: first, it accomplished the greatest transfer of wealth the world will ever see over so concentrated a period; and, second, even while the fat cats were gorging themselves on the flow of cream from West to East and back again, it debased the million, through general inflation, more precipitately still.

To look at the inflationary process the other way around, a 1986 million in dollars represents only $400,000 in 1973 money, $180,000 in 1948, and a little nest egg of $90,000 in 1914. If the score is in dollars, moreover, that exaggerates the degree of wealth in terms of international buying power. The violent fluctuations of exchange rates since President Nixon opened Pandora's box by freeing the dollar from gold have wreaked further havoc with the value of the magic million. The clearest measure is gold. For much of the postwar period, $1 million bought you 31,250 ounces; at Christmas 1986, the sum purchased a mere 2,538 ounces—so low had the once-mighty dollar fallen.

As inflation has belittled the score, so the scoring has become easier. The apparent, or monetary, value of assets has steadily risen, so that a man buying any treasure, from a cider press to a car dealership, has an overwhelming chance of reselling at a profit, which is the basic activity of every Croesus who ever cashed a check. For one example among the millions: in 1986, a Brancusi *Muse* that had originally cost the Bulova Watch family $7,000 was sold for $2 million; the family had sold back in 1981 for $800,000. Art, houses, farms, horses, business sidelines, stocks, gold, real estate, collectibles, whatever the wealthy have turned their money into has with little effort turned itself into still more wealth in the era of inflation.

The rackets of the rich are as various as their assets. They cover a range of real-life fairy tales that even Scheherazade, given a million and one nights, could not exhaust. Ballpoint pens, ball bearings, demolition, construction, shipbuilding, shipowning, brokeraging, banking, farming, not farming, molybdenum, milling, holes in the ground, filling holes in the ground, stealing, borrowing, lending, foreclosing, carpets, convertibles, soup, soup cans, pictures of soup cans, salad oil, nonexistent salad oil, betting, taking bets, extortion, exemption, junk bonds, junk food, software, hardware—the catalogue rolls on endlessly and with as much variation as the names and backgrounds of the blessed.

It's not exactly a roll of honor; nearer, at times, to a roll of dishonor, since, in a significant bevy of cases, the basic wealth-creating activity has been augmented, if not by fraud, by tricks, devices, stratagems—all variants of the conjurer's game of doing it with mirrors. The basic activity, however, never changes. The millionaire earns his title by selling, or being able to sell, some property, some product, some service, some idea for more than cost. The wider the gulf between cost and realized value, the more rapidly the player gets to his ultimate reward. There are two invariable extremes of technique. The player can choose between selling to a myriad of customers at low profits (10 million customers at a dime apiece) or to a select clientele at high profits (ten suckers at $100,000 a throw). But in the golden and silver ages, the resultant wealth was measured certifiably in cash, negotiable gilt-edge securities, and real property, all of which took time to accumulate.

That measure was only natural at a time of low or no taxes, of minimal inheritance tax, and of a political dispensation that enshrined inequality. The truly kingly fortunes all stem from this golden age: the Rockefellers (at least $6 billion in 1986), the du Ponts (some 1,700 of them, worth over $7.5 billion in the mid-1960s, were supposed to benefit from $24 billion before the 1987 crash), the Mellons (once supposedly neck and neck with the Rockies, thanks to heavy holdings in the Mellon National Bank, Gulf Oil, Alcoa, and so on, but with a worth now listed as less than half the Rockefeller total).

As the changing ratio of Mellon money to Rockefeller riches indicates, nobody truly knows the actual wealth of the super-rich, probably not even the latter or their advisers. The Rothschilds weighed in collectively at $100 billion long ago, but that can't have been more than a reasonably educated guess. Not only is the full extent of their holdings unknown but the value of individual items is uncertain. What price do you put on Château Lafite or Château Mouton Rothschild, each owned by a different member of the great banking family? At these exalted levels, the actual numbers quoted are merely another way of saying that the owners are very, very rich.

Nor have any calculations been made of the proportion of the world's wealth that is held by the 300 richest families. Their share is plainly that of a particularly greedy lion. Including the three imperial fortunes listed above, *Forbes* counted no less than thirty-three billionaires or billionaire families in 1986. The combined total of these outstanding American nest eggs handsomely exceeded $50 billion, or

3

approximately the end-1985 book value of the all-embracing IBM; and there is, of course, that definite likelihood that these mighty aggregations, which are only the chapter headings, so to speak, in the golden book of wealth, are under-, not overestimated. In most cases, if the concept of people's wealth is widened to include all assets which they can enjoy exclusively, all business interests which they can influence while holding only a proportion (or none) of the shares, they emerge as richer by far than even an expert optimist can guess.

The tip-of-the-iceberg argument probably applies even more strongly outside the United States, where privacy is guarded by the rich as closely as any of their treasures. The Reichmanns of Canada, the Thyssens of Germany, the Matsushitas of Japan, the Agnellis of Italy, the Paos of Hong Kong—these are among the famed families whose names are attached to financial empires at least the equal of the prime American fortunes. The Rockefellers, for example, are no longer New York City's largest commercial landlords. That palm has passed to the three Reichmann brothers of Canada, whose total worth, estimated as greater than that of the ten richest Americans put together, in 1987 was surpassed only by the yen-rich Japanese with their vastly inflated property holdings in Tokyo.

The 50 million square feet of Reichmann property rubs in a general monetary truth. Land probably constitutes or lies behind and beneath many of the greatest fortunes. This remains true even in Britain, whose aristocrats, because of their touching faith in primogeniture and distrust of newfangled financial devices, often frittered away their wealth in estate taxes. The Duke of Westminster, who died in 1953, bequeathed a tax liability of between £15 million and £20 million. Thanks to the efficiency of his advisers, the bill could be met without touching 270 priceless acres in the little villages of Belgravia and Mayfair.

Of the nine richest Britons identified by the London *Times* in the mid-1980s, four derived their fortunes primarily from real estate: including the latest of the well-advised Westminster line; there was another duke (Buccleuch); and, at the top of the tree in every sense, sat the treble-billionaire Queen Elizabeth II. Her Majesty's truly regal wealth, no less than that of the Rothschilds, Rockefellers, and du Ponts, is evidence of the staying and multiplying power of aristocratic fortune in the Age of the Common Millionaire.

Yet this sumptuous survival can be misleading. The predominance of imperial old-line families led one careful researcher, Ferdinand Lundberg, to conclude that "there is less and less room for new millionaires." But an old-new billionaire contradicted him. "Large fortunes will be made," wrote John Paul Getty, "in the next two decades by men who are beginners today." As usual in money matters, the thinker was wrong, the Midas was right.

The three richest people found by *Forbes* in 1985 were all of little or no financial account in 1960. Sam Walton's Wal-Mart discount store chain only became public in 1970; fifteen years later its near-1,000 stores were valued at over $11 billion, of which the sixty-seven-year-old founder controlled 39 percent—or $4.5 billion. H. Ross Perot quit IBM to found Electronic Data Systems in 1962 with $1,500; already super-rich in 1970, on paper, before the value of his stock fell by a billion dollars, Perot became even richer in real coin when General Motors first bought him out, for $1.5 billion, and then kicked him out, with a 1986 cash payoff that exceeded $700 million.

The tale of David Packard and his partner, William Hewlett, is another fable of startling progress from a tiny start: in this case, the time-honored garage workshop. By 1986 Packard's share of Hewlett-Packard was worth a couple of billion dollars. In both Packard's and Perot's cases, you could argue that their contributions to business efficiency and American electronics have materially improved the national well-being. It's harder to demonstrate, however, that the gross domestic product or the general national welfare would have been affected one whit if Sam Walton and his brother had never opened a store outside Rogers, Arkansas.

Yet consider this proposition: even among America's greediest boards of directors, relatively few men earn million-dollar salaries. To match Walton's wealth in the fall of 1985, not allowing for taxes, they would have to labor for 2,800 years, or some seventy working life-times—and that takes no account of the dividend income flowing to the Walton family. If they had sold out, using the late 1985 market value as a yardstick, the proceeds would easily have yielded a million-dollar income every working day—before the $1.7 billion leap in Walton wealth in 1986 and still true after its $300 million October 1987 crash.

That is one spectacular American example of the democratization of wealth. The aristo-plutocrats may stay on top of some lofty, reserved Olympus, but on the lower slopes (and now hardly any further down) a new and different breed has been climbing fast, propelled in part by the natural force of rising mass. The Common Millionaire creates himself by skimming the cream off the general pool of wealth. The deeper and wider the pool, the smaller the amount of skimming required to fill the same size money pot.

Thanks to the sheer abundance of natural and human resources, aided by stupendously lax political control, the United States has always spawned the bulk of the world's millionaires, from the gold and silver kings to the stock-option fat cats of today. From 1914 onward the gross national product (GNP) of the United States—the annual stream of real wealth—has multiplied prodigiously. Back in 1914, the sum of $100 million was 0.4 percent of the GNP; in 1972, measured in 1914 dollars, it was only 0.04 percent; today, tinier still.

Despite all the supposed efforts of politicians to curb and spread the wealth, the share of property and income held by the few has, according to several studies, remained more or less constant. Possibly there is some natural law, like that of water finding its own level, that constantly forces a given ratio of the national income into the hands of those who already have more than their per capita share or are burning to do so.

But the simple, mathematical growth of the pool of wealth is only the start of the story. Equally important has been the discovery of the modern philosopher's stone, the authentic way of creating thick wealth out of thin air. An heir to many millions and creator of a fair few himself once observed that in talking about modern fortunes, people "confused wealth and money." He was, it turned out, distinguishing between the wealths of the mint and of the mind, but his remark holds the key to the Age of the Common Millionaire. For the Common Millionaire has succeeded in divorcing real wealth—property, the creation of new resources—from money.

In the first Rockefeller's day, to create money you had to create an equivalent amount of assets. True, Wall Street in those days had no hesitation about multiplying such real objects by unreal accretions of paper, a pastime known agriculturally as "watering the stock." J. Pierpont Morgan in 1901 poured forth "securities" (an interesting euphemism in the circumstances) to a face value of over $1 billion in launching U.S. Steel on a gullible world. On the official count he printed $726.8 million more in paper than the company, in visible material form, was worth. In 1929 and by similar zealous work at the printing press, Goldman Sachs issued $250 million in securities in a mere month. Even the most ambitious and hot-handed financier in the steaming Manhattan markets that boiled over in the terrible days of October 1987 would have been quite impressed by this torrent of paper—but only quite.

Even in 1929 currency, $250 million looks positively modest compared to $150 billion, this being the total value of the junk bonds extant in November 1986, the awful month in which Ivan Boesky and the insider trading scandal broke. Boesky was among the leading artists in financial *junk*: pieces of paper that are officially rated as "less than investment grade." In other words, their worth lies only in the high

6

interest rates attached. If that interest flow ceases, so does the value—and $3 billion of junk went bad in the good times of 1986.

The day of the old pirate, like Morgan, has gone; come is the time of the new piranha. The sharp-toothed discovery of operators like Boesky or Ted Turner (whose Turner Broadcasting alone issued a stunning $1.4 billion of junk bonds to buy MGM) is that the wealth represented by real assets could be gained in exchange for no assets at all. If the deal succeeded, the purchased assets could then be aggrandized by the paper multiplier, with an ease and a perfect legality that makes Boesky's machinations inexplicable as well as inexcusable.

The Age of the Common Millionaire has made possible the ceaseless repetition of a trick that would have thrilled J. P. Morgan himself. The open sesame to Aladdin's cave is the "discounting of growth." That is, the Common Millionaire sells not what he owns, but what (God and the stock market willing) he *will* own one day. The cardinal invention of capitalism, the joint stock company, had become an engine for the creation of endless wealth, which might, in extreme cases, be unsupported by any concrete foundation.

A man can sell, to an overjoyed public, a fraction of his shares for a price that, on a traditional basis of valuation, would purchase the entire caboose. He can retain total control of the company through paper, valued at several times the cash fortune now safely in his pocket, which can be used as currency to purchase more assets, to which a similar multiplier can be applied, and so on, not quite ad infinitum.

In actuality, such operations reverse the historic process of capitalism. Instead of the equity holder taking all the risk, and consequently all the rewards, he now partly offloads his risk for the highest price the market will bear and takes his reward in advance. Bear traps aplenty lie along such paths. But the essential truth remains unchanged. The market capitalization of major companies has risen to such unthinkably large sums that possession of a tenth of a tenth of the stock equals a monumental fortune, even by Morgan standards. Bill Hewlett, for example, owned only 9 percent of Hewlett-Packard stock at the end of 1985; that molehill was worth a mountainous $780 million. A mere 6 percent of CBS accounted for most of William Paley's $290-million pile at the same date. Armand Hammer's minuscule share in Occidental Petroleum, still controlled by his iron eighty-seven-year-old hand in 1987, made him a millionaire thirty-seven times over.

A case much lower down the corporate scale is more typical than those of the three corporate veterans above. Sy Syms, owner of fourteen discount stores selling designer clothing, took Syms Corp. public in 1984; after trousering the cash from that sale, Syms ended up worth

$200 million or more—and still held 80.2 percent of the company. His fortune, though, rested largely on the market price of the stock, on how much investors were prepared to pay for the present earnings and anticipated capital gains on shares whose availability was by definition limited to 19.8 percent of the supply.

Market capitalization is always an entirely hypothetical figure obtained by multiplying the number of shares in issue, only a small proportion of which are generally on the loose (even in the case of a General Motors), by the market price of the day. That would inevitably drop to calamitous effect if even a quarter of the shares were offered, let alone 80.2 percent. This explains how an entrepreneur such as Philip Hwang, once a half billionaire thanks to making more VDUs (visual display units) than anybody except IBM, can see his fortune dwindle in a couple of years, first to $150 million and then to $60 million as the stock's upward spiral goes into reverse.

At that, $60 million is well clear of penury. What's true of less successful players such as Hwang is a fortiori true of their betters. The rich sought to achieve via the stock market the condition that their predecessors contrived by paying no tax: the combination of massive real assets with maximum personal liquidity. To put it crudely, you couldn't take your cash out in income, because the government grabbed it; so you took the booty in stock, which the government touched either lightly or not at all. It's a sweet paradox. The efforts of governments to restore equality by soaking the rich have led directly to the development of methods that have created far more rich; and any efforts to inundate these with taxes would probably make still more millionaires.

And the rich today *are* different. Not just because (as Hemingway correctly argued against Scott Fitzgerald) they have more money, but because they are a different breed of furry cat. The millionaires and billionaires of the golden age were would-be princes. Deprived by fate of royal stature, they outspent those who had it. In the mid-1960s it was noted with astonishment that one spectacularly successful Texas oilman, Algur H. Meadows, with $55 million to his name, had shelled out only $500,000 on his dream house, less than the first Rockefeller, most parsimonious of all the billionaires, spent in a single year on the upkeep of one family estate, his $30-million, 7,000-acre Tarrytown pad.

The Common Millionaire lives in the same way as the good bourgeois citizen, only more so—and even the Common Billionaire may do much the same. J. P. Getty bought his splendid mansion, Sutton Place, from the third Duke of Sutherland for a supposed £500,000. A Vanderbilt would have regarded that kind of money as a decorator's bill (Cornelius spent $5 million on a Newport cottage that he used for only ten weeks a year). Almost the only lavish similarity among the ultra-rich of the golden and silver ages is the passion for paying great prices for art; even then, demand for a greatly diminished supply of Old Masters waned so markedly that it took over a generation before the Duveen prices charged to the earlier merchant princes were seen again—and that was in depreciated money. *The Mall in St. James's Park* by Gainsborough cost Frick $300,000; the same artist's wonderful *Mr. and Mrs. Andrews,* at 1973 exchange rates, fetched only $357,000.

Mostly, today's new millionaires come from the amorphous mass of the middle classes, from upper to lower, and bear the stamp of their origin. There are titled exceptions, but they, too, start to amass their millions in a down-to-earth or déclassé way. Baron Marcel Bich, for example, is a French aristo whose nine-figure fortune was accumulated on the humble base of the disposable ballpoint pen and magnified by the equally lowly disposable razor. Bich's pens were launched after the war with capital of $1,000. The margins on the products totted up to infinitesimal sums, such as .0066666 cents per Bic. Multiply that by a billion and a half units, however, and you get $10 million, which is a perfect example of the multitudinous-small-profit approach and a perfect explanation of the richness of Bich.

The foresight of the rich is their prime justification. Although nearly all owners of big, middling, and small money owe much of it to multiplication by mirrors, many derived their riches originally from some flash of true inspiration, the equivalent in the material world of Nijinsky's leap, Picasso's Cubism, Proust's memory: Land's instant camera, Getty's Kuwait oil, even Bich's ballpoints, Perot's computer services, and Turner's cable news represent breakthroughs from which millions of people have had real benefit and from which, therefore, millions in currency have naturally flowed.

The breakthrough, the searing stroke of genius, lies in spotting a demand, latent or blatant, and simultaneously noting how that demand can be satisfied at the necessary premium over the cost of supply. Characters such as David Sarnoff, the genius of RCA, are in this sense great philosophers and artists; and very few artists or thinkers in other spheres can boast a dramatic series of achievements to excel Sarnoff's triple.

In 1916, almost alone in his faith, Sarnoff wrote, "I have in mind a plan of development which would make radio a household utility"; from 1922 to 1925, sales of his "radio music boxes" came to $83 million. In 1923 he wrote, "I believe that television . . . will come to pass in due course," a belief that cost him $50 million before a payoff of incalculable size. He then pumped another $130 million into his final bonanza, color TV. Although Sarnoff laid one large egg—correctly seeing that computers would boom, but incorrectly assessing RCA's chances in this unfamiliar, booby-trapped market—verily he earned his reward.

Whether the return is proportionate to the contribution is another matter. In the overpowering majority of cases, there can't be any argument. The balance between capital and income has been tilted grossly in favor of capital, and the capital gains of the cut-price variety of capitalist often bear only the slightest relation to the value of their work to the society that cost sets them.

In the Age of the Common Millionaire, the possession of 50 million as opposed to 500 of them has a primarily social connotation. The billionaire is an uncrowned monarch; the multimillionaire is a global potentate; even the Common Millionaire is a welcome, highly placed courtier (like Bebe Rebozo at the court of Richard Nixon or the cronies of Ronald Reagan), and a potential folk hero. At each of these three levels, there is a common denominator: the affirmation by the rich that money means nothing to them. They are telling the truth and lying in their Sulka socks at one and the same time, because the possession of money bestows the ineffable power to make more money still; and power, for most of the rich, is the name of their game.

All wealth equates with power, which has as many forms as there are Rolls-Royces. To Andrew Carnegie, once he was through with giving steel rivals and steelworkers hell, wealth equated with the power to establish free public libraries; to George Armstrong, a Southern millionaire, wealth meant the ability to offer a staggering sum to a small military college in Mississippi if, in its curriculum, it stressed the racial superiority of the white man (the college, to its undying credit, refused); to a legion of rich men, it means the power, free of any fear of the sack, boot, or ax, to dominate the corporations they have created. For instance, Antony Jay, the management writer, once asked a tycoon wherein lay his own contribution, given all the brilliant and forceful men in his employ. "I'll tell you," said the Croesus. "I own sixty-seven and a half percent."

But for the mass of millionaires, the loot is a by-product of achieving some other end, although the objective and its results get mysteriously intertwined. That doesn't matter; the clue is still that the budding Walton or Perot has to decide what he wants. This is the first step along the yellow-brick road, and most businessmen—9,999 out of 10,000— never get even that far. But lack of focused intention, of truly moving motivation, is only part of the story. While nearly everybody vaguely "wants" a million, few are prepared to work for it. Lack of knack is equally crippling. Tall Texan stories abound of the brilliant men who drilled on land known to be stiff with oil, but found nothing but dry holes.

There are hundreds of millionaires who have only one gift—making money. In this they resemble the master chess player who is good at nothing else. Making money resembles chess in other ways, not least in its cozy relationship with mathematics, still more in its abundance of traps, ploys, gambits, stratagems, variations, even its recognized offensive and defensive openings. As in chess, the moneymaker gains more through his opponent's mistakes than through his own immaculate brilliance; and for every winner there must be at least one loser.

The First Law of Millions states that "every millionaire creates his wealth at somebody else's expense," and it is this law that the new techniques for divorcing capital from income and taxes have exploited to such wondrous effect. The sale of shares to the public to guard against estate taxes or whatever has almost inadvertently created a new dimension of wealth: it has enlarged the number of those whose finances can be tapped by the resourceful few.

As long ago as 1968, the Internal Revenue Service calculated that the total of U.S. millionaires, having risen by 150 percent in a decade, had passed 100,000. More recently, the Federal Reserve Board came up with a much larger figure for households with a net worth in seven figures: 1.3 million. That fits well with the observation of one downy investment banker, sitting on nest eggs belonging to some of the choicest U.S. clients, that, for all his experience, he was constantly amazed by the number of unknown, substantial private fortunes—lump sums that lie forever protected in the giant investment portfolios of the banks. The bankers of Switzerland, long among the champions in this arena, look after $125 billion in so-called fiduciary accounts. Thus the great lumps lie, silently sleeping and fructifying in their sleep, behind the anonymous nameplates in which banks rejoice.

Trusts and nominee (or dummy) companies are two of the more obvious ways in which the wealthy can squirrel their wealth away from view (and sometimes from their nearest and dearest). There are doubtless banks in the United States still storing cash—reportedly a million—belonging to the bank-hating W. C. Fields, under names like Mahata Kane Jeeves and Otis Criblecoblis. Fields had hundreds of bankbooks and once claimed to have $50,000 in wartime Germany "in case that little bastard wins." For the same reason, many of the war rich put their money in Switzerland; and here, too, some of the famous numbered accounts doubtless contain wealth whose identification has passed into the grave.

Many of these rich, old or *nouveau*, have no more knowledge of three-dimensional monetary chess than the novice player, although the moves may be played for them brilliantly by some well-rewarded functionary. The novice, however, must make the moves himself, and knowledge of them is not enough to turn the graduate into a grand master. He needs, like a supreme player of real chess, an extra and indefinable quality that, in making money, manifests itself in different forms: as luck, as timing, as genius, as ruthlessness, as insight, as opportunism, as stubbornness.

Some of the qualities deployed are admirable, others deplorable. But is this, the issue of personal right or wrong, the only moral question raised? In the bad old days of the robber barons, there could be no doubt. The barons robbed their fellow citizens and in doing so accumulated political, economic, and social power, which they systematically and cynically abused. Gustavus Myers concluded his superb *History of the Great American Fortunes* in suitably admonitory fashion: "And so, having a roster of more multi-millionaires in reserve, we call a halt to this edifying history, the facts in which impart their own moral and conclusion."

The nature of that conclusion can be drawn from some of Myers's headings: "Great Thefts Compromised," "Law Brushed Aside," "20½ Per Cent Profit—and Wage Reductions." The Myers roster not only featured malefactors of great wealth, he could find precious little evidence of great wealth without great malefaction. Apologias for the lives of his heroes have indeed been hard to come by since their misdeeds were first published in 1907—about the only arguments ever raised in the barons' favor are that all economic takeoff must rest on mass exploitation (false), and that the malefactors gave away much of their ill-gotten gains (true, but irrelevant).

Today, even without such evidence as the Boesky crimes, nobody doubts that wrongdoing and wealth sometimes go hand in hand. But this is no longer the burning issue that possessed Myers and the muckrakers. Nor are thinkers bothered by the socioeconomic-political implications of huge riches. True, the $125 billion in those Swiss "fiduciary accounts" is greater (by $25 billion) than Switzerland's gross national product a year or so back, and so is the $134 billion estimated net worth of the Forbes 400 in 1985. But does the wide spread of those holdings mean that the issue of their aggregate size is no longer important?

In *The American Economic Republic* (1963) Adolf A. Berle decided that property had changed out of all possibility of recognition by Gustavus Myers. Berle had been a close adviser to President Roosevelt in the first hundred reforming days that so shocked the contemporary men of great property. Thirty years later, property, opined Berle, no longer counted: "Property is active and productive—but is so because it is organized and administered, not because it is 'owned.' It sets up passive, exchangeable wealth, thanks to surrender by the wealth holder of owner's power, and to state-fostered mechanisms giving liquidity to this wealth."

Berle went on to ask, "What quality of it can fairly be called private?" It was meant to be a comforting question: not that much comfort is apparently needed by Americans who, in five of the past seven presidential elections, have voted millionaires into the White House. But think more carefully about the implications of Berle's question and it clearly goes to the heart of the Age of the Common Millionaire. This book will seek its answer. It is an easier answer to find in an America softened by the great sell-off that may have burst not only the stock market bubble but the public's too adulatory acceptance of the private pursuit of superwealth and its abuses.

I wrote with anxiety in *The New Naked Manager* about the "folderols and hot flushes of greed" that were disfiguring the America of 1986 and noted that "history is, unfortunately, repeating itself. The point shouldn't need stressing that the excesses of the 1960s were followed by, or led into, the period of American management's most abysmal postwar performance, as technology and market leadership in industry after industry passed to other companies, mostly Japanese ones—events that in 1960 nobody would have thought remotely conceivable."

Nor would anybody then have expected the further humbling of America that took place as, in the wake of the Blackest October, the reality came home: that the mighty United States is subject to the same financial disciplines as any overspending Third World client state. In the aftermath of the '87 crash, stronger disciplines were being imposed both on Washington and on the markets, and the manipulators, in an effort to ensure that the excesses and folderols of the 1980s would not, like those of twenty years before, be repeated. One message of this book, though, is unavoidable. They will.

Book I

THE NEW ARTS
OF
INHERITANCE

1

NOTHING LICKS
A
SILVER SPOON

Should you leave it all to the children? So ran the headline of a 1986 article in *Fortune* that surveyed the intentions of thirty multimillionaires in this respect. Six planned on only minimal bequests to their progeny. Against this fifth of the sample, "almost half" were going to benefit charities as much as children. This left about a third who intended to act as old-money millionaires did—and do, according to one Wall Street lawyer quoted. Eleven out of a dozen old-money clients with $20 million or more kept the money where they reckoned it belonged—at home.

That doesn't necessarily keep the money. As the magazine pointed out, you won't find that many people named Dodge, Reynolds, or Vanderbilt in the big chips today. Imitate one Minnesota family, with sixty-three idle heirs in the fourth generation, and you can easily run a fortune into the sands. So the reluctance of the modern super-rich to enrich their children sounds laudable enough (although receiving only half of a $100-million will is not being cast friendless into the world).

Yet the reticence runs counter to an undeniable fact: inheritance is the most common route to riches.

Among the Forbes 400 of 1985, all with fortunes of at least $150 million, 181 were beneficiaries who had "mostly or entirely" inherited their wealth. The ranks of the heirs outnumbered the 165 who enjoyed "no significant inheritance"; and the latter included a goodly number who, if they inherited nothing of immediate material value from their forefathers, did step into family businesses, however feeble. It follows from the sheer increase in numbers of millionaires that the number of rich inheritors must greatly increase; if that *Fortune* rule of only 20 percent disinheritance is followed, four-fifths of the 1.3 million million-dollar wills means a great many wealthy heirs.

Yet inherited wealth, like all fortunes, comes in different shapes as well as sizes. The styles represented by the late lone eagle Howard Hughes and the flock of du Ponts are as different in their ways as Greta Garbo and the Marx Brothers were in theirs. In Europe, more than in the United States, the governing principle is plainly dynastic: financial powers cluster in tidy family groups—Peugeot and Michelin in France, Agnelli and Pirelli in Italy, Thyssen and (until their recent sell-off) Flick in Germany, Cayzer and Vestey in Britain, Rothschilds all over Europe, and scores of financially incestuous Japanese.

There are at least as many Rothschilds as there are du Ponts, many of them doubly related—twenty-nine of fifty-eight weddings of the founding fathers' descendants united first cousins, which at least kept the money in the family. But the Rothschilds have managed their interests in an active sense long abandoned by the du Ponts. Like the latter, over a hundred of the Forbes heirs, a quarter of the entire 400, are passive inheritors. Theirs has been the simplest path to a million: gratefully receiving it. There's a powerful reason why, even in this age of people's capitalism, most millionaires achieve their financial paradise in this manner. The secret is time and the magic of compound interest.

It works this way. By dint of luck, labor, and loose laws, an ancestor in some midwest Bible belt or California oasis put together $1 million in 1920 when a dollar was a dollar, a pound was a pound, and a mark was a bad joke. It has never been especially difficult to achieve 7 percent tax-free growth, which doubles your money every ten years, quadruples it every twenty, octuples it every thirty, multiplies it by sixteen in forty years, and in half a century turns that million into 32 million. You have to be especially inspired in your choice of investment or adviser (and remember, with a million you can afford advice) to do worse, although it's not impossible.

Sir Winston Churchill seems to have managed this discouraging feat. His Boer War escapades, journalism, and American lectures netted him £10,000 in his very early manhood. The young Churchill, who had a shrewder eye for the main chance than for money, entrusted the lot to Sir Ernest Cassel, an old family friend. That was his first mistake. The fact that somebody was on dining, golfing, or even advising terms with your parents is no qualification for employing him to mind your own money or (as Churchill put it in his instructions to Cassel) to "feed my sheep." Churchill himself ruefully admits that in a few years all the sheep had been roasted and devoured. Had the capital been preserved intact and grown by only 8 percent per annum, Churchill would have died worth £1.3 million from that single source.

To revert to that lucky scion of a 1920s millionaire, if he had survived his parent for fifty years, secured his 7 percent capital growth, and spent only the interest, he would then, from a starting point of a nice, steady, rich income in the Roaring Twenties, have been pulling down $7,000 a day for doing precisely nothing. He was, moreover, in a position to make thirty-two further millionaires out of his heirs. Had they exercised the same prudence, by 1980 the fortune would have totaled $64 million, and by 1985 that original million would have multiplied nearly one hundredfold. This story glosses over painful subjects such as the Great Depression, inheritance taxes, and taxes in general. But if the million was safely locked up in a sound private business with good marketing connections, tolerable growth, and efficient financial advisers (as hosts of family millions were), the scenario is perfectly credible.

Some sagas far exceed this fictional rendering in their true fantasy. Charles Stewart Mott, for instance, was a successful wheel and axle manufacturer in the days long before the motor industry had spawned its megamillions. He sold his business to the infant General Motors for a parcel of shares in 1913. While Mott continued to labor sagely and well in the vineyard of the great corporation, the shares worked for him to so gratifying an extent that the Mott fortune, in the old man's nineties (he died at ninety-seven in 1973), was valued at some $800 million. The family, which has been well shod ever since it started selling Mott's Apple Juice, was worth some $300 million in 1986 despite its philanthropy ("I'm not a leech on society," says the latest Mott). And the Motts still held plenty of GM stock when the '87 crash came.

Wall Street slump or no, GM shares have fructified in a way that is characteristic of the huge concerns born in the age of affluence before World War I. A decade or so back, a London stockjobber sold, to his pride, a £1.5 million line of shares in Shell Transport for a Scottish broker. Later he met the Scot, who told him their origin. Back in 1910, a canny father had left his sons £10,000 (the same sum as the young Churchill had put by). The jobber had just offloaded the holding of one son.

In like style, the heirs of Henry Phipps (200 of them at the latest count) have reason to bless the day in 1901 when the old boy, unlike his partner, Andrew Carnegie, took stock from J. P. Morgan instead of bonds. His $50 million, put in a trust named Bessemer after the steel process that made the Carnegie-Phipps fortunes, has now swollen to a total estimated by *Forbes* at $1.8 billion. By a fascinating arithmetical coincidence, that is precisely what $50 million compounding for eighty-five years at 7 percent would have achieved.

Many sizable fortunes such as that of Henry Phipps, the cobbler's son, have been turned into great piles of shining gold by the 7 percent progress on which even untalented heirs can reasonably rely. But suppose the heir is actually bright and, even better, lucky. Doubling the compound growth rate to 14 percent turns $1 million into $32 million in only twenty-five years. In just forty years, the family fortunes will stand at a whole quarter of a billion. Had the Phipps pile multiplied at this doubled rate, it would now in theory stand at over $90 billion, or $450 million per Phipps.

Even at a mere quarter billion, no matter what happens to the value of money in the next four decades, no matter how intensively the family breeds, the inheritance will spell great riches for all. At going interest rates on corporate bonds, it would have yielded at the end of 1986 an income of $20 million a year. Continuing 14 percent capital growth would have been worth far more: $35 million. Nor is the 14 percent compound accumulation out of this world. Warren Buffett, perhaps the only man to have made $1 billion from pure investment, multiplied the worth of his corporate vehicle, Berkshire Hathaway, by 22 percent for over two decades.

The mathematics explains how, despite heroic philanthropy, even on a Rockefeller scale, the surviving fortune is still enough to keep a large family in regal condition, although it also explains how vital philanthropy is simply to prevent the mushrooming of great private fortunes from undermining the economic foundations of the state. Indeed, the U.S. government felt obliged to bring suit against one wealthy, dead eccentric, who left his fortune in perpetual trust: there his bread was to do nothing save breed compound interest, which would be plowed back to breed still more interest, compounding in its turn; within a perfectly foreseeable period, the trust would have cornered all the liquid wealth in the United States ($100 million compounding at 10 percent ends up after a century at over $2,000 billion). This lunatic scheme was not so far-out: in 1906 it was calculated that if John D. Rockefeller's wealth simply grew at the current rate of interest, he would own $90,000 billion by 1936. The would-be mini-Rockefeller's trust was duly overthrown by the courts. But, more intelligently applied, geometric progression keeps personal fortunes marching on, seemingly forever.

There are, of course, several catches in this beneficent process. Fortunes can dissipate rapidly in the second generation, let alone the third and fourth, as family members (and the proportion of incompetents and wastrels) also multiply geometrically. It can be taken almost for granted that the money won't be thrown away in some harebrained manner, such as actually paying the full inheritance taxes that the law lays down. But, for compounding to work its magic, reasonable time is required in the early stages. If the money has been made in business and is still invested there, it is dangerous for the scions to abandon all interests save their own enjoyment.

In some cases, the managers of the good old family firm would gladly pay their heir a million dollars a year to keep clear of the office. No doubt, the supermarket satraps minding the A & P (the Great Atlantic and Pacific Tea Company) for all Huntington Hartford and the other heirs were worth were delighted to see Hunt engaged in losing millions at a safe distance on wild projects for establishing Shangri-La on Hog Island or, single-handed, reversing the remorseless flood of modern art with a fretwork museum (since abandoned) on Columbus Circle in New York City.

Given that Hartford contrived to lose $90 million, it is said, on such endeavors, it's unlikely that he could have made any positive contribution to the affairs of the supermarkets. Not that A & P benefited from the heir's abstinence. The greatness fled, even though the Atlantic and the Pacific (and the tea) remain. The downgrade of the 1960s, when earnings per share declined by 9.4 percent annually, was the sorry prelude to disastrous losses in the mid-1970s. Despite recovery under new management (whose leader, Englishman James Wood, has been earning $1.9 million income *and* $5 million capital per annum) the return on the investment over the last decade has been mediocre, and over the last quarter century, dreadful: an outcome owed entirely to internal incompetence. If a family owns a store, or a thousand stores, somebody in the family should mind it.

The management mafia at Du Pont has long been eager to point out that du Ponts play hardly any part in the company's affairs. Yet there have always been family members or representatives in the best observation place of all: the summit. Senior vice presidencies and a solid, dominating phalanx on the finance committee, which is where they keep the money, are a standard formula for this kind of non-managerial control. Apart from backsliders such as Lammot du Pont Copeland, Jr., who achieved one of America's brightest and best bankruptcies on Wall Street, keeping the money is something at which du Ponts have usually been good.

Compounding, for this family, has taken $36,000, the cost of their original gunpowder plant on the Brandywine River in 1802, to the estimated $7 billion-plus of the early 1970s to the $10 billion of 1986. Even with a few hundred descendants putting their fingers in the pie—632 of them sat down to celebrate the one hundred fiftieth anniversary—that leaves plenty of succulent slices all around. The same arithmetical curiosity noted with the Phipps fortune applies: $36,000 to the magic $7 billion in 170 years is again a compound growth of 7 percent a year; for the du Ponts as for the Phipps family, time has been money.

The addition of only (that's some *only*) $3 billion since 1973 suggests either that the score hasn't been accurately kept or that the rate of growth has slowed to below the apparent 7 percent norm. In fact, if all the cousins are thrown in, the family was worth far more—perhaps $24 billion. But in truth, the great company hasn't been a great investment of late, as the Bronfman family has some cause to rue. Their 22.5 percent holding in Du Pont, held through their basic Seagram drinks business, has held back the latter's profits; and the Bronfmans, a managing clan, with assets worth $30 billion or so, are apt to be less patient with such performance than the du Ponts (who still own a quarter of the family firm).

Even with the Du Pont blip thrown in, Joseph E. Seagram had averaged a 19 percent return on stockholders' equity; in a good year, Du Pont just about makes double figures. Watching your pile from a close vantage point is a reasonable strategy for the inheritor, who has no alternative if he lacks the taste or the ability for management. But managing the fortune directly, as the Bronfmans do, sounds more likely to produce truly satisfying results, and it's a route that many heirs are driven to take—by both internal and external pressures.

Their fathers, powerful and puritanical about money (especially their own), inflict the work ethic on their children, imbue them with the business from early days, and persuade them, without much difficulty, that if you want to reach the top the easiest way is to start there. Wealthy descendants such as the grocer Sainsburys in Britain (with a supermarket fortune well in excess of $1 billion) or the food-rich Cargill descendants in the United States (revenues $30 billion, fortune heading toward $2 billion) have developed their inheritances beyond the imaginative powers even of the family begetters. Yet folklore still has it that the primrose path to managerial ruin is nepotism, that with each successive management generation the original impetus and talent get progressively weaker, until they disappear, usually in disaster.

This theory is hard to square with the facts of companies such as Sainsburys, led by one sound Sainsbury after another, or S. C. Johnson, still literally waxing strong in Racine, Wisconsin, on a dose of fourth-generation management. Sam Johnson, in the saddle since 1967, can't be accused of acting as a mere caretaker. The nonwax products, such as Raid and Glade, added at his urging, have been instrumental in generating highly profitable growth to some $2 billion of sales. They also engendered a typical Johnson quote to *Forbes*: "Whenever you get bit by a mosquito, remember I'm smiling." Smile he may: the privately held company is worth, on a conservative estimate, $1 billion.

Is Sam Johnson the exception that proves the rule? When one toy firm, once worth $25 million to its ruling family, dissolved into a worthless puddle, a newspaper smugly observed in the received manner that "second and third generation managements are not usually the best"; and in truth it's hard not to sneer when somebody called Raymond C. Firestone is made chairman of a rubber company founded by someone called Harvey S. Firestone, or even when one Edgar M. Bronfman decides to appoint one Edgar M. Bronfman (Jr.) to run Seagram's in his stead. The sneers will be none the less for dutiful observations in the press that Firestone, Jr., "started work with the company in 1933 as a gas station attendant," or that Bronfman, Jr., according to *Fortune*, attracts from all sides comments that "on and off the record, were remarkably uniform and favorable."

All the same, the sneers are too facile, reminiscent of the cracks that Premier Harold Wilson made at "the fourteenth Earl of Home" when the latter was elevated to prime minister before him. As Home reasonably remarked, there was presumably a fourteenth Mr. Wilson. Everybody is second or third generation. The fact that pa or grandpa was a business genius doesn't mean that son or grandson must turn the former's silk purses into sows' ears.

In his *Up the Organization*, the arch antinepot Robert Townsend points out that "Gerry Eskow succeeded his father as president of Yale Express in 1960. Five years later the company went bankrupt." This merely proves, not that son should never follow dad, but that Gerry Eskow should never have followed his progenitor. Nonfamily managements are just as capable of allowing events to drench their balance sheets.

For every weakness of family management there is an almost exact balance of strengths. Genetics is a bad management selection system, true; but you have to find managers somewhere—and the family does provide an immediate pool of people who should be deeply versed in, and deeply committed to, the business from birth. True, a nonfamily manager of real talent will doubtless shy away from a company where the way to the top is barred or narrowed by birth; but the family provides a built-in focus of loyalty and continuity that can make even nonfamily managers work above their natural level.

True, the family develops a vested interest in the company as it was then, is now, and ever shall be, a fondness that can prove fatal if events (as they must one day) overtake the formula; but on the other hand, the family manager—being proprietor, shareholder, and executive rolled into one—finds it easier to take the long view, while continuing to watch the short-term pennies (because they are his or her own).

How do the pros and cons balance out in practice? *Fortune* looked at the question and came up with a negative answer: "The laggards' performance may suggest that, by keeping management in the family for generations, a company is not getting the best management," and quotes a New York investment banker to even more dire effect: "Sometimes you have to wonder whether the blood is getting thinner." Yet the accusation isn't really supported by the accompanying statistics on ten family-managed firms: Anheuser-Busch, Loews, Motorola, Seagram, Weyerhaeuser, Marriott, McDonnell Douglas, Corning Glass, Wang, and Safeway.

Their average return on equity in the decade to 1985 works out at just under 20 percent, which would rank at 140 out of the Fortune 500. True, the average spans the great gulf between Weyerhaeuser's lamentable 1.9 percent per annum and the 44.5 percent of Wang—already, though, a troubled company by the time of these calculations. (Seagram comes in just above the average with 21.1 percent, or nearly three times the figure for the nonfamily-managed Du Pont.) But coming in the top third of all large American public companies is no mean performance, especially when the identification of family with firm is less than total in one most important respect.

This is the amount of the equity owned by the family: under 1 percent in the case of the Magowans and Safeway (which has since been taken private), 7 percent in that of the Galvins and Motorola, 10 to 12 percent for the eponymous Weyerhaeusers, and 14 percent for McDonnell. Only the Tisch family (in Loews), the Bronfmans, and the Wangs own more than a quarter of the companies they run. Because even 32 percent of the equity may be no protection of the family management (Richardson-Vicks, despite that percentage, went to Procter & Gamble in a $400-million payoff), it's plain that the tenure of the family managers in many cases rests not on equity, but on the normal stockholder sufferance.

The family stockholders are truly in the same boat as the unrelated. They should insist on getting the best management available, irrespective of birth. Western families, however, are all too prone to put family first and their own financial interests second. According to Peter Drucker, they organize things better in Japan, where the family fortunes are watched over implacably by the elder womenfolk (a much tougher breed than bankers). If any honorable nephew is no good, grandma gives him the chop.

As this variety of women's lib is unlikely to wear well in the West, families have to exercise self-discipline in other ways—although Guinness tried out a Western variation. For many decades now the magic stout, having brewed incomparable riches for the Guinnesses and transformed them into Earls of Iveagh, Viscounts of Kelvedon, and various other nobilities, has been managed by nontitled non-Guinnesses with such care and attention that one year a French magazine, to the amusement of the many Guinnesses, elected their company as the most dynamic in Europe. At that time, the board was festooned with Guinnesses, including a nub of titled ladies, representative of large family holdings, whose appearance at the annual general meeting was likened to "a forest of cock's feathers and fur."

Far from being dynamic, Guinness got stuck in a groove of mediocrity, and only appeared to escape when a marketing professional from Nestlé, Ernest Saunders, moved in, shattered the old, production-led norms, supplanted the complaisant reigning earl as chairman, and in an acrid struggle took over the national Scotch giant, the Distillers Company. In the process, unfortunately, the new broom not only swept too close to Ivan Boesky, but committed so many share-dealing illegalities that the saga changed almost overnight from successful family abdication to Britain's biggest City scandal, with heads (including Saunders's own) rolling in French Revolution style.

Nothing, not even the appointment of a nonfamily wonderman, can relax the rules of family corporate discipline. They are exactly the same as for firms of the nonfamily variety. Never allow anybody to become indispensable—or rather, to think and act (like Saunders) as if he or she is. Never appoint incompetents, related or unrelated, to any position of significance. Never allow the board to become overburdened with age, even if it means forcing the dominating father figure to retire at the same age as the lesser fry. Bring young talent into positions of real power while it is still young, but always ensure that wise, prudent, unambitious, and trusted elders watch what the young are getting up to, especially with money. (The Texas oil millionaire Tom Wagoner, chided by a barber for tipping less than his son, pointed out that "my boy's got a rich daddy, but I ain't.") Don't let indifferent performance drift by. The iron law is that stagnation leads to decline. The time to act to avert the former is when the signs of stagnation first appear, before huge deposits of inertia have had time to silt up the entire works.

The crunch comes when stagnation cannot be averted without severe discontinuity, and discontinuity is the process that heirs in general are worst at achieving. They can be superb at developing a great and soundly based business along more or less established lines: thus did the Sieffs at Marks & Spencer triumphantly overcome the difficulties, for a bunch of hereditary millionaires with expensive tastes, of serving mass-market desires in food, clothing, and other consumer joys. But never let heirs try to prove that they are better than good old dad, or grandad, by striking out in brave new directions.

That's what Gerry Eskow attempted at Yale Express and, in an even more bizarre episode, Herbert Hoover, Jr., at Hoover. This would-be chip off the old block, dissatisfied with the narrowness of the view from North Canton, Ohio, set up an expensive international headquarters in New York, staffed by his own protégés, to revolutionize the company. Sadly, the only obvious focus for young Hoover's energies was the British subsidiary, which Hoover neither wholly owned nor ever controlled to much effect.

The architect of Hoover's British upsurge retired, with a then record payoff, to make dishwashers, and Hoover's U.S. and U.K. halves stewed together in so complete a mishmash that the suffering professional managers in North Canton finally mobilized the family and gave Herbert, Jr., the old heave-ho. That is the only correct treatment for any descendant who rocks the family's solid silver boat, is rude to its servants, or wastes its compounding wherewithal.

Not that the ousting of the junior Hoover marked the end of the company's travail. The European interests, spearheaded from London, never did regain the lost momentum, and the family, as often happens, was bailed out only by takeover: Hoover succumbed to a bid from Georgia-Pacific. The other inheritors would have been far better off had the last managing Hoover originally decided to do something else with his time—and their money.

There's nothing heinous in the rich heir who shuns the business (such as most of the assembled du Ponts): the only son of the great retailer Lord Marks preferred painting to stores; the top Rothschild, socially speaking, preferred biology to banking—and ended up in his sixties running the prime ministerial think tank in Downing Street. But dropouts should be discouraged from overspending their income or dissipating their capital in support of expensive hobbies—unless, that is, the family luck sticks to their fingers.

One sprig of a great fortune was having a boat built when he heard to his fury that the builder was going bankrupt. He thereupon told his factotum (good factota, stewards, or bailiffs are a privilege of the rich) to buy the business. On completion of the deal, the heirs found to their horror that the company also made nasty little wingless aircraft whose propellers were in the wrong place, whirling above the fuselage. They stuck with this unfortunate acquisition until one day a government decided to merge the aircraft industry, helicopters and all, into fewer companies. In the reshuffle, the family found itself several millions better-to-do, all because originally one prince of the blood wanted his boat finished. The justice in the world tends to favor the rich.

Should it? In the ultimate, the answer hinges on ability and results. That is what determines how much you should leave to the children: the expected outcome. That, too, answers the corollary: Should you leave them to run your business? The passive inheritors can be coupon-clipping drones (in which case they shouldn't have been left the money), or proper trustees for all concerned, including the employees and any other shareholders. In that guise, they will ensure that the inheritance is well managed (by others) and that the proceeds are well spent internally (on benefactions within the firm, such as the pioneering employee benefits at S. C. Johnson) and externally, on outside philanthropies.

The active inheritors can earn their inheritance by developing the established business, like the Johnsons and the Sainsburys, or they may succeed only in demonstrating their unsuitability, like Eskow and Hoover. Or they can totally revamp what they inherit. Again, only the results can deliver the verdict. That on Henry Lea Hillman, however, has to be favorable, even if, as he told *Forbes*, his Pittsburgh coal-brokering father has "turned over in his grave many times with some of the things we've done."

Keeping the founder's bones at rest is no part of the active inheritor's duty. His obligations are owed to the living, not the dead. By moving out of $300 million in old-industry assets in 1969, the younger Hillman was able to create a billion-plus empire in electronics, real estate, and venture capital. (The provision of funds for new ventures is one of the better justifications for inherited wealth, and one of the more promising ways of enhancing said fortunes.)

On the other hand, J. Peter Grace has rotated everything in sight, including (no doubt) ancestral bones, switching from shipping to chemicals to energy, without producing a convincing shape for the still huge W. R. Grace (sales $5.4 billion). The period from 1975 to 1985 saw an average annual decline of over 6 percent in the company's earnings per share, while the profitability, at 6.1 percent of stockholders' equity, was stuck firmly in the bottom third of the Fortune 500. Yet the supreme commander was the same Peter Grace who was once voted an enormous special bonus by his co-directors for his invaluable services.

The insuperable difficulty for the wealthy parent is to determine in advance whether or not his heirs deserve the inheritance. The ghost of H. L. Hunt cannot today think well of Nelson Bunker Hunt and his brothers. Yet until the Hunts foolishly attempted to corner the silver market, to the tune of $6.6 billion, much of it subsequently lost, their record was brilliant. Under them, Placid Oil, which filed for a humiliating Chapter 11 protection from bankruptcy in 1986, was a match, thanks to Libyan oil, for father Hunt's own fabulous achievements.

The Hunt sisters, Margaret Hill and Caroline Schoellkopf, wouldn't touch the silver folly, thus proving that the female of the species is often brighter than the male. Each rides herd on billion-dollar or thereabouts fortunes in a style that should certainly leave their father's grave and ghost undisturbed: Margaret told *Forbes*, "We're workaholics—that's the way of our father and mother." As for Caroline's $350 million of lush hotels (not to mention her enormous development, The Crescent, in downtown Dallas), they "are not the whim of a rich woman, but a calculated real estate investment."

So inheritance poses a paradox. You should leave the money, and/or the business, to the children only if they are so able that they need neither the money nor the management seat, because they could do equally well on their own account. If they can't make it on their own, which means that they truly need the money, you shouldn't let them have it, or much of it. Yet the results of inheritance, which is a fact of capitalist life, are not uniformly undesirable. It is not the worst system of transferring assets or economic power—a verdict subject to one enormous *caveat*: that the only people, nine times out of ten, who can ensure that the overwhelming privileges of inheritance are not abused are the inheritors themselves.

2

THE GRAVE
IS A VERY
PRIVATE PLACE

Between old and new multimillionaires, one great gulf is usually fixed. The new recruit to riches is far more likely to share ownership of his prime asset with the citizenry at large. The newcomer takes early advantage of the stock market, because he needs the multiplier effect as a rocket booster. The older fortune, being already in orbit, requires no such assistance, although the chances are strong that, at some point in dynastic succession, private will become partly public.

Traditionally, when private firms that have deposited great wealth into the hands of their private owners yield their virginities in this way, the proprietors give many a sigh and heaving of the breast as they sell a modest chunk of their shares. The suffering is mitigated by the fact that they receive a goodly volume of cash for their pains—and there is always some plausible explanation of the self-sacrifice: fear of inheritance taxes, difficulty in raising money for expansion, trouble in attracting or keeping smart enough hired help. But none of these obstacles is insurmountable.

The clear proof is that so much of the world's wealth is in wholly or largely private hands. The public had no more than a look-in, if that, at the fortunes of Howard Hughes and H. L. Hunt in an older generation whose survivors into the mid-1980s included the equally secretive empires of Forrest Mars and Daniel K. Ludwig. The customary British reserve likewise extends to the largest fortunes. Of the country's nine biggest, three belong to the hereditary aristocracy (the Windsors, Grosvenors, and Buccleuchs); of the remaining half dozen in 1985, four were private.

It does happen that 1985's three wealthiest people in America, according to *Forbes*, took the public route to their riches: Wal-Mart Stores, Electronic Data Systems, and Hewlett-Packard being the respective golden founts for Sam Walton, H. Ross Perot, and David Packard. But they are the public exceptions that prove the private rule; from then on, with occasional interruptions by rarities such as Warren Buffett (Berkshire Hathaway) and Leslie Herbert Wexner (The Limited), the tale is largely one of privacy. Sometimes it's diluted by the odd public interests, such as the investment positions built up by the Bass brothers in companies such as Disney. But the Newhouse brothers, Si and Don, with their private media interests, ranging from *The New Yorker* to cable television, are as typical as the Swigs.

The latter (brothers Melvyn and Richard and brother-in-law Richard Donner) brought up the rear of the 400 that year with assets such as the four exclusive Fairmont hotels. They are typical in one other respect: their fortune derives from real estate. Not only did land and buildings account for 83 of the 400 fortunes: they fueled the self-making of 38 fortunes (almost double the next largest self-made category) and 27 of the active inheritances. Nearly all these real estate piles, moreover, are privately held.

From these two facts—the numbers and the privacy—a clear deduction follows. Real estate has offered the easiest route to great wealth, both in its rate of capital appreciation and in its financing and basic economics. The deduction is perfectly correct. Harry Helmsley, the New York billionaire whose wife, Leona, runs their hotels, puts the capital point succinctly: "You don't have to do anything. You just have to sit. The values go up." In Manhattan alone, they have gone up sufficiently to account for thirty-three of the real estate fortunes listed by *Forbes*, a remarkable testimony to the concentration of wealth and power in one metropolis.

As for the financing, *Forbes* noted of the flamboyant forty-year-old Donald Trump, "Boy wonder attracts top institutional bankrollers." The beauty of a building is to provide its own security. The issue of collateral is resolved by the asset, with its capital value underwritten by the rental income secured. So long as the net revenue exceeds the financing and operating costs, the owner can, like Helmsley, just sit while the rentals and the values rise and the tax breaks keep down his payments to the Internal Revenue Service. Tax reform may remove some of the bloom from this rose, but it won't remove the immense value locked into the equity ownership of Helmsley's 50 million square feet of office space, including the Empire State Building, or the Swigs's four hotels (worth some $100 million apiece).

Even the one disadvantage of properties—their immobility—has been diminished by innovative financing, such as the syndication that yielded the eponymous family $1.3 billion from Rockefeller Center. But the real estate rich have come under little pressure to change their act or share it with the public at large. Their holdings therefore stand as the most obvious example of a basic truth: that what the rich have, they prefer to hold, all of it, if they can.

None of the standard excuses for selling shares to the public has any convincing validity; the only point in doing so is to exchange assets for real money at a time when the switch is advantageous. The advantage of publicity is clearest if the private owner has it in mind to take his money and run. But even if the private owner has every intention of staying put, going public has considerable financial benefit—simply because the parts can be made wondrously more than the whole. Nobody ever got richer faster than that former wizard IBM computer salesman named H. Ross Perot. But this wasn't simply because his computer software business grew like the giant mushroom (as it did). The U.S. public fell over itself to buy the tiny amount of shares that Perot generously released—15 percent of the total equity. At its palmiest, this was valued at over 100 times earnings. Nobody in his right mind would have paid that kind of multiple for the whole of Perot's company; if he was exceedingly lucky, it might have fetched a third of the putative but fictitious market valuation.

In the end, when Perot got $2.2 billion in cash and stock for under half of Electronic Data Systems in 1984 to 1986, the earlier valuation looked less absurd. As that deal with General Motors emphasized, the private asset always has a public value. The only questions are how, at what price, and when that value should be realized.

The stock-sale route, though, has enormous inherent attractions: it multiplies the values and enables the owner to grab real money but leaves him total control over the cornucopia. There has to be some nonfinancial explanation of why so many wealthy citizens, on generally spurious grounds, reject the benefits of public sale, preferring to cling

31

to absolute ownership of vast private assets such as the *Reader's Digest* or Milliken & Co., the biggest private textile company, whose three third-generation owners are worth $1.3 billion.

The practical advantages of privacy are minor compared to the loss of financial flexibility. Even Howard Hughes found the public route indispensable when his legal dispute with TWA put him in possible need of several million dollars. Hughes won that case, and needn't have bothered. But note that the crafty recluse hung on to all his assets except his daddy's original business in oil-drilling bits; for that he got $140 million off the stock market, although the profits had dribbled down for three years, and three once commercially significant patents were shortly to expire (not to mention the fact that the U.S. oil industry, after Hughes's death, would plunge into its deepest postwar depression).

The Hughes case is self-explanatory: the private person avoids public ownership because of his very lust for privacy, which in Hughes's case amounted to mania. At a less manic level, the lust can still be obsessional, blotting out common sense as well as financial self-interest. The dictatorial boss of one retailing and gambling empire, with over $1 billion of sales coming in, once explained his position in language worthier of a small storekeeper than a tycoon: "If we were public," he said, "and I didn't make enough money, they [the shareholders] would be after me."

Useless to tell such a Midas that a holding of well under 50 percent will yield absolute control (witness, among countless other examples, the suzerainty of Dr. Armand Hammer over Occidental Petroleum); useless to say that shareholders seldom speak unless spoken to; useless to argue that large public firms have reported indifferent results for a decade or so without the directors attracting more than a unanimous vote of thanks at the annual general meeting (an event that usually vies with a Reagan press conference in its irrelevance to anything of practical import).

Many a Midas is motivated by deep inward fear: anxiety lest his personal control be weakened by dilution. The proprietor has a simple, all-or-nothing approach to proprietorship, and the psychological attractions apply across the whole range of business brains, from simple men who all but keep their money under the bed to international jet-set sophisticates of the Onassis or Niarchos variety. In especially cunning hands, moreover, privacy can be made to yield profits equal to even the greatest stock market killings.

Indeed, in the latest phase of the Age of the Common Millionaire, privacy has been making a strong and interesting comeback. Some of the most rapidly growing American fortunes—notably that of the Basses—are as private as any European economic dynasty, nobody's business but that of the ruling family. The Basses, though, were continuing in the Texas oil and gas tradition in which their fortune began. Billionaire John Werner Kluge and Leonard Norman Stern (worth $550 million) are, however, two examples of turning the tables: the major part of their wealth derives not from going public, but private.

Kluge's exploit will resound among the towers of Wall Street for many years to come. The device he used so brilliantly, the leveraged buyout (LBO), was originally designed to free corporate managers from the toils of groups that no longer wanted their businesses. A benevolent financial institution provided the bulk of the cash for the buyout, and the fact that most of the cash was financed by long-term debt supplied the leverage. The managers put up money for the equity that they shared with the financiers, and, all being well, or managed well, everybody cleaned up big. The size of Kluge's cleaning-up, though, was phenomenal—and this was no imprisoned, depressed, downtrodden hired hand, but a successful media empire builder.

Because Kluge owned 26 percent of the resulting company, Metromedia, he naturally received part of the $1.2 billion raised to purchase the company. This came to $115 million in cash. Thrown in with the deal, though, was three-quarters of the new corporate entity, together with all but 7 percent of the votes. Kluge had thus been *paid* $115 million to enlarge his holding threefold—the reverse of the normal order of events. Since the seven TV stations in the package were valued at $2 billion in Kluge's later sale agreement with Rupert Murdoch, Kluge had no cause to complain of his financial treatment of himself—and there were billions more to come.

By those standards, Stern's coup is merely spectacular. Stern came by an interest in pets by heredity: his father emigrated from Germany with 2,100 canaries. But the resulting pet supply business, named the Hartz Mountain Corp. after the homeland, was only built into a major business by Leonard after taking charge in 1959. Thirteen years later he went public at $22 a share; seven years after that he went back to privacy, paying $14.50 a share. His turn on the transaction was thus a profit of around half. Small wonder that he could afford to pay $100 million in an antitrust settlement, cough up $55 million for *The Village Voice*, and say to *Forbes*, "When I think of the degree of my worth I find it ungraspable."

That of the Pritzker family must be far harder to grasp, totaling at least $1.5 billion, and again wholly private, thanks to one of the first buy-backs. Jay and Robert, the controlling sons of father Abram, who died in his late eighties in 1986, no longer have to share the results of the high-powered buildup of the Hyatt hotel chain. Again, real estate is the foundation of private superprosperity (pet food king Stern is also big in real estate, in New York).

Father A. N. began as a lawyer whose real estate investments finally elbowed out other clients in 1940. Law school remains the traditional training for family members, with the object, it's said, of equipping each Pritzker with the ability to confront the battalions of lawyers who beset American business. Each Pritzker, too, has a job, if so desired, on the family estate, which takes in $5 billion of sales in the Marmon manufacturing conglomerate, the Braniff airline, and much besides, all managed, alongside the Pritzkers, by carefully selected *Yummies*—young upwardly mobile managers who share ambitions such as building the world's biggest and best upmarket hotel group. Why conduct so public an expansion on so private a base? "We're not," says one of the Yummies, "subject to the whims of Wall Street or to economic ups and downs." That is typical.

The graspable freedom to do what they like with what they have is certainly a powerful factor in the private proprietors' psychology, although it's difficult to see what more freedom they might want to deploy than Robert Buckley, no proprietor, did at Allegheny International. He spent a million bucks on a corporate home away from home in the hometown of Pittsburgh, ran five private jets, lent some $30 million at 2 percent interest to top executives, bought a New York hotel for $6 million, and installed his son as manager and as occupant of a $1 million penthouse. Nemesis only caught up with Buckley because his financial results became addled; but the private proprietor is secure, given mere solvency.

This can't be said with equal confidence of the family that shares its act. As a Chicago money manager told *Fortune*, "A lot of old-line family businesses may think nothing could happen to them, but these days they could be vulnerable." The very fact of large family shareholdings tends to reduce the stock market valuation, simply because the professionals don't expect a bid. Paradoxically, that undervaluation could make a bid more likely. With half ownership or more, however, the family management need fear no man or woman, and that may be an even more compelling motive than reluctance to let outsiders, in return for nothing but their savings, share publicly in the loot created by your private efforts.

This private passion is no prerogative of the ultra-rich. One of the main causes of bankruptcy is the refusal of the unwise, or unwised-up, infant entrepreneur to let others into his action at an early stage. The explanation is human enough. The man knows how wonderful his idea is, how irresistible his own managerial force, how dynamic his growth rate (if you start from zero, almost any growth looks marvelous). If he lets somebody else in on his ground floor, no matter what that person provides in capital or knowledge, the interloper is getting in dirt-cheap; cheap, that is, by the standards of the unrealized future supergrowth.

This denial leads straight to the dread condition known as over-trading or undercapitalization, in which the sufferer tries to cure his shortage of money by desperate means—such as not paying his bills to suppliers and praying that his customers pay theirs on the nail. If these makeshift means fail (they do, with depressing regularity), the proud and private independent casts around, at last, for outside money. Only it's too late. The time to swallow private pride is when you are not forced to do so; diplomats call it negotiating from strength.

By all odds the craftiest exponent of this art was the wily Armenian Calouste Gulbenkian. Zen masters teach pupils the essence of swordsmanship by striking at them with sticks when the student isn't watching. The Armenians in much the same way have acquired such dexterity from dodging their persecutors down the ages that only the foolhardy ever tangle with a businessman whose name ends in "ian" or "yan"—and that prohibition included Anastas Mikoyan, the craftiest trader and most professional survivor thrown up by Soviet Russia.

Gulbenkian's contribution to the world's welfare was to lay his hands on the rich oil concessions in Mesopotamia. His wiliness emerged in his readiness to give up all but 5 percent of this treasure trove to the mighty oil companies that were eager to share the gold. That 5 percent not only gave Gulbenkian his nickname of "Mr. Five Percent," it generated, painlessly and annually, one of the world's great fortunes, and it demonstrated the truth of an unforgettable maxim: a little of a lot is better than all of a little.

The small, would-be-big entrepreneur ignores Gulbenkian's gambit to his own detriment. In any event, giving away some equity early on isn't a final, fatal step. If the business flourishes like a green bay tree, the entrepreneur can always buy his partners out. That was the course favored by Henry Ford I, who began his rise with a motley crew of faithful supporters and devoted much of his time in later years to liquidating their interests.

By and large, despite Henry's appalling mismanagement in the 1930s, the other shareholders were wrong to sell out (although the cunning old fox left them with little option). Ford shares were worth more than dollar bills. But few people can resist the lure of cash, even in small amounts. The great majority of the oilmen who, at the point of John D. Rockefeller's economic gun, were forced to sell out either for cash or for Rockefeller shares, took cash; it proved to be a ludicrous error. Keeping a Gulbenkian-size corner in somebody else's gold mine is one of the easiest ways to wealth, so long as, like Gulbenkian, you are in a position to safeguard your interests.

The private imperialist values his privacy partly just because there are nobody's interests to safeguard save his own. This enables him to build the company in his own image and for his own sake. Power, in these circumstances, is plainly more important than its full expression in money terms. Britain boasts one Quaker company that is kept resolutely private by the will of the family—or, to be more precise, the managing members thereof. As usual in these circumstances, a formula exists to put a price on the shares in the event of death or dissolution. It prices the holdings far below even a conservative estimate for the company's stock market value. This undervaluation robs the family of many tens of millions: the price of allowing the few actively ruling family members to preserve totally untrammeled management control.

Why do the family outsiders suffer such penalties? Aunts may be intimidated by Cousin Dick; nephews may fear that, unless they comply dutifully with Uncle Al's wishes, he will pull up stakes in a huff and retire to the nearest tax-free island. Apart from paranoia, they are victims of ignorance. Almost as if they were uninterested in their money (which, in a sense, they are), they are happy to have the anxiety of its care lifted off their shoulders. Tell them that they are being defrauded of the odd million and you turn contentment into a state of acute anxiety. It is kissing cousin to the equally ill-founded apprehensions of private family managers that, without the protection of all-family ownership, their management grip will first be loosened, then contemptuously knocked away.

If their abilities are defective, so much the better for one and all—including themselves as shareholders. But managers of the blood are seldom eager to recognize their own incompetence, no matter what it costs. The beauty (or horror) of privacy is that mistakes are more easily buried here even than in big public corporations (where funerals can be fully as discreet as Mafia disposals in the East River). Only rarely does a scandal reach such dimensions that the veil is lifted, not merely from the management failure of a family business but from the very facts of its life.

When Tino de Angelis, the great salad-oil swindler, finally ran out of empty tanks, a company called Bunge discovered to its horror that $15 million of the nonexistent oil belonged to it, so to speak. Another $3 million had oozed away in a simple check fraud. To mislay $18 million, even to the second-greatest swindler of all time, you have to be adequately rich, and Bunge belonged to one of the richest private kingdoms of them all. At that time its sales were $1.2 billion a year; it held one-fifth of the entire American trade in grain, oil seeds, oils, and fats; the whole Bunge y Born earthly paradise, known in its Latin American home as "The Octopus," was in the ownership of two families: the Borns and the Hirsches.

The reigning Hirsch was said at the time to know "if a typist blows her nose in São Paulo," despite the fact that he had never visited Brazil. Yet here was a single, suborned employee in New York waylaying checks to the value of $3 million, and nobody noticed. The closefisted, close-controlled approach typical of the private empire had failed before the depredations of a determined con man; of four tanks supposed to contain 160 million pounds of salad oil, for the ultimate benefit of the Borns and the Hirsches, three contained gasoline and the fourth was empty. Being big, it seemed, had even greater drawbacks than the one highlighted by a family member: "The bigger you are, the more tax you pay. The smaller you are, the more tax you evade."

The quieter you are, what's more, the better the chance that nobody will notice your size. The Michelin tire giant used to pretend that its sales, privately owned in entirety, came to only $18 million a year when the true number was over fifty times higher: the current figure of over $5 billion can be trusted, since the company is now public (and rewarded its followers with a 31 percent compound gain over the five years to 1986, the kind of profit worth keeping to oneself).

Privacy not only retains the profits in the hands of their producers, it protects the tender personality from bruising. One real estate developer had a few outside shareholders, thanks to a quirk of fate. He once turned up at the annual general meeting wearing a rubber mask to protect his anonymity. More practically, privacy allows the truly gifted proprietor to practice management experiments without hindrance. Whether the subtleties of Howard Hughes count in this context is debatable. But in the age of passion for communicating, for man-to-man, eyeball-to-eyeball confrontation, Hughes showed that a monster conglomerate could be managed through a Mormon bodyguard, telephone kiosks, and a tame lawyer or two. Practically the only business that Hughes botched up, in fact, was the one to which he was nearest, right on the proverbial spot, in Las Vegas.

Another equally secretive tycoon also used a hotel as his nearest thing to a head office, but certainly operated one of the most effective management machines: Forrest Mars of Mars, a man photographed hardly more often than the elusive Hughes. Rubbing in the fact that second-generation incompetence is a myth, Mars left a successful father (who was glad to see him go) behind in the United States and went to Britain to build a confectionery giant so rich that, reversing the usual compliment, Mars finally took over the original parental business back home. He provides his disciples with a management grounding that is direct, steeped in common sense, and founded on a simple notion, as expounded by another émigré to Britain, Canada's Roy Thomson, in an immortal phrase: "You make a dollar for me, I'll make a dollar for you." Within that scheme of things, Mars has felt free to experiment with marketing approaches, production methods, incentive ideas, knowing that, if they worked, he would benefit; if they failed, he would foot the bill (as he did after a misguided decision to stop all advertising of his dominant cat food in Britain, which came near to destroying the brand).

Nobody can say that the Thomson-Mars philosophy is ineffective. In 1985, having abandoned such painful possessions as the London *Times* and the *Sunday Times* (to the great good fortune of their ubiquitous purchaser, Rupert Murdoch), members of the Thomson family were still the largest shareholders in the International Thomson Organisation, which enjoyed $2.2 billion of sales and had enlarged investors' capital by the scarcely believable compound growth of 54 percent annually for five years. Roy Thomson's old associate, Jack Kent Cooke, who presumably had made more bucks for Thomson than anybody else, was meanwhile enjoying his buck-for-buck proceeds. After retiring in 1960, at age fifty-seven, Cooke relieved his boredom by interests such as the Los Angeles Forum, two L.A. sports teams, 14 percent of Teleprompter (sold for more than $100 million), horse breeding, the Chrysler Building, the Washington Redskins, and sixteen acres of downtown Phoenix: all resulting in a $600 million-plus fortune.

Without bothering to diversify at all, the Mars trio (Forrest and two sons) have been sitting on $2.6 billion of wealth, thanks to their private ownership of a $5 billion company that has over 35 percent of the U.S. market. In his eighties, Mars, Sr., was having fun with a specialist candy company in Las Vegas, while his sons ran a business whose fondness for outside inspection earned the industry nickname of "the Kremlin." Yet the secrecy and privacy do carry a price, judging by the prices recently paid for the owners of great brands; after all, Chesebrough-Ponds, with sales of around $3 billion, went to Unilever for about that amount. Can the $5 billion of Mars sales really be worth less than $3 billion?

The wholly private emperors probably always lose very substantial sums, in terms of immediately available cash and marketable securities and in borrowing power, by retaining their privacy. If they deal primarily in solid assets—real estate, ships, oil in the ground—the problem becomes minimal, because any banker will gladly lend on such triple-barreled security. But their fate could then be akin to that of Gerald M. Ronson, the seventh-richest person in Britain and proprietor of its second-largest private company, who paid himself well over a million dollars in salary to cover the interest on his vast debts.

Ronson, although still in his forties, controlled entirely a billion-dollar business that has been growing at 28 percent compound. He has never flirted with the idea of going public—though he has said, "I wouldn't say we will *never* offer any shares to the public. Never is a long time." That is true enough. Even an outfit rooted in real estate, such as Ronson's Heron Group, and most of the greatest American private holdings, can't foretell the future or rely on the future succession. Family difficulties may destroy privacy if business needs don't.

The business fix may appear genuinely painful if, like the Sainsbury family in Britain, you find that the solid assets in the form of stores are small in relation to the volume of sales, and that, in a business such as supermarkets, it's hard to earn fat enough cash margins to finance needed expansion. When the Sainsburys bit the bullet in 1973, they pocketed some $20 million by going public and still had over $140 million left, in and on paper. After Black October 1987, their business was still worth over $3.4 billion; two managing members of the clan owned $700 million of equity.

You can have your supermarkets and eat them. But if the cake is cooked like Daniel K. Ludwig's, there simply is no incentive to share the assets ($2 billion at home and abroad), the borrowing power, the tax advantages, and the gigantic profits with the suckers. The Ludwig ploy, or play, was as simple as real estate development (at which Ludwig is also adept—he was actually photographed, for the first time in many years, when signing up a ninety-five-acre New Jersey development in 1985). To quote *Forbes*, the Ludwig formula is "get charter to move oil, use as collateral to borrow, build tanker, repeat." That's perfect, and can stay perfectly private—so far as it goes.

The limit is obvious. What the private business always lacks, unless the family is exceptionally gifted, reasonably prolific, and blessed with an especially rich racket, is the ability to generate decades of endless growth and diversification. Exxon no longer even bears the Rockefellers' Standard Oil name, though plenty of Rockefellers and allied families can still bless it for their daily bread—and caviar; but Exxon's $69 billion of assets leave even the wildest Texas fortunes in the minor leagues. Like Krupp in German industry, or the Rothschilds in finance, the private business inexorably gets overtaken by the public concern as the years roll by, and maybe that's no bad thing.

The resurgence of the private owner in the United States only faintly calls to mind the days of the robber barons, because the main items of private proprietorship—office buildings, hotels, shopping malls, condominiums, medium-size businesses, sports teams, TV and radio stations, local newspapers, and so on—are not the commanding heights of the economy. True, they command the heights of many a city; and the question will one day have to be faced: How much power over the local townscape, and thus over local politics, can be safely placed in private hands?

The very attraction of privacy, the lack of outside control, is the very thing that will one day concern the public if the private empires continue to wax and spread. As it is, the issue has been deferred by the tendency of private groups to self-destruct. The sobering thought, however, is that, if the Hunts, armed with $5 billion, had grown as fast as the Basses, starting with only one-hundredth of that amount, they would now be worth an unthinkable $500 billion.

For the sake of democracy as well as economic efficiency, the unthinkable had best stay that way. But the self-destruction of Bunker Hunt, down to a humble (but not humbling) $400 million in 1986, isn't only the consequence of his own incompetence. It reflects the fact that privacy is ultimately an inferior platform for growth. Big-time corporate managers can create money out of the air by issuing stock. The big-time privateer, like his golden age exemplars, can only create his loot by some form of real economic achievement, and that must be a hard trick.

3

LET YOUR
NEPHEW
TRY

Nepotism has acquired an increasingly bad name as the generations have passed—and as finally, in firm after firm, one generation of heirs has been found sorely lacking. That is another advantage the public company has over the private empire. In theory, the former can choose from the entire array of executive talent eager for the stock-option millions that wait at the top of the tree. The private family business is doubly strapped for candidates: confined for senior positions to family members, certain to miss out on ambitious outsiders who will never join a company where the top posts and top gains are reserved for the kin.

Arguments in favor of nepotism, as noted in Chapter 2, tend to run thin. For every August Busch III, who runs his great-grandfather's brewery better than any hired hand in the beer industry, and whose family thus enjoyed a $600 million-plus fortune, there's a bunch such as the two hundred timber-rich Weyerhaeusers, who shared $620 million, but have brought outside shareholders little joy. The family creed, quoted approvingly by one business professor, is "This is not for us or

our children, but for our grandchildren." At a midget capital appreciation of 1.2 percent over the decade to 1985, against 17.1 percent for the
Busches, the grandchildren might not be too impressed.

The Weyerhaeuser stake is only a tenth of the company, against
more than a quarter for the Busches, which makes the nepotism and
the poor performance much harder to defend. Within the wholly private possession, like the Pritzker empire, standards of performance are
relevant only to the family, and the outside world has no direct interest
in the competence or otherwise of the clan. It can carry on regardless
in the Hollywood tradition exemplified in the gibing rhyme: "Uncle
Carl Laemmle / Has a very large faemmle."

Evelyn Waugh expressed the same movie mogul tradition in his
novel *The Loved One*, where after one summary execution, a producer
suggests a relative of his wife's as replacement. "All right," is the
answer. "Let your nephew try." In the context of a family business, that
answer may not be as stupid as it sounds. In business, as in genealogy,
adoption has much the same effect as birth. But the son who inherits
the trappings of office, and its loot, by divine right may try to manage
in the same inherited way. The adopted protégé, whether he's the lucky
fellow who married the right daughter, or was born to the right sister,
or went to the right college, really has to work for his keep.

Rich fathers-in-law, for example, are generally suspicious of sons-
in-law, especially poor ones, until the nuptial acquisition proves himself
in battle. Like Tamino in Mozart's *Magic Flute*, any adoptee probably
has to pass through ordeals by fire and water before receiving full
initiation. Once accepted, however, he has all the advantages of his rich
protector, including cash and power, strengthened by his own drive and
guaranteed relative youth (girls tend to marry men younger than their
fathers).

Compared to a natural son, moreover, the adoptee has an irre-
placeable asset—the old man isn't his father. This doesn't remove the
possibility, even the inevitability, of conflict between generations, but
with luck it subtracts from the brew the ingredients of inferiority complex, dark primal hatreds, and contemptuous love. Many a son-in-law
has found that Tamino's trials don't cease with initiation. But many a
father-in-law has had cause to thank his daughter's natural instincts.

The great Philips electrical business was successively run by two
sons-in-law. When Konosuke Matsushita, founder of a more wondrous
electrical enterprise, retired to the position of "rear echelon chairman,"
he was succeeded by his son-in-law—who adopted Matsushita's name
(in much the same way as the Krupp in-laws added that family's
patronymic). In British retailing, Simon Marks and Israel Sieff formed
the second generation that transformed Marks & Spencer—and it was

the Sieffs's in-laws, not the Marks main line, who provided the management succession.

The most prominent son-in-law in the Western electrical and electronics industry is Arnold Weinstock, ennobled for his efforts in creating the General Electric Company. The future Lord Weinstock led his new family's firm out of the valley and into the broad uplands, where the old GEC paid a price that gave the family and its friends 15 percent of a corporate edifice then crumbling unsteadily toward bankruptcy. When the son-in-law, backed by the family equity, announced that he would attend no more meetings of a time-wasting management committee, he was hastily invited to take total command, and within a couple of years the profits were zooming upward.

So were the shares, multiplying ten times in five years and making that 15 percent, if still intact in 1986, worth around $1 billion. Weinstock's father-in-law, Michael Sobell, had the good sense to bow out early in this saga, sharing with Weinstock only in the management of their sporting horseflesh. It's a moot question whether it's always comfortable for the adopted successor to have his patron—especially his wife's father—hanging around the shop when the latter's day is officially done. It takes more than the honorary title of life president or some such (normally the corporate equivalent of the Holy Roman Empire, which was neither holy, Roman, nor an empire) to keep a self-made family superboss seen and not heard.

In his pugnacious seventies, a supermarket tycoon, who was succeeded, one after the other, by two sons-in-law, defined his role succinctly: "I'm a nagger. All I do is find fault." Performed tactfully, that's almost as valuable, in business terms, as finding a pot of gold. One slip on the wrong side of tact, however, and the son-in-law can readily be driven to drink or hibernation—after all, the man has been made rich by his father-in-law's shares and his own efforts, and he doesn't actually have to work.

In one set of circumstances, the old boy's interference can be ruled out of court, no matter how irresistible the governing urge: death. What comes to all men has had curious results in the case of women—curious because it casts a critical light on the prevailing they-shall-not-pass attitude of the dominant American male to the would-be female top manager. The Forbes 400 of 1985 included only 72 women; the number, 77, was no more impressive (especially if the numerous du Ponts are extracted) in 1986. Some were daughters. But the wealthy widows who stepped into their husbands' shoes did so with a success that should, perhaps, not be startling.

The saga of *The Washington Post* combines both the son-in-law syndrome and the widow's might. After Eugene Meyer had turned a bankrupt newspaper, purchased in 1933, into the capital's most powerful organ, his daughter's husband, Philip Graham, took charge. Philip killed himself in 1963, and under Katharine Graham's management, the Post company has prospered to the benefit of all (including billionaire Warren Buffett, who took a large and profitable position in the then undervalued stock).

No great U.S. fortune ($1 billion in sales, $350 million in 1986 family holdings) has been more worthily earned. It's easy to understand why Mrs. Graham's son, who is publisher of the *Post*, told *Forbes*: "My mother has given me everything except an easy path to follow." David Copley could say much the same of another media madam, his mother, Helen, who took charge of Copley Press and its nine dailies. That was a decade after Katharine Graham's assumption of the *Post*. In 1986, Mrs. Copley ran eleven papers that made her worth $335 million.

These women are no caretakers, although they have taken care of their fortunes as effectively as any macho business male. Helen Copley approached her role in the classic turnaround vein. So shy in public that she needed a speech professor to cure the condition, she instilled the sorely needed commercial ethos and disciplines into the papers (of which the *San Diego Union/Tribune* is best known), tidied up the corporate holdings, and added to the improved newspaper properties in cautious, effective style.

The formidable Dorothy Stimson Bullitt, yet another media queen, showed the more adventurous spirit to be expected of a lady who went down the Colorado rapids by raft in 1977, aged eighty-five. Opening the first TV station in the Northwest must have seemed at least as risky when there were only 6,000 sets in the entire region. Her King Broadcasting now has four TV stations, six in radio, and strong cable interests. Mrs. Bullitt came by her inheritance through her lumberman father, but took over the business in 1932 on her husband's death. The postwar media expansion to what, according to *Forbes*, was a value of at least $275 million in 1986 is the widow's work.

The combination of a husband's demise and media appears to be preternaturally potent. The *Houston Post* (which she later sold for $130 million) came into Oveta Culp Hobby's orbit through her marriage to former Texas governor William Hobby. The *Post* sale left the widow and her family dependent on the broadcasting interests she has been instrumental in adding, and which contributed powerfully to a family worth of over $400 million.

Maybe media ventures, with their highly personalized and generally autocratic ownership, and their clear division between the commercial and editorial sides, are particularly easy for a strong-willed and intelligent person to grasp and control without running into the complexities and chauvinism that block women's progress in other fields. Certainly the media widows have been fortunate in their landfall: newspapers, magazines, and broadcasting have been the most prolific sources of big money, outside of real estate, in recent years.

Media owners accounted for 69 of the Forbes 400 in 1985, up from 59 the year before. The explosion of communication and entertainment took most people by surprise in an era when printed media faced a seemingly deadly threat from electronics and when the television market was fragmenting. But fortunate positioning doesn't detract from the extraordinarily high activity and success ratio of the eleven super-rich widows. They proved financially wise in their choice of husbands, and still wiser in the business skills they brought to bear.

In truth, entrepreneurs are thrice blessed to have managerial talent visited on them from heaven by matrimony. Their luck lies in the essential difference between the creator and the critic. When Picasso died, the supply of Picassos (genuine ones, that is) ceased for all time, but the supply of critics of Picasso is timeless and inexhaustible. Business breakthroughs, too, are a form of creative art, and therefore often fail to conform to theoretical formulas—which is why so many wildly unorthodox approaches have achieved highly orthodox fortunes.

The critic mentality, and the son-in-law syndrome, come in at the next stage: when the big idea has turned into reality, when the small holding has become a fertile, king-size ranch of many acres, or has the chance to spread. At this point the creator finds himself in the additional, and often unwelcome, role of administrator. He needs a supply of managers, the artisans of business, to run his artistic shop. And he needs an analytical, understanding, critical intelligence to run the artisans.

These henchmen, of course, are disposable and replaceable, but, then, so is the Picasso himself in his new role of manager-in-chief. Very few masters are detached enough, or sufficiently interested in the wide world outside business, to recognize this reality—unless a son-in-law (real or metaphorical) fits naturally into the slot. The West Coast Croesus, Norton Simon, is a rare example of total abdication—maybe because this one-time scrap metal merchant had developed rare, expensive, and profitable tastes that absorbed more and more of his attention.

Simon progressed from metal to Old Masters on the unlikely back of the tomato, becoming the dominant force in U.S. ketchup with scarcely a false step. Outside of tomatoes, there was an ill-judged venture into non-scrap metal, when he bought a big steel firm. And the house that Norton Simon built had in its rooms the usual batch of misfit investments the Croesus type always collects: all collectors, even of businesses, are magpies.

45

Simon not only badly needed somebody to tidy up the collection. He wanted to retire to devote himself (very profitably, as it turned out) to paying (and, when he sold off the occasional work, getting) the world's highest prices for paintings. That is where nepotism comes in handiest—when the founding father wishes to hand on, or has to because of impending death. Without a family successor in sight, so that despotism cannot develop into nepotism in the normal way, the despot has to find an unofficial nephew.

Simon chose a hard-jawed former advertising agent, David J. Mahoney. Quickly satisfied by his protégé's performance, Simon sold virtually all his stock—leaving little behind but his name, and taking little with him, except for $100 million, which isn't so little. Simon was doubly wise. Not only has his fortune at least doubled since 1969, thanks largely to art, but the shareholders who stayed with Norton Simon, Inc., suffered severely when, later on, Mahoney ran out of luck, steam, interest, or all three. The company disappeared into Philip Morris, while Mahoney departed clutching a multimillion-dollar payoff that ranks among the less merited rewards in the history of hired hands.

The parting gift came on top of Mahoney's earlier rewards after his first four, far more glorious years at NSI. His stock options and largely company-financed preferred stock took Mahoney to a net worth of $14 million. Note, however, that Mahoney's money would not have bought too many Rembrandts. The adopted nephew always plays second fiddle financially to the godfather, and protégés who are unrelated by birth are most unlikely to make the Olympian monetary grade on which perch many relatives by marriage or blood.

Take the case of a miller named J. Arthur Rank, whose flour had already earned him more loot than he could conveniently spend. An ardent Methodist, Rank wanted to make good, wholesome films to counteract the insidious evil he saw creeping over the screen. Making films, he found, was one thing, getting them shown, another. By putting the two necessities together, Rank ended up owning the largest cinema chain in Britain, plus virtually all of the local Hollywood (a midget, hand-me-down copy of the real thing).

Since movies were not like mills, or film stars like flour bags, Rank came to rely on an accountancy-trained professional manager named John Davis. He proved no more able than the Hollywood moguls to avoid foundering before TV and the death of the star system. But one day a small Rochester, New York, company, desperate to exploit the expensive new invention on which its survival depended, made Davis an offer he could easily have refused. For under $850,000, Davis bought half the world rights outside North America in the unwieldy document copier the boys from Rochester had humbly lugged over to a London hotel.

In a decade, profits from Rank Xerox, less than $700,000 at the start, blossomed to $75 million. The only begetter of this bonanza, Davis, certainly made a couple of million or more as a result. But there's no doubt who profited most lavishly from the arrangement. The Davis take compared miserably with the nest egg of $600 million in the various Rank trusts at the end of that dramatic decade. To him that hath, much shall be given, remains the rule, even in enlightened nepotism.

Where the nepot should look for a surrogate son, if neither genetics nor matrimony have obliged, is a tricky question. Selecting some stalwart who has risen from the ranks seems the safest step. But there are a couple of hurdles (not counting the first of all, which is that the struggle for the crown prince's diadem will waste much energy that is better dedicated to the care of the founder's fortune).

One higher barrier is that the prince will have served so long at his master's feet that he may find it difficult to stand up straight, even if the master does a Simon-like abnegation (which he probably won't). The other main disadvantage is that tycoons are often unwilling to put total, unquestioning trust in a man whom they have ordered about for many years. The logic sounds weird, but is akin to the inability of fathers to have uncompromising faith in their sons. One such overlord, having finally been persuaded that his newly named, loyal, and able president was underpaid, reluctantly told him to put through a salary increase. After deep thought, the man gave himself $25,000 more.

The aggrieved chairman promptly summoned him and demanded an explanation. "You've only been in the job a few weeks," he expostulated, "and you've already cost me $25,000 of profit." If the tycoon looks outside for a protégé, he is less likely to show contempt and is certain not to get his man on the cheap. But unless he stumbles on a Davis or Mahoney by chance (Mahoney was working in a Simon acquisition, Canada Dry, and climbed to the top over the recumbent body of an adversary), the tycoon is apt to be terribly disappointed—and it's usually all his own fault.

He draws up an ideal blueprint, a job specification, for which the combined skills of Napoleon, Henry Ford I, and Winston Churchill are required—along with the humility and sweetness of Little Nell—and then is terribly disappointed when his choice turns out to be merely human. One such visionary was always discovering a new wonderchild, who never had time to don the purple before he was being shown to the door marked exit.

Harold Ross, the editor of *The New Yorker*, was a perfect example of this kind of proprietor. He wore out managing editors at a depressingly fast rate in his endless search for perfection (the choice even fell, in one spate of inspired lunacy, on James Thurber). Another ace practitioner of this deadly art was Charles B. Revson, creator of the Revlon cosmetics fortune. Revson's imminent appointment with his maker was, in fact, the main reason that Michel Bergerac was the first of many hired wondermen to stay the course. Others fell prey to an unattractive trait of Great Business Dictators. They will court potential nephews with every blandishment in their power, only to wonder, once the seduction has succeeded, why a man supposedly so good has given in.

The nephew-to-be is thereupon subjected to a bombardment from the resident Mussolini that guarantees failure. In Bergerac's luckier case, the inducements to leave ITT included an executive package that was rich even to American tastes, giving him the 1985 distinction, according to *Business Week*, of being the chief executive paid most for doing least for the stockholders. His stewardship culminated in an impudent takeover by a Florida company named Pantry Pride, which Charles Revson would have spat out whole.

Thanks to one of the most golden parachutes ever stitched together by a board, Bergerac departed with a payoff of bizarre bounty: $35 million. That still left plenty for the victor, Ronald Perelman. He paid $1.8 billion for Revlon, recouped $1.4 billion by selling off Bergerac's least attractive acquisitions, and was left with sales of $1.7 billion, on which operating profits of $195 million should have been a cinch. The sales accounted for just over half of Perelman's total trade, all achieved by the acquisition know-how originally learned at father's knee.

His father, Raymond, told *Fortune:* "When Ronnie was a boy, whenever I was thinking of making an acquisition, we would drive out to look at the company and discuss the pluses and minuses together." The crucial point in this endearing tale of family life is that the younger Perelman left his father's business and advice behind in 1978, aged thirty-five, to embark on a far riskier and higher-flying expansion, replete with massive debt and junk bonds.

That tale encapsulates an important truth about nepotism and supreme business talent. By and large, the latter is inherited. That may sound unfair, but it would not surprise a geneticist. In the Forbes 400 of 1985, well over half came from business families. Most were sons, of whom 103 continued in the same line of business as their fathers (just as Ron Perelman, born to a conglomerator, conglomerated in turn). In contrast, only 18 branched out in totally different directions.

The environmentalist wouldn't let the geneticist have it all his own way. He would note the effect of father's knee (as in the Perelman case).

The infant businessman acquires knowledge as well as genes, ethos as well as aptitudes. He also probably acquires either capital or access to capital. Moreover, he never has to resolve the most basic problem faced by any entirely self-made man or woman: where to start. Nature and nurture point the family member in the direction of the flight path.

There's some evidence, though, that the takeoff is most explosive when the second generation, either through choice or necessity, flies solo. Perelman is an example of a far more successful breakaway from the paternal success. But there are many more instances of sons who have far outdone their fathers—often in full awareness of their motivation. Leslie Herbert Wexner is a case in billion-dollar point. After starting in his father's clothing store, Wexner quit in 1963 to start on his own with $5,000 supplied by an aunt. As he told *Forbes*, "I wanted to show my dad." That explicit motivation built a specialty retailer that went public in 1969 with six stores in the Columbus, Ohio, region. In 1986 Wexner had some 2,500 stores and sales of $2.4 billion. He had rewarded the investors (including himself, above all) with a 4,045 percent gain between the end of 1976 and March 1986. His big regret was, "My father did not live to see it."

In the case of the Gallo brothers, Ernest and Julio, their father was dead, by his own hand, before their saga even started. In the wine business where Joseph Gallo had failed, destroyed by the Depression, the boys progressed in a straight line from bulk sales at cut price to dominant force in the U.S. market, making more wine than anybody else—and more dollars. "I've never lost money," says Ernest, who followed up the first inquiry for their product with a personal visit to the customer and, traveling onward, and eastward, didn't come home until the entire first year's output had been sold. The Gallos now share at least $700 million.

The key to men such as Wexner or the two Gallos is that, while every son no doubt wishes to surpass his father, many doubt their abilities to do so, and doubt still more when their father's living shadow lies over their desks. The breakaway combines strength of motivation with freedom of action. In exploiting these advantages, moreover, he tends (just like Perelman) to show greater daring as he strives to outstrip his parent's progress or, sometimes, to redress his wrongs.

The tragedy of Sir Keith Murdoch's otherwise successful career in Australian newspapers, for example, was his failure to capitalize on his creation of a leading national chain. On his death, Murdoch left more ambition than estate to his son Rupert. The latter, in contrast, has never repeated his father's mistake. Oxford-educated, he brought a gut instinct for pop journalism to make his first fortune from an inherited, ailing newspaper in Adelaide, moved decisively from Australia into

Britain, where he performed the same trick to far greater financial effect with the *Sun*, tried the same formula (with poor results) in New York with the *Post*, bought the London *Times* and *Sunday Times*, destroyed the power of the London printing unions with the most brilliant employer coup in the history of labor relations, switched his main attention to TV and film screens in America, and consolidated one of the largest media empires worldwide—all while retaining 49 percent ownership control through his private company.

The crowning, more-than-symbolic moment came in 1986, when Murdoch, worth over $725 million from his labors, bid for and won the company that owns the *Melbourne Herald*, the very paper Sir Keith had edited without owning. No doubt Murdoch, like Wexner, only regretted that his father wasn't there to see it. In many cases, though, if the father had been around, there would have been much less, maybe nothing to see. Fathers and sons can work together in financial harmony. But for every Lester Crown, who worked with Chicago's great Col. Henry Crown in building up a $1.3 billion fortune, partly in General Dynamics (23 percent), largely in real estate and other investments, there are many other sons whose only hope of achievement is escape.

Those who stay must often endure harassment, even humiliation, as they wait for death to us part. There is, for instance, one magnate of notable capacity who, by great good fortune, conceived a natural son possessed of every necessary virtue: a calm, methodical, intelligent manager, with none of his father's passion for the big deal (of the double or single variety). The son quietly and sensibly developed the business, while his father prowled about looking for anyone whom he might devour. Every now and again, seemingly as a tease for the good son, the father would fall for some simulacrum of his own young self: a fast-draw gunslinger who had made millions while still (in business terms) in short pants.

The father's favor would be publicly blazoned forth, often by the new nephew; this new love was cemented by details that were once or twice semipublicly criticized by the good son. The implication was that Big Daddy, disappointed with his son's lack of adventure, might shift some of the inheritance to the dashing shoulders of Little Nephew.

In all the excitement, few people, even the nephews, noted that the terms of their business relationship were, as was his wont, unduly favorable to the old maestro. His favor, suddenly and warmingly given, could be just as abruptly withdrawn, at which point the former nephew would find himself clutching the short end of the deal. A sound policy when dealing with wealthy veterans is to assume that the wiliness and power that propelled them to their wealth has in no wise been dissipated by age. Their favor, like that of any absolute monarch, is fickle; the sane courtier protects his front at all times and never turns his back.

Those adopted nephews who neglect this truth are liable to end up like the numerous potential pilots at Occidental Petroleum, whose dropping had the not-so-incidental effect of leaving Dr. Armand Hammer in total charge into his eighties. Harold S. Geneen, still sitting on the board at ITT, made chief executive life untenable for his first chosen successor. Harry S. Gray of United Technologies went a bridge too far by splitting the board over the dismissal of his heir apparent. Gray's board meekly caved in while the corporation's virtual creator clung to as much power as possible. But Gray obviously couldn't hope to repeat the performance, and the crown finally and inevitably slipped from his grasp.

It's desperately difficult for potentates to select successors who might outdo them from any source, kin or no kin, kith or no kith. Plainly, everybody's interests, including their own as shareholders (if they survive) and creators, are best served by finding the best man or woman. If the paragon can be discovered among the kin, so much the better; it keeps all, instead of nearly all, the money in the family. But nepotism, even in its remoter reaches, is probably a mistake in businesses that have already adopted all the standard corporate characteristics, including the routine bureaucratic defense mechanisms, of an ITT or a United Technologies.

The du Ponts may just have got away with naming Crawford H. Greenawalt, a du Pont by marriage, as president, although the results, the start of a long Du Pont profit stagnation, don't support their case. Where professional, hired managers will accept a son, especially if they have been schooled to do so, they may balk at seeing nephews, cousins, and in-laws stepping on to all the top rungs. Wallace Barnes, the fourth-generation boss of an engineering company with $432 million of sales, discovered this difficulty when seeking an outsider to occupy his throne. *Fortune* reports that Barnes found it "a bit of a shock" when candidates "always inquired in great detail about my children and my cousin's children and their career plans."

The applicants can't be blamed for their suspicions. In family business, it's usually all or nothing. Nepotists try to get around this by adopting the odd henchman as "almost one of the family": in one case, where blood was not only thicker than water but also strongly Sicilian, the few stolid Wasps who had been admitted to the inner councils were obliged to become honorary Italians. One even grew a Godfather mustache. The successor, though, was the real godfather's son.

To put it another way, water is thinner than blood. On the face of it, Richard Rainwater, the college friend of Sid Bass, had no cause to regret his years spent making Bass and his three brothers richer than the Hunts—turning a $50 million starter into wealth that *Forbes* places at $3.2 billion and *Business Week* at maybe $5 billion. Whatever the sum, Rainwater's genius at making deals (notably the $850 million raked in from saving Walt Disney) played a key part in amassing that total.

"He just loves to make people rich," according to a former associate: that includes himself—Rainwater, says *Business Week*, is thought to have accumulated $175 million since he joined the Basses in 1970. But that hardly compares well with the lion's shares of the Bass brothers, any more than Rainwater's authority could compete with his boss's: "Sid always had the final say, of course, but as the two disagreed more frequently, Rainwater chafed under the restrictions." His departure to run his own operations in 1986 was less surprising than his staying so long.

Family owners have a strictly limited chance of attracting and certainly retaining top-class outsiders, even ones with less protean powers than Rainwater. The acid test is whether there is any chance in this life of a nonfamily executive being promoted over the head of a family member. It can happen: after 131 family years at the F & M Schaefer brewing giant, a seventy-two-year-old father plucked a management expert-cum-academic from outside to replace himself as CEO, passing over a forty-two-year-old son. If family boss follows family boss forevermore, the nonkin will never be better than faithful family retainers— and some other, brusquer solution than Schaefer's will have to be found, one day, to the inevitable management and business problems.

Other brewing dynasties—witness not only Anheuser-Busch but also Coors—have been unnaturally successful at breeding capable family managers. Despite the Busch family's remarkable feat, selling the average American 122 bottles of Budweiser per year, the Coors family, with a collective $560 million, run the Busch fortune close, with non-beer interests (industrial ceramics), and two of the kin have won plaudits for managing Coors upward from the earnings trough created by indifferent marketing and misguided attitudes on minorities.

But the trough, not the salvation, might easily have been the final fate of Coors. The childless or effectively childless emperor could be luckier than he knows. If he can stumble across the right protégé, the person who can make sense out of success, he can leave a lasting monument and enjoy his own last years. If he can't, or if it falls into the hands of feckless sons, the empire will eventually dissolve.

Men seldom toil to create gold alone; the business itself, their creation and dearest child, is the name of their game. Rather than lose its glory, it's far better to "let your nephew try."

4

WHAT'S BAD ENOUGH FOR GRANDPA

At the heart of the issues of nepotism, of dynastic perpetuation, and of family control lies a fundamental problem of all business management. The answers are more difficult, but the question is the same. Every business has to tread a frayed tightrope between conservatism and change. If it fails to move with the times, it risks falling behind, as Krupp did during the forlorn effort to prolong a nineteenth-century patriarchy into the 1960s. If an old established company tries too hard to turn newfangled, as Hoover did under Herbert W. Hoover, Jr., it risks destroying the very strengths that made it great.

Theoretically, it's a toss-up which course is more dangerous, sticking too long to the old or shifting too zealously to the new. But more once-great companies have vanished from sight through being swamped by the tides of history than through swimming too hard in an effort to keep up with the Marxist dialectic. That famous news photograph of the aged Sewell Avery being carried, chair and all, out of the Montgomery Ward offices to end his resistance to President Roosevelt's order to accept a union symbolizes the fate of all firms and financial heroes who resist history. They get beaten—Montgomery Ward, once a name to mention in the same breath as Sears Roebuck, became but a shadow of that mighty shape.

The issue isn't only that what's good enough for grandpa can't be equally good for every succeeding generation. Often it's the old boy himself who is the purblind villain. All great entrepreneurs have grave weaknesses, the blindest of spots, both in their business attitudes and in their treatment of other people. As they grow older and more hallowed and even wealthier, the partial blindness tends to become more severe and to affect the way in which the company does its business.

The natural belief of the rich, shared by their publicists and their public, is that the methods that brought them their yachts, mansions, and Monets are not only right, brilliant, and socially desirable but also everlasting. The heirs of founding fathers and grandfathers usually share this pious delusion, but worse damage may well be done by the old gentleman himself as he pursues his star to the illogical conclusion.

The postwar history of European business contains some ripe examples. A devastated Continent catching up on U.S. standards of living, with the aid of U.S. finance, offered inordinate opportunities to men of courage, men who often, because of the lost wartime years, came into their glory late in life. They were older in years and in background than the men who ran U.S. business, and the concepts of public ownership or what passes for modern management were as far removed from their minds as Mars is from Earth.

Not that American business was free from the same syndrome. Henry Ford I and Sewell Avery were conspicuous examples of old men who had long outlived their commercial usefulness. And even the ranks of entrepreneurs who had waxed with the war effort included titans whose territory dwindled in the peace—for notable example, Henry J. Kaiser, the herculean builder of Liberty ships. The aberration of believing that he could market a car called the "Henry J" successfully by the same techniques was only one stage in the decline of the Kaiser empire. In 1985 only Kaiser Aluminum & Chemical survived in the Fortune 500, and no Kaisers rank among the richest American fortunes.

At that, the Kaisers lack not for wealth. They have fared far better than the heirs of a European Kaiser, Cornelius Verolme. The future czar of Europe's shipbuilders, Verolme only began his career in his later forties, when he conceived the notion that, since 5,700 Allied ships (many of them built by Henry J.) had gone down during the war, an insatiable replacement market must exist. He worked up from reconditioning old marine engines to running the most modern shipyard in

Rotterdam (whose higher-toned shipbuilders promptly blackballed the upstart from their exclusive club).

Blackballs and all, Verolme built over a hundred ships in under two decades to a value of more than $330 million. His was the archetypal cry of the victorious grandfather: "Never have any doubts about your own ability. Never ask, Can I do it? No, do it!" The catch was that, like most powerful, self-made men, Verolme not only did it, but sought to do it all himself. A professional manager, called in to man the pumps of the sinking group, said, "I warned him several times that in the end he would not be thanked if he went on running the show himself as long as possible. . . . It is nonsense for a man to travel round the world personally to win orders."

Nonsense, however, is what takes control when the grandparental diseases of inordinate ambition, overweening self-confidence, and inadequate systems take control. Verolme knew no principle of business other than keeping everything to himself; nobody else knew much about profits save that they were mostly plowed back—though some of the money went into furrows such as the large yacht from which Verolme kept in constant touch with his office on shore. Even with his group almost bankrupt, this doughty old man went on fighting to regain control of the $150 million empire he created and all but destroyed.

This repeated tragedy is of Greek dimensions: the old king who pulls his kingdom down by clinging too long to the methods that originally raised him to the throne. Among the similar doomed rulers who abound in business history, the Italian appliance millionaires had one of the sharpest rises and falls. They began after World War II, in an Italy that lacked both a market in consumer durables and manufacturers. The Zanussi family, the future lords of this slice of creation, had actually started by making iron-age products such as wood-burning stoves.

As Italian housewives began to clamor for more electric labor saving, the Zanussis, Ignis, the Borghis (Guido, with sons Gaetano, Giovanni, and Giuseppe), and the Zoppas expanded at a furious pace, built the most efficient and productive plants in the world, and barged so heavily into other European markets (essential to keep their productive monsters satisfied) that they virtually destroyed much of the competition. In the process they so saturated their own market that the Italian boom in refrigerators was over by the mid-1960s; that in washing machines ended by 1967 or 1968. The rest of Europe peaked out only slightly later, and the Italian tycoons were left with a tortuous management problem—and no managers to solve it.

Fortuitously, the families were hit by dynastic and business disaster simultaneously. Lino Zanussi, the entrepreneur nearest to managerial stature and builder of the strongest group, died in an air crash with his heir apparent. Only one Borghi survived to take Ignis into the multinational embrace of Philips. The three Zoppas brothers died within twelve months of each other, leaving $75 million-odd in bank debts and a company, taken over in extremis by Zanussi, losing about $1 million each month.

Another Zanussi buy, Triplex, was losing only marginally fewer millions, as the workers, the original beneficiaries of the appliance boom, acted as the final wreckers by staging a spate of strikes, staved off only by ruinous wage increases. Accidents aside, the families paved the way for their own dissolution by continuing to manage businesses of international scale with methods insufficiently remote from the old wood-burning days. In 1986, the wheel of ill fortune completed its turn. Zanussi, crippled by debt, succumbed gratefully to Electrolux, a group run by hardheaded, nondynastic Swedes.

The appearance of simultaneous dynastic disasters emphasizes the chief danger of family enterprise: a bad genealogical run can ruin the act. In Lancashire textiles, where the heredity failed almost universally, the saying used to be "clogs to clogs in four generations." These days, though, it's far harder to return to square one—tycoons may lose their businesses, but seldom all their baksheesh.

There are cases of yacht to dinghy, triplex apartment to farm, Cadillac to Chevrolet, in one generation, more often in one lifetime. But in the Age of the Common Millionaire, few families are foolish enough to leave all their eggs in one locked-in basket, and few husbands imprudently forget to set up their wives in the manner to which they have both been accustomed. The two devices that have created and perpetuated the Common Millionaire, the partial sale of equity to the doting public and the "provision for the family" in a man's lifetime by the formation of trusts, both also serve to keep the family in bread and butter in the event of failure by grandpa or his heirs.

Following the draconian law of business (that incompetence breeds more incompetence), few sights are more awe-inspiring, however, than the completion by heirs of the crumbling begun by the progenitor. Had William Randolph Hearst possessed less megalomania, less talent as a newspaperman, less obsessive extravagance, and more business acumen, the Hearst empire would today be fit to share the same paragraph as Ford or possibly even Mellon. But Hearst's dictatorial methods and disdain for economics left his two sons a dwindling empire with a managerial heritage they proceeded to dissipate by squabbling with the managers.

The thirty papers that remained at the old man's death, still a formidable collection, shrank to eight. Unheard-of and relatively diminutive figures (in both senses) such as Samuel I. Newhouse overtook the giant with stupefying ease. In one generation, it was almost as if W. R. had never rejected an editorial; after two generations, there was even less evidence that W. R.'s father had ever exploited the Comstock Lode.

But the Hearst money was big, the biggest, and it's this size of accumulation that is all but impossible to destroy—as Henry Ford I proved by the survival of a colossal family inheritance through a decade of grotesque mismanagement and inept financial provision. Even though the Ford Foundation siphoned off much of the family loot into philanthropy, the three grandchildren of Henry Ford were worth nearly $700 million in 1985. The comeback of the Hearsts, under the direction of William Randolph's son, Jr., has provided a still more dramatic demonstration that new wine in old bottles can work in business, if not in oenology.

After 1974, when the family repurchased control from the Hearst foundations, and the Hearst holdovers who ran them, the restructured and revitalized corporation emerged as a $2 billion collection of dailies (fourteen), magazines (twenty, including *Cosmopolitan* and *Good Housekeeping* at opposite ends of the female spectrum), TV stations (seven), radio stations (another seven), and other interests of which both the dynastic founders would have been proud. Note, however, that under William Randolph's original testamentary dispensation, the renaissance of the family fortunes could never have occurred.

The old man was eighty-eight when death, as it comes to all men, came to him. The Hearst case, like that of Henry Ford, reinforces the logical belief that fathers and grandfathers, however brilliant their past achievements, should be compelled to retire from executive action at the ripe young age of sixty-five, at the latest, and that the arrangements for the succession should be ratified by outside decision. However, that flies in the face of both the realities of power and the fact that many ancients are not only powerful but also effective in their biological dotage.

Many lasting fortunes have been supervised day-to-day to a great age by people who share the attitude of Edward John DeBartolo, the king of shopping centers, with fifty-five major malls around the United States. According to *Forbes*, "Mr. D" alters his 6:00 A.M. to after-dark routine only on Sundays, when he works a mere seven hours. He has never taken a vacation. At the age of sixty-eight, and a worth of $900 million or more, DeBartolo affirmed: "I'm going to keep going until somebody hits me in the face with a spade. Period."

For the son and daughter in the business, that implied, while wishing their father an exceptionally long life, wishing him still more fervently an even more exceptional ability to adapt to change with advancing years. The clue lies somewhere along that tightrope between change and continuity. If the progenitor possesses some instinct, maybe only the desire to maximize a profit, which keeps him flexible into his physical decline, he can do more good than harm. Once he gets glued into his ideas and ways, however, damage is inevitable, not least because his successors, probably lacking his genius, will be as heavily indoctrinated with the allied arrogance.

It may take a long time before the vultures come home to roost. A family can be undermined, while still staying rich enough to take care of every need of subsequent generations—provided, that is, that the generations are neither excessively prolific nor overfond of disputation. In the 1920s the German family of Stinnes possessed one of Europe's premium fortunes, not of Rothschild rank, but fit to vie with Krupp and the like. In the nineteenth century, shipping and coal had founded the fortune; with the third generation, Hugo, known as the King of Assyria for his stern black beard, added steel, oil, and papermaking to the mix. Within two years of Hugo's death, the family had to turn to U.S. banks for $25 million.

The family kept half the U.S. company, which now held most of the Stinnes assets, but lost these (as enemy property) in the war. Through all this period, and thereafter, the main problem was the total inability of the three sons to abide one another. One was bought out; the other two had to be forcibly parted by the widow, who sacked the second son. This Stinnes, Hugo, Jr., went off to found his own empire in engineering and plastics. When that came unstuck in 1963, the rest of the family interests, still presided over by the King of Assyria's widow at the age of ninety-three, were also on the rocks, despite, or very possibly because of, the fact that the final manager of the truncated empire was Franz von Papen, the last German chancellor before Adolf Hitler.

Dynastic succession is a hit-or-miss game. It used to be a matter for marvel how superbly the successor generations at Pirelli, Fiat, and Olivetti, the three jewels in Italy's industrial crown, had carried on the founders' good work. Men such as Leopoldo Pirelli or Fiat's Giovanni Agnelli (after the latter gave up playboying for business) won heroic reputations. If they claimed the credit for the earlier success, all three have to take the responsibility for the later reverses. In the third management upheaval in Olivetti in seven hard years, that hard truth was grasped: Roberto was retired to a nonexecutive position—even though the family had 22.9 percent of the equity.

Even that didn't save the good old family firm. It took an outsider, Carlo de Benedetti, to rescue Olivetti from incipient bankruptcy and to create thereby a new, Benedetti fortune that bid fair to outstrip the old Olivetti money. As for Agnelli, he grew older, mellower, and, with the passage of time, much richer and better at management. Fiat never did become the clear leader of the European car industry that its dominance of the Italian market (cemented by the acquisition of both Lancia and Alfa-Romeo) should have enabled. But as in the analogous case of Ford in America, the historical strengths carried the company through the worst efforts of later managers to sabotage the fortunes of the firm—and the family.

Managements that suffer such monumental reverses can't have been doing everything right. Fiat was, after all, once forced to omit its dividend. The Agnellis, whose tentacles spread into every corner of Italian business life, can manage without the money. But could their main company have done better without the one-man Agnelli pinnacle? To judge by what happened after 1980, the answer is obvious. That was when Cesare Romiti took over as premier to Agnelli's constitutional king and proceeded to raise profits to $1.3 billion from the awful $60 million he inherited. Necessity is usually the mother of such handovers. Without external pressures, if your father and grandfather dominated the show, you are unlikely to settle for less. This is rarely a source of strength—the exceptions prove a different rule.

Sam Johnson, the reigning wax emperor mentioned approvingly in Chapter 2, is no exception among the four successive Johnsons who have headed S. C. Johnson. The quartet have taken their private realm in Racine, Wisconsin, into personal care, financial services, recreational equipment, and venture capital as they have moved beyond the bounds of wax and polish to world sales of around $2 billion. Sam Johnson's business philosophy exemplifies the conservatism with which the family has gone about its business: "I go into things with my little toe first," he told *Forbes*. But a conservative approach to novel ideas is not always the worst business strategy, and it's one that seems to have come naturally (the best way) to the Johnsons. According to one admiring executive, there's "not a drop-out, not a lemon, among them. Each one has been more aggressive than his father in business terms. They've all had different ideas about what could and should be done, and each seems to have had the very strong feeling that anything the old man could do, he could do a lot better."

The Johnsons, in addition to inculcating business sense into their sons, have indoctrinated their scions in a social ethic of good works. This has given the company a frame of reference more specific than the general Italian paternalism, as practiced at Fiat and other places. But Fiat still has an autocratic style that the old Agnelli, and his strongman successor, Professor Valletta, would have recognized. The reasons are not just Italian (although from medieval and Renaissance times dynasties have wielded most of the country's real power). The autocracy also reflects a curious internal logic of car companies the world over.

Historical accident produced car companies that were structured around one man, largely because the successful car empires (a handful of survivors from a legion of competitors) were built around one automotive hit; and a wonder car almost always springs from one man's instinct and inspiration. The Ford company under Henry II, though perforce utterly different in most ways from the creation Henry I left behind, still bowed its collective head to the reigning Mr. Ford, who was less a *primus inter pares* than a king among courtiers.

That was the truth that Lee Iacocca signally failed to grasp. Kings and queens have ever distrusted overmighty courtiers. The burning ambition to be Duke of Dearborn led Iacocca to behave in the way that has lost impetuous subjects their heads since history began. He started to enjoy the perquisites of majesty while the throne was already occupied. He intrigued against the mighty one. He forgot that, without the favor of the monarch, the courtier has no power base.

The realities of power and those of common sense may not be the same. The one-man say-so that made Ford managers jump in the heydays of the two Henrys produced generations of dangerous subservience. Trundling up for pats or kicks makes perfect sense in the atmosphere of a court. It makes no sense in the conditions of modern competition for world markets, in which professionalism, not prostration, must be decisive. And if dynastic firms lag behind in adapting their management styles to changed days and ways—including the irritating wish of the workers to have some say about their work—the fortunes of the dynasties are sure to suffer, as they have done in Italy.

Leopoldo Pirelli, returning to work in 1973 after a car crash that killed his brother, had to face the hard fact that management autocracy coupled with technical failure had laid his company appallingly low. A dozen years of hard work later, sales of $3.65 billion were safely tucked away in Swiss ownership, along with $101 million in net income, showing how shrewdly the tire and cable giant had climbed from low to high; and how much the Age of the Common Millionaire has reduced the chances of widespread devastation for those families that are sensible enough to spread the risk, either by diversifying away from the main business or by spreading the wealth (or at least the ownership) to the public at large.

That has much the same effect, since the cash received for the family shares will be deployed elsewhere. The consistency of the Forbes 400 from year to year is quite remarkable: of the 1984 roster, only 23 suffered financial reverses. The 1985 list showed even greater resilience—only 9 went down by reason of poor performance. That lends a certain distinction to cases such as that of the Murchison brothers of Dallas. They were among the first Texans to come riding out of the Southwest into the canyons of Wall Street in the 1960s, launching an acrimonious but ultimately successful attack on Investors Diversified Services, then the largest mutual fund group. By the mid-1980s, one brother was dead and the other financially moribund, weighed down by debt, in Chapter 11 bankruptcy protection, and worth nothing like the $250 million of the year before.

Still, that counts as a mere oversight compared to the dwindling of Nelson Bunker Hunt's fortune from a world-leading $16 billion before the seizure of his Libyan assets to perhaps $400 million as he battled with the banks, the oil slump, and the aftermath of the great silver disaster. This wasn't a case of what's bad enough for grandpa, but of ignoring what was good for him. "Dad said," so Nelson's brother William Herbert is quoted in *Forbes*, "never borrow money unless you can get it paid back. I guess I didn't listen well enough."

The Hunt boys are a perfectly imperfect example of the conflict between conservatism and innovation, in which conservatism (caution over incurring debt) lost and innovation (speculating in silver rather than prospecting for oil) won a Pyrrhic victory. The good son would approach his inheritance in the same spirit as any professional manager taking over a new corporation. He would survey its strengths and weaknesses, ascertain its opportunities and threats, and then devise a strategy to accentuate the positive and eliminate the negative. Only, an heir may never get the breathing space in which to deploy the professional approach—his own conditioned reflexes, and those of the kin and nonkin who surround him, may call the tune to which he marches.

The wreckage a truly determined family can wreak on grandpa's legacy is demonstrated in reverse by the work done on Waterman by the unlikely Madame Francine Gomez. Waterman once enjoyed all but a tithe of U.S. fountain pen sales, but the U.S. company, battered by ballpoints, had been sold in 1958, while the French company, which had the European rights, struggled steadily toward the grave. Madame Gomez, taking control of the inheritance from her mother, had to sack nine out of ten top executives, cut the labor force by 485 persons, reduce the head office to a quarter of its former size, move it, buy back the U.S. company, and refurbish everything in sight—thus converting a half a million loss into a $1.5 million profit and creating a business that was still setting the pace in fountain pens in the mid-1980s.

If grandpa and his heirs are to hang on to their hats, that ideal balance has to be struck between conservatism and radicalism. The principles are quite easy. First, no cow can be sacred—anything can be changed, and anybody can be put out to grass, if change or grassing appear necessary. Second, there's an obvious distinction between those traditions that are material to the business and those that are merely nice to have around—much like a clump of mistletoe at Christmas. Leave the latter alone, so long as they don't cost much and people like them. As for the former, meticulously question every one, and if the answers come out wrong, found a new tradition.

Finally, suppose that the business is running quite beautifully; don't succumb completely to the correct urge to leave well enough alone. Search for one area of inadequately exploited opportunity; find one function or part of the company that isn't running with the same degree of smooth beauty as the rest. Concentrate on these two fields— good grandpas always do, before their arteries begin to harden.

But that leads to the hardest trick of all: removing or immobilizing the old boy (or boys) before he (they) start costing the rest of the family a deal of money. Short of parricide, which isn't legal, there is no sure method. The older the family incubus gets, the harder it becomes to insult him, to intimate that he is no longer wanted. There is only one gun that his juniors can level at his head—a threat that, if he doesn't go, they will. But heirs are generally too intimidated (and too scared, often with good reason, of their chances of finding acceptable employment elsewhere) to fire that weapon. They prefer, unwittingly but surely, to go down with the captain—and the ship.

Book II

THE CHANGING STYLES IN BOOTSTRAPS

5

GREAT OAKS
FROM LITTLE
ACORNS GROW

Short of inheriting, stealing, dealing, printing, or finding the stuff, the millionaire has to work for his apotheosis. And for self-made millionaires, there is only one method: commercial arboriculture. He has to start from the earth, planting one seed, nursing it to sapling and then tree-size, and next encouraging the good work until he has a whole forest, or at least one towering California redwood, on and in his hands.

Any old seed will do: a drive-in hamburger joint in Des Plaines, Illinois; a recipe for a bread substitute; a garage in Tokyo; a women's sportswear shop in Columbus, Ohio. The list could roll on through every possible avenue of wealth. But these particular fortunes (the McDonald's chain that made Ray Kroc's multimillions, Kellogg's cereals, Honda motorbikes and cars, the stores of The Limited) all have one thing in common: they began with one thing. From that point the laws of geometric progression took over. The little man who runs one shop or garage well can probably (but not certainly, so watch it) run two. If he can operate two successfully, he can with equal likelihood cope with four . . . and thus his progress continues until he comes up against the sound barrier created either by his own competence (or incompetence), by competitive conditions, or by the nature of his market.

For most little men the exact speed at which they either pass through the barrier or stay permanently subsonic is academic. The overwhelming mass of small-business ventures remain single, small, and unadventurous. On one estimate, 10,000 enterprises fail for every one that climbs or multiplies out of sight. Although in the golden glow of hindsight the tycoon's advance from doing his one thing seems inexorable, almost preordained, that transformation is a rare event, something like spotting a four-leaf clover in a cabbage patch.

To start with, running one small business efficiently is less easy than it sounds. The activity isn't especially demanding, but the ability to analyze the shop or sweatshop, to work out the key ratios on which it depends, to understand instinctively what is good business and what isn't—these are uncommon gifts. Without them, the would-be entrepreneur not only can't exact the maximum toll from his little enterprise, but can't hope to control much more as he sets out on his geometric route.

On his way to becoming Lord Forte, a keen young businessman worked out in his little milk bar the set of ratios that was still serving him well in a $2.5 billion empire nearly forty years later. Britain's seaside is festooned by catering emporiums operated and owned by various members of the prolific Forte family. But only Uncle Charlie made the big time, and his ratios, together with the quality of business mind that saw their magical relevance, had much to do with his dynastic progression.

The proprietor has to be brilliant at tending his seeds and saplings to have any chance among the great oaks. There are, no doubt, exceptions where astounding fortune, or the advent of a fairy godfather, made a vital difference; and even the brilliant single proprietor needs further propulsion than simple efficiency. He must want, truly and deeply, to aggrandize his business—and this quality is almost as rare as competence.

The fact that he runs one successful and reasonably appetizing eatery, owns one monopoly newspaper, produces one low-powered motorized bike that actually sells like the dream of its name, or brings in customers for sportswear in one outlet financed with $5,000 from a relative imposes no obligation to open more outlets (à la McDonald's), add twenty-eight more newspapers (like Samuel Newhouse), advance through every size of bike to become one of the world's most respected carmakers (the feat of Soichiro Honda), or expand from the single store into a $2 billion empire. Growth is an optional extra. For every retailer in women's wear such as Leslie Wexner, whose success with The Limited has made fifty more millionaires out of his executives, and who enjoyed a personal wealth of over $1.5 billion before becoming a main sufferer of October 1987, hundreds of thousands are buying and selling away who can't, won't, and don't want to see beyond a single dress rack.

The world knows many small builders who made it big—construction being one of those helpful industries where, since the main item of expense is labor, you can start with nothing. But nothing is where most builders end, building being the West's fastest route to bankruptcy. John Murdoch Harbert III was fully aware of this potential of his trade: "Our creditors," he told *Forbes*, "remained unaware of the seriousness of our situation." Harbert invested $6,000 of wartime crap winnings in a concrete mixer and tools, moving on from building a local bridge via everything from pipelines to high-rolling deals in the Third World, to arrive at a $600 million fortune. But for every Harbert there are hundreds of thousands who, while evading bankruptcy just as successfully, have also avoided the accumulation of anything more than a financial nubbin.

The bitter truth is that most proprietors who stick with a restricted lot are only capable of a strictly limited amount of success. There is a small shop selling riding gear in London that perfectly epitomizes the true situation. For decades it has sported a notice saying that "owing to pressure of business this shop will stay closed on Mondays." The small businessman grown big never has that lack of energy.

Those whose little acorns grow are often astonishingly fast at performing calculations in their head. One statistically trained boss is supposed to go through complex operational research routines in his head while cruising along in his Rolls; another had total recall of the latest figures, or the old ones for that matter, of every one of over a hundred divisions.

This encyclopedic knowledge of the firm is in itself a good sign, evidence of both flair and thoroughness. But a specialized computer facility in the head is no substitute for paperwork. The headwork tycoon is also capable of placing his figures where they belong, which is on paper: a location that has the advantage that others can also get at those precious digits. And the fundamental difference between the acorn and the oak, let alone the forest of business, is that with greater scale the proprietor needs to deal with greater numbers of those awkward objects known as people.

The methods of managing men employed by the self-propelled proprietor often include arrogant repression or heavy selection from his own ethnic group—and the business grown from small beginnings often does have an ethnic flavor. A high proportion of little-acorn-to-great-oak cases are of immigrant stock. There's even a plausible case for arguing that the superbillionaires of the United States are the supreme exponents of the immigrant drive; after all, a century ago practically everybody in most of the United States was a first- or second-generation immigrant.

This factor almost certainly explains a great deal about the fervent thrust of the business empires created by men such as Andrew Carnegie (whose father was a desperately poor Scot) or the du Ponts (refugees from France) or the seemingly endless list of German-Jewish merchants and financiers (Belmont, Kress, Lehman, Salomon, Kahn, Guggenheim, Schiff, Altman, *und so weiter, und so weiter*).

The same phenomenon occurred in Britain before the war with the creation of Shell (Samuel) and ICI (by three geniuses named Brunner, Mond, and Nobel). The biggest single benefactor of British business, you could assert, was an Austrian whose immigrant thrust destroyed the whole of Germany—Adolf Hitler. The Führer completed the work of Polish and Russian pogrom specialists by exporting to Britain, as well as to the United States, families that, having nothing to call their own, proceeded to create prosperity from that nothing.

But the impetus is not confined to any specific nationality or ethnic set. The immigrant wave in Britain included Armenians, Hungarians, Italians, Germans, Persians, Australians, a clutch of Canadians (Thomson, Murdoch, Weston, Beaverbrook), and even Americans (Forrest Mars). It's the transplant, not the root, that is the turning point; witness the astonishingly high proportion of recent immigrants among the great contemporary U.S. fortunes. A quarter of the $500 million or more fortunes listed by *Forbes* in 1986 were in the possession of people who were either born outside the United States or were the children of immigrants. They include Russians, Germans, Belgians, Austrians, an Armenian (Kirk Kerkorian), an Australian (the very same media tycoon, Rupert Murdoch), a Swede (Curtis Leroy Carlson, a former Procter & Gamble soap salesman, then a one-man conglomerate worth $550 million), a Chinese (word-processing wizard Dr. An Wang), and a Pole (Jerry J. Moore, who builds shopping centers, owns more Duesenberg cars than anybody in the world, and reconstructed all forty rooms of a French château to obtain a comfortable pad in Houston, Texas).

This select group also includes the proprietor of *Forbes*, and thus of the Forbes 400: Malcolm Forbes, whose father emigrated from Scotland and whose entry in the aforementioned list is a perennial pleasure of American capitalism. To quote part of the 1986 version: "Owns Colorado ranch, South Seas island, Tangier palace, French château, 1 dozen Fabergé Imperial Eggs (2 more than Kremlin), presidential letters, toy soldiers, toy boats, etc., etc." He also owns 100 percent of *Forbes* and believes in lineal succession ("Nepotism isn't a dirty word in our family").

Whether Forbes is worth half a billion or a billion is beside the point ("Anyway, I'm solvent"): his career, his accumulations, and his strong sense of family are characteristic of the transplants. Their impetus often seems to run as readily in the veins of the next generation as in those of the founders who had the courage to vote with their feet—and their lives.

Most such immigrants, being broke, have a driving and burning need to achieve economic security. That need strongly reinforces the true businessman's innate expansionary urge, but it isn't the only essential carried to Ellis Island or the East End of London. The newcomer has the golden asset of entering the new culture and its markets free from the culture's values, preconceptions, prejudices, received ideas, and general stupidities. This capacity for what the British theorist Edward de Bono has called "lateral thinking," or not looking at a problem in the obvious way, is the common ground from which most uncommon businesses have grown.

The successful grower usually does the obvious thing—there is nothing, after all, very original in activities such as selling people food—but he seldom does it in the obvious way. The outsider (and all immigrants are outsiders) is not blinded by the knowledge that things simply aren't, or can't be, done in the way they want; and that, consequently, is the way in which outsiders win.

Although that combative, competitive urge is invariably part of the do-it-yourself millionaire's kit, the immigrant must win, not only for winning's sake, but to survive. This double urge gives him a thick edge over the Establishment firms, which have all the continuity of Old Man River and Old Father Thames but have often forgotten quite why they are rolling along.

Rarely does the small man grow in a field the Establishment hasn't been tilling for generations. Like two ex-servicemen who seemingly invented, but only improved, the diecast model car to provide postwar generations of children with inexhaustible toys, the new boy bursts into a field in which some somnolent giant has been thoughtlessly earning an easy income. In Britain, not one of the large existing food chains caught on to the significance of the supermarket—plain enough to anybody who could afford a plane ticket to the United States, or even a seat in the movies—until their minds and profits had been jogged by a crop of eager newcomers.

Economic motivation, the desire to profit personally from geometric progression up the business scale, is vital; and this, too, has an especially awful and useful clarity for the outsider. To him, managerial success is directly associated with individual wealth. The business empire, the family fortune, the public prestige, are all tied together in a bundle of total personal involvement that the professional company manager can scarcely grasp, let alone rival.

Failure of recognition was the key to the extraordinary battle in which the pro management of Trust Houses, a big hotel chain, sought to oust what they regarded as the amateur management of Forte, a company with which an ostensibly amicable merger had just been concluded. The pros failed to note that the seat of the pants and the rule of the thumb were only part of the future Lord Forte's managerial armory. The critical difference, however, was that Forte owned a large chunk of the merged business—it was his money, his thing, his maximized milk bar, in a sense that could never belong to his opponents.

In short order, demonstrating canniness as well as tenacity, Forte plunged most of the many millions on which he could lay his hands into buying more and more shares. He bided his time, let the opposition do all the running and make the risky statements, then struck when the iron was hot by forcing a timely boardroom vote. His payoff by 1987 was a $40 million personal stake and family shares worth another $110 million in the middle of that fateful market year.

It was a classic display of the true entrepreneurial drive, abetted by many of those tricks of the trade that are best learned the hard way. If the margin between a good and bad decision is personal failure, it wonderfully concentrates the type of mind that is capable of concentration. And that's another essential characteristic. Dragging a shoe business up by its bootstraps, so to speak, takes long years and a deep devotion to footwear; any lag in concentration, any sign of boredom, is an awful omen—one that appears fatally in the big insider firm that has outgrown its outsider origins.

The insiders, however, have always done the outsider one gigantic favor: they exclude him from the large-scale, capital-intensive, respectable, established industries. Thus do the insiders generously force the immigrants into nonestablished areas that, by definition, include those (like movies in the first half of the century or electronics postwar) with the most explosive potential. It's reported that the father of Max Palevsky, who founded Scientific Data Systems and later sold his computer firm to Xerox, came to the United States from Russia in the erroneous belief that the streets were paved with gold. Once he saw the wonders of SDS's price-earnings ratio (it was sold to Xerox for $900 million and promptly started losing money) father Palevsky changed his mind. "Max," he said, "the streets *are* paved with gold."

It took from 1961 to 1969 for Palevsky to achieve his golden payoff, from which he personally pocketed $100 million. You can easily understand why Palevsky told *Forbes*: "In my dreams I see a $100 million company that we will sell to Xerox again." (He blames the SDS collapse and eventual disappearance on a Xerox management that "didn't know how to run lean and cut costs.") Palevsky has stayed on the golden pavements, but the rewards from his latter-day high-tech adventures (including the spectacular microprocessor firm, Intel, of which he is a director) don't seem that wondrous: the magazine estimates that his fortune has merely doubled since 1969.

Maybe the immigrant's essential hunger was slaked by that early payoff—although Kirk Kerkorian, who also trousered $100 million from selling out (his bauble was a charter airline), was merely stimulated into much more ambitious success. Palevsky, however, was diverted into activities such as reasonably lucrative moviemaking (*Fun with Dick and Jane*) and very unrewarding support for politicians such as George McGovern, which turned him into a pillar of the liberal Establishment.

Disestablishment is usually fundamental, though it isn't everything. The small man, the immigrant above all, tends to be impoverished. He must find some racket that needs hardly any capital, or in which others obligingly provide the ready. This delicious category still includes movies and real estate—even though outsiders now mourn the passing of the glorious heyday when some Establishment muttonhead would put up all the film or property cash, take all the risk, and pocket none of the profit—and it embraces retailing at all times.

This, quite as much as any innate shopkeeping or peddling ability, explains why so high a proportion of the great retailing names have nothing of an Anglo-Saxon ring about them. Gimbel, Saks, Marks, Strauss, Ohrbach, Wolfson, Wexner—they all demonstrate that if you can peddle from one tray, barrow, stall, or store, you can peddle from the next step up, and that if you have no money, peddling is the quickest way to get some and to go on turning it over.

Again, the phenomenon isn't peculiarly ethnic. In the Outer Hebrides in 1972 Pakistani peddlers were following the same route that sixty years earlier took Michael Marks from Russia to Leeds (then a magnet to displaced Jews) and to his first stall in his first market. For the outsider, or the beginner seeking commercial lessons, retailing provides still more joy than its most obvious pleasure, which is that of a high profit in relation to capital employed. Allied joys include the fact that suppliers finance you, providing goods on credit while the customers are made to cough up either on the nail or at stupendous rates of interest. Few enterprises teach more business knowledge more rapidly or familiarize an outsider with new markets at greater speed, or respond more satisfactorily to the laws of geometric progression—or give a more thorough grounding in thievery of all descriptions.

Sensitivity to crooks and crookedness is a talent the man not made by himself finds it curiously hard to develop. The biggest victims of the great cons, from Kreuger to Estes, have mostly been bred behind their desks, which is no place for developing the seventh sense that protects the not-so-innocent from those who are not innocent at all. Even as Cornfeld's IOS sank slowly in the east, several highly reputable houses actually believed there was great treasure left for honest men to salvage. One even sent a team of bankers over to Geneva to investigate—only to be told by them to tear up his file and forget about it.

The immigrant outsider has an unfair edge, naturally. One Chinese can nearly always spot a Chinese con man. But to Anglo-Saxons (as some of the barely believable lending fiascos on London and Wall Street have proved) all Chinese look alike, and maybe all Asians. Johnson Matthey, a British metals business, was nearly sunk by the inane lending of its banking subsidiary, almost all to two borrowers of Asian origin. It's a hard truth that, just as an unfair proportion of small men grown big carry exotic names and scanty backgrounds, so do a good (or bad) many crooks. There are two paths to wealth open to the outsider—the shortcut and the long. A few take the crooked path at the fork, and many stay confused all their lives over which road they are actually on.

Nobody illustrates the crookedness and the confusion more obviously than the arch inside trader Ivan Boesky, son of a Russian immigrant, or his partner in the Guinness caper, Ernest Saunders. The latter's gynecologist father brought him to England from Middle Europe, thus launching the career that led via Beechams and Nestlé to the fatal empire building at Guinness. Winning or losing the takeover battle for Distillers was not the beginning or the end of the world, or of the world drinks colossus Saunders had in mind. But the tactics Saunders adopted were his terminus as a multinational tycoon. In the cases of both men, the end justified the means to so excessive an extent that ordinary prudence vanished. Personal aggrandizement can become an overwhelming attraction to the personally insecure. Boesky once inadvertently gave perfect expression to this truth, speaking of arbitrage: "It's a sickness I have in the face of which I am helpless."

The moral confusion usually stems from a powerful psychological force. When you have started with nothing, avarice, the lust to hang on to the something you have grasped, can achieve truly terrible power. To Rockefeller I, a man of upright personal morality, there seemed nothing wrong in offering his victims a choice between takeover and commercial extinction. That wasn't vicious, crude blackmail, it was good business, sensible progress.

This curious ethical distinction crops up in case after case. One self-made entrepreneur sold his chain of shops to a like millionaire in exchange for shares; the purchaser suggested that since the vendor now had several millions of low-taxed capital gains, he hardly wanted horrible, high-taxed dividends. The vendor agreed to waive his dividend. Later, when the two predictably failed to get on, he agreed to accept the market price for his shares, but was horrified when this turned out to be a million or so less than he expected. The purchaser gently explained that since the stock had never carried a dividend, it had been listed separately on the stock exchange and had never risen a penny since the day of its issue.

In this case the victim won (at the door of the courtroom). But the sagas of small businesses growing up are littered with tales of immoral advantages obtained and ruthlessly seized. And the annals of big businesses are scarred by stories of moral gentlemen failing to recognize the fundamental amorality of their once-small exploiters.

But nemesis is in store. Even as he outwits and outruns the Establishment, the outsider hankers desperately after its established joys. His biggest risk is the desire to come in from the cold; titles, honorific, time-wasting invitations, and all the corruptions of respectability are highly tempting to somebody whose formative years were spent in Saskatchewan, Stepney, Alice Springs, or the Bronx—let alone Lodz. The danger sign isn't only a propensity to lavish money on Tudor manor houses, yachts moored in Florida, Rolls-Royces, and diamonds from Cartiers; if you have wealth, after all, you are apt to spend it. The weakness is, rather, seduction by daydreams that have nothing to do with business and that may be dreamed by people of ostensibly modest ways.

The hagiography of self-made men is full of references to the battered station wagons they prefer to drive, or the simple life-styles they pursue on their usually rolling acres. These self-denials are no more relevant than the self-indulgences that, to tell the truth, are far more common. Corporate raider Carl Icahn, according to *Fortune*, "lives quietly." The quiet in his Manhattan co-op and thirty-acre Westchester estate may indeed be sepulchral, but it certainly comes as expensively as Icahn's ventures into Thoroughbred horseflesh. The crucial question is not whether the outsider indulges his or her tastes, but whether the outsider, once inside, preserves the dedicated heresy from which commercial magic springs.

Frank Lorenzo's iconoclastic attitude to the airline industry, as much as his insouciant attitude to debt, is what gave him his edge; typically, he is the son of an immigrant—a Spaniard who had a beauty parlor in New York. The fact that the outsider viewpoint mellows with time is inevitable. It's when the obsession mellows, too, that far greater problems are created. The great once-small companies all share the common factor that the founder is as passionately, obsessively involved with his game at seventy as he was at twenty-seven. He not only runs the business on the same motivation, he runs it in much the same way, or tries to. The supermarket chain is the corner store writ large. Tenacity, in a real sense, is the essence of his career, because, even though the process of arboreal growth takes less time in business than in a forest, it is still measured in decades rather than years.

From the day when Michael Marks laid out his first stall to the time when his son reigned over a hundred shops was forty years. Even the elapsed time from Thomas Watson's arrival at the future IBM in 1914 to its emergence as a $100 million corporate deal was thirty years. The protean John D. Rockefeller, true, controlled the world's largest oil-refining business, with $1 million in assets, by the age of thirty—but Rockefeller was about to grow far more phenomenally as one of the earliest and most ruthless amalgamation experts. In most cases since World War II, only the merger and acquisitions route has been fast enough to produce sudden empires and rapid fortunes that are significant, at least in size. Even then, spectacular success generally comes later rather than sooner.

John Kluge was forty-five when he and his associates muscled in on Metropolitan Broadcasting. He was a septuagenarian when, in the junk bond era, he privatized the resultant Metromedia and made his billions. While Sam Walton was only twenty-seven when he opened his first store, that business didn't make it. Walton tried again in his thirties, but still took another fifteen years or so before he became America's richest man. Henry Crown (not then even a colonel) was fifty-seven when he bought the Empire State Building. Kirk Kerkorian's $100 million killing on the sale of his little airline came when he was fifty-one; he took another eighteen years or so to multiply his millions sixfold.

If the average time span a small businessman needs to grow organically into a true king of commerce is around thirty-five years (roughly the span of a generation), it follows that a business started immediately after the war could not have made it big by organic means until the 1980s. The normal expectation would be something like the saga of Milton Petrie. He was twenty-five (and also the son of an immigrant from Russia) when he opened his first clothing store in Cleveland, thirty-five when it went bust ("I paid all my creditors 100 cents on the dollar," he proudly told *Forbes*), and in his forties when he started on the long haul toward a chain of 1,400 stores in which his 51 percent 1986 stake largely explained a $700 million fortune.

But Petrie Stores is in low retailing, not high tech or high taste. In both those fields, businesses have been built, not over a thirty-five-year generation span, but before the proprietor has even reached thirty-five. The archetype of high-tech success (with a strong high-taste element thrown in) is Steve Jobs of Apple Computers. Jobs was only born in 1955, and his company twenty-one years later. Within seven years, Apple had passed $1 billion in sales faster than any company in history as it led the personal computer revolution. Jobs's personal fortune bounced up and down with Apple's share price after the onslaught of IBM and an army of others remade his revolution. But in 1986, Jobs still had $185 million to his name—and he was still only thirty-one.

Yet, like Max Palevsky, Jobs has proved short on staying power. Maybe his ousting from Apple at the hands of the PepsiCo graduate John Scully (a chief executive handpicked by Jobs himself) will be followed by enactment of a new Jobs saga. But that's uncertain; Silicon Valley has spawned many an early multimillionaire, and many an early blow-out. Technical brilliance is the forte of such people; they lack that commercial tenacity that is built into the true grower's fiber.

You can see it in sagas such as that of one family that, after starting in wallpapers and paints in Minsk, in 1917, moved out as the Germans moved in. The next stop was Berlin, where the family jewels were sold to finance a small restaurant; like Sam Walton's first business, and Milton Petrie's, it failed. A technically minded member of the now penniless family started earning new pennies by making radios in the kitchen. The clan finally struck it rich again in small transformers. The arrival of Hitler moved these indefatigable refugees on to London, where they at last found a permanent home and several millions— making door chimes.

The super-rich Reichmanns were no different. On their way to a tile-importing business in Toronto, and from that base to the biggest real estate operation in North America, their route led from Eastern Europe via Vienna, Paris, and Tangier. Robert the Bruce's spider had nothing on such people when it comes to sheer persistence. The grower is never deterred by anything, even failure (Henry Ford I, after all, failed twice). Possibly, when they look back, growers romanticize their small beginnings. But there is, after all, a truly romantic quality in sagas such as that of the fourteen-year-old who (when "I hadn't a penny") hired a horse and cart to move a load of earth—and ended up, the standard generation later, as General Motors' biggest distributor of earth-moving equipment outside the United States, with a real estate fortune thrown in.

Stories like his, or that of Luigino Francesco Paulucci, are legion: the latter, yet another son of a poor immigrant, was selling produce at sixteen. At twenty-nine he turned $2,500, plus deep knowledge of the bean sprout, into Chun King canned food. At forty-eight, he cashed in for $63 million, and he multiplied the proceeds some eight times in the next two decades. Rags to riches to super-riches is a genuine romance, and the sense of romance is felt, and forcibly, by the men themselves. Romanticism is part of their dynamic, but heavily interlarded with realism—not so much that of figures, but the realism of whatever trade they have stumbled into.

During the fits and starts of his struggle upward, the man is palpably learning; usually, however, more about doing business than handling men. This is the Achilles heel, the location of the wound that cuts off many half-fledged empires in mid-growth. Every commercial Napoleon needs his marshals, but few are able to choose their assistants as well as Bonaparte, and nature may not oblige by providing a usable son.

Most business Bonapartes—as shown by the trail of sellouts by the self-made—never reach the point of developing self-perpetuating growth, proving that self-made millionaires who have grown the hard way, by stages from the bottom up, are seldom surrounded by the brilliant teams of which they like to boast. The final distinction between those who rise like self-rising flour and those who stop or are cut short lies in the ability of the survivors to keep enough able men around during the decades of growth (as Ken Olsen did at Digital Equipment—without which he could never have mounted a successful frontal assault on IBM after the long years of relative safety in his famous minicomputer niche). If you can't keep, breed, or develop good people, you can't in the end grow a business—even for your own posterity.

6

THE BETTER
MOUSETRAP
GAMBIT

High technology is an expression whose very coinage implies a step-change in man's relentless advance—and there's no denying the height and speed of that climb. In an age when fabulous inventions and miraculous innovations are spilling over each other into the marketplace, in areas as far apart as genetic engineering and consumer electronics, research and development should surely be the equivalent of the California gold rush. The California high-tech rush—and its contemporaries around America and the world—have indeed spawned numberless fortunes. But making (and still more important, keeping) these fortunes has been far harder than making the high-tech breakthrough itself.

The gold rush is an apposite metaphor. For while invention is as famous and heavily trampled a road to fortune as prospecting, it is rockier than the deserts of Colorado, more hazardous and less hospitable than the North Slope of Alaska. Great manufacturing companies, though, continue to be built on technological advance. It may be scientifically sensational, such as the germanium dioxide semiconductor, a mystery to all but the electronic elect; or humdrum, such as the moving fly button, alias the zipper.

The idea may be revolutionary, like the internal combustion engine in its day, or the notion might have been kicking around for years, like television. Whatever the circumstances, if the gimmick meets a real demand, works without need for too much ministration by white-coated specialists, and can be sold at a profitable price, millions are there for the making. The more astounding the innovation, and the greater the technical discontinuity with the past, the richer the prize available to the technological prospector—and it can be as fabulous as the technology.

Enormous wealth has accrued to David Packard and William Hewlett since they converted their high-innovation business into the publicly owned Hewlett-Packard. In early 1987, thanks to high-tech achievements ranging from audio-oscillators to scientific calculators and small computers, the company was valued at $15 billion. Perhaps surprisingly, few other cases of high-tech triumph exist among the Forbes 400 (it shouldn't be surprising, for reasons to be explained). But the youngest paper billionaire of all time, Bill Gates of Microsoft, then thirty-one, could never be cloned outside the high-tech world.

Even America's most flamboyant real estate tycoon and oldest boy wonder, Donald Trump, senior to Gates by a decade and in business since 1968 (it was 1975 when Gates dropped out of Harvard), ranked well behind the software champ's billion, despite making $8 million a month (almost double Microsoft's total net) from a single Trump property in Atlantic City. Just as Visicalc burgeoned on, and greatly helped to create, the success of Apple, so Microsoft has been indispensable (and vice versa) to IBM's onslaught in personal computers.

But thereby hangs a warning. Visicalc and the company that so recently marketed that one-time wonder are now as dead as the dodo or the dinosaur. High technology, to the chagrin of Wall Street and venture capitalists, has proved even higher in risk than they supposed—not so much because the technology may fail, but because it may not endure. The searing pace of technology that creates the abundant opportunities also generates attendant chances of being overtaken, leap-frogged, lapped. If IBM had dropped Microsoft for its vital second-generation PC (which was the giant's original idea), Bill Gates and his company might have survived, but his 45 percent would never have been worth the billion that shrank so spectacularly fast in Black October 1987.

Even more than in the past, the great innovator must deploy low cunning, low-tech management, and low-cost money manipulation to capitalize permanently on his breakthrough. The package isn't readily found in one human skull, which is why high-tech prospectors have often failed to collect their prizes. Many a brilliant, ineffably creative inventor has seen other men garner his harvest—while he gets a grain or two as total recompense. The case of polyester fiber, an innovation that is literally one of the world's record money-spinners, is guaranteed to bring tears to the eye.

Manufacturers of Terylene and Dacron (the former ICI and Du Pont near monopoly), Trevira (Hoechst), and the rest, before the post-1973 depression, had amassed a worldwide total of Midas proportions. The two intellects that created this cornucopia, you might think, must have been laden with honors and wealth: you would be wrong. Their names were J. R. Whinfield and Dr. J. Dickson. They worked for a company, the Calico Printers Association, that bowed to nobody in its knowledge of printing calico, but was in no fit state to handle the Whinfield-Dickson discovery, made in its labs. In 1947 the bonanza was sold to ICI in return for royalties that kept CPA shareholders in easy money for many years.

Whinfield went over to ICI with his discovery (which caused its purchasers no end of problems in its early days—the first all-Terylene trousers practically stood up by themselves). His booty from one of the century's premier achievements was just $900 a year. Dickson didn't even climb on the ICI bandwagon—he went to work for a company manufacturing linoleum, a product the Victorians knew well. While no mean invention in its day, lino was a long journey away from the product of the finest modern polymer chemistry.

Hired hands such as Whinfield and Dickson hire out their genius, as well as their hands, for the salary. That's no way to make millions, as increasing numbers of high-tech employees have been quick to spot. Hence the drain of brains noted in Chapter 15, "Inside Every Fat Company." Curiously, the dearly departed (such as the Apple founders, Steve Wozniak and Steve Jobs, or H. Ross Perot at IBM) usually do try to interest their superiors in their innovatory masterstroke. But that's no easy task in a large corporation—as Gifford Pinchot demonstrated in his book *Intrapreneuring*.

Art Fry, the hero who invented Post-it pads for 3M, had to endure blood, sweat, tears, and outright opposition before his innovation became reality. The path of another corporate hero was equally bloody, sweaty, and tearful: he directly defied an order to cease work on his project (which eventually came good) from the corporate supremo. That boss was Dave Packard, whose Hewlett-Packard also employed Steve Wozniak and showed total lack of interest in his visionary plan for a microcomputer.

The innovator is almost forced to be a lone eagle, with all the vulnerability that implies. The jet engine was probably the most influential invention of the mid-century. Compared to the polyester pioneers, its inventor fared well, relatively speaking, but in absolute terms his money fate was much the same: others made millions out of his discovery; he did not, depending for his main reward on a government handout. Sir Frank Whittle's principal misfortune, perhaps, was that his jet made its slow progress toward realization under the war clouds of the late 1930s. This inevitably made the government intensely interested in his little private company, Power Jets, which had originally been financed by City investment bankers.

In the end the government purchased the entire kit. A few weeks before the historic moment in 1941 when the Gloster Whittle E28 made an unintentional 200-yard flight during the taxiing trials, the total government investment was put at £96,000. Whittle was given £4,000 more than that—or £100,000 tax-free—in 1948, a sum that sinks to its proper proportions with the knowledge that, three years later, the U.S. government alone (another amazing bargain) paid $4 million for the use of the patents.

History is littered with men who similarly made the breakthroughs for others to exploit. The liability of the innocents in these cases is their very innocence. Like the stock character of the absent-minded boffin-brained professor, they truly are an unworldly bunch. Build a better mousetrap, they fondly believe, and the world will beat so many paths to your door that the problem will be merely which road to choose.

In fact, when the improved, Mark II, all-electronic mousetrap does appear, the world says it will never work; if you prove that it does, the world (or rather the worldly) will try to steal the drawings. The skepticism and the thievery are in a sense both justified: every year hundreds of thousands of patent applications are made, many by private individuals whose ingenuity is matched only by their incompetence. Of the small minority that does have a worthwhile wonder on its hands, an even tinier minority has digits adroit enough to exploit the opportunity it has created. If some more capable, cunning fellow doesn't lift the invention from its parent, the chances are that it will be stillborn.

The most likely scoffers are the giant corporations, even such innovative heroes as 3M and Hewlett-Packard, first, because it goes against the grain of top managers to accept any idea from outside or from outside the company's set parameters, except on their own initiative, second, because the acceptance of the new, the untried, the unknown, must involve the corporation, or somebody within it, in time, trouble, and expense. It's the unknown, more than any other psychological deterrent, that is most off-putting.

The same phenomenon that caused the two Hewlett-Packard gaffes just mentioned will occur in any company, however strong its innovatory tradition, unless the all-but-immovable body of corporate obstruction meets an irresistible force. In *Made in Japan: Akio Morita and Sony*, the hero tells how he was that force, pushing through the Walkman innovation against the united opposition of his supporting cast. Sony's marketing people said "it wouldn't sell, and it embarrassed me to be so excited about a product most others thought would be a dud. But I was so confident the product was viable that I said I would take personal responsibility for the project. I never had reason to regret it."

Significantly, Morita is no technologist, high or low. His vast success was founded on (1) early partnership with a technical genius; (2) adequate financial backing from a friendly source (his father took shares in the infant company and thus became one of history's most successful venture capitalists); (3) timely conversion of himself into a marketing man; (4) obtaining other people's technology—and improving thereon; (5) building a highly efficient and talented corporation—as he writes, "Your business and its future are in the hands of the people you hire."

It's plain that many inventors in the West, like many corporations, miss out on some or all of these five stages. The Japanese don't—which is why, when Minolta introduces the first autofocus SLR and scores a runaway success, you know that before long Nikon, Canon, and Yashica will hit the shops with rival and, if possible, improved products. Behind most Japanese high-tech successes lurks a controlling entrepreneur or family, whether in high-tech ceramics or numerically controlled machine tools—and this personal leadership has helped Japan sustain the innovative thrust American firms such as Eastman Kodak have struggled to recapture in the 1980s.

Kodak's ossification had set in much earlier—and rejection of the unknown was the fatal sign. True, Eastman Kodak listened to the two concert pianists who dreamed up Kodachrome in the bath, but film was its business. It rejected xerography because Chester B. Carlsson's invention had its potential and technology in areas where Kodak didn't, at that time, feel that it belonged.

Kodak's loss was the Haloid Corporation's infinite gain. The executives of that obscure New Jersey operation waxed adequately rich even by the standards of the George Eastman family, and Carlsson, while lagging behind, did stand financially among the inventing elite: his royalties themselves created a substantial fortune.

That pile, however, was negligible beside that of Charles F. Kettering, inventor of the self-starter and other handy gadgets, who, on his death, left at least $200 million, the proceeds of his long and lucrative association with General Motors and automotive technology. The closer the inventor nestles to business itself, the better-heeled he must become—even if invention itself is his business, as in the case of a Dane, Karl Kroyer, who authored such benefactions to humanity as the nonstick frying pan; he also thought up an ersatz hosiery elastic during World War II, worked out that expanded polystyrene granules could be used to salvage ships, and devised a detector for death-watch beetles. All this inventive activity was masterminded and promoted through a series of companies; a man with a commercially viable mind must have a better chance of developing a commercially viable product.

Unfortunately, from the pecuniary angle, the inventor is more often preoccupied with the problem for its own sake. Without that preoccupation, he would never have possessed either the stamina or the concentration to solve his conundrum. When Dr. Jonas Salk was working toward the discovery of polio vaccine, or Dr. Selman Waksman toward streptomycin, their thoughts may conceivably have drifted toward the fortunes that attend all pharmacological breakthroughs; but the mind finds this notion as hard to believe as the idea that pharmaceutical companies are devoted, disinterested, altruistic benefactors of mankind.

The profits from genuinely new drugs are larger than from any enterprise except a successful bank robbery. According to the industry's standard defense, the astronomical profits are required to finance research into the new drugs from which greater medical progress will result. But that progress, as the apologists fail to mention, inevitably goes along with still more nourishing profits.

The happiest event to befall any drug company postwar came to Smith Kline and French—the discovery by British researchers of cimetidine, the histamine blocker that, by counteracting the secretion of stomach acid, put gastric surgeons out of a substantial part of their business. Even after the invention, marketed as Tagamet, had met formidable competition from Glaxo's Zantac, the renamed SmithKline Beckman had a market value of $7 billion and profits of $521 million. The largest single beneficiary of the bonanza, however, was the Beckman family in the new title—handsomely overpaid when the now-fat company diversified into instruments in a too-successful effort to offset some of its fat pharmaceutical profits.

Some idea of how fat such profits can be emerged when the British government once decided that the world's biggest drug company had been overcharging it by unholy percentages for two tranquilizers, Librium and Valium. The British offshoot of Hoffmann–La Roche, a Swiss company so secretive that even elementary financial figures had to be pried loose by detective work, was charged by its parent $925 a kilo for Librium supplies and $2,300 for Valium that can't have cost the parent company more than $22.50 and $50 respectively (the prices at which Italian pirates, who have made fat livings out of Italy's lack of patent protection for drugs, were willing to supply the same compounds).

In seven years in Britain, according to the investigators, Roche pulled in $55 million, most of it siphoned back to the Swiss parent in the transfer price. Small wonder that Roche was among the pet investments of millionaires. At a mid-1987 cost of 136,000 Swiss francs each, a dozen cost $1.1 million; the stock has become so heavy that trading has long been conducted in "mini-Roches," worth a tenth of a share apiece.

What the millionaires were buying, in addition to a share whose price kept it beyond the reach of the masses, and whose limited supply helped keep the price aloft, was an entrance ticket to the inventor's perfect product. The sick man is in no position to haggle over price. He isn't the direct customer, anyway; that role is filled by the doctor, who doesn't have to pay a penny. The situation, provided that government can be kept out of the act, is perfect: urgency of demand, total elasticity of price, and floor-level costs of production.

Most inventors design their wonders with no thought for the market's demands, ignore the fundamental importance of price, and don't understand that, since profit is the sum of price less cost, if the relationship between the two gets out of hand, their work will go for nothing. The perversion of that essential basic marriage tends to begin at the beginning, with the cost of development.

Anybody who has financed any noble try in research and development sooner or later stumbles over the fact that inventors always grossly underestimate the cost of getting even to a working prototype. Even then, the final 20 percent of progress toward the crock of gold at the end of the technological rainbow seems to cost as much as the first four-fifths put together—plainly, the process is governed by inexorable laws (those discovered, no doubt, by the Italian economist Wilfredo Pareto).

That successful and enormously profitable inventions still emerge is a measure of the wondrous gap that lies between development cost and market potential of any product that fills a human need, such as Tagamet, Valium, the Walkman, and the instant camera. The last two products, however, provide a fascinating corporate contrast and an important guide to the proper exploitation of better mousetraps. Once Akio Morita, a businessman, had got the message, Sony was marketing-led; Polaroid, run by an inventor, was product-led—and therein lay a mighty and painful difference.

The first Sony breakthrough was in tape recorders; Morita's technical partner spotted the model American professional machine in a studio while delivering the infant company's first, and crucial, order for broadcasting equipment (this is a classic example of fortune favoring the prepared mind). The pair couldn't sell their own tape recorder after its successful development, which is how Morita realized that "having unique technology and being able to make unique products are not enough to keep a business going. You have to sell the products, and to do that you have to show the potential buyer the real value of what you are selling." That truth resulted in twenty almost-instant sales when the Sony recorder was demonstrated to the Japanese Supreme Court.

Morita's marketing breakthrough was no more important than his repetition of an economic discovery made long before by King C. Gillette, who made little profit from his razors, but dollars by the hundreds of millions from the blades. Morita and his partner saw that tape was a consumer item, too, and determined to make tape themselves—before they even had a marketable recorder. Their reasoning was more than marketable—to make sure that, from the stream of money between the technological start and the financial finish (when the ultimate customer buys), they got their hands on the optimum amount.

Dr. Edwin Land, perhaps the best inventor who ever went into business, did not obey all the necessary economic injunctions. He obeyed some, but only by accident, just as his original success had been fortuitous. Land's preoccupation with the polarizing of light was wrongly founded on the notion that he would create a breakthrough in car headlights, not sunglasses.

But the launch of Land's nonglare glasses in 1937 set him up in a business that, thirty-five years later, was still selling twenty-five million pairs of lenses a year. This supported him through lean times and fat—the leanest coming after the war, when the loss of military business plunged Polaroid into a $2 million loss. In addition to the indispensable tools of a good basic business and luck, however, Land was saved by his high degree of the inventor's highest uncommon denominator: single-minded persistence.

His original experiments took nine years to pay off. The first instant camera, appearing in 1948, had been in the works for five years. Its apotheosis, the SX70, was seven years in the making. As time scales go, these were probably unusually short. The inventor has to prepare for a long investment of time, which is money, and of money, which is time—the more you have to invest, the quicker the heavy returns must come to produce the desired payback.

In obeying the demands of this iron law, Land helped himself mightily by aiming at the top-volume end of mass markets. Just as Polaroid sunglasses are relatively expensive but still sell in millions, so the first Polaroid camera was no toy for the poor at a price of $89.75 (nor was it a plaything for the weak—it weighed in at nearly four pounds).

Another draconian law rules: prices of innovations always fall after the innovatory honeymoon. Land profited greatly from the virtue of this necessity. That virtue lies in the constant widening of the market as prices decline; he simultaneously improved the product, with five major developments between 1960 and 1971, so that it kept the upmarket cream while, at the bottom end, its appeal widened into Kodak's mass-market preserves.

But Land's weaknesses had begun to appear. Unlike Sony and Morita, the Polaroid inventor hadn't in all these years fully exploited the virtues of the Gillette gambit. Every buyer of a Polaroid camera is a captive customer for Polaroid film, without which he cannot use his captivating purchase; and buyers of consumable necessities, as Morita and Gillette saw, are notoriously indifferent to price. By an interesting coincidence, the culmination of work on the SX70 was accompanied by a Polaroid decision to make its own film, instead of buying from Kodak. Looking for ways to build new and recurring turnover and profits on the initial sales is a neglected avenue to making money: many great prizewinners of invention have this key characteristic—like the usage charges on Xerox machines. The two approaches—the financial and the technological—are equally important: lesser inventors fail because they are one-dimensional.

The market in Polaroid stock tells the tale of the price of single dimensions. At the peak of the excitement over the SX70, the shares were valued at over a hundred times earnings, making the Land family worth some $700 million. The valuation meant, incidentally, that if Polaroid doubled its earnings every three and a half years, the company's earnings were being purchased well into the twenty-first century. Such are the wonders of technological sex appeal. But they seldom last; within one more year of the twentieth century, the Land fortune was down to $350 million and still dropping as the SX70 fell behind schedule and into problems. Only with the coming of the Spectra in 1986 did Polaroid break out of the long slump that from 1975 to 1985 reduced its earnings per share by 4.6 percent per annum compound.

That's why Bill Gates was well advised to be "leery of counting paper assets as real wealth," as he told *Forbes*. The Microsoft pioneer supposedly pulled off a magnificent coup on taking his software company public and becoming a millionaire a mere 350 times over. Yet within a year the price had more than quadrupled. As Gates noted, what goes up can just as easily go down the same fast escalator (and did by half a billion in October 1987). The downside risks have increased for the same reason that the upside potential has widened—the galloping and gathering pace of technology. In a world in which an IBM (Microsoft's principal vehicle, remember) can lose a quarter of its PC market share to clones, nothing is either sacred or safe.

There are precious few monopolies anymore, though, curiously enough, Polaroid found itself enjoying one all over again. The decision to make its own film had backfired, landing the company with Kodak's own instant camera on its neck at a time when improvements in conventional cameras and film (and the videos that killed Land's instant movies) were shrinking the instant market. After Kodak's final retreat from that competition, forced out by the courts for breach of patent, Polaroid had a hot camera ready that actually did what the customer wanted (the Spectra), not just one that the company wanted to make.

Just like Polaroid, so Gates—with no built-in monopoly—is locked into a race to keep his technological prowess ahead of competition whose identity he cannot even know. After all, in 1980, when Gates won his breakthrough contract to make IBM's PC work, he had never written an operating system. Buying the bones of the one that became the industry standard PC-DOS cost Gates $50,000: one of the greatest bargains in technology—high, middling, *or* low.

In fact, neither high nor even new technologies are needed for financial success. The $150 million fortune that Ewing Kauffman, owner of the Kansas City Royals baseball team, boasted in 1972 was started in 1950 with $5,500 and a pharmaceutical product, Os-Cal, confected from crushed oyster shells. His fortune was made by another wonder of medical science, Pavalid, an opium derivative for dilating blood vessels, which had been known since 1848. The proceeds from these preparations enabled two of Kauffman's executives and one salesman to retire with a million in their money boxes.

By 1987, Kauffman himself had more than $315 million in his own kitty, but, according to *Forbes*, Marion Laboratories still spent not a nickel on primary research—like Gates, with his $50,000 program, Kauffman buys in research products and develops his purchases (he also developed the Royals to the very satisfactory point of getting $11 million for just under half the franchise).

There was nothing much more sophisticated in the way that an immigrant of Greek extraction, Demetrius Comino, scored his millions with a construction device called slotted angle, which worked on exactly the same principle as the child's building kit known as Meccano. Robert H. Abplanalp rose to wholly private means estimated at $100 million from a single basic improvement in a common product, the aerosol spray-can valve. Cutting down its propensity to leak enabled Abplanalp to grab a patent, 60 percent of the world market, and some notoriety as the financier of Nixon's San Clemente.

Genius is seldom required to see whether a market exists for an unknown but wholly innovatory product such as the above. But you do require perverse genius of a different sort to say (as various worthies did) that the automobile, the electric train, and the instant camera would never sell. Again, those with a vested interest in the technological establishment naturally reject a challenge to their sacred and financially consecrated way of life, like the British motorcycle firms who refused to believe that bike engines could rev at the breathtaking speeds Soichiro Honda developed.

But challenge to established ideas need not mean the pursuit of far-out technology; that chase offends against the well-known rule that the further out you go, the longer it takes to get home. The Japanese genius has been to use well-known technology (even the Walkman incorporated no new marvels) to meet unfamiliar market needs. In cars, however, Honda's vault, from a standing start, to number three in Japan is much more remarkable than its decimation of British motorbikes; the opposition in Japanese cars was infinitely tougher—and technological leapfrogs were impossible. The car, the dominant, if not overdominant product of twentieth-century civilization, has seen relatively few revolutionary inventions since Model T days; possibly the can opener has changed more.

Recent years have seen an acceleration in progress mostly in minor details (such as electronic dashboards) and in the performance of major units (engine and braking systems, for example). Honda's strength was to be ahead or abreast in all these improvements in the motorized mousetrap—even though, atypically for a Japanese company, Honda will not buy in technology. The current chief executive admitted to *Time*, "There are some technologies that we didn't have. . . . But when you buy technology from others, it remains frozen, a foreign thing that is not part of yourself, and in the end you don't know where to go with it."

That flies in the face of the experience of Sony and many other Japanese companies. It's hard not to hear in this philosophy the echo of his master's voice; of the spirit of the indefatigable inventor who prefers to create his own technology (as Soichiro Honda did with the first nonpolluting engine) because, if he leaves tasks to others, there will be that many fewer fields to conquer.

Honda, like Land, served a long apprenticeship before becoming a master. That, too, is characteristic of inventors. Their tenacity is bred by their experience, and in a world peopled with far richer prowlers, they need to be as tenacious in business as they are at the bench. Witness the doggedness of Harry Ferguson, who let Henry Ford use his revolutionary tractor principle (the engine drove both tractor and tools) on the strength of a handshake. When Ford abused that handshake, Ferguson filed the heaviest breach-of-patent suit in history and stuck with it until he won (he collected $9.25 million).

This eccentric genius from County Down proved equally hard to pin down when his Canadian partners decided to buy him out. A powerful delegation from Canada found Ferguson willing to talk anything but business—then its leader overheard his host telling the butler that the Canadians could be kept cooling their heels. The Canadians threatened to return home at once unless Ferguson signed; he did. One queer feature of the case is that Ferguson was not profoundly interested in money: he once lost $1 million to his Canadian partners on the toss of a half crown—they generously had the million-dollar coin mounted at Asprey's and gave it to Harry as a present.

Would-be Fergusons need that selfsame quality of eccentricity combined with deep understanding of the ordinary. Ultimately, the invention has to find its reward and justification in a marketplace formed by people in the mass; it must find its expression in a business apparatus manned and managed by people who have neither genius nor inspiration. Invention, like most of the admirable qualities in life, is not enough—certainly not in a world where the key to fortune isn't the complex structure of DNA but rather the simple mathematics of the price-earnings ratio.

For instance, which of these two high-tech companies, both in the same racket, would you value more highly? Company A has sales of over $1 billion, Company B of $134 million. The A team made a phenomenal $238 million of profit in 1986, which meant a stunning 39.2 percent return on equity and a 28 percent improvement on 1985. B *lost* more than A made: minus $352 million, a highly negative 160 percent on equity. It had lost money the previous year, too—indeed, it had never done anything else.

In logic, B must be worthless and A worth many mints. In actuality, their market valuations in early 1987 were almost identical at $4.7 billion. The first company is Syntex, whose invention of the Pill (with a vital ingredient extracted from yams grown in the Mexican jungle) ranks with the jet engine, antibiotics, the microcircuit, the transistor, and so on, for its impact on human society. The second company is Genentech, which at the time of writing had created nothing of great commercial value—except, of course, its own pieces of paper.

The architect of this strangest of high-tech fortunes, Robert Swanson, who started the company with $1,000 (half his own) in 1976, expected to have $1 billion of sales in the early 1990s. So how could it equal the value of a company that already sold $1 billion in 1987? The only answer is that the genetic engineering mousetrap is more seductive than the old hat (or old pill) of Syntex. Wall Street simply (very simply then) believed, with *Fortune*, that Swanson was "The Man Who Could Make Biotechnology Profitable—At Last."

At last, indeed. The high-tech world is one in which great expectations are valued even more highly than great achievements, and where small disappointments, conversely, have consequences almost as grave as great disasters. If Genentech's hoped-for triumph had come (Wall Street was betting mainly on Tissue Plasminogen Activator, for dissolving blood clots), Swanson will have been wise to don the clothes, metaphorically speaking, of Sieuemenon Indaba, whose Fanuc controls for machine tools created one of the hottest investments to emerge from the Japanese miracle. Indaba has dominated his high-tech field, not only by setting the pace in innovation, but by refusing to look at any activity that won't give him $400,000 of sales per employee and an operating income that runs at no less than 35 percent of sales. His motto is "Precision"; he hates meetings and conferences ("They're a waste of time"); and like Morita he is a better model for the would-be inventive maestro than the genius locked in his lab.

The inventor has to start by selling himself, continue by selling his invention, capitalize by selling the product of his inventiveness, cash in by selling, at least in part, the business that produces the product—and preserve his birthright at all times by refusing to be sold down, up, or across the river. He can get off the gravy train at various stages, but the earlier the exit, by and large, the smaller the spoonful of gravy. Those who want all the rich juices that invention can provide must stay on to the end of the line. This is their toughest test.

7

CAN *HE*
SELL SALT

There was once a young son of Polish immigrants who began his business career as a vacuum cleaner salesman. He sold some of his wares to people whose homes had no electricity—a feat that may be easier than the traditional selling of refrigerators to Eskimos, but not by much. The sprig convinced the customers that electricity would eventually arrive, as no doubt it did. Plainly, though, the salesman was going to make a brilliant career in business—as he did.

Jerry J. Moore deserted vacuum cleaners for real estate, where his specialty is the shopping center, in which others do the selling while Moore rakes in enough cash to make him worth $500 million, according to *Forbes*; the magazine also reports that Moore rises at four every morning, so that "I gain two hours" on you, and proceeds to work for anything from twelve to sixteen hours.

Without doubt, workaholic hours are a less significant factor in business success than the sales power that can sell vacuum cleaners to unelectrified prospects. Selling is often regarded as a mere regrettable necessity of commerce, regretted especially by its more respectable exponents. Yet even in the upper realms of high technology or higher art, selling is the open sesame. The foot must still get in the door; the pitch must still be delivered; the sale must still be clinched.

The whole embarrassing process is as important to the business-man or professional manager as to the door-to-door huckster. But the god among businessmen pretends otherwise—he hides selling under covers such as "marketing," or "customer relations"; he sometimes severs himself almost completely from sales operations manned by a caste of company untouchables. Most businesses prefer their customers to buy, thus apparently removing the disagreeable imperative of selling. From this weakness, rooted in the same psychological depths as fear of money, the supreme salesman makes his mint.

An illustrative Jewish fable tells of the grocer whose store and storerooms are heaped high with cartons of salt. "My God," says his visitor, "you must sell a lot of salt." The grocer shakes his head slowly. "I don't," he answers. "But the man who sells me salt, can *he* sell salt." Salt sellers rely on their powers, techniques, and tricks to persuade their marks to buy goods the marks may not really want or need.

The purchase may be perfectly good value, although the champion salt seller also aims to get the highest price the traffic can bear, even if the customer can't. But the image of the forlorn housewife standing helplessly on her doorstep holding a set of brushes or encyclopedias she never intended to buy is what gives salesmanship its bad names—and they even come in Latin. It's the *emptor* who has to beware; nobody ever says *caveat vendor*. Nevertheless, selling is a two-sided relation-ship, and the bargain can easily work against a seller—as many who have tried selling a family heirloom to a dealer have found to their cost and the dealer's profit. As Marcus Samuel, the first Lord Bearsted, a seashell merchant who moved on to higher things and Shell Oil, once remarked succinctly, "The price of an article is exactly what it will fetch."

But what determines that? The most successful salesman on record was a dealer, Lord Duveen. Precisely how successful can be gauged from the sums collected by his covert partner, the learned art authority Bernard Berenson. While supposedly independent and impartial, the distinguished expert in twenty years pocketed $8.4 million in commis-sions on the art sold by Duveen, often with Berenson's help. In his excellent book, *Artful Partners*, Colin Simpson values the rakeoff at $150 million in present prices. Since Duveen was committed to pay Berenson first 10 percent and then 25 percent of the profits, but by no means on all the firm's transactions, and unquestionably cheated him (like everybody else), the firm's profits must have gone over the $2 billion mark with some ease.

Like all the greatest salesmen, Duveen to a substantial extent created his own market, in this case the transfer of European art treasures to American millionaires. To a substantially higher degree, he created that market's prices by paying (or saying he had paid) exorbitant amounts so that he could charge still more extravagant sums. He stalked his prospects with a whole armory of blandishments, from bribing their servants to simple acts of friendship, and devoted years to the pursuit of an indispensable target, notably Andrew Mellon, the supreme millionaire of his day. The tycoons came like lambs to the slaughter. Duveen and his uncle paid only $1 million for the magnificent Hainauer collection, whipping it away from under the kaiser's infuriated nose (he wanted the Berlin Museum to steal it for $375,000). The Duveens told J. Pierpont Morgan they were going to pay $5 million; had the nerve to borrow the actual million-dollar price from the great banker (in return for first choice, not for interest); and collected $5 million from Morgan, P. A. Widener, and Benjamin Altman just for sculptures from the huge array of works. Simpson notes that when a later Midas, Norton Simon, bought all the Duveen stock in 1964, over a hundred pieces from the Hainauer purchase were still unsold.

So long as Duveen lived, he went to remarkable lengths to defend the market that made him rich. For instance, Alfred Erickson, of the McCann Erickson advertising agency, bought Rembrandt's *Aristotle Contemplating the Bust of Homer* from Duveen for $750,000. Hit by the Great Slump, Erickson sold it back for $500,000. Duveen then stored it for his customer until Erickson could afford to repurchase that noble work (the storage cost him $90,000, but was worth it from his heirs' point of view: the picture fetched $2.3 million at auction in 1961, when it passed to The Metropolitan Museum of Art in New York).

Duveen made himself the social superior of his customers; spending and living like a prince, acquiring a title (by long, apparently disinterested courtship of Labour Prime Minister Ramsay MacDonald), moving in exalted circles, deploying a considerable scholarship to which the clientele could never aspire. But the whole bravura performance was rooted in the Garden of Eden of all selling: faith. The great art dealer had surpassing faith in himself, bounteous belief in what he sold.

Insecurity is the enemy of selling, and insecurity is the normal condition of man. Cross that psychological barrier and you are in the promised land. The difficulty of making the crossing, however, shouldn't be underestimated. Its hardness and stress explain why so many salesmen, at all levels of the art, hit the bottle with unending percussion. They don't drink to be sociable with their customers; they drink to obliterate the shock to the psyche of overcoming the instinctive urge to hide away in safety.

Selling is no simple activity. It has as many subcultures as the Polynesian islands, each with its own complications. Even the ostensibly simplest form—selling something that is actually better—is complex (and relatively rare). This problem confronted Procter & Gamble in acute form with Crest, the first fluoride toothpaste. P & G's Cincinnati millionaires had developed to a superfine art the second main division of the sell: flogging a product or service that is not at all superior to the competitor's offering.

This is usually the case when the salesman claims that his goody is superior; just as, if the fellow boasts that the thing is new, you can bet that it is merely an old offering mildly revamped. With such basic techniques did the boys from Cincinnati make P & G world-famous. Crest, discovered in a university, threw them into mental confusion. It truly was a more effective toothpaste—and P & G, having cried wolf in reverse so often, simply didn't know how to advertise the truth, the whole truth, and nothing but the truth.

In the end, Cincinnati was taken off its painful hook by the American Dental Association, which made Crest the first toothpaste it had ever endorsed. Straight ads retailing this fact, with none of the huckster devices P & G and its agencies had perfected, swiftly turned Crest into the best-selling brand in the United States. But selling the genuinely better product, in addition to such subtle problems, has the more obvious heartache of limited life span. Sooner or later, somebody is going to match the new marvel, and its superiority will be lost and gone forever.

For instance, the Randolph family of Wilkinson Sword had for years been minding its own genteel business, manufacturing superb swords and good, if clumsy, razors. They then suddenly burst forth with a stainless steel blade that left all other forms of wet stubble remover far behind. As word of mouth spread like stubble, the Randolphs' only difficulty was to produce blades. At the point when a flabby, out-of-condition Gillette had finally caught up, the selling had to start; then, although the Randolph family was already worth many millions, its managing members found it increasingly hard to hang on to their seats—and their company ended up in the arms of the high-living Americans of Allegheny Corporation.

The product that sells itself only does so for a time. The extreme potency of word of mouth dwindles with familiarity, and the management (as Wilkinson Sword's professionals did with fair success after the family vacated the premises) must master marketing—deliberately giving the customers what they want, instead of doing so by inspiration and luck. Marketing is the crucial arena of modern competition. But marketers forget at their peril, as many have, that the brute power of selling is still the force that drives the profit through the firm.

That power has seldom been demonstrated in more brutal form than by Lowell ("Bud") Paxson and Roy M. Speer. In their forties, the two went into business to combine huckstering with television. It was an inspired combination, for (as every producer of fast-moving consumer goods knows) television is the most powerful of all mediums. Exposed to vigorous selling over the partners' Home Shopping Network, the viewers poured $1 million a day into its coffers for the huckstered products.

Only nine years after kicking off in Clearwater, Florida, the partners went public. The shares quintupled in a year—the company was still worth $1.8 billion (of which Paxson owned 45 percent) even after the stock had plunged on diminishing returns and the appearance of other hucksters eager to cash in on the same easy money, and doing so more effectively. That is the common problem of a fortune built on selling alone—it is too easily imitated and, perhaps, outsold.

There is only one absolutely sure method of maintaining the "company superior" position—eliminating the opposition entirely, by fair means and (inevitably) by very foul. The father of modern selling, John H. Patterson of National Cash Register, was a devoted adherent of this faith. His techniques, illegal even in their day, included setting up dummy companies to corner the secondhand market and undermine his competitors. The henchman in charge of this department of dirty tricks, Thomas J. Watson, Sr., went on at IBM to refine both Patterson's ways of objecting to competition and his more orthodox approach to organization of the sales force—including the heavy use of evangelistic commercial theology.

The differences among the sales evangelisms of Patterson, Watson, W. Clement Stone (ace inspirer of insurance salesmen), or, for that matter, Billy Graham, are very small in principle. They all use the Group, the Cause, the Leader, the Message, the Slogan, and the atmosphere to induce in the subject precisely the reaction the psychological theory of salesmanship demands: faith, the suspension of insecurity, the elimination of disbelief in oneself, its replacement by belief in the company and the product.

Patterson and Watson worked their wonders in a field, office and shop machinery, where the salesman always makes the running. Most other selling armies, no matter how similar the generalship or inspirational technique, face the logistical difficulty that they cannot penetrate to the ultimate customer. They can use a multitude of methods to get goods on the shelf, but the goods won't move off the shelf unless the mass public buys; and that means advertising.

The distressing truth for ad-hating puritans is that clever ads have translated several modest fortunes to imperial heights; from the celebrated Doyle Dane Bernbach campaign for Levy's Jewish rye bread ("You don't have to be Jewish") to the campaign that not only made Bartles and Jaymes the biggest-selling wine cooler, with 30 percent of the market, but in a sense invented the product. Adman Hal Riney, according to *Fortune*, thought of the name, dreamed up and cast the two rustics who appear in the commercials, and even had a hand in the labels and packaging.

Riney's agency was well rewarded from the $50 million account— and deserved to be for the bizarre, and bizarrely successful, idea of casting old country codgers in commercials aimed at people between twenty-one and thirty-four. But the rest was up to the proprietors, E. & J. Gallo. They had to make the stuff—and, above all, sell it. But selling is Ernest Gallo's lifework, and his technique is not so subtle as Riney's. Before the Gallo brothers burst into the market, wine coolers were a nice, fast-growing niche with pleasant profit margins. Bartles and Jaymes blew it apart, converting the market to the low-margin, high-volume sales that the Gallos, with their unmatched hold over both production and distribution, can dominate with awesome ease. Small wonder that their cooler sales doubled in a year—and not just thanks to Riney's inspired commercials. The big money spent on ads can't be divorced from the intrinsic appeal of the product, the strength of the distribution setup, the use of other promotion methods, and the power of selling (as demonstrated by Gallo).

Generally it's an illusion that you can start with nothing and turn yourself via a collection of TV spots into a mini-Rockefeller. In fact, the more spectacular sellers from a zero base usually rely heavily on other techniques, even if they also use the media. The appeal of direct mail, for instance, lies in eliminating the infuriating gap between buyer and seller. If some worthy citizen will fill in a coupon cut from a publication, or return some junk mail dropped in his letterbox, you have a ready-made mark. The game even has the charm of being measurable. Replies to coupon ads can be tabulated; the conversion of replies into sales can likewise be measured; offers that fail these statistical tests can be dropped and others substituted.

Then, the tiny percentages required for a successful operation look deeply encouraging. Get 1.5 percent response to a properly designed mail shot, and you're in business. Get 2.5 percent, and you have real money on your hands. Get 4 percent, and you can start thinking in seven figures. Unfortunately, a selling method is no substitute for what is actually being sold. The frenzied efforts of U.S. publishers to boost sales of magazines hit by television succeeded all too well. The circulation of *Life* shot up from 6 million to 8 million, but since the sales were being serviced for substantially more money than the new, expensively purchased subscribers were actually paying, the operation merely brought forward, instead of warding off, the evil day of the death of *Life*.

Direct marketing has soared as the most direct form of selling—door to door—has sunk. Using individual salesmen on commission (such as Jerry Moore with his vacuum cleaners) to sell individual items to individuals is wasteful and inherently expensive, especially in an age when salesmen come dear, appliances are cheap, and other forms of promotion are ubiquitous. The changes in marketing and the market have had a profound effect even on companies that potently combine the agency gambit and the catalogue caper.

Adding amateurs to this powerful combination, such as the hundreds of thousands of Avon ladies ("independent businesswomen," according to the company), once created the most profitable company in the entire United States. From 1961 to 1970 Avon increased sales and earnings by 19 percent annually. By 1973 its stock was so avidly desired by the big institutional investors that, at $7.9 billion, this one cosmetics firm was worth more in the stock market than the entire U.S. steel industry. In the decade to 1986, though, no cosmetics could disguise the awfulness of Avon's results: its annual increase in earnings was only 1.2 percent; its 1987 market value, at $2.2 billion, was 72 percent lower than all those years before. The psychology of women selling to women in the highly conditioned atmosphere of the home has proved far less effective in an era when women are far less likely to be in that home.

Today, the telephone (like the television) is mightier than the doorbell, than even the mailman. Straight mail order, which has produced more than its fair share of millionaires inside and outside the United States, has become far less effective as a means of mass-marketing. While Sears Roebuck now turns over $120 million a day, the mail order on which Julius Rosenwald thrived has long ceased to be the engine of what, in any case, has been unimpressive growth.

Not that mail order, used in the right place, has lost its financial potency: witness the great good fortune of Gary C. Comer and his fundamental error. The former Young and Rubicam copywriter spent a year literally learning the ropes of the sailmaking trade, and then started selling hardware and other sailing equipment by catalogue to avid amateur sailors like himself. The recipients of his catalogues (not surprisingly, well written) started asking for items of clothing. When profits on apparel proved far higher, Comer, like any good sailor, changed tack. His Land's End company, with its monthly catalogue, high levels of service, and large range of clothing (no longer for sailors only), earned $21 million in the 1985/86 fiscal year. Translated by the stock market arithmetic beloved by Common Millionaires, that made the fifty-nine-year-old Comer worth $179 million at the end of 1986; the value of his retained holding after the company had nearly gone public a year before Black October.

Land's End is a convincing example of the lucrative identification of the seller with the sold. As Comer told *Fortune*, "I treat customers the way I want to be treated." But beyond that, the Land's End payoff (a decade after Comer dropped sailing equipment from his mix) is only one example of how the selling action around the world has swung to the differentiated retailer: what were once mere departments in large stores are now independent businesses generating fortunes that outstrip those of many old-line department store magnates.

The explanation lies in the fragmentation of modern markets into segments capable of attracting affluent customers who (unlike Avon's erstwhile captive audience) are more likely to be in the shopping mall than the apartment. Leslie Wexner spotted his first segment, sportswear for younger women, in 1963. According to *Forbes*, Milton Petrie— another ace exponent of specialty stores for women—advised Wexner to stay small. But in 1986 Petrie was worth only half of Wexner's The Limited fortune from 2,500 stores (though, since Petrie weighed in at a precrash $700 million, derived from 1,400 middle-priced, mostly teen-loving outlets, his practice definitely proved more effective than his preaching).

In just the same style as the specialty makers and retailers—in everything from running shoes to cosmetics—have expanded at the expense of the generalists, so individually managed and focused food retailers have torn chunks out of the flesh of the industry giants. The two Weis brothers, Sigfried and Robert, inherited a grocery business that their grandfather had begun with a single Pennsylvania store in 1870. The 121 stores run by the old boys (one seventy, one sixty-seven) managed over five times the average supermarket margins in 1986— operating in only four states.

It's these localized sticklers for detail to whom the race goes time and again. Sam Walton is merely an extreme example of the genre. Running the biggest stores in small towns has turned out to be vastly more rewarding than joining the crowd in big cities. As Walton observed to *Forbes*, "There was a lot more business in those towns than people ever thought"—multiply that unconsidered business by 950 Wal-Mart towns and you arrive at $11.9 billion of sales and $450 million of profits, even at the 3.8 percent margins that go with discount prices.

That gave Wal-Mart in spring 1987 a market capitalization of $15.9 billion, a staggering four times the sum fetched by a great supermarket chain, Safeway, once the preserve of the Magowan family, when it was taken private in the second-largest financial deal of 1986. As that shows, the front of selling moves radically over time; and as the waves of changing markets sweep toward the shore, the old leaders are beached and new ones emerge in unsuspected places to change the seascape for keeps.

The supermarket tycoons helped beach themselves by getting locked into sterile battles for market share that unnecessarily savaged their margins—hence the ability of such as the Weis brothers to quintuple the average. One of the oddities in this sacrifice of margins was the trading stamp. What should have been profits were shoveled largely into other people's pockets, notably those of the Beinecke family. The Beineckes sold by catalogue to captive customers, imprisoned for them by the supermarkets that gave discounts in the form of stamps that, to its inordinate profit, could only be cashed in for the stamp company's goods.

The decadence of the trading stamp age had some dismal results—especially for the Beineckes and their Sperry and Hutchinson pink stamps—in Britain. The Sainsburys, showing the Weis-like grip that made them the richest Anglo-Saxon grocers, resisted the evil pink tide like the Greeks repulsing the Persians. Allied with most of its competitors, Sainsburys organized a boycott of S & H's biggest outlet—the Fine Fare supermarket empire built up by Canadian billionaire Garfield Weston.

His misfortune was that he also sold flour and bread to Sainsbury and his retail allies. After a spirited attempt to sell himself out of trouble by exhorting his salesmen to supreme endeavor, Weston surrendered—in what is possibly the last example of a full-bore restraint of trade that Anglo-American business will ever see. That left a boycott-proof supermarketeer, Jack Cohen of Tesco, almost alone in taking his stamps from a business that (like S & H) was 100 percent in the hands of its proprietor: the Green Shield of Granville Tompkins.

In fourteen years the said Tompkins had built up a $60 million turnover and $7 million profit with no visible sign of either financial strain or undue effort. As for his insistence on keeping this handsome possession entirely within his own bosom, along with a nationwide discount chain and a public furniture business, that's one of the eccentricities to which self-made millionaires are prone. If your posttax income is high enough (Tompkins long ago, when sitting on gold mines, paid himself nearly half a million dollars one year, at 1987 exchange rates, and collected an estimated $2 million more in dividends, which is presumably the taxable tip of his particular iceberg), who needs more capital?

High-intensity sellers often fall into this colorful private category—especially if they are in a position to conceal from everybody, including the tax collector, just how much they are paid. Hence the self-evident, but secretive, profits of those in the ancient trade known as export-import. The little-known private fortunes often cluster around this admirable activity—not only the Bunge y Born commodity trading empire, but those of Anton Besse, who made enough out of import-export in Aden, the most godforsaken spot in the British empire, to found his own postgraduate Atlantic College in Britain; or of Juan March, who made one of Europe's largest piles by bringing tobacco into Franco's Spain; or of a former egg dealer's son, Count Volpi, whose father's tobacco beat was the trade between the Balkans and the Middle East.

The count, Mussolini's "financial wizard," was crowned with enormous estates in Libya by his patron, and ended up with a hotel chain, a power company, shipping, resorts in Venice (of which he became uncrowned Doge), and a Palladian villa, equipped with priceless frescoes by Veronese, not far from Bassano. The export-importer buys in one place and ultimately sells in another, often far removed in time and space, and after a series of barters and other deals that totally obscure (except in his computerlike brain) precisely where the profit was made—and there usually is a profit.

Because the export-importer seeks to buy where his commodity is in surplus and sell where it is short, the profits may well be high beyond the dreams of usury. But so long as he stays in line with prices prevailing locally, nobody is likely to notice, still less care. It's the position into which every salesman hopes to maneuver—selling where supply is demanded but questions aren't asked. Obviously this happiness is harder to achieve in a less exotic trade than Balkan tobacco.

Very basic commodities can nevertheless produce great wealth for generations of families who, like the lilies of the field, do not sow; but they certainly reap financially. The greater the privacy, as noted, the higher the profit tends to be; and Cargill Inc. is the largest private company in America. Since the 1860s, when the founder had the sense to go West from Long Island, the Cargills and the Macmillans (who came in by marriage to the first Cargill's daughter) have dominated the ownership and the midwest grain trade. Together, the three main branches own three-quarters of a company with revenues of $32 billion.

That's more than the turnover of Du Pont: the *Forbes* estimate of $1.8 billion for the three principal family fortunes is almost certainly too low—for who can accurately value a worldwide trading empire that also has boxed beef processing and even steel mills in its collection, and that need account only to itself and the Internal Revenue? Another largely private grain empire is that of the Fribourgs, started in Belgium in 1913 and now, as Continental Grain, boasting sales of $14 billion; it is under the firm control of Marc Fribourg (worth over $800 million), who surrounds himself with talent, according to *Forbes*, on the theory, "many egos but only one opinion."

Notoriously, other private traders have been far keener on their egos than on the Internal Revenue. Tax evasion to the tune of $50 million was among the charges that led abruptly to the Swiss residence and Spanish citizenship of Marc Rich, who shares a billion-dollar fortune with partner Pincus Green (now a Bolivian by the same cause). Why the pair, after creating two great commodity trading businesses, one now part of Phibro-Salomon, one their own, felt it necessary to affront the U.S. authorities is an easily explained mystery of wealth: riches stimulate greed.

They also encourage gluttony, which is how the transparently simple device of charging enormous, nonnegotiable prices and making that fact part of your sales appeal can bring the pleasures of the export-import equation to the High or Main Street. This particular pitch is the key to the rich specialty shop, the Tiffany or Cartier; the pitchman need only ensure that, like Duveen, he has the best that money can buy. Harry Winston evolved from son of a small New York jeweler to purveyor of million-dollar diamonds to the new aristocracy (the Burtons and such Texans as Mrs. Robert Windfohr) by this well-trodden route. At one point or another he owned the Hope, Jonker, and Vargas diamonds; the latter was sold to Mrs. Windfohr, who couldn't even bend her finger with it on. "Harry says," she would remark, "it's the third greatest rock in the world."

The technique reached its most stupendous manifestation, feeding off the gargantuan appetites and incomes of its native state, in Neiman-Marcus, possibly the only general department store in the world regularly to stock million-dollar bijoux. Long before it found fame by putting His and Her private airplanes in a Christmas catalogue, its ambition was only the praiseworthy idea of dressing a whole community beautifully. It was started in 1907 in a two-story building by Mrs. Carrie Marcus Neiman, and her brother Herbert Marcus; by Christmas 1960 it could afford to lose $5 million, almost entirely in stock, in one fire.

In the process of providing beautiful dressing, the Neiman-Marcus duo discovered that people with an inexhaustible supply of money required an equally endless supply of goods on which to spend it. One vitally important corollary is that the more expensive the goods, the greater the amount of the money supply that can be absorbed. The second corollary is that the more guaranteed the intrinsic virtue of the expensive goods, the less their well-provided purchasers will care about the expense.

As Stanley Marcus once explained to an interviewer, at their start, "many of these millionaires never had the money to buy fine clothes . . . to provide comfortable, gracious decor. . . . But because there was a recognizable authority in the form of a store a hundred miles away, they were able to avoid many of the pitfalls of the rich." It's a selling pitch that never misses. In fact, nobody would regard the Marcus clan, or the lineal descendants of Mr. Fortnum and Mr. Mason, or their equally exclusive counterparts in France, Germany, and Italy, as salesmen, as pitchmen; but that they plainly are.

The suave, forceful expertise of purveyors to the rich, however, has had far less effect on the reputation of selling than the slick, aggressive confidence tricks of another important group of salesmen—those who are actually selling an inferior article. Paradoxically, their task is relatively easy: if the sucker doesn't recognize the shoddiness of the goods, he'll fall for anything. By its nature, however, this nefarious branch of the trade is self-liquidating: the shoddy seller runs out of suckers and must move on to a different pitch.

The inferior breed are unfortunately hard to distinguish from hard sellers in general (since the techniques of persuasion are identical) and from cheap sellers in particular, although the latter are not only respectable but social benefactors. The sell-it-cheap merchants are the alternative method of cracking the monopoly of established retailers, who, if given an inch, have tended to take a mile of profit margin.

The supermarket chains began as price-cutters; the discount stores turned cutting into a religion. Eugene M. Ferkauf, whose very name means "sell," deserves immortality for the concept that created E. J. Korvette and a personal fortune of $50 million for its boss by the age of forty-one. The idea of a department store without frills, from which the customers carted away their own purchases, made high-speed mileage until it fell foul of two predictable developments. On one hand, the frilly department stores began to compete in price in the area where the discount stores hurt them most, on big-ticket appliances; on the other hand, the discounters began to get ideas above their station and above their management ability.

Ferkauf's management consisted mostly of former high school friends from Brooklyn who practiced techniques of a certain basic simplicity—like marking up all appliances at $10 over cost, irrespective of that cost. As Korvette spread, so did its administrative problems and costs; it became harder and harder to maintain the low prices. Much the same thing happened, earlier and more disastrously, to Ferkauf's imitators. Before many realized what had happened, they were running full-scale department stores at substandard profit margins. The subsequent spate of setbacks and crashes rubs in the same old lesson: a seller makes his living from the difference between his costs and his prices, and if the prices are low, the pressure on his economics must be high.

This explains why the larger and lasting discount fortunes have been made by those who, like Sam Walton, have their roots in the simple, low-cost country districts such as Bentonville, Arkansas, far from the big-city lights and big-city rents. Wal-Mart's offices are deliberately kept Spartan to discourage executives from occupying them; deserting the uncomfortable desks, they spend more time where the selling is and where, too, the best experience—both for would-be millionaires and managers—is obtained.

Lee Iacocca spent long years as a red-hot Ford salesman—and continued to demonstrate supreme pitching skills after his Chrysler metamorphosis into America's most famous big-time corporate manager. Even Harold S. Geneen, who became renowned for his unmatched financial management skills, got his start in selling—he learned the arts from a book that taught him:

1. Never make your sales pitch right away. Sit down with the client and talk to him about the advantages of your product.
2. Listen to what he says. Don't interrupt him.
3. Pick out his main objection or doubt and focus your sales talk on that.
4. Finally, before you leave, don't forget to ask for the order.

Hardly anybody has risen to the financial summit without, like Geneen, selling something—even if it's only himself or herself. That is the type of selling into which, regardless of his basic activity, every salesman is forced. He must sell himself before he can sell his product.

In a sense, most supersellers who float their companies do two distinct selling operations: the basic one that creates the business, and the ancillary self-selling, the one that offloads the business, in part or in whole, on the public, and thus creates the capital wealth—maybe out of very little present substance, as in the case of Genentech, the long-profitless company with a one-time stock-market value of $4.7 billion, and its boss, Robert Swanson. By 1987 he certainly hadn't sold drugs anything near as successfully as he had marketed the company in the late lamented bull market. But could *he* sell shares. . . .

8

MONEY
IN THE
MAKING

In the golden and silver ages of wealth, manufacture, transportation, oil, and big money ruled most roosts. In the Age of the Common Millionaire, transportation is an area of major and minor disasters, oil is an arena of idle rigs and slashed prices, the big banks are struggling to earn a big living, and much of the manufacturing industry has retired to the sidelines and the dustbin—thus, the largest relic of J. Pierpont Morgan's steel trust, USX, lost $1.8 billion in 1986.

At that, the company had vast interests outside steel. Behind it, the once-mighty Bethlehem Steel ranked only eighty-ninth in the Fortune 500—just below a couple of soup companies, Campbell and H. J. Heinz. The latter made half a billion between them (to the pleasure of the Dorrance and Heinz families); Bethlehem lost $152 million. Small wonder that Wall Street has turned its back on the former giants of manufacturing.

Brains these days are valued much more highly than brawn: the heavyweight Ford Motor Company, riding the winning streak that took its profits above those of General Motors for the first time, was actually valued at fewer billions in spring 1987 than Digital Equipment—a computer company with only 12 percent of Ford's sales and a quarter of its profits. Just as extraordinary, the manufacturing and marketing king of the supermarket shelves, Procter & Gamble, had a lower market value than one localized nonfood retailer, Wal-Mart, with only 59 percent of P & G's profits.

These days manufacturing per se has gone out of fashion, probably forever. Only smart manufacturing attracts the smart money. That doesn't necessarily mean smart industries, such as computers and drugs; it means shifting away from the highly repetitive, heavy grind of the assembly line and the mill toward the varied, multifaceted, marketing-led manufacture that has turned upside-down the old ideas—including the notion that making things is difficult: making them well, that is.

True, the pain of turning inert materials into articles of use and beauty is so exquisite that down the centuries the master craftsman has always been able to name his own price. But the Benvenuto Cellinis, the Thomas Sheratons, the Paul Lameries, made only one artifact at a time. The task of achieving their standards of excellence over and over again, with each product identical to and as satisfactory as its twin, triplet, sextuplet, and million-uplet, used to be of an exceedingly expensive order before new technology changed the name of the game.

A mass culture demands mass products, and the great manufacturing fortunes went to the masters of mass-producing, not Cellini cups, Sheraton chairs, or Lamerie silverware, but products that, made in the millions, satisfied the multitude. The greatest fortune ever assembled, after all, was that of Henry Ford, a mint put together, appropriately enough, from being the greatest assembler of all time.

The Ford family, had it played its tax and management cards right, could still own, directly and indirectly, every lock, stock, and barrel of the Ford Motor Company. Without counting the immense millions piled up in income over the years (at the top of the Model A's earning power, Henry pocketed $13 million in one year and his son Edsel another $8 million), the Ford Motor Company fortune came to $37.9 billion in assets and $14.8 billion in stockholders' equity, all valued in the market at $21.2 billion at the start of 1987. That aggregation would have left even the Reichmanns in the shade (a rich enough shade, admittedly).

Ford emerged from the welter of competing car firms at the turn of the century, not merely because the Model T offered the best value for money, but because it was designed for mass manufacture by Ford's own mass method. Every manufacturing millionaire has exploited the same basic formula: vfm + cn + dfm = m², where *vfm* equals value for money, *cn* equals consumer need, *dfm* equals designed for manufacture, and *m,* of course, stands for the inevitable financial reward, even in an industry where, as in cars, the competition has always been intense and potent.

The product can be widely manufactured by firms in every industrialized state—and still millions are there to be made, simply by making it better. In Germany, the already super-rich Hermann Quandt demonstrated the possibilities by turning BMW from a highway wreck into the world's most successful maker of sporty executive transport. But the German achievement is as nothing compared to the Japanese. Well before the yen climbed to the dollar-defeating heights of 1987, Toyota had become the largest manufacturer outside the United States—sustaining growth rates, what is more, that doubled those of Chrysler, which is now a smaller company than Toyota, for all the enormously paid efforts of Lee Iacocca.

Before World War II, the Japanese company, the pride of the Toyoda family, already rich from sewing machines, was so inept that its initial product, a small truck, broke down all over Japan in what was promptly dubbed the "praying" posture. After World War II, the first Toyotas shipped to California blew up on the freeways. As in shipbuilding and steel, however, the Japanese not only mastered the secrets of American mass production—they bettered them. Yet the successes are transient, in the sense that today's new manufacturing fortunes are determined not so much by how the product is made but by what it is.

The true modern makers are companies such as Merck and DEC, Hewlett-Packard and Abbott Laboratories, IBM and Bristol-Myers: companies that are in the main highly efficient in their manufacturing methods but that are instantly clobbered (like IBM in the clone era) if the products lose face in the market. Two of the above (Hewlett-Packard and DEC) are linked with large current, self-made personal fortunes. But most of the drug companies, like most of the largest manufacturers, have passed out of entrepreneurial ownership; and in the ranks of the richest (two of the exceptions being mentioned above), the manufacturers are few and far between.

A billionaire family such as the Pritzkers may have large manufacturing interests, but none of those plants are such as to make world markets tremble. The typical manufacturing fortune is that of John H. Krehbiel, Sr., who in his eighty-first year controlled both the management and $235 million of shares in Molex, a company that makes electronic connectors and whose sales are a relatively small $844 million annually. As Krehbiel's years indicate, it takes a long time to build even a middling manufacturing enterprise. The old principle of victory through nothing but economies of scale, lowering costs Ford-style by pouring out more and more identical copies, and then lowering prices to raise demand still more, no longer works so simply.

The gambit of making cheaper to sell more cheaply never was by any means the only approach; there is also making things more expensively to sell at a higher price. Thus, Johnson's Wax once proposed to bring out a car polish for sixty-nine cents. It was persuaded by the ad agency that the price was simply too low for so passionately protective an activity as polishing the beloved car. So the company added some expensive ingredients and marketed the wax, with much heavier advertising, at $1.47. The cynics might wonder why the Johnson boys bothered to alter anything about the mix except its price, but there is a curious morality in your true manufacturer. It was, after all, Henry Ford who promised his customers a cash rebate if sales climbed above three hundred thousand; that cost the old boy $13 million.

The Peugeot business in France, possibly even to the surprise of the Peugeots themselves, became the most profitable carmaker in Europe in the early 1970s (not, by the way, a great distinction in those hard times) by the paradoxical device of extravagance. They would spend far more on a component than their U.S. rivals. A Detroit mogul found it all too much to take. "How can you waste money like that?" he demanded after watching Peugeot's pains. "In Detroit we run them all straight through and scrap the defective ones at the end."

That single sentence could serve as the epitaph for America's former dominance of world manufacture. The words are the antithesis of the efficient quality-control methods that, when that foolish mogul spoke, had been pioneered several years previously—by an American, of course. The quality ideas of W. Edwards Deming, assiduously adopted in Japan, were ignored with equal stupidity by Peugeot and were one important reason for its collapse into loss.

The last family to run a major French carmaker, the Peugeots were forced to retire to count their millions while other men began the painful task of marrying modern engineering to scientific management. America's manufacturing millionaires have suffered still more serious damage from their neglect of both. By 1986, the consumer electronics markets where the likes of the Sarnoffs (RCA) and the Galvins (Motorola) had made their mints had been surrendered—all but 38 percent—to the foreigners. Of this rump, too, much was Japanese-owned. The loss of markets such as machine tools (down from 23 percent of world exports to 4 percent, while imports multiplied eleven-fold) devastated another area of manufacturing fortunes.

The toolmakers, in turn, were inevitably affected by the horrendous rise of car imports to 30 percent of the U.S. market. The $31 billion adverse balance in America's automotive trade represented a gigantic loss in profit to everybody connected with the auto business—except dealers in foreign cars. The new car rich are people such as Norman Braman, also owner (at a cost of $67 million) of the Philadelphia Eagles. After breaking one of the several early retirements in the chronicles of wealth, Braman started collecting Cadillac dealerships. He then switched to the foreigners; according to *Business Week*, his twenty-plus franchises, which include Rolls-Royce and Toyota, sell half a billion dollars worth of cars in a year. The $15 million Braman invested (not wisely) in one new model—British Rover's Sterling, for which he gained U.S. marketing control—is some measure of the bonanza Detroit's manufacturers have missed.

The malaise of such mass producers has been shared by people who should have been immune. As the Japanese demonstrated that Deming's and their own methods could combine high volume with top quality, the squeeze also fastened a fierce grip on U.S. manufacturers, such as Zenith, that had adopted the Peugeot approach—old-fashioned engineering combined with what, in an industry dominated by careless conglomerates, had become old-fashioned quality. Under founder Eugene McDonald, Zenith built a formidable reputation for its TVs and radios. By 1986, however, its most successful products were microcomputers; but consumer electronics losses dragged the whole business into a $10 million deficit in 1986—on $1.8 billion of turnover.

The Zeniths and the Peugeots banked on the old knowledge that every market contained a premium product, commanding a rich extra in price and profit, manufactured to better specifications and with more-consistent performance than any other, and made by, in most cases, a smaller specialist competing with the gross generalists. What they didn't allow for was the advance of technology that made it impossible to recover higher labor and other production costs in higher prices for higher quality. Today the specialist manufacturer such as BMW has to be as efficient in production as the mass maker such as Toyota. To defend its marketing strength (from which its higher prices flow) the specialist must love that product. This oldfangled product orientation is despised by the big corporations, and it's their contempt that makes them unable to compete against the manufacturing freak. The image of the founder-millionaire wearing overalls, tinkering with some mechanical marvel in workshop or lab is often reality—that's where Soichiro Honda made his multimillions, where Ken Olsen of Digital Equipment is happiest.

A born manufacturer loves to have his office at the plant; it's the professional managers who fly to the skyscraper aeries of the big city, where, safe in their nests, they can forget about nuts and bolts. But the plant orientation can work economic miracles fully as startling as those created by the passion for production. Love that plant, too, and it will grow.

It could even grow tenfold in under four years—at least, that was the pace set by Nelson Peltz and Peter May after they walked into Triangle Industries. The list of products from which these Jacks built their $2.7 billion beanstalk included aluminum cans, copper wire, bottles, and cable—the very kind of smokestack products on which ambitious managements and investors have long since turned their backs. Yet, after a stunning performance in 1985, the shares rose 562 percent in the first two-thirds of 1986—how?

According to *Business Week*, the recipe was indeed "love that plant." Peltz and May thought, for instance, that "by keeping overhead lean, giving their managers an investment stake in the business and *being unstinting with capital spending*, Triangle will prevail as the world's low-cost producer of containers." They became the largest force in American containers by acquiring American Can's packaging business, whose chairman, Gerald Tsai, epitomizes a different breed of modern millionaire—and, indeed, one who made his name in a different era.

The Chinese-American was the hottest-shot investor of the hot-stock 1960s. On the strength of name alone, Tsai pulled in a sum of public money—$247 million—so large that it was impossible for him to produce the mutual fund performance investors fondly imagined they were buying. Tsai's fund (despite one of Wall Street's pathfinding million-dollar personal incomes) hardly performed at all. He finally sold out for $30 million—and little was heard of the genius until he reappeared as head of American Can and began to convert the suffering mammoth into a financial-services conglomerate designed to exploit the bull market's final throes.

That is the new conventional wisdom: dismantle the smokestacks, build a downtown skyscraper with the financial bricks that result—and let manufacturing America go hang. The precrash results for Tsai were eminently satisfactory. American Can's stock soared 60 percent from high to low in the twelve months that straddled its transition to postindustrial. And Tsai once more rejoiced in a seven-figure income: $1.2 million, to be precise.

That was conspicuously larger than the take of another container buff, Richard M. Ringoen, whose management of Ball Corporation (return on equity 16.1 percent versus 11.6 percent for Tsai's masterpiece) has long shown that fat profits can still be wrung out by lean management of dull manufacture. At Crown Cork and Seal (14.1 percent return), John F. Connelly collected over three years only a fifth of Tsai's total pay for increasing his investors' wealth by 176 percent, double Tsai's performance. Connelly, like Ball, is a love-that-plant man who founded his own company after World War II and merged it with Crown in 1957, when sales were $40 million. He now presides over a business forty times that size. His miserly reward in income shouldn't mislead: Connelly in May 1987 owned Crown stock worth $17.2 million, while his foundation had another $182 million under its belt.

That's far more than Peltz and May had garnered after their three-year charge up the smokestacks—and the question has to be asked: where and what will their Triangle be after a forty-year run like Connelly's? The pair were certainly right to tell *Business Week* that "there are a lot of opportunities in the manufacturing industry today." But their opportunities arose, first, because plants like those of American Can, in Peltz's words, have been "starved of capital," run down, and second because junk-bond financing had made it childishly simple to pick the bargains from the basement. The future of U.S. manufacturing is on shaky ground if its profitability rests on the power of smart money to buy neglected businesses at low or even zero cost; the latter was the case with Hanson Trust's purchase of SCM's lucrative typewriter business. It cost effectively nothing after the conglomerate's other assets had been profitably sold.

All over America, without benefit of financial wizardry, solid managers such as Connelly are beavering away at the task of maintaining a competitive lead in the "low-tech, zero-sex-appeal" products on which an economy turns. The phrase is *Fortune*'s description of the door and window seals and trim that former lawyer James Reid makes at Standard Products. This style of manufacturer, in the quest to out-Japan Japan, puts up with dreary offices in dull districts, simplifies everything (Reid concentrated the business on laminated extrusion products only), and makes much money—Standard's $27 million in 1986 represented a quadrupling in four years and a 24 percent return on equity. The family's then stake of $50 million shows the amount of money there still is in the making—for those who follow simple rules.

Britain's Sir Jules Thorn, the lighting and television tycoon who took Sylvania for a ride (see Chapter 15), though nobody's ideal of the delegating pro of scientific management, exemplified the simple rules. Rule one, the vital factor is cost: if a change will bring down the cost of production, change. Rule two, cost is a function of modernity: if a new machine will improve efficiency and lower cost, buy it. One of

Thorn's associates, recalling the early days, said that Sir Jules "did certain things that absolutely shocked me." He bought the key machine on the fluorescent lighting side "before we had the volume to support it."

That leads on to rule three: unless you can get a suitable buildup of sales, expenditure on the latest million-dollar wondergadget is the way to bankruptcy. That rule in turn leads to the Vertical Gambit. A big enough market at the far end of the line opens up subsidiary markets all the way back to the raw embryo. This perspective is all the more beguiling to the truly acquisitive tycoon because going vertical promises to transfer to him all the annoying profits made by his suppliers— profits he tends to resent.

The true productioneer never believes that anybody else can manufacture a component more cheaply than he can himself. If he doesn't like a supplier's quality or price, he simply makes his own. If the end market isn't enormous enough to support his ambitions, he buys somebody else's end-market share. Big corporations try the same popular trick, but lacking the entrepreneur's exclusive interest in ultimate profit, they mess up the formula. They are decentralized into product groups and divisions, each with its own target for profit, and each expected to charge prices, even to other divisions in the same group, that will hit the profit bull's-eye.

At each level of the corporate chain of production a profit gets taken, which in turn is compounded into the price and profit of the next link of the chain, until at the end of the line, when the product actually escapes into the hands of the customer, the final price carries an accumulated profit that is vastly greater than the selling division's final margin. That compounding chain produces a final price that a truly integrated entrepreneur can savage.

This helps to explain how one textile maverick was able to produce an uncomplicated product such as a nylon sheet for $1.50 when the nearest competition was $2.50. As one of his sidekicks remarked of his rivals, "It may be one company, but the yarn is spun in one place, woven in another, and finished in another. Here, bales come in at one end, and the finished sheets go out at the other."

The aim (as Thorn knew so well) is to make widgets more cheaply, so as to lower the price and/or raise the profits on the gadgets into which the widgets disappear. The true return, the real money, lies in the saving over the lowest available bought-in cost; it's the achieving of lower cost by submanufacture, not the notional profit on selling the submanufactured part to their own companies, from which the vertical fortunes are made.

The vertical corporation, though, has been forced to reverse engines by the advance of technology and of foreign competition. Electronics has become assembly—the easy availability of standard components manufactured outside is what, along with its own tactical errors, made IBM vulnerable to the clones. Indeed, this once most vertical of giants became, for the PC and even more for the failed PC jr, something of a "hollow corporation"—the evocative phrase for a "manufacturing" company that makes nothing of what it sells. *Business Week* cites the Galoob family, creator of the Golden Girls action figures: the Galoobs actually create hardly anything—even the product ideas mostly come from outside.

At a more exalted level, some of the greatest names in manufacturing—General Electric, Honeywell, Caterpillar Tractor, Olivetti—market products that are made entirely elsewhere (usually in Asia). For those lines, the multibillionaire giants, like the $58 million Galoobs, are little more than glorified wholesalers; and so is clothing "manufacturer" Liz Claiborne. She runs what Raymond E. Miles of the University of California calls a *dynamic network*—meaning a small outfit that does big business by masterminding the activities of a mass of outside contractors.

Miles sees this as a trend: "What you'll have is a switchboard instead of a corporation." The dynamic of Claiborne's extraordinary rise and one-time $80 million fortune—derived from a twenty-eight-times rise in the stock price after going public in 1981—lies not so much in the network as in the identity between her design ideas and those of the sensible dressers who buy her Asian-made clothes.

In the same way, Britain's greatest hollow fortune—and one of the country's largest of any kind—was made by Alan Sugar. He spotted, first, that he could sell computers by having them designed and made from standard components—just as he had previously and expertly packaged hi-fi equipment; second, that the obsolete eight-bit computer technology had left a lot of cheap components and many hungry manufacturers stranded; and third, that a huge gap existed between the cost of a typewriter and the cheapest personal computer.

Sugar's Amstrad offering came in at only $600. Despite manifold imperfections, it sold in vast numbers, encouraging the maestro to launch an IBM clone for only $150 more. As his paper fortune soared to hundreds of millions, Sugar told the secrets of his success. They included attracting as employees "people who either catch on quickly or last two minutes"; telling them "rise or fall by your own decision or get out"; teaching "engineers to think on a commercial basis"; assuming that "a component is going to work and cut out delay" with "a contingency plan if it does not"; calculating advertising spending "by the amount you can afford from the quantity you plan to sell";

and making "the accountants take risks" in areas such as credit control.

No respecter of Americans ("On balance, they don't hold a candle to the Japanese"), Sugar noted that "if we get the same market share . . . in all the countries in the world we would be bigger than General Motors"—without owning a single factory. Yet much of Sugar's formula is immediately recognizable as the secret of the success of those Japanese who, he said, have taught him, among other things, "attention to detail. I was asked by one of their salesmen what color I wanted. When I replied 'white,' I was shown twenty-five shades."

Overwhelming attention to making things, as opposed to marketing them, or flooding the stock market with paper, has distinguished not only Japan but also the other most durable economic miracle of the postwar world—that of West Germany. Millions of customers bought the Beetle (the single most important ingredient of Germany's great recovery, and Adolf Hitler's only lasting achievement) not because it was cheaper, smarter, more economical, or more comfortable than the opposition (it was none of those things) but because it didn't, unlike competitive cars, fall apart in the driver's hands (even if, in Ralph Nader's, it tended to roll over).

The Japanese, possibly because they started by imitating other people's products, founded what are probably the most staggering postwar fortunes by finding better ways to make and design the identical products. They achieved apparently impossible feats, such as making better Leicas than Leitz, before proceeding to advances in design that left Leitz behind. In the dawn of new genuinely Japanese technology, the insistence on quality and efficient manufacture remained in the risen sun.

The results for such as Konosuke Matsushita have been dazzling to behold—on a par with the creations of wealth in the second American Industrial Revolution, after what Aldous Huxley called the Year of Our Ford. In chalking up his series of world-record incomes, Matsushita ran far ahead not only of U.S. salaries but also of the nearest Japanese; for instance, when Matsushita earned $660,000 one year in the 1960s, the runner-up was a $360,000-a-year gentleman whose job, obviously a nice number, was baldly described by the taxman as "son of the president of the Kondo Textile Company."

Small wonder that Matsushita wrote a work titled *The Words of Peace and Happiness Through Prosperity.* His own prosperity stemmed from apprenticeship to a maker of charcoal braziers, which led via meter reading for the Osaka electrical system to starting his own electrical firm in 1917. He made electric lamp sockets in the proverbial one room on 200 yen of capital.

In 1987 the Matsushita interests controlled the seventh-largest firm outside the United States, with assets of over $21.4 billion and sported (which is almost unheard of in Japan) both high profits and a decently sized shareholders' equity. At a time when most Japanese companies were in hock to their eyebrows and only minimally in profit, Matsushita sat on over $1 billion of stockholders' equity and by far the most exalted profits in Japan, at $165.7 million; fifteen years later, the numbers were over $10 billion and $1 billion in profits. The 5 percent Matsushita stake in this combine is one of the world's largest fortunes, a long, long way from 200 yen.

The company song ends with the stirring anthem "Grow industry, grow, grow, grow! Harmony and sincerity! Matsushita Electric!" This enthusiasm is reflected in the less lyrical fact that one division alone had 553 quality-control teams, holding, what's more, "many voluntary study sessions." Matsushita, for all his moral fervor, is one of the easier Japanese entrepreneurs for a Westerner to understand; he even adopted, down to the last form, the Philips' control system, but made it far more effective by applying rigid personal supervision. According to one story, each division had to telephone its results in *every day*, so that Matsushita had them on his desk next morning.

The autocratic style is by no means atypical of Japan's manufacturing giants, as *Fortune* once pointed out. The family-owned Suntory with $4 billion in sales, which makes what the Japanese fondly think of as whiskey, has a boss who believes in management by inquisition; that is, he forces executives to master their subject, to do their homework, to have facts to justify their theories and ideas. "At a meeting someone will suggest something. I ask 'Why?' I want more detail. He will answer, and then I ask, 'Why?' I ask 'why' five times, and then I stop."

The largest shipbuilder in Japan, another personally owned fief, doesn't believe in the nonsense that only a limited and small number of managers should report to him. No less than 300 line managers report directly to the boss, who models his regime on that—believe it or not—of Joseph Stalin. According to *Fortune*, the shipbuilding tycoon, Hisap Tsubouchi, was impressed by the devotion of his Russian wartime captors to the Great Dictator: "They said that Stalin didn't exploit them and led a simple life"—which is just what this tycoon does. He has almost no staff and lives modestly. The title of Tsubouchi's best-selling audiocassette is "How to Reprimand Your Subordinates," which figures.

Then there's a red-hot firm in advanced ceramics that is run just like the old Imperial army: people even salute their bosses and do nothing, apparently, but work hard, obey orders, and put up with the occasional rages of the dictator. But there must be method in his madness—the firm makes profits of $132 million from dominating the world market for the ceramic packages used in advanced electronics. Its leader says, "When I talk to the managers of our subsidiaries in America, I tell them to listen to their subordinates. They tell me 'I'm the boss here.' But I tell them that nobody is perfect, so listen with humility." That is, no doubt, an order.

He is a blood brother to a ball-bearing magnate who believes that American managers waste too much time in "meetings, meetings, meetings." This man is known as "Mr. Hurry-Up" to suppliers and is made very unhappy when he comes across senior executives in the West who don't know their business down to the last detail—such as how long it takes to grind a bearing (four to five seconds for a 15 mm effort). He believes, too, that the best overhead cost is no cost at all. "I cut, cut, cut."

Here sounds the authentic voice of the true manufacturing entrepreneur: as lean, mean, driving, and dedicated as Henry Ford, the spiritual father of them all. The title of "the oriental Henry Ford I," though, belongs not to Matsushita but to a blacksmith's son, Soichiro Honda, a man who baffles even Japanese business journalists. "Mr. Honda," said one, "is a management executive who always wears red shirts and tells naughty stories when drinking." Honda learned the importance of efficient production quality when, out of 50 piston rings tested from a batch of 30,000, only 3 passed. That was his first manufacturing venture, which understandably led nowhere.

In 1947 he started to make motorized bicycles with two-stroke engines adapted to run on pine-root extract. Five years later, however, Honda came of technological age. With the Japanese market in recession, Honda spent $450,000 on German, Swiss, and American tools, for the sound reason that they were the best in the world. He then began to take apart the European bikes he was copying—and discovered that their best was not good enough.

European manufacturers believed it was impossible to run motorcycle engines at 15,000 rpm, with even faster bursts. Honda not only proved that you could but also started to win Grand Prix races all over the world. Once again, the superdesign went with superefficiency in production engineering. At Honda's motorcycle plants not a single storeroom existed for parts, raw materials, or finished machines; deliveries went in at one end, up to one every seven seconds, and finished bikes moved straight on to the double-decker trucks at the other.

Building up a $10 billion company on the pillion of the motorbike is not only a prime economic achievement. It's one that, before Honda demonstrated the technique, would have been disbelieved—especially by the established British companies, bearing once-proud names such as Norton, Matchless, and BSA. In the Honda era, their decline and fall ended in pathos, with the workers at the once-famous Triumph factory fruitlessly defying the management's efforts to close the works down forever.

But millions from manufacture, more than most other seven-figure breeds, are closely linked with personalities. It's the aura, drive, and design passion of the resident Our Ford that provide the impetus and maintain the edge. Remove that presence, replace it with mere mortal men, and the manufacturing operation runs the risk of losing its inspiration and becoming merely routine. That's when, if the product has been selling on a quality reputation, the public begins to notice that the quality differential no longer exists, and when, if the product has been living off inspired design, the competition begins to overtake in the fast lane.

This process overtook the Beetle—the recalls of bugged VW bugs in the United States marked the end of an era dominated by the personality of the late Heinz Nordhoff. Brilliant manufacture is a highly creative activity, and those who don't make millions at it (or throw them away) fail because they approach this act of creation with all the imaginative flair of a cop testing doorknobs. The result, as in much of British manufacturing and too much of American, has been to throw away the company—or at least the plant. It's no surprise that the numbers of the 400 cited by *Forbes* as manufacturers have dwindled (from 103 in 1985 to 92 the next year). They still represent the largest single group, though few are manufacturers as Henry Ford would have understood it, and some make little or nothing in the United States. The ratio is about the same as the sharply reduced share of manufacturing in America's gross national product. It's an illusion to suppose that America's factories can continue to slide without affecting the welfare of all citizens, including the Common Millionaires—whatever the source of their own millions. Somehow, Americans have to recover the money in the making—or it will continue to be made by others, at America's expense.

9

A TASTE
OF
MONEY

The wondrous new fortunes of the Age of the Common Millionaire have gone, not to the manufacturers of the basic products that dominate the world markets in numbers, but to those who find value in the interstices—the "gaps in the market." A typical exemplar presciently called his company exactly that—The Gap. Don Fisher was forty-one when he started catering to the San Francisco college generation. He made his first fortune from jeans supplied by the family firm, Levi Strauss, that, somewhat to its own surprise, had transformed world taste with a single denim product.

The jeans giant then dealt Fisher one body blow by undertaking its own distribution; the change in taste away from the basic product, which also hit Levi Strauss in the solar plexus, finally forced Fisher onto the ropes in 1983. The blows of fate were the knocks of opportunity. Three years later, the reborn Gap, selling casual clothes to the postcollege generation, weighed in at 688 stores and a $335 million *Forbes*-estimated fortune—at $68 million of sales, Fisher had found one of America's neatest niches.

By the same token, Levi Strauss had missed one of the essential lessons of the age—that fashion rules the factory, not the other way around. It's what you might call "demand-side economics." The supply is useless, redundant, without meaning—unless the supplier meets a demand that is strong, but in this age will probably be fickle and fast-changing. That's why the money in the making described in the previous chapter now goes largely either to those basic, unpublicized souls who supply basic, unseen components efficiently to final products, or to the publicity-hungry sophisticates who—no less than Fisher in his second coming—find that *gap in the market*: a phrase that means nothing more nor less than an unfilled demand.

In filling that demand, the better mousetraps of technology may be crucial. Television, compact discs, disposable diapers, hi-fi, long-playing records, latex paint, personal computers, magnetic tape, paperbacks, power mowers, refrigerators and freezers, man-made textiles, transistors, transparent tape, washers and dryers, VCRs—all these are products based on new technology and, according to an exhibition at New York's Cooper-Hewitt Museum, are among fifty innovations that in fifty years have radically changed human life.

In most cases the innovation sold itself, sometimes after a faltering start. But the race has not always gone to the first off the mark, and sooner or later (in recent times sooner rather than later) the ultimate winners have been the suppliers most adept at following the shifts in taste or the followers who, likewise attuned to the market, have later found its most lucrative gaps.

That truth applies to services as handsomely as to goods. Thus, in a country constantly on the move, it's no surprise that overnight accommodation has been in constant demand. But even in a market with so many suppliers, the Holiday Inn founders discovered, from personal observation, a gap in middle-class, midpriced hotels with standardized but higher levels of comfort, just as the son of a Baptist minister, Cecil B. Day, while traveling with his five children, regretted the lack of comfortable motels at budget prices—and with no liquor.

As a real estate man, Day promptly set about filling the gap with 40,000 rooms (the total when he died). *Forbes* recounts that his widow, Deen, another of those females of the species who have proved at least as mighty as the male, greatly improved the Days Inns chain—and finally sold her 45,000 rooms to Saul Steinberg for $615 million.

In employment services, another much-trampled field, William R. Kelly's perceived gap was the unfilled demand for temporary workers. By his eighty-first year, that gap had burgeoned into $876 million of revenues, 650 offices, and $380 million of personally held shares. "Fill that gap" is an even stronger policy than "Love that plant." It's a truism, though, that gap fillers (like plant lovers) are far more commonly found among individuals than in the mighty corporations—even though the latter devote as much time to future tastes as to the expensive search for technological novelty. Their success ratio is equally miserable. A survey in the grocery market showed that, out of 3,087 new products introduced in a seven-year period, two-thirds had disappeared without trace four years later—and of the survivors, many must have earned exiguous profits.

This insensitivity to trends in taste is what distinguishes the common manager from the inspired entrepreneur, and the mature corporation from its origins. All consumer goods companies spring from fertile anticipation or understanding of customer desire. Back in time there truly was a Dr. Clarence Birdseye, whose deep-freeze innovation foreran and facilitated the explosion in convenience foods (which also radically changed human life). Back in that past, too, a Dr. John H. Kellogg, running a sanatorium in Battle Creek, Michigan, in 1894 invented the health-faddist's bread substitute that his Seventh-Day Adventist brother, William K., a dozen years later began turning into a world cornflakes neomonopoly.

Ask the successors of John H. and William K. to parade their own major innovations and the comparison is meager. The Kellogg companies are now in their tenth decade of making millions from a public taste successfully identified while Queen Victoria was still eating her morning porridge. Public taste changes far more reluctantly than the marketing apostles have persuaded businessmen to believe. Hence the latters' penchant for churning out unwanted new products in the hope that they will create their own demand (the supply-side delusion).

The entrepreneur of true taste rarely makes this error. He recognizes a demand that is apparent or latent. Often in these lucrative satisfactions of taste, the tin has been waiting around for somebody to open. Although the opener needs courage and initiative, he needs above all to share the taste; self-identification usually gives the entrepreneur his instinctive appreciation of the market's hungers—as in the hunger for sublimated sex, for transmogrified cheesecake, which existed in full, nubile glory before Hugh Hefner burst into gatefold view.

In *Esquire*, the combination of good masculine living, pinups, jesting sexual innuendo, and sexual frankness, sugared with excellent prose, had worked successfully for decades. But *Esquire*'s come-on girls, originally only painted, had a defect: however languorous their poses, their pudenda and nipples were more or (mostly) less covered. Hefner used the basic *Esquire* formula, plus techniques of nude photography no more advanced than those that experts in naked calendars had employed for years, and published wholly nude nudes by the yard. He took *Esquire*'s sexual themes and suggestiveness and handled them with heavy-handed frankness.

Hefner added one special ingredient to this borrowed, improved concoction: an orgiastic, populist philosophy, every man his own Casanova, that bound the soup together. It was useless to argue that no man lived as *Playboy* suggested: Hefner did. With his philosophical outpourings, accessible maidservants, pluperfect pads, personal Bunnified jet, round bed, and millions, Hefner was the Playboy King made manifest.

Just as Henry Luce was the quintessential reader of *Time* and *Life*, so Hefner acted out the role of his own public. His achievement in strictly business terms cannot rank with Luce's triple hit of *Time*, *Fortune*, and *Life*. But at a time when publishers such as *Life*'s were giving away subscriptions in their forlorn effort to attract advertising, Hefner founded a mass-circulation magazine that made money from subscriptions alone, and then proceeded to establish a prime medium among advertisers who would once not have been seen dead in the company of full-color, let alone full-fronted, nudes.

The magazine cashed in on the sexual Walter Mitty in every man. The Playboy clubs gave middle-class Babbitts the key to a door of private enjoyment that had previously been reserved for the rich. The whole operation was, of course, a tease, another come-on: perfect for customers who fundamentally prefer teasing to reality. Hefner's dreamworld left room to his left for harder-nosed, harder-headed practitioners such as Bob Guccione of *Penthouse*. As noted, trailblazing innovators often do get pushed off the road and left behind by forceful followers. Guccione served an audience that preferred its vicarious sex neat. While Hefner allowed his fantasy life to spill over destructively into the real world of business, Guccione, the fired dry cleaner, built a group whose diversifications (including seven other monthlies) were more soundly based and efficiently managed than the Playboy forays into fields such as gambling.

Where Hefner, like Levi Strauss, stayed locked into variations on a single concept that aged along with its innovator, Guccione catered to broader tastes. There's nothing intrinsically erotic about *Four Wheeler*, another of the magazines that made Guccione worth some $225 million at the age of fifty-four. Specialized titles such as the above (or *Hot Rod*, *Guns and Arms*, and *Teen*, the products that helped make one Robert Peterson worth $235 million) are the clearest evidence of the rich fragmentation of markets, which explains the many media fortunes made in a magazine world that many had given up for dead.

As Helen Gurley Brown showed in performing the sex change with *Cosmopolitan*, it wasn't the market that was dead but the managements.

The necessary skills to syndicate sex probably existed in defunct houses such as Curtis Publishing. But the respectable magazine establishment missed, because of its respectability, the blatant information that human beings, male and female, are passionately interested in sex and that, for the best part of three decades, they have become less and less inhibited about expressing that interest, from Hanover to Grand Rapids, and from Oswego to Yokohama.

It required no great genius from Rupert Murdoch to spot that the basic yens for sex and sensationalism were not being satisfied by the London tabloid newspapers printed by the unaware publishing giant that foolishly sold him the *Sun* newspaper. Mostly, gaps are that obvious; they must be to yield revenues of a sufficient size to produce a fortune like Guccione's or to fuel an ambition like Murdoch's to power the creation of a worldwide media colossus.

The auto industry is a long-running example of how colossal companies lose contact with the tastes that made them great. The Cooper-Hewitt Museum listed the following pre-1966 life-changing autos: the 1959 Austin-Morris Mini, the 1965 Ford Mustang, the 1942 Jeep, the 1941 Nash 600, the 1949 Oldsmobile/Cadillac V8, the 1965 Toyota Corona, and the 1951 VW Beetle. In all these cases save one, the cars were either developed ineptly or not developed at all—either the days of glory faded, or the brand flopped.

The exception, of course, was Japanese. From failing totally with cars that blew up on the Californian freeways, Toyota learned painstakingly how to meet the U.S. preference for smaller cars. Detroit never did, though it should have been forewarned by events such as the $250 million collapse of Ford's big Edsel and the Beetle-led rise in sales of European cars. By dismissing the latter as mere whim, the Detroit tycoons opened the door to George Romney of American Motors, with his onslaught on the "gas-guzzling dinosaurs." Had Romney ever produced a series of excellent compact cars, he might have created America's greatest postwar fortune. Instead, he left the field to the Japanese (and left a died-again AMC to become grist for Lee Iacocca's mill at Chrysler).

The attack on the gas-guzzlers undoubtedly sprang from deep Mormon convictions in Romney's own healthy-mind-in-healthy-body, up-at-six-to-play-golf philosophy. In much the same way, the heady cocktail of sex, schmaltz, patriotic Americanism, violence, melodrama, and wisecracks that poured forth from Hollywood in its golden age mirrored tastes of the mainly Jewish tycoons who gave birth to the industry and presided over its Arabian Nights accumulations of wealth, including their own. In movie mythology, these cold-blooded inhuman monsters ruthlessly plotted the exploitation of mass tastes. Monsters they often were, but the tastes they exploited were their own.

The whole history of mass exploitation revolves around the four ancient appetites—sex, food, drink, escape. Of the four, drink has probably been the most reliable mint, a staple flood of riches through several family generations, and an easy opening for brand-new talent. People need to eat more than they need alcohol. But the price competition in booze is less intense than in food—the need (real or apparent) to generate new products is less pressing, and the outlets are more various.

Produce a new breakfast cereal and you are stuck with the supermarkets and their avaricious, price-cutting monopoly buyers. In contrast, booze flows in bars, clubs, homes, restaurants, trains, planes—and in consequence it takes a rare genius to go bust. The longevity of alcohol-producing families (as in Britain's brewing aristocracy or "beerage") proves the point. It's a source of eternal wonder, given the small evidence of management skill shown by most beerage barons this century. The continuity of their American counterparts suffered severe interruption from Prohibition, although the leading legitimate (so to speak) bootleggers of that era were still up among the leading lights of hard liquor after World War II.

Muscling in on these long-running acts is no joke—but not impossible. Two Scotch whiskys cracked the critical U.S. market open, stealing first and second places from the Distillers Company Ltd. (itself an amalgam of old Scotch families), entirely by emphasizing an attribute of taste. Drinking palates worldwide were moving to lightness and dryness. But nobody had ever thought of blended Scotch whisky as something heavy until some unsung hero started the idea of the "light" Scotch. Whether those who flocked to Cutty Sark and J & B Rare could tell the difference, blindfolded or with their eyes open, from any other Scotch is in grave doubt. But the magnificent results make the question and the doubt irrelevant.

The full magnificence of the family wealth created for Berry Bros. and Rudd, proprietors of both Cutty Sark and a wine shop two centuries old in St. James's, has never been calculated. But even in the late 1980s, when taste has drifted somewhat away from their potion (as from hard liquor in general), the two families concerned must have shared at least $75 million. It would have been far more if, like Guccione and unlike Hefner, they had followed the market into the lighter and even drier zones where another booze-rich British family, the Burroughs of Beefeater gin, had located their premium product.

But whiskys, gins, and even vodkas all run behind another, in essence unlikely taste, that for Bacardi rum. In ten years, no other brand has toppled the product from its leadership in the U.S. market and the world. Exemplifying (again) the law that great wealth and great privacy go hand in hand, the Bacardi empire is a family possession veiled behind a rarely raised curtain. In 1987, in fact, the descendants of Don Facundo Bacardi, a Spanish émigré to Cuba, decided to lower the only lifted veil: they took totally private the marginally public Puerto Rican company that, so its last public figures revealed, made $44 million on $234 million of rum shipped to the family's Jacksonville bottlers.

At the Florida plant's 1972 start, a mere 3 million cases were sold in the United States; that all but trebled in a decade as the Bacardis cashed in on "bottle and glass" ads, naïve drinkers, diet consciousness, mixers, the under-twenty-six baby-boomers of the 1970s—in other words, a whole complex of social and fashion change, unforeseen by the Bacardis, and by everybody else. Rapid reaction, though, is as formidable as foresight. "We may not be trendsetters ourselves," Luis Echarte, the family member by marriage who heads U.S. marketing operations, told the *Herald Tribune.* "But we follow the trends very closely and we can bring out something new in a hurry and get it to market."

This simple formula is the indispensable strategy of the 1980s, when failure to catch opportunity on the wing may mean losing the feast entirely. Before the long Bacardi boom began, the rum market appeared to offer no hope: rum was one of the countless products that, though selling in significant amounts, was stuck in a historical rut that led in no obvious direction. But the commercial persistence of a taste—any taste—provides a clue for the true entrepreneur. Instinctively, he knows that if hundreds of thousands or millions of people insist on buying some product, or attending some entertainment—even if, according to the profit-and-loss account, death is at hand, there must be a fortune lying in that old taste mine waiting to be picked up. For example, the film box office smashes of all time started to pour forth black ink at the very moment when the last rites were being uttered over the cinema, and have done so all over the world; in Hong Kong one Run Run Shaw and his brother made eastern Westerns and, says Run Run, "have hundreds of millions. Hong Kong or U.S. dollars—it doesn't matter."

The products (such as *Love Story* or *Rocky* or *Jaws*) that create mass taste breakthroughs are often mysterious to more sophisticated palates. Sophisticates can't understand the worldwide enthusiasm for a sweetish, fizzy pink wine from Portugal called Mateus Rosé; they deplore the rush to view another saccharine cinematic confection such as *The Sound of Music*, which cost $7.6 million to make and made $72 million in the United States alone; they shudder at the names of Irving Wallace, Harold Robbins, Jackie Collins, James Clavell, and Arthur Hailey (whose millions, and those of their publishers, have been made from another supposedly unlucrative art form, the novel).

Possibly this explains why most mass tastes have been created by American men of the people, often from the populist South or Midwest, in sagas such as that of McDonald's (whose founding genius, Ray Kroc, left a widow worth $640 million) or Kentucky Fried Chicken. The secret recipe of Colonel Harland D. Sanders enabled Jack C. Massey and John Y. Brown to turn twenty of their executives into millionaires—one secretary made $3 million; Brown collected $35 million when he sold out, immortalizing his decision in the words "One day I asked myself: 'Is this all you're put on earth for? To be a chicken man?' " (So, among other things, he promptly became a hamburger man instead before further translation into governor of Kentucky.)

Coke, tomato ketchup, cornflakes, hamburgers, instant coffee, standardized hotels, standardized restaurants, other franchised eating chains—all these inventions have crossed the United States and then the world on the simple strength of a mass taste simply satisfied on a simple formula with simple economics. But of all these invaluable simplicities, that of down-market taste comes first, and it is desperately hard for the up-market mind to master.

Even tastes at the top of the market, actually, tend to come from the bottom up. Sociologists and psychologists alike should rejoice at the fact that Ralph Lauren and Calvin Klein grew up a few blocks apart in the Bronx. In an aspirational age, those who have risen are most likely to satisfy the tastes of those who want to rise. The pecking order in fashion fortunes appears to be led by Liz Claiborne, with her middle-of-the-road appeal to the modern executive woman. But neither Lauren ($1.3 billion of 1986 sales, $300 million of riches) nor Klein (maybe three-quarters of the Lauren lucre) has cause to complain about the rewards of aspiration.

They have been magnified by the process that goes under the unlovely name of "globalization." The U.S. market is rich enough in all conscience, but as lush American living standards have been matched around the world, tastes have become global in ways that once seemed impossible. Just as an Italian family making color-conscious clothes under their Benetton name can straddle the globe with franchised outlets and create a billion-dollar empire from middle-class trade, so a Lauren or a Klein can build an up-market franchise anywhere that people have money to spare.

The path to the paradises of taste is generally hard. Lauren is that typical son of immigrant stock (the Lifshitz family came from Minsk) who began early on his own (aged twenty-four, in menswear, with $50,000 backing from another New York clothing manufacturer), who ran into equally early calamity (he almost went under in 1972), and who then at last found the winning blend. It revolved around the right-hand man or manager that all taste leaders need—Klein has one, too. Lauren and his aide, Peter Strom, wisely deserted manufacturing for licensing deals, save for the Polo menswear, which, so to speak, has always been Lauren's strongest suit—definitely more than women's wear.

The taste leader doesn't sell a product, though; he sells an image, a life-style. *Time* magazine needed a whole battery of evocative words to describe what Lauren vends: "the up-and-coming customer's appreciation for things and dreams that last"; an "aura of rich romance" (in contrast to Klein's "sizzling sexiness"); "prestige and marketing mystique"; "an image of ready-to-wear prosperity"; "He lures customers who think high-fashion styling is too faddish, and traditional business garb is not quite sporty enough"—in other words, he fills a gap. The gap filler himself told *Time*: "I want to make all the things I love. A lot of people have nice taste. I have dreams."

By the standards of most other clothing companies, the dreamiest aspects of Lauren's formula are his prices: well over $300 for a cashmere sweater, $1,200 or more for a woolen suit—dreams, indeed. The virtue of selling an image, a dream, instead of a reality is that dreams come dearer but cost the supplier no more. That is the equation that basically accounts for Lauren's apartment on Central Park, house on Montego Bay, 1,500 cattle on a ranch in Colorado, and third residence on the ocean in Long Island—all connected by private jet, chartered helicopter, monogrammed limo, or all-black customized Porsche Turbo Carrera.

It's easy to be spooked by such evidence of evident success. But Lauren and Klein have the edge over forerunners such as Bill Blass and John Weitz only in the social and global expansion of their markets with rising affluence, and in their own ability to seize this expanded opportunity with both eager hands. Otherwise, there is nothing strange in the phenomenon of better-off people wanting clothes that assure them that they are indeed better off, any more than it is odd to find better-off black people wanting a better magazine of their own such as *Ebony* (the key to the treasure chest of sixty-eight-year-old John H. Johnson, which contained some $185 million in 1986).

The continuing, continuous social revolution can be tracked, not through the fashion houses alone, but through the supermarket. At first they merely supplied staple goods at lower prices, but they rapidly moved on to the trade-up that has been the basic modern evolution in taste and spending. Even Bartles and Jaymes, with its overtones (or undertones) of old-fashioned goodness, belongs in the game of making exclusive tastes, in reality or in appearance, available to a panting public. Trading up, fed by education and travel, feeds them in turn. Sometimes the elevation is vicarious: humdrum sex lives trading up mentally to Hefner's playgirls or Guccione's Penthouse pets. Sometimes the process is real: the broiler revolution, changing roast and grilled chicken from middle-class treat to everybody's protein. Old-line money has been among all these golden eggs: the Rockefellers, for example, had a big stake in the broiler boom.

But, as usual, new men have been more tastefully conspicuous. John Eastwood, a perky Briton, became worth plenty of millions, representing the proceeds of 900,000 broilers a week, plus 4.5 million laying hens: he claimed that this total made him the largest producer of protein on two feet, not excluding the beef barons of Texas and the lords of the Argentine pampas.

Those who fail to trade up, by and large, slip slowly down. Once, F. W. Woolworth, whose British chain was the main source of profit, did a third more turnover than Marks & Spencer. The latter increased its quality, prices, and range, and repeated in food the process of integrated retailing and production begun in textiles. In contrast, Woolworth's remained solidly, stolidly, and stupidly stuck down market. After ten years of this inertia, Woolworth's relative turnover had fallen to two-thirds of its British rival's.

The fact of social change is as obvious as the eternal determinants of taste: trading up has been as clear as the fact that human beings have a continuing yen for sex. The evidence, moreover, is omnipresent, blasted out in the pop culture of the day. And it's from the pop pastures that taste changes are picked up, pocketed, and turned into quick cash by the left-hand men and women of all modern business, the advertising agents.

When Bill Bernbach, in his campaigns for Volkswagen and Avis, plugged the underdog theme, he consciously or subconsciously reflected another social change: the death of the leadership idea, the realization, in the era of the dropout, that you don't have to try to be first, it's a matter of choice. The admakers have an advantage in spotting trends. They live in a world of words, pictures, music, and media, and they automatically pick up its coloration; instantaneously the new images and hard-won visions of artists get stolen for the artwork used in ads.

Pop artists, in fact, sometimes seemed to be in a race with their own material (and a highly profitable one: at his tragic death in 1987, Andy Warhol was certainly worth 60 million avant-garde dollars). The sharper pencils on Madison Avenue or its European equivalents are quick enough. But in monetary terms the admen are still appreciably slower than those who earn their bread in pop itself. Every member of the Beatles ranked as a multimillionaire in the 1970s, not on the strength of past earnings, but from the future income of a group that hadn't performed together since 1969. This calculation didn't count their loot as individuals, before and since parting.

The possibility of making a pop mint has waxed exponentially with the international market in records and tapes. The astute singer or promoter need only corner one-thousandth of that market to be Beatle-rich; a ten-thousandth has him or her well on the way. The odds in the pop stars' favor are actually better than that long shot. One in 25 records has a chance of survival; if 1 out of 25 survivors hits some kind of jackpot, the odds become 1 in 625. Clearly, this is one of those ideal scenes where taste plus initiative can equal a million without the uncomfortable extra ingredient of capital.

Accumulations worthy of a major industrialist have consequently always dignified the pop scene, from Rudy Vallee via Crosby and Sinatra to Presley. In the mid-1960s Elvis was earning a hot $5 million a year and sending teenagers into screaming hysteria from pole to pole. In the 1970s, however, the number of Elvis-style fortunes had plainly expanded: expansion was actually inevitable, since pop singers developed an irresistible tendency to come in multiples.

There have been hit groups before. But the Inkspots and the Andrews Sisters never had it so rich as the Beatles, the Rolling Stones, the Who, or even the wholly synthetic Monkees, and their various, numerous Svengalis, and all their numerous, sometimes seemingly numberless successors, from Abba to Culture Club. Fragmentation has been facilitated by an enormously enlarged market. Consequently, the big music companies, while fat enough by most standards, have lost any advantage over the small man; and the latter has been quick to seize his golden discs.

Long ago, Lou Adler, former manager of the Mamas and the Papas, who sold one record company to ABC for $3 million, promptly founded another whose assets included an album that made $5 million on a $400,000 investment. Adler also earned from *Time* magazine an oddly uplifting accolade: "Lincolnesque in bearing and probity." Since Adler also had houses in Malibu, Bel Air, and Jamaica; Britt Ekland; bell-bottoms; and Jesus sandals; things had plainly changed since Abe was a boy. Another uplifting take was that of Ahmet Ertugen, who sold Atlantic Records for $18 million. This so-called Pop Sultan had to his credit Sonny and Cher; Otis Redding; Roberta Flack; Aretha Franklin; all four of Crosby, Stills, Nash and Young; a Long Island estate; and a Manhattan town house, which boasted a floor apiece, no less, for the bedroom and living room, respectively.

These two were mere beginners compared to Berry Gordy, the only challenger to *Ebony*'s John H. Johnson for the title of wealthiest black. The launch of Motown Records, the idea of a Detroit dropout who had already failed in his first business (a record store), showed touching faith on the part of Gordy's family, which put up $700. Its reward, the backing of Diana Ross, the Jacksons, and Stevie Wonder, is the equivalent in pop music of Henry Luce's triple-threat in journalism. Gordy's own taste was brilliant, but it worked commercial wonders only because of the explosion of buying power in the entertainment market.

That same atomic effect explains the translation of Dick Clark from a top disc jockey, via a painful brush with the 1960 payola scandal, to a highly profitable career making TV programs. Clark's role as "America's Oldest Living Teenager" paid off in a 1986 net worth that *Forbes* estimated at $180 million—a number, however, that ranked well behind the $235 million fortune of Aaron Spelling. This former scriptwriter, the son of a tailor from Russia, has scored as many smash hits in his field as Gordy and Luce, including "Charlie's Angels," "Starsky and Hutch," "Hart to Hart," and the amazing "Dynasty."

Society reserves special favors for those who put cherries in its cocktails. Popular entertainment wins these cash prizes because of the magnitude of its audiences. Each attendee pays a modest fee for his cherry; multiply that fee by the millions, and you have a whole orchard, created where nothing grew before. In the higher reaches of faddery, although various priests and priestesses of fashion, from Dior to Quant, have borne plentiful financial fruit, their deployment of taste used to have lower turnover attached; the mass markets, as Helena Rubinstein knew, make more money from making less-exclusive products.

The key change in the Age of the Common Millionaire is that higher taste and higher turnover can go hand in hand. Lead the masses up-market, and you can hope to win mass sales at upscale prices. The unchallenged queen of cosmetics since Rubinstein's death has been Estée Lauder, the Hungarian immigrants' daughter who began her own business in 1946 and multiplied the million dollars of 1960 sales 1,000 times in a quarter of a century to a level unthinkable in a genuinely exclusive business.

The billion-dollar fortune she shares with her two executive sons is one of the more impressive monuments to the supremacy of taste in the modern marketplace. *Forbes* credits this "Blue Lady" of indeterminate, or undetermined, age with an "uncanny sixth sense for consumer trends." As the Bacardi example shows, extrasensory perception may not be necessary. But extraordinary sensitivity to observed or suspected trends does open the door to the ultimate storehouse of riches in the modern economy—to the gaps in the market that, at the high and low end alike, often contain more profit than the main market itself.

The same rules apply both high and low. First, follow your own instinct: that always applies. Second, choose a soft target, a market where demand is already heavy or where existing suppliers are panting behind the pace of unmistakable change. Third, always aim for a sector of massive spending, where, like Ralph Lauren and Calvin Klein, you need only a midget proportion of total expenditure to make a giant fortune. Fourth, build a proper business organization to support the gratification of identified taste, but without ever supplanting it. Fifth, watch for the inevitable change in taste that will alter even the markets of the taste-changers.

The waves of public likes and dislikes are coming more strongly and at shorter intervals than ever before. Filling the gap is the immediate name of the game. But filling it permanently is a challenge that few of yesterday's taste-makers have survived, which, of course, is why their successors have found, and will go on finding, shopping malls that are paved with gold.

10

FINDING'S
KEEPING

The clearest-cut way to new money is finding it, and always has been.
The forty-niners after gold, the East Texas wildcatters pursuing oil, the
Geiger counter gangs hunting uranium, the postwar Americans after
the last great pools of Arab oil—all had the same, and the right, idea.
Those who lack any other form of financial ability may still have just
enough wit to find a pot of gold and just enough strength to pick it up.

The idea is not, however, quite as right as it used to be. For a while,
after crude oil prices quadrupled and then doubled again, the gold
gushed from the wells as never before. Large companies paid great sums
for oil in the ground as they scrambled for a commodity whose price
had octupled to over $30 a barrel. As the price tumbled during the
mid-1980s, those who got out while the going was great could congratulate themselves. Those who stayed in oil, though, entered a depressing
new era of idle rigs, eating off their expensive heads, heavy overhangs
of debt, declining capital values, and an uncertain future.

In many other commodities, the situation was no different. As the more-accessible sources of mineral wealth were exploited, so the less-accessible—and thus costlier to develop—had to be sought, at a time when prices were falling and demand was lagging well behind supply. In the fall of 1986, for example, the hard-pressed Hunt brothers, in hock to the banks for $1.5 billion, had poured an alleged $100 million in six months into a new oil field 100 miles into the Gulf of Mexico. It was a gamble against time and the perils of the new technology on which the project's economics depended—a far cry from the easy Libyan bonanza that made Nelson Bunker Hunt super-rich.

But for his catastrophic silver plunge, Hunt, like the shrewd and strong prospectors before him, could have founded one of the lasting empires. Their names still resonate: Getty and father Hunt, Hirshhorn and Hearst. The most interesting Hearst may not have been William Randolph, the czar of San Simeon, for all his newspapers and noise, but his father, exploiter of the Comstock Lode, a hard, warm man whose interests expanded into most of the unmined metals and untracked deserts in which his day abounded. Hearst, Sr., functioned in a more-primitive age, when finding had an annoying drawback: the finder (unless he sold out smartly) had to wrest his mineral from the good earth; then he had to exchange the wrested rock for hard cash. He couldn't find it, sell it, and still keep it—a trick modern Hearsts manage with prestidigitatory ease.

The truly modern and imaginative prospector sets forth on his mission armed with a bundle of share certificates, along with the more traditional tools. If he strikes it rich, the next stage is to engender enthusiasm for shares in his company. Mining shares can soar to more fantastic heights at faster speed than any other form of paper wealth as investors all over the world, although personally unable to distinguish between nickel and molybdenum, or to separate geographically Wagga-Wagga from Addis Ababa, flock for a piece of the finder's action.

Before long the momentum of the share price ceases to bear any relation to the prospective value of the new hoard. The shares themselves, though made of nothing but engraved paper, become the equivalent of the Comstock Lode: buyers desire and devour the stock because they find it so amazingly valuable—and it is valuable solely because buyers desire and devour it so avidly.

While this bubble swells to prodigious size, the finder and his friends can take generous reward in cash—and still retain total control of the claim and all that lies therein. Without an ounce of their metal on the market, they are already rich and can only get richer when the wonder company actually comes to have some wonder earnings.

This convenient arrangement makes the methods of earlier prospectors, such as Vernon Pick, seem positively self-abnegatory. Pick believed in both the "self-sustenance homestead" and the existence of uranium in the Four Corners area, where four of the states neatly come together. He was proved right, and was amply sustained by the $9.37 million handed over for the property by the Atlas Corporation. A whole army of would-be Picks promptly descended on the U.S. deserts armed with Geiger and scintillation counters. But many years passed before other self-sustainers discovered the still greater surface riches lying around on the stock exchanges of the world.

That discovery wonderfully enlarged the horizons of the finding industry, which previously lived off the no-less-wonderful profit margin between the cost of discovering, extracting, and refining a mineral and passing it on to the customer. In the good old days, before the Arab natives got restless, virtually the entire price of a barrel of oil extracted from the Middle East sand was pure (or, as J. P. Getty would put it, "clear") profit. Getty himself lovingly charted his own progress from the first $12,000 profit on a well in 1915 to the $6,387,946 clear profit on the Nordstrom Lease from 1921 to 1937, with stopovers such as the $400,000-plus "excess recovery" on the Athens Lease in 1924.

But what made such excesses the foundation of an excessive share of America's wealth was more than simply the initiative, intelligence, and industry of its finders; it was fine, old-fashioned freedom from tax. Not a single writer or thinker on taxes or oil has been able to explain precisely, let alone convincingly, why U.S. oilmen should have received the blessing of an exemption that did for them by law what latter-day mineral explorers must achieve by dint of hard stock-market graft.

The sovereign notion goes beyond the idea that, before getting around to paying tax, oilmen should be free to deduct the cost of drilling all their wells, wet or dry. (Although this convenient fact became the basis of countless schemes, some of them fraudulent, for sheltering the rich from the Internal Revenue Service.) A beneficent federal government went much further. Noting that a barrel of oil, once removed from the ground for sale, cannot be replaced, the law decreed that the owners should be compensated by tax relief for this "depletion of their resources." On the same line of thought, a man finding a Ming vase buried in the woods, who then sells it for $100,000, would be allowed to knock a huge chunk off his tax (not the vase) because he no longer has Ming to sell.

Until 1969, the oilmen got $2,750 in every ten grand knocked off their Ming equivalents, and great was the outcry at the reduction of the sacred depletion allowance, as American as apple pie, but many times more fattening, from 27.5 percent to 22 percent. At the former rate, an oilman had trouble getting into a taxpaying position no matter how hard he tried—and most didn't try too hard. One of the least-determined triers must have been Robert O. Anderson, chairman of Atlantic Richfield, which in four years paid no taxes on $465 million of profits—and ended up with the federal government owing it money.

That should have been some help in the care and maintenance of Anderson's personal fortune, which included over a million acres, mostly of ranchland, at its peak. In 1985, however, *Forbes* was moved to comment that Anderson, after recent land sales and in a money-losing year for Arco, had "only $200 million." While a notable advance on the $50,000 cost of his first little refinery (all borrowed from a banking father), that obviously seemed, in the writer's eyes, scant reward for a sixty-eight-year-old oilman of legendary prowess.

Anderson was not, however, especially venerable as oil multimillionaires go. Of twenty-two oilmen listed in the Forbes 400 in 1985, all but four were sixty or over, compared to just under half of the whole list. The veterans included one ninety-year-old (William Alvin Moncrief, Sr., of Fort Worth, now deceased) and another of eighty-four (Claude B. Pennington, a one-time optometrist from Baton Rouge). The more the years, the more the millions, is a logical result of the workings of time and compound interest. But the exceptional years of the oilmen may partly reflect the fact that tax avoidance isn't what it used to be.

This would explain Pennington's reported hatred of taxes on interest and royalties. With oil reserves accounting for the bulk of a $600 million fortune, however, he might seem to have little cause for complaint, especially since oil and gas escaped relatively lightly from the historic 1986 tax reforms. These were supposed to finance lower taxes by abolishing or greatly diminishing exemptions. But independent producers retained both the depletion allowance and the writeoff of "intangible" drilling costs; for the bigger integrated companies, the only new restraint was a 70 percent limit to the first-year writeoff of said intangibles.

That still adds up to highly tangible tax savings, sauce for the corporation and ketchup for the individual. The Penningtons and the Moncriefs can still benefit from a most happy combination of events. If the finder can retain all his income free of tax, reinvest the surplus in still more properties that will yield even greater tax-free earnings, and borrow heavily against the security of the proven oil in his ground, he has no need to let the public or anybody else into his act.

This impeccable financial logic enabled the oil barons to form a separate, politically powerful kingdom within the empire of the rich; their realm was as important, relatively speaking, as that of the Dukes of Burgundy in medieval France. Of the thirty-five richest men listed by *Fortune* in 1957, no less than fifteen were either oil finders or entrepreneurs who had grown rich from the tidbits from the oilmen's table, suppliers of services, bits and pieces, valuable odds and ends. H. L. Hunt, Sid Richardson, and several other ducal figures of the new plutocracy owed their eminence and their fortunes primarily to the oil riches of Texas.

Like Pennington and Moncrief, they kept their dukedoms to themselves. Public companies and holdings were and are rare among the oil-rich. Their typical member is independent in every sense. But their preeminence is a thing of the past, lowered, not just by higher taxes, but by fundamental changes in the pattern of supply, demand, and, above all, price. Compared to this, changes in the tax law are of no account. As one Houston accountant told *Business Week*, "Market conditions are such a powerful force that it is difficult to assess the impact of the tax law": what screwed down OPEC has had an equally lowering effect on the oil plutocracy.

At first sight, true, the situation in the latter 1980s may seem little different from the past. There were sixty-four fortunes in the Forbes 400 of 1985 that were based primarily on oil—and this included such mega-accumulations as those of the Bass family (scions of the legendary Texan, Sid Richardson) and the Hunts (whose misfortunes, confined anyway to the three brothers, Nelson, William, and Lamar, didn't initially flow from the wells). Look closely at the sixty-four, however, and the picture changes. They form only the fourth-largest group, headed by manufacturing, real estate, and even the media.

Read through the accounts of the oil sixty-four, moreover, and you see a litany of woes. This man's company is "troubled"; the decline in oil prices, plus real estate difficulties in Denver, meant that Philip F. Anschutz might no longer quite be a billionaire; John Lee Cox consoles himself with "at least $300 million" and the thought: "The price of oil has to go up. I don't know when, but sometime." Even Ray Hunt, whose North Yemen strike of 1984 may be one of the last, old-fashioned giant discoveries, told the magazine: "We'll never go back to the good old days of the oil industry."

The smart oil money, like Ray Hunt's, has diversified widely into other investments from real estate to entertainment. The truth is that the supply of satrapies from oil and gas was already drying up in the early 1970s, the result of the millionaire's besetting disease: greed outdoing itself. As the richer fields of the United States were steadily sucked dry, the signs first appeared that new and lush finds were becoming far harder to hit. The costs of production climbed inexorably closer to world prices, which have long been determined, not in Texas, but by the superabundant oil fields of the Middle East.

The reaction of the oil moguls, aided and abetted by all the political friends oil money could buy, was to get the American oil out while the getting was good—at the highest possible price. Quotas were slapped on by President Eisenhower to minimize imports of cheap foreign crude (selling at prices of, say, $2 compared to $3.75 for the Texas variety). How much money the quota system pumped into the U.S. oil industry's bulging pockets nobody can ever calculate—one estimate runs between $40 billion and $70 billion over a decade. The cold certainty is that it rushed on the day when the United States would run short of energy.

The affluent Americans who found their oil supplies rationed in the winter of 1972, following which crisis the quota system was finally scrapped, were the direct victims of the brilliant deployment by the oil lobby of the billions that its previous lobbying had won. As the shortages of that winter developed into the Arab boycott of the next one, Americans had even more cause to regret their failure to grab all the Middle East oil they could when the sheiks were quiescent and the price was four-fifths lower.

If there is any consolation, it lies in the fact that few of the Texas fat cats, mostly being too old and too rich, had the sense or muscle to follow the oil trade's trend and head east. For those who did—notably Nelson Bunker Hunt, a partner in British Petroleum's great Libyan fields until they were expropriated, and J. P. Getty in the "neutral zone" of Kuwait—the richest rewards of all were still to be made. In his advice to would-be executives Getty stressed the pain of paying $12.5 million for the Kuwait concession and of investing many times more before a drop of oil came to market. He failed to mention, however, what financial pleasures he received in return for all that pain.

Even after his death, Getty's dolor was still yielding monetary delights for his heirs—and gigantic fees for lawyers. It says little for the shrewdness of son Gordon Peter Getty that he was willing to sell a billion barrels of his family's hard-won reserves to Pennzoil for a bargain-basement $3.6 billion. When that deal was trumped by a $10.1 billion bid for all of Getty Oil from Texaco, in the same week of January 1984, the result was an $11.1 billion lawsuit (initially won by Pennzoil) and a neat $750 million package for each of the four Getty family branches.

The almost unthinkably large sums demonstrate the high temperature the race for reserves such as Getty's had achieved before the 1986 price collapse; and they show what a gift some eager Japanese won when they bought 45 percent of Abu Dhabi, another lately developed gusher region of the Persian Gulf, for $780 million. The vendor was British Petroleum; since the sale took place only a year or so before oil prices quadrupled, it can't have been the greatest decision in the great company's history. But even at the low valuations of the Abu Dhabi price and the Pennzoil offer, the Getty family won a return hardly less wonderful than that from Scott Fitzgerald's solid gem of a mountain in *The Diamond as Big as the Ritz.*

The elder Getty, though, was lucky as well as wise. He got in early, when a sheik was still a sheik—and not the next victim of a nationalist, ex-military, revolutionary politician. The first batch of Arab plutocrats, men such as the lecherous Ibn Saud or the complaisant Sheik of Kuwait, and their numerous henchmen were notably (although the competition for this title is stiff) the least deserving of all the multimillionaires. Their successors, surrounded by still more lushly rewarded acolytes, also rank low in the merit tables. But they shared a common problem. Even though the oil companies kept the ruler on as short a string as possible, the oil states inevitably became so loaded with unspendable loot, even before the quadrupling of the oil price, that the simple process of investing their wealth itself generated fresh millions. As with the American comeuppance, greed undid the Arabs. Their gluttonous plunges into absurdly costly and often absurd projects diverted much of the oil money back into Western hands and achieved the apparently impossible feat of leaving the oil states strapped for cash.

Doubling the oil price in 1979, the classic response in such situations, produced the classic economic effect: a slump in demand. As that worked back inexorably into the oil price, the financial embarrassment of the Near East billionaires became still greater (although it had no impact on their grandiose life-styles). Oil will remain the world's richest industry. But just as Texas has probably run out of future H. L. Hunts, and the West Coast of future Gettys, so the non-American world has probably seen its last giant private operation.

In areas less politically tempestuous than the Middle East, such as the North Sea, the bonanza has also fled. It began inauspiciously for the British public when, to the chagrin of many citizens, various oil companies, mainly American, were allowed to gobble all the cream, and much of the milk, under tax conditions the most stupid old-time oil sheik would have considered generous. But the independents who flocked to the feast found themselves on a starvation diet in 1986. You don't have to be an expert in oil economics to see that, if average operating costs are $20 a barrel (as they are in those inhospitable waters), and the oil price is $18 (let alone the $8 of the nadir), profits will not be available.

Small wonder that one North Sea independent saw its turnover cut in half—a drop of $120 million—in a mere six months. The big squeeze between high operating costs and low prices has by no means been confined to oil. Other commodities, hard (metals) and soft (the rest), all suffered from the prolonged slowdown in world growth. The Klondike pioneers would have rubbed disbelieving eyes over what *Business Week* described in October 1986 as "a new gold rush in the West." The new forty-niners use modern technology to scrape gold from old, formerly played-out mines; while traditional gold miners live on a knife edge. The balance is between the price of gold, which fell to $284 an ounce in 1985, and the cost of mining—$300 an ounce in the case of traditional Homestake Mining. As the gold price boomed in 1986, rising to over $400, the much cheaper costs of the newcomers yielded much higher profits than Homestake's. Indeed, that company's earnings in the first half of 1986, despite the gold boom, were down by nearly 60 percent.

That's because Homestake, in its second century of life, has diversified into uranium, lead, zinc, oil, and gas: mostly rich sources of millionaires in previous happy years, all sectors where it has become much harder to win even a dishonest penny, from the wastes of Alaska to the wilds of Australia. There, a new generation of prospectors in the 1960s exploited with several vengeances that prime advantage of finding, as opposed to making, wealth, which is that the riches are created almost from the moment of discovery. If the finder can prove, or get somebody to believe, that he has located a million tons of mineral-bearing Mother Earth, that find or purported find immediately has a value. That is not the price times the recoverable quantity (even the suckers know it costs money to get the stuff out), but the valuation may still be a very reasonable proportion of a staggering sum.

The wild Aussie boom demonstrated what perfect material mining stocks are for a speculative share surge. Profits in one company multiplied thirty times in five years, and a related share rose fortyfold in four years, despite a peculiar economic characteristic of the boom. It was founded largely on finds of nickel, a metal that, at the start of the saga, was in short supply. With all those lovely new discoveries being announced, however, before long—before, indeed, all the new mines could even open—shortage was bound to turn to glut. In the world of commodities, as burned-out speculators constantly have to be reminded, even a little glut means a large price fall.

The phenomenal Poseidon, "the share of the century," earned its title on both the way up and the way down. One pair of nickel-rich millionaires decided that, although the price would cool from the then level of $180, it couldn't possibly drop below $120, which still yielded the huge profits that had made their millions. Hadn't one stockbroker actually written that "at any price below $270, they're a snip"? In fact, the shares crashed to $7.50, and the partners had invested 19 percent of the fund they controlled in this single stock.

It requires faith, as well as other people's money, to put trust in geologists' reports couched in meaningless technicalities and emanating from the back of beyond. For every honest prospector, there's always one who isn't above salting the mine. No salter ever swung the trick more daringly than one keen entrepreneur, who got hold of an insignificant little company by various means and persuaded much of the populace, including normally shrewd financiers, that he had found a mine that contained almost every valuable metal known to man (a cautious type, the promoter stopped short of diamonds).

A brilliant scientist had discovered a new secret extraction process that only stopped short of turning dirt into gold. In fact, it would have had to. Visits by curious pressmen to the Eldorado, which was valued at numerous millions, discovered a ramshackle lab but no scientist, and a mine of uncertain title, more or less in the middle of a housing estate, but no gold and no mining. Even then there was a delayed reaction before the promoter decamped with his loot, leaving the sadder and wiser investors to contemplate the wreck.

It pays to be skeptical. The catch, alas, is that it sometimes pays more to have faith. In 1961 an Irish-Canadian prospector named Pat Hughes, then thirty-seven, made a sentimental return to the old country bent on doing it and himself a bit of good by finding some mineral wealth. Now, the Republic of Ireland, as everybody knows, is good for cows, Guinness, Arran sweaters, and leprechauns, but the idea of a Klondike in those soft green hills was plainly the wildest Irish-Canadian blarney.

Hughes announced, however, that he had indeed made a find, of lead, zinc, silver, and copper to boot, and shares in his company, Northgate, began to move in the accustomed manner. In the bars of Dublin, where many wonders have been seen, the discoveries seemed perfectly acceptable. But elsewhere people were harder to convince that there was anything more valuable than fairies at the bottom of Irish gardens.

Hughes even went to the extraordinary lengths of flying in and entertaining right royally journalists and investment men from all over Europe and the Americas to inspect his new mine. The inexpert looked at Hughes, arm in sling after a recent accident and looking like the pirate king, observed a newly mined pile of dirt, noticed a few suspicious silvery twinkles in the heap, and went back to their Old Bushmills whiskey as unconvinced as ever. But the silver was of sterling reality, and Hughes went on to discover yet another crock of money called Silvermines.

Those who invested in these two companies, and Hughes in particular, did better than a lucky draw in the Irish Sweepstakes. In no time at all, Northgate was earning $6.3 million a year, and soon Hughes sold just 6 percent of another Irish find for $5.6 million. Unfortunately, there is no guide, no touchstone, to help the outsider distinguish between the phony and, as here, the fruitful claim. You need the same tool as the prospector himself—a sensitive, quivering nose.

Expertise in the geology, characteristics, and technology of whatever mineral you are hunting, and in whatever terrain the hunt has reached, is of course useful. As Getty tells it, he and his father spotted one of their most lucrative hauls by noticing a locomotive laboring uphill; this convinced them that they were looking at the top of a dome full of oil. Normally a prospector (provided he can afford the fee) turns to an academically equipped expert to tell him the good news. But experts have a disconcerting habit of being wrong—and you never know when.

Their failure is understandable. An expert is somebody who has been taught all that is already known about a subject. But he doesn't know what *isn't* known, and he tends to dismiss any information or observation that contradicts his knowledge. The true prospector—indeed, the true business genius of any kind—listens carefully to the expert, but he goes right ahead when instinct tells him that the expert may be wrong.

The great D'Arcy was almost alone in believing that oil could be found under the sands of Arabia; Dr. Armand Hammer made one of his Libyan hits on a concession that Mobil Oil quit after drilling nothing but dry holes; British oil experts turned up their noses at Kuwait, the richest pool of them all. Two of the world's great oil companies, Shell and British Petroleum, are based on England, a country that for decades was devoutly believed to contain no oil or gas whatsoever. All that time the British moguls were sitting in blissful ignorance within seventy miles of some of the world's biggest untapped deposits beneath the North Sea.

True, the drilling and extraction of this bonanza would have presented insurmountable problems to the technology of an earlier age. But a U.S. company even turned up a major field in Yorkshire, of all places. Geologists are not trained to look where they don't expect to find—but that is often where the true finder finds what is truly worth keeping.

As time goes by, however, the ignored and overlooked areas and chances must get fewer and farther between. Robert Anderson is said to have drilled 200 dry wells before he made his first New Mexico strike. That kind of hitting and missing is a rich man's pastime, and a time-consuming one. Anderson was forty before his crude oil holdings were impressive, and even then a shrewd property-cum-oil deal with some California gas stations was his chief claim to industrial fame.

Anderson bought the chain for some $4 million and sold it for $25 million to one of the helpful giants, Gulf Oil, to whom many of the individual rich should daily sing hosannas. The big play, however, was again in the stock market. Anderson got 700,000 shares in Atlantic Refining for his oil business; the leverage he applied to this holding, by merging Atlantic with Richfield and making the big strike in Alaska, is what pushed his oil fortune, at its peak, to something like $100 million.

Anderson is by no means the only proof that the path to oil and other commodity fortunes lies, not through the canyons of the West, but through those of Wall Street. Hugh Liedtke, the man who won the $11.1 billion judgment against Texaco, headed a $2.3 billion giant at the time—small only by comparison with the likes of the defendant. Liedtke had seized his first big chance only twenty-four years before, with a helping hand from the great J. P. Getty in person. As *Business Week* tells it, Liedtke spotted the charms of South Penn Oil in an investment manual and approached Getty, the controlling shareholder.

Told to come back when he owned as many shares as Getty, the tyro did just that. He merged South Penn with his own little Zapata Petroleum; the magazine lists the following subsequent milestones in Liedtke's climb. "1965 . . . takes over United Gas—ten times its size. . . . 1970 . . . sets up POGO, the first of two affiliates that sell securities to finance aggressive exploration. . . . 1974 . . . spins off United Gas Pipeline." While the catalogue contains some other items of interest (such as a Pennzoil plane carrying campaign funds linked to a Watergate burglar, plus insider trading charges and legal wrangles in the pipeline spinoff), it doesn't record a major oil strike until 1982, a full twenty years after that auspicious encounter with Getty.

Even then, the heavy oil strike off California was made by Texaco on a tract where Pennzoil had only a quarter interest. Liedtke has been a whiz—but on and for Wall Street, not in the oil fields. Anybody who gambled $60,000 on Pennzoil in 1963 would have been rewarded with $2.7 million in 1986. Liedtke himself had $25 million—though, significantly enough, the value of the holdings has been maintained by repurchases of the company's stock and by closures (notably of copper mines) in the face of slumps in the oil and gas prices on which finders' fortunes used most to blossom.

The old days of the lone prospector with his pick or his rig or his Geiger counter are no likelier to return than those of the fur traders from whom John Jacob Astor made the first of the great American fortunes. The Hochschilds, whose molybdenum mine in California stood in their books at $3,000, netted $15 million more when in 1957 they merged it into the corporate complex of American Metal Climax. Like Bob Anderson, Joseph H. Hirshhorn, the richest of the Geiger men, went corporate, turning over his massive Canadian uranium interests to Rio Tinto Zinc; and like Anderson, too, Hirshhorn was already a long way from the breadline. He is alleged to have read the storm signals in 1929 and to have left the stock market to its slump with $4 million in his kitty.

As a miner and speculator, Hirshhorn was big in uranium by 1950; from this base he made the superstrike of 1952 and 1953. He obeyed the sound principle of listening to a maverick expert, one Franc Joubin, who was almost alone in suspecting that the Algoma Basin of Ontario contained uranium. It cost Hirshhorn $30,000 to prove Joubin right— in return for which proof, transmuted into a mining giant, Hirshhorn was worth over $130 million in 1961. He sold out his stake for Rio Tinto Zinc shares not cash, whereby hangs another story.

In the palmiest days of that mining corporation, it seemed unstoppable, but in the early 1970s, the giant's market value almost halved. Over the whole decade to 1985, the earnings per share retreated, falling by almost 3 percent annually. It must be a galling experience for a gambler to see his winning chips dwindle in as mysterious a manner as they grew—and even the hangers-on in the finding's-keeping boom have suffered along with their patrons.

The Schlumbergers became the richest industrial family in all France thanks to their fifth of the greatest of the oil-service companies. In 1980, that added up to a fortune of $5 billion. As the number of rigs operating in the United States dropped from over 4,500 to 800, though, so did the Schlumberger profits and the share price—and with it the family fortune, all the way down to $2 billion. Anderson had a similar kind of experience as Atlantic Richfield ran, first, into the massive Alaskan pipeline blockage, then the general unhappiness of U.S. oil in its degenerative phase, and next the downward price spiral.

At least the oil fortunes had soared so high that they had a long, long way to fall before crossing the border between super-richness and mere wealth. In lesser commodities, the damage had been so great that by 1985 *Forbes* listed only one minerals fortune among its 400, and that $365 million belonged to the widow of Charles Engelhard, dead for fifteen years. In its heyday, the conversion of wealth in the ground into your very own paper money worked wonders. But in harder times for commodities its practitioners have learned a new lesson: by playing finding's keeping you can have your cake and eat it; the catch is that you can no longer control the size of the cake.

Book III

THE
CORPORATE
FORTUNE
HUNTERS

11

THE COMPANY WAY
IS BY ME
OKAY

The balance of economic power (that is, the place where they keep the money), when it shifted overwhelmingly to the side of the big corporations, might, for lovers of the free and rugged entrepreneur, have spelled a sad reduction in the individual's ability to wax exceeding rich. Not to worry; the coming of the corporation has spawned a host of new, easy methods of making millions—and several of these lush avenues are within the corporation itself.

For those who lack a rich daddy the safest method is to join a rich company. After all, with sales of $1 billion, profits of $100 million, and a stock market value of $2 billion, you only need 0.1 percent of the first, 1 percent of the second, and 0.05 percent of the last to pass the seven-figure mark and head off toward the upper reaches. And if the gambits fail, for reasons of incompetence or accident, the player can still fall back on the soft cushion of a plump salary and a fat pension.

Minneapolis–St. Paul is said to be littered with the millionaires made by 3M, for this salesman's conglomerate, permeated through and through by the commercial ethos of the Midwest, carries the typical characteristics of the big corporation to extremes. Its whole system of rewards, from the commissions paid to salesmen to the dummy stock by which managers got their profit-linked bonuses, to the stock options that grace the top echelon's safe deposit boxes, has always been geared to the creation of individual riches through both capital gains and income.

In any country where the tax man knew what he was doing, and couldn't be bribed to do otherwise, it used to be much harder to assemble $1 million out of income—let alone $5 million. It's not impossible, though. At $400,000 a year, by no means an uncommon U.S. reward, an executive can pile together $8 million in twenty years at the top. At a time when no American paid as much as half his income in taxes, that left at least $4 million; if he banked half, that gives him today $100,000 a year on which to live—plus, presumably, some income and capital gain from the accumulated savings.

As with companies, moreover, a heavy cash flow has uses and charms of its own—which, no doubt, is why inordinately wealthy men such as Henry Ford II (who resided in his company's salary grade twenty-eight) insisted on paying themselves inordinate salaries and bonuses. After allowing for inflation, Henry's $878,746 in 1973 compares brilliantly with the $1.4 million salary (plus $255,000 in long-term compensation) earned by his successor as chairman, Donald E. Petersen, for 1985. The Ford top echelon, however, had guzzled much deeper in the trough in the previous year, when stock options, granted in the automotive industry's slough of despond, came home to father.

These giant payments were assailed with notable scorn by Chrysler's regenerator, Lee Iacocca. Noting that Philip Caldwell, former CEO of Ford, had earned $7.2 million for his 1983 efforts, the Chrysler boss noted: "If these bonuses were scandalous, ours will be only half that. You reach a point of asking 'How high is up? How high is tolerable for a public corporation?' " A year later, however, Iacocca's scorn was muted (or should have been) by payments that brought the critic $11.4 million, or well over double the total compensation of all four top men at General Motors and Ford—companies that have seven times the sales of Iacocca's company. So how high *is* up? And how high *is* tolerable for a public corporation? Plainly, Iacocca can't be taken as a guide to the answer or as an example of benign self-denial.

There is, of course, an argument in favor of these mighty handouts. Large corporations, it is said, will not obtain or retain the services of large professional talents such as Iacocca's unless the talented can gain the rewards of an independent entrepreneur in return for enriching the collective body of stockholders far more than themselves. More: the carrot of executive millions motivates and concentrates the managerial mind. More: simple justice is involved on the "you make a buck for me, and I'll make a buck for you" lines of Lord Thomson, the Canadian media tycoon, previously mentioned.

It never quite worked out that way, naturally. The Thomsons always end up with more bucks than all their employees put together. That doesn't invalidate the principle, although there is a curious fact; the wealthiest to begin with are by no means shy when it comes to using devices originally invented to enrich the underprivileged executive. The Watson family of IBM joined the best-heeled clans in the world, once worth an estimated $400 million in IBM stock alone—and that's not counting what was left from the founding Watson's salary, which was running at $1,000 a day back in 1934. Yet Tom Watson, Jr., though by no means the most avaricious or self-assertive of tycoons, didn't say, when the stock options were being slung around, "Count me out, fellows, I've got enough already." No, he dipped his fingers in the bran tub and came up with a paper profit, on exercising his option—to take one year as an example—of $1.9 million.

At Wang Laboratories, the return to shareholders over three years to 1985 had been very negative: a fall of a third. Yet, founder An Wang took out $5 million over three years to add just 1 percent to a fortune worth $500 million even after the slump in the performance, and the share price, that caused investors so much pain. In fact, major companies such as Wang, with the founder's name on the label, have become rarer in the United States. Managing, as opposed to ruling, dynasties are now far less common: the Watsons, the Fords, the Rockefellers, the du Ponts, and the rest have retreated into the background, and few have come forward to replace them. But the Wang principle still applies: wherever there's a dynast or an heir in the executive suite, usually he to whom much is given is given much more. That should give the lie to the otherwise engaging theory that stock options are there to motivate, sustain, and finally reward executives for their labors on behalf of the shareholders. On the contrary, the options have one purpose and one purpose only, which is to make the executives as rich as possible and in the most painless possible way, without risk and at the shareholders' expense.

They also serve as a handy cushion in case the profits falter, and with them the profit-linked salary and bonus. Even here, though, the fate of John J. Murphy, who received only $847,000 in three years as his Dresser Industries struggled to perform in a deeply depressed oil-equipment business, is the exception that proves there is no rule. Far more typical is John M. Richman, chairman of Dart & Kraft, the shortest-lived marriage of major companies in U.S. history. Richman earned $100,000 more than Murphy in salary alone in 1985. *Business Week* calculates that for every dollar Richman earned (if that's the right word) the shareholders lost $154 as the stock slumped. The beneficiary of the shareholders' involuntary largesse usually doesn't have to pay a red cent until he chooses to take up the option—and he only makes that choice, to nobody's surprise, if the shares have risen sharply enough to offer him a pretty piece of immediate profit. In that blessed event, he can finance the payment by borrowing on the collateral—and if the price holds up, can eventually convert his paper profit into the real stuff without having run any risk or spent any money. If there's no paper profit, being no idiot, he shuns the option.

The cost to the shareholder is wrapped up in mythology and mechanics. The myth is that, without these inducements, the cosseted executives either wouldn't work for the company at all, or wouldn't work as well. There is no proof that executives garlanded with options are any more effective than those who simply work for their livings—and Japan and West Germany, whose economy and companies have vastly outperformed the United States, did so without benefit of these devices.

If options are so effective, anyway, why would a company also need profit-linked bonus schemes? There is no sensible answer, yet most big U.S. corporate nests are feathered in both ways. The object, again, is to maximize, optimize, and generally elevate the executives' wealth—and it presumably never occurs to the beneficiaries that every extra $2 million paid to the management cadre is $2 million off the pretax profit, thus to some extent negating the executives' good work on behalf of themselves as option holders.

The shareholder-robbing mechanics of options are less blatant but still apparent to the discerning eye. Take the Iacocca case again. He got $9.8 million from his option; whence did the difference between that figure and the option price arise? At first sight, the money seems to have been created out of thin air; at the most, surely, you could say that it came from the pockets of unknown, mythical investors who might have bought Chrysler shares at the lower price at the same time and instead are buying them from Iacocca now (if he sells) at a much-inflated figure.

The inflation wasn't, as it happens, the result of any recent wonders; according to *Business Week*, only five other CEOs gave shareholders less value for money than Iacocca in 1983 through 1985. That sounds a grotesquely unfair judgment on the hero. The apparent unfairness results from the way in which the rankings were calculated. First, the salary and bonus over three years were divided by the average industry pay. Then the three-year return to shareholders in dividends and capital gains was also divided by the industry average. The first figure was then divided into the second. This evidently expressed a philosophical view—that an executive should not receive more than the average unless the shareholders do, and that the quantities should move in step. Whether or not this philosophy is sound is beside the point. For it bears no more relation to reality than do the options, bonuses, and other gimmicks.

Of the nine executives who accompanied Iacocca into 1985's Hall of Shame, two (like him) had been highly successful in generating wealth for the investors, which they more than doubled. Two had been moderately successful, including the outspoken raider and corporate critic T. Boone Pickens. He picked up the largest three-year package in America—$31.7 million for only a 40.2 percent boost to Mesa shareholders' fortunes. Floyd D. Gottwald, who almost quadrupled the return for shareholders in Ethyl Corporation, collected only $1.7 million for his efforts in selling industrial chemicals—and Ethyl is five times Mesa's size.

To put Pickens's disproportionate reward another way, all but three-quarters of the $41 million after-tax profit Mesa made from his failed attempt to acquire Phillips Petroleum went, in effect, into the Pickens pocket. (He actually collected $4.1 million of the Phillips payoff directly.) The analogy expresses a hard and clear reality about stock options—whether they are dubious, like Wang's $5 million reward for a negative return, or virtuous, like Iacocca's. The effect is exactly the same as if, at the date when the option was exercised, Chrysler had sold the same number of shares to the public in a money-raising operation, but turned over $9 million of the proceeds to the chairman and chief executive of the day. It is a straight gift of cash from the shareholders' equity to the executive. The main difference between the option and straight pay is that circumspection demands that the latter be kept within reasonable bounds, while the sky is the limit for the option, also the gift, if cashed in, pays lower tax than the salary.

The shares, of course, have to appreciate handsomely to make the beneficiaries into instant millionaires; in that case, the shareholders are less likely to complain than in the contrary case, where the company slides to perdition and the options aren't worth a burned-out match. It used to be said of Litton Industries, a company so red-hot for capital gains that it paid out stock instead of dividends, that Charles B. Thornton and Roy Ash, Litton's inventors, had in a mere decade made themselves millionaires thirty or forty times over, creating a score of other executive millionaires along the way.

Unless their fortune reached $10 million or they sold out along the road, none of that happy score stayed stock-option millionaires as Litton sank from decline into fall, piling up horrendous losses, mostly under the impact of its shipbuilding fiascos, and the share price slumped to a tenth of its former glory. Options can thus backfire for the executive as well as the shareholder, although that will never stop companies from offering instant millions as long as the law allows.

There is rough justice in options, in one sense. Running a big corporation is no idle game; it may even be excruciatingly hard work, executed under a mighty weight of responsibility. General Motors does, after all, employ some hundreds of thousands around the world, a force that is larger than most armies. Surely, the argument runs, the men with this awesome burden on their shoulders deserve better recompense than the dealer who merely sells and services GM cars. Yet a $200,000 straight-pay executive in Detroit, without financial schemes, would have no capital value outside his pension rights, while a dealer generating $200,000 of net profits (and there are plenty of those) is worth anything from $1 million upward: one fairly typical Ford dealer in the United States, for instance, had multimillions of net wealth that included thirty-three oil wells and plenty of real estate.

The share option thus appears merely a rough attempt to redress the balance, before all the guys running GM charge off to open dealerships. But there is, of course, no guarantee that the management magnates either could or would build up a business of their own from scratch. By and large, the man who does possess that drive and talent proves the point in practice. The man who heads for a big corporation has other drives and satisfactions—and it's stretching the argument to suggest that he, alone among all classes of salaried individuals, deserves to share or surpass the rewards (possibly disproportionate anyway) of the true entrepreneur.

Warren Buffett, the super-rich investment genius behind Berkshire Hathaway, gives short shrift to the notion that options put managers and owners in the same boat. "In reality, the boats are far different," he told *Business Week.* "No owner has ever escaped the burden of capital costs, whereas a holder of a fixed-price option bears no capital costs at all. An owner must weigh upside potential against downside risk. An option holder has no downside."

Buffett's clinching argument applies even more strongly to straight gifts—such as the cunningly named "performance share," or the 300,000 Chrysler shares (worth another $12.4 million in the spring of 1986) that Iacocca stood to collect by staying at Chrysler until

December 1987. With the "performance share," companies such as CBS, PepsiCo, Polaroid, General Telephone, and Sun Oil decided simply to give executives shares, provided that they met certain predetermined targets—predetermined by the executives, that is. The idea is that these large gifts—one company set aside $16 million for them over ten years—should *supplement*, not substitute for, regular stock options. But why are supplements needed at a company such as Coca-Cola, where the new magic phrase is "performance units"? Chairman Roberto C. Goizueta and president Donald R. Keough will eventually be able to cash in these performance units for stock. That little gratuity, awarded in 1985, was worth $6.4 million and $3.5 million, respectively, by March 1986, when the chairman of the compensation committee (an investment broker whose outfit received substantial Coke fees that year) explained to *Business Week* that the duo "had the courage to put their jobs on the line, and that's rarely done today at major American companies."

Once upon a time, a British admiral was shot *"pour encourager les autres"* after failing to engage the enemy. Now, it seems, American executives are to be encouraged by being rewarded for failure—the one in question being the fiasco of new Coke. While the company made spirited (but costly) efforts to undo the terrible damage Goizueta and Keough had inflicted on the main brand, the chief beneficiary of the change in formula was the enemy: PepsiCo. Once again, the remuneration had neither rhyme nor reason, only the result of enriching further another pair of multimillionaire executives. Quite apart from the non-performance units, Coke's leaders shared $2.5 million in their 1985 pay packets—$723,000 of which was Goizueta's option money.

Looking only at one year, or even three, moreover, gives very little idea of the real payoff, or rip-off, from the options racket. At the exultant PepsiCo, now possessed of the top-selling cola, chairman Donald M. Kendall took home less than Goizueta—a mere $1.2 million, half in options. Indeed, employment consultants Sibson & Co reckon that, by rewarding shareholders with $876 for every dollar earned personally, Kendall provided exceptional value for money. But Kendall, good and true friend to Richard Nixon in the latter's White House days, has been around for a long time. Back in 1972, he exercised options worth $8.1 million; the following year another $3.5 million flowed into the family fortunes. In constant dollars, that far outstrips Iacocca's three-year haul from 1983 to 1985.

Without doubt, that kind of money—risk-free and added to relentlessly year after year—easily beats the variety of loot made, at their own risk, by most individual entrepreneurs. Not that big-time corporate managers, and even little ones, fail to go into business for their own account—this can be as sure and rich a route as the stock option. Early in 1987, for example, a company named Telecom Plus International figured prominently in *Fortune* magazine—not because of its performance or size (the company had lost nearly $21 million in twelve months on $255 million of sales) but because some powerful shareholders objected to the management, specifically to chairman Stephen R. Cohen. The latter led a group that in 1983 invested $125,000 in a deadbeat company that then received valuable chunks of Telecom business. Surprise, surprise; in 1985, the Cohen management of Telecom arranged for the purchase of all outstanding shares in the former deadbeat. Profit to the Cohen gang, $2.4 million.

The aggrieved shareholders were also complaining about options, arising from another takeover deal, worth $2.5 million more to the cabal. Cohen & Co., however, can cite all manner of precedents for their amazing strokes of good fortune—and not from the annals of the small- and medium-size firms, either. There is the illuminating case of Ernest R. Breech, savior of the Ford Motor Company, the man who simultaneously rid the company of Henry I's appalling legacy of company goons and corporate mismanagement and brought Henry II along to super-manager status. Breech seems to have been slow off the mark—initially he refused an offer of 30,000 Ford shares at $40 apiece, which could have made him a clear million just for starters.

But never mind. He easily made up lost ground with the Dearborn Motors caper. This company was set up solely by active Ford executives to distribute Ford tractors; the most active and the largest stakeholder was Ernie Breech, who got 20 percent of the action. Setting up Dearborn cost these inside investors $200,000; their employer finally took the encumbrance off their hands for a modest return of $11 million.

The payoff was invested first in a finance company, then in a securities firm, along which road Breech's original $40,000 was turned into $6 million. By then Breech had recovered from his early false start in other ways: $1.9 million of stock options had been converted into holdings worth $10 million. Although Breech did mighty deeds for Ford, and although there seemed to be an element of bitterness in his parting words, "Henry doesn't need me anymore," nobody can say that Henry Ford left Breech to the mercies of the poorhouse.

Latter-day Breeches, however, have made sure of avoiding that fate before even accepting the job, none to greater effect than one Lester Hogan. He was the outstanding managerial beneficiary of the convulsions that struck the semiconductor industry in the late 1960s when the prices of these electronic masterpieces slumped from $15,000 a thousand to $750.

In this contest, two scions found themselves eyeball to eyeball: Robert W. Galvin, who had inherited a fifth of Motorola, and Sherman N. Fairchild, who derived heftier financial muscle from a far lighter stake in the company of the century, IBM, but who had Fairchild Camera as his own thing. As the two companies wallowed in a change of fortune akin to that of Pharaoh when the seven fat years ended and the seven lean ensued, Fairchild reached out not only for Hogan but for seven other members of Motorola's hot semiconductor management.

For agreeing to rescue Fairchild Camera, Hogan accepted in short order, first, a salary rise of a third to $120,000; second, an instant cash bonus of a quarter of a million; third, stock options with a paper value of $5.4 million; and fourth, a loan of $5.4 million, enabling Hogan to purchase the aforesaid options, advanced by the good Sherman free of interest. When the path to the executive suite is carpeted with such goodies, who needs to go into the risky business of business on his own account? Not content with this largesse, Hogan acted in the same way as junk-bond king Michael Milken in a later era. He got the action moved from New York to California, the place where he preferred to live (in a house, what's more, provided by Fairchild). The final sad word, the proof that the managerial magic of stock options is strictly in the eyes of the recipient, lies in the Fairchild record after Hogan's arrival: it lost $27 million in a couple of years.

The Hogan deal, which stirred an indignant Motorola to sue Fairchild (unsuccessfully) for damages, looks like a mere midge bite compared to the self-serving deals of later generations. Among these arrangements, that of Michel (Mike) Bergerac passes all others for mind-blowing creation of wealth out of all proportion to value received. The soon-to-die Charles Revson, founder of Revlon, granted this recruit from ITT, among other goodies, a severance clause including a five-year salary and bonus scheme worth $7 million, plus stock options and other capital benefits to a value of $13 million. Not content with this massive provision in his signing-on fee, Bergerac and his fellow directors later added a "golden parachute" to protect the Revlon executives in the event of takeover. The effect was to add $15 million to Bergerac's payoff, making up the all-time record total of $35 million.

That's "an enormous amount of money," according to somebody who should know: Bergerac himself. The vulnerability of Revlon to takeover arose from the fact that, while quadrupling the company's sales by acquisition, Bergerac had failed to sustain either its profits or its share of the original core market in cosmetics. The defense proposed by one outside director has a hollow ring: "It would have been worse without him." There are echoes here of the Coke apologia for the so-called performance units: once again, it's an investment banker speaking; once again, the justification for a ludicrously large award is negative—the recipient is being lavishly rewarded, not for exceptional achievement, but for not performing to still-worse effect the duties for which he is already being handsomely paid.

The golden parachute is a monstrosity in any event. Although Bergerac's $35 million is more than the landing fee for the next nine parachutists put together, that isn't because their payoffs were small—the ninth and tenth got $2.3 million apiece: both worked for Revlon. It's highly unlikely that a couple of senior vice presidents would have swallowed such sums as normal reward even in a company far larger and more successful than Revlon. Plainly, the opening of the golden parachute, which makes the beneficiaries instant millionaires, may well be the greatest financial good an executive can expect.

His incentive is therefore to so manage or mismanage the company's affairs that takeover results. That is by no means the same thing as maximizing the return to shareholders. Bergerac's defenders (including Bergerac) argue that he earned his parachute by making Ron Perelman of Pantry Pride cough up $2.7 billion—or $800 million more than the initial bid. But what would a well-managed Revlon have been worth?

In any event, it was Bergerac's highly paid duty to obtain the best possible deal for the shareholders from whom the high pay derived. There is no defensible advantage to the shareholder in the golden parachute, only advantage to the executive. Small wonder that Congress acted to penalize those evident abuses by tax penalties; small wonder that nothing changed—a long line of executives in other companies were waiting for their loot as Bergerac collected his (he conveniently escaped the penalties thanks to a deal that anticipated them by seven months). Companies such as Borg Warner have even promised to compensate their parachutists for any extra tax.

These displeasing devices come on top of a battery of executive compensation techniques: a manager may have salary, bonus, options, incentive compensation, and deferred incentive compensation, leading the uninitiated to wonder just how much incentive, deferred or otherwise, a manager needs. Is there an incentive effect, anyway? The findings of some Rochester business academics, who thought they had established a link between executive reward and investor welfare, have been challenged by experts such as David Larcker of the Wharton

School. The data of 400 companies over a fifteen-year period didn't throw up "much of a correlation between stock prices and salary and bonus," he told *Business Week.*

The magazine's allies in its indispensable annual salary survey, Sibson & Co., looked at five years of figures for America's fifty largest companies—and predictably found an utterly random pattern. For running 3M, Lewis W. Lehr earned salary and bonus of $829,000; from 1981, every dollar of Lehr money returned $1,486 to the 3M shareholders in capital gains and dividends. At United Technologies, in the last days of his clinging to power, Harry J. Gray earned $1.1 million; his return to shareholders per dollar from 1981 onward was a mere $85.

The only rationale in this comparison is that United Technologies is a far larger company than 3M, with $15 billion of sales against $7.9 billion. What mathematicians call a Pareto distribution does have some rough-and-ready application. The more people a company must pay, the higher the salaries at the top must be to allow sufficient room underneath. This has some effect on intercompany comparisons, but not much; thus, in the same aerospace industry, David S. Lewis of General Dynamics earned only $57,000 less than Gray, even though his company's sales came to little more than 3M's, at $8.2 billion.

Lewis also pocketed $2.2 billion in long-term compensation. Do the options act as incentives where the salaries and bonuses don't? The evidence again is unconvincing—and is bound to be, given that the booming stock that brings joy to the shareholders also boosts the take for the executive millionaires. Which came first, the chicken or the egg? The option may in fact be counterproductive, making its beneficiaries so wealthy that the impact of later fluctuations in the corporate fortunes is of little account. For instance, Mark Shepherd, Jr., earned a mere $455,000 in a heavy loss-making year for electronics leader Texas Instruments. Serve him right, no doubt. But in 1972, the same Mark Shepherd put away $2.7 million of options, adding the chips to the pile of $5.9 million set aside the year before.

Since then, the alleged incentive force of his shareholdings and options hasn't prevented Shepherd from leading TI through one messup after another—including the humiliation of a $400 million write-off on its withdrawal from home computers. The loss of world semiconductor leadership to the Japanese, and the buffeting of profits by the downcycles in silicon chips, are shared by TI's U.S. competitors, true. But they still don't speak well for Shepherd's "incentivization"—while TI's specific snafus have been traced to precisely the kind of clumsy mismanagement that long experience and financial self-interest should alike prevent.

The point is made just as emphatically by the case of a largely forgotten man, Richard C. Gerstenberg. When elevated to the top spot at his company, this executive pulled in $551,575 in salary and other payments. With his basic needs thus cared for, he was given a $251,550 bonus payable in stock, making a cool half million in a couple of years. Lest this, too, fail to suffice, he took home $15,000 in company contributions to a stock-purchase plan (921 "stock contingent credits" at $78 a throw) and exercised $297,587 of options, on top of more than half a million the previous year, as a further support for his old age. It was imminent. When these benefits were heaped upon him, Gerstenberg was sixty-three, one of the long succession of General Motors executives, senior in both senses of the word, who became chairmen just in time to build up their finances before retirement, and whose efforts did nothing, and could do nothing, to arrest the great company's long slide into mediocrity. To the eyes of almost any nationality outside the United States, the fortunes lavished on mediocre men who happen, by dint of long service and noses pressed to the company grindstone, to have reached the ranks of the executive committee are no less amazing than the fantastic inducements, unmatched since the days of absolute monarchs arranging dynastic marriages, offered to men such as Shepherd and Hogan.

Other countries have lagged well behind these practices and will never catch up, despite earnest attempts and the direct importation of U.S. patterns. As the City of London approached the liberalization known as the "Big Bang," Wall Street firms led a frenetic competition for talent and clients that thrust vast signing-on fees into the hands of supposed financial aces and more millions into the bank balances of purchased stockbrokers than they had ever dreamed possible.

At the same time, hired hands among local executives began to demand a piece of the action that, traditionally, they had shunned. For example, Glaxo has been a wonder company of the 1980s. Under the influence of the wonder drug Zantac and its amazing impact on stomach ulcers, Glaxo's profits grew sevenfold in five years, from $120 million to nearly $1 billion. Its shares not surprisingly soared by over 2,000 percent in a decade. Only $135,000 worth were shown as beneficially owned by the chairman, Paul Girolami, who had steered the company right through this saga, and whose salary likewise took a long time to reach respectable sums ($360,000 in 1985).

Plainly, some other incentive than money was at work—and the same observation could have been made of virtually all British executives, hits or flops, until an American, Dick Giordano, arrived on the scene. Giordano had been chief executive of Airco before that industrial gases business lost a disputed takeover struggle with its British shareholder, BOC. Knowing a good man when they saw one, the BOC directors placed the erstwhile opponent in the driver's seat, where he naturally insisted on the same high and "incentivized" remuneration that any red-blooded American manager would expect.

That catapulted Giordano immediately into the position of highest-paid British executive, a position he held for many years—although the top salaries of far larger local firms, no doubt drawn upward by the magnetic effect of Giordano's pay (over $1 billion in 1986), began to narrow the gap. That year, the hugely successful chairman of ICI, Sir John Harvey-Jones, earned $590,000. Giordano was eclipsed, however, not by the leader of a great multinational, but by the thrusting boss of a retail chain, Burton Group. A passionate believer in bonus payments, and equally keen on sharing his passion with himself, Burton's Sir Ralph Halpern became the first Briton to earn a million *pounds* in salary.

Not content with an American income, Halpern also wanted American-style capital gains. His board agreed to a scheme that, subject to performance targets being met, would have given the executives much financial joy—above all, Halpern, who stood to gain £8 million. Stock options had by then become quite common in Britain; outlawed under a Labour government, they had received the blessing of Mrs. Thatcher, a woman who believes profoundly in the power of the purse. So does the City of London. Yet the investment institutions took so unkindly to the plan that Halpern's payout had to be limited to a maximum £2 million. At that, it was no small recompense—though tiny in relation to Halpern's achievements. From 1982 to 1985, Burton sales had grown by 429 percent to $1.8 billion; from 1976 to 1986, the shares by 5,282 percent. That, however, raises a fascinating question. Nobody knew better than Halpern that the retailing wonders he had wrought were bound to boost the stock. So how much did he buy?

The even more fascinating answer, on the face of it, is very little. Halpern was shown in August 1985 as owning only 8,229 shares, worth under $25,000 and representing only 0.7 percent of his stock options at that date. Like the lack of Glaxo stock in its chairman's hands, this points to the same conclusion that Warren Buffett drew. Corporate executives will not risk their own or borrowed capital even in—or maybe especially in—their own corporations. In that, they are wholly unlike entrepreneurs, which makes it distinctly doubtful whether they truly do deserve entrepreneurial rewards.

Nevertheless, the indignation of the City of London over Halpern's millions has its paradoxical aspect—for as it happens, nobody in the wide world, not even in the stock-option executive suites of the United States, is more adept at feathering nests from the inside than your fully-fledged City gentleman. Behind that immaculate suiting and off-hand manner lies a sharp eye for a passing bank note—and not too many pass. The bankers and brokers feed their young and their old from pieces not only of their own action but of other people's, and in a perfectly legal manner. For instance, suppose that a promising, youthful, growth business comes a bank's way. In exchange for what is called its financial expertise and for loans of hard cash, the bank picks up for a song perhaps a quarter of the equity that, with growth, will be sold to a fond public at a far higher multiple.

At various points along this route, the bank may choose to cut its executives in on the profits—and may even lend them the cash (à la Sherman Fairchild) to finance the cut. The technique has certain virtues compared to the stock option. First, there is no nasty area of doubt: the capital gain is dead certain. Second, the bank's shareholders never know a thing—and what they don't know can hardly hurt them. Third, the process can be endlessly repeated. The snag is that the game shades over all too easily into the dubious zone of insider trading, or buying shares on the basis of knowledge, fed to the bank either in its professional capacity or on the back of deals the bank can promote or control.

In the case of the venerable Lloyd's of London, the temptations were so extreme that the only wonder is why they were resisted for so long. The underwriting of insurance is financed by *names*—wealthy individuals who are attracted to Lloyd's, not by the intrinsic profitability of insurance, but by the tax and other breaks that can bring them a 40 percent annual rate of return. That, however, depends on the scrupulous honesty of the managers of the "syndicate" to which the "names" belong. Some unscrupulous managers noticed that, by reinsuring the best risks with offshore companies owned by themselves and leaving the dross with the syndicate, they could skim off the profits to their hearts' desire.

Since they were very big-hearted people, millions flowed into the tax-haven bank accounts—and out of the resources of the syndicate, whose names suddenly found themselves facing the consequences of unlimited liability; that is, they stood to be wiped out by the losses made. While those who fleeced the names enjoyed their gains in sunny areas outside British jurisdiction, the names not unnaturally argued that the liability had been morally and perhaps legally limited by the lax supervision of Lloyd's.

But the whole world of executive recompense is laxly controlled, if controlled at all. Long before the Boesky scandals, a list of inside enrichment included kickbacks to a couple of American Airlines executives in connection with printing the in-flight magazine (called, appropriately enough, the *American Way*); profits made by Kaiser Industries executives from inside dope on a Canadian subsidiary; and some fast moves by Ling-Temco-Vought in the days of Jimmy Ling—such as paying Ling and three others $1 million for a ranch later sold for $1.4 million to another L-T-V interest, or selling warrants in a stock to L-T-V insiders, which enabled them to triple their money in the most painless manner imaginable.

Even if stock options have not made the executive a millionaire, fringe benefits can enable him to live like one, which is the next best thing, or to die like one (not quite so satisfactory). Retirement benefits are not peanuts. If an Englishman goes out to pasture at £350,000 a year, his pension entitlement could be £233,000; but a benevolent law allows him to "commute" a quarter of this sum for lovely, tax-free cash. A standard multiple would be thirteen times £58,000, easily a dollar million, simply for still being alive at the blessed age of retirement.

It's not only corporate executives, and it's not only the capitalist West, that share such fruits. A well-directed labor leader in the United States can garner a decent harvest: former convict and current missing corpse Jimmy Hoffa was said to have a million-dollar pension entitlement, while his successor, Frank E. Fitzsimmons, a confidant of President Nixon, not only shared the use of the Teamsters' family jet, Lincolns, and Cadillacs, but also enjoyed $125,000 of salary, a free house, and a freely disbursed expense account, one almost worthy of the champions of expensive expense living, the Japanese.

Those industrious easterners are supposed to churn through many billions of expending every year, plunging 1.5 percent of the GNP into gross bills for booze and beauty. Activities that in the West are concealed for fear of dismissal, such as recording fictitious entertainment of a friend, are a frank part of the Japanese game. Their ingenuity beats even that of W. C. Fields, who once padded his expense account with $25,000, allegedly disbursed on milk for entertainment of newsmen. According to *Time*, there is even a Japanese phrase for it—*shayo tengoku*, or "paradise for the corporate set." But, for some, expense accounts are not enough.

The same Stephen Cohen, mentioned earlier in this chapter, whose self-enriching deals aroused the ire of powerful shareholders, was provided by the company with a $2.9 million apartment in Trump Tower because of his frequent need to visit Manhattan. A further $1.1 million was needed to renovate and furnish this pied à terre. In fact, Cohen, with the shareholders howling around his head, later unwound this deal; but the case of Allegheny International (see Chapter 2), where the beneficiary of some spectacular interior decorating was the chairman's son, is yet another piece of evidence, rarely seen, of how deep executives can dig into the corporate till—with perfect legality.

Custom and practice, maybe as much as individual scruple and restraint, govern what is acceptable and accepted. *Business Week* notes, for one massive instance, that over five years the number of executives receiving total remuneration of $1 million or more had risen from 4 to 146. That thirty-six-times expansion bears no relation to any other corporate or national economic statistic. Indeed, the final year in the series was one of poor corporate profits, one in which a third of the executives surveyed actually suffered cuts in pay.

Obviously enough, chief executive officer 1, seeing that CEO 2 has a seven-figure take, isn't going to rest until he has likewise. That provokes CEO 3 to the same action, and so on ad infinitum, or at least to CEO 146. In this process, vice is virtue and virtue nonexistent. Thus, the modestly low salary paid for the immodestly high performance of Floyd Gottwald at Ethyl Corporation has to be offset by one signal fact: his is a family business (bought from Standard Oil, N.J., and General Motors via the use of heavy debt) in which the underpaid Gottwald has a comforting stake worth $230 million.

Ownership conveys rights, including the rights to its rewards. But should the rights and the rewards of employees be left to their own decision? The institutions set up to control executive pay and perquisites are lamentably weak. One of the cheerleaders on the Revlon compensation committee that handed Michel Bergerac his $15 million golden parachute is the gossip columnist known as Suzy Knickerbocker of the *New York Post*. Shrewd though she may be, Ms. Knickerbocker is a long way short of judicial standing. As for the investment bankers who, as noted, figure prominently on such committees, the people-who-live-in-glass-houses argument applies: five of the twenty-five highest paid executives in corporate America in 1985 worked for Wall Street investment banks.

This can't have been what Adolf Berle meant when he wrote about the change in personal property. The diffusion of ownership among the many has been used by the few to feather their nests with the richest down. No logical defense exists—certainly not in the relative performance of a U.S. economy that has dropped so far off the international pace. Legal defenses against the abuses could be erected with some ease, but that isn't a subject in which legislators—or, for that matter, shareholders—are much interested. The only consolation—and it's not much—is that even today's greediest chief executives are moderate by the standards of the past.

Business Week noted of 1985 that "top pay numbers aren't really as big as those in years past, when a few entrepreneurs were pulling in $40 million or more." For the sake of still more nostalgic comparison, Sir Henri Deterding, the omnipotent between-the-wars boss of Royal Dutch Shell, pulled down $250,000 in the solid sterling currency of those bygone days. The great earners of today are thus not truly in the same league as the prewar emperors or the postwar Japanese. As far back as 1961, the founding Matsushita pulled in the small annual matter of $500,000. But Deterding and Matsushita were supermen of world industry, not company men, not corpocrats. The company man, in any country that lets him, contrives to win both ways. With the left hand he dips into the corporate cash flow for the comforts and luxuries of bureaucratic life, all neatly docketed and documented. With his right hand, he dips into the shareholders' pockets for the pleasures, without the pain, of the individual, infallibly successful capitalist.

True, the withering of Wall Street in the fall of 1987 removed the bloom, not only from shares held as a result of past options but, just as painfully, from those yet to be cashed. However, the pain was fully shared by investors in American business. Now, the rationale of stock options is to encourage management to enrich investors through the stock market. The bursting of Wall Street's bubble thus also pricked this pretension. Since executives can do nothing to ensure shareholder enrichment, why reward them for trying to—especially as many of them fail?

The evidence for this statement comes from events *before*, not after the Great Crash. A writer in the *Harvard Business Review*, Ben C. Ball, after a painstaking study of corporations over the years from 1970 to 1984 found that "Many companies' profits simply never found their way to shareholders, either as dividends or as higher stock value over time. For more than half these companies, a large proportion of retained earnings simply disappeared."

Who were these delinquents? They include 3M, Coca-Cola, American Express, Eastman Kodak, and Sears Roebuck. The conclusion is inescapable: the fat options pocketed by such fat corporations' boards weren't earned. Nor were those of the American corpocracy as a whole: and it wasn't just the investor who suffered as a result.

12

IT CAN'T
GET ANY
WORSE

The good reward can come more easily from a bad situation than a good. Thus, quick and risk-free fortunes have been made by managers seduced to move into deadbeat and dying companies. They have cleaned up doubly, both for themselves and for the moribund corporations. Their rewards are out of decent proportion to their turnaround contribution—though it isn't easy to heave a corpse out of the industrial graveyard.

Still, the can't-get-any-worse artist has a saving grace or two. Bad needn't become best to produce the financial transformation he seeks. A mere improvement from murderous to moderate suffices, provided that the manager is prepared to use every trick in the trade of adjusting earnings per share sharply upward. If investors believe that a corporation is headed for the slaughterhouse, they will shed the shares like so much molted skin. The price will slump deeply below the physical value of the assets. (The one certainty of a deadbeat situation is that, in effect, dollar bills will be on sale cheap.)

More: since the company hasn't actually collapsed in a smelly heap of bad debts, the odds are that it won't. The Chrysler Corporation has been a rich source of bounty for its top executives despite, or rather because of, its past propensity to drive into acute crisis. This potential was first convincingly demonstrated after the mid-1950s slump, when the market share had been shot to ribbons, the earnings were barely visible, and the debts were monstrous. However, the company was still sufficiently intact for George M. Love (custodian of a Hanna fortune that was once among America's finest) to mount a swift and enriching rescue operation.

The executive in charge, Lynn A. Townsend, paved the way, both by his ripe rewards and by his later management, which did still worse damage to the Chrysler finances, for the spectacular performance, in all respects, of Lee Iacocca. When the latter, ousted by Henry Ford, moved up the road from Dearborn to Detroit, the number-three car company was a virtual basket case. Bankrupt, bleeding cash from every pore, Chrysler came within a million dollars of running out of ready money. The corpse could only be resurrected by federal backing. Once that had been negotiated, however, Iacocca had nowhere to go but up—and up.

The backed loans gave him the breathing space in which to force through a celebrated revamp that restored profitability, repaid the loans, revived the market share, and royally enriched the corporate saviors—Iacocca far above all. The foundation of Iacocca's turnaround wealth ($9.8 million in 1985) came from the stock options granted when the company was flat on its back, when things couldn't get any worse. Small wonder that Iacocca felt no personal need for the millions more made by his autobiography. (The co-author, William Novak, might well have felt that need, but he received a fee that was flat in every respect.)

Note that Iacocca didn't take long to reap his phenomenal return—only three years to reach the kind of fortune that takes even successful entrepreneurs a lifetime. The possibilities for such swiftness are another virtue in the turnaround situation. If a company is on the floor, it's probable that the management that dumped it there lacked even the normal self-preserving executive attributes. Sweeping away the expensive cobwebs, a straightforward task for an educated manager, must produce an immediate and lush saving.

To give some idea of the potential in a really large company, IBM came under financial duress as its growth slowed to a crawl and disrespectful competition chewed away at its margins in 1985 and 1986. Among other cost-cutting measures, such as persuading employees to take early retirement from the company that never lays off, and pruning a gross excess of capital spending, IBM found *$700 million* of savings in its bill for travel, meetings, and outside consultants and services. In relation to IBM's $51.5 billion of sales, neither the earlier uncut figure ($2.5 billion, or 5 percent of sales), nor the reduced number was especially large. But $700 million exceeded by almost half the total 1985 revenues of Compaq, one of the jauntiest of IBM's competitors in personal computers.

IBM had the reputation of being perhaps the world's most efficiently managed company. Like all outside reputations, this one no doubt contained plenty of exaggeration. But the relative excellence of IBM's management isn't in doubt. If a relatively efficient firm can squeeze out that much juice, imagine the joy that can flow from a rotten apple. And, again, the juice will be compounded by the mathematics of any stock set for a turnaround operation, and therefore lying in the stock exchange rubbish bin. Assume that the company used to earn $2 million a year and that earnings have collapsed to $200,000. The market may value the entire misfired shooting match at $2 million. In comes Sir Galahad with his team of trusty knights, throws out the old-line management, and hauls out all the skeletons from their cupboards in the first year's accounts.

That year a thumping loss results. But the shares, buoyed up by Galahad's reputation and his press interviews, advance 50 percent to a $3 million capitalization. Galahad & Co. don't mind this at all—they have stock options at the old price, a quotation they now proceed to leave far behind in their gleaming wakes. They push profits up to $1 million: only half the company's old earning power, true, but think of the steep rate and angle of climb. If the knights-errant merely return to $2 million, the next year around the course, that will mean doubled profits. No investment analyst can resist a proposition of this kind—so the shares go to twenty times the million-dollar earnings, or $20 million, a tenfold rise; the knights cash in their options; and, if they are lucky and keep their noses sharp and their lances clean, there are years of pickings to come—if.

In truth, the qualities needed for a turnaround artist and those required for the long haul are not one and the same, and seldom occur in the same body, which explains the regrettable tendency for turnarounds to turn again, like Dick Whittington, only to much worse effect. The five ghastliest returns to investors in the Fortune 500 of 1985 included Control Data, whose fortunes have risen and fallen yo-yo-style as different strategies in waging war with IBM have been tried, succeeded, failed—only for the cycle to be repeated again.

Over the longer haul, the decade to 1985, the five greatest dogs included American Motors, whose original resuscitation under George Romney propelled the latter into wealth and the national political limelight—and which seemed to have another revival under way as recently as 1985. The problem of sustaining recovered success contributed to the troubles of the conglomerates. Their game was basically a variant of the turnaround: buying underexploited companies and, by exploiting their assets and earnings potentials, enhancing the capital value to the joy of all mankind (especially themselves). The conglomerates ruined an imperfectly viable system for the creation of paper fortunes (readily convertible into more-solid assets) by misunderstanding the nature of their own rackets.

The essence of conglomeration was, and is, the exchange of paper for earnings; by this unprepossessing trick were the conglomerate millionaires created. But the front behind which they executed this stratagem was a beauteous but totally illusory vision of a new management world, brave and unprecedented, in which finely honed minds using razor-edged techniques would manage diverse businesses in a manner leaving far behind the contemptible efforts of the older, switched-off generations.

The snag behind this noble facade was that the conglomerators, who (like all con men) believed their own publicity, in reality had to manage convoluted, complex, ill-assorted bundles of companies, at which they had no greater success than any previous generation of managers out of their depths. The consequences were cruelly exposed by the sell-offs, low market valuations, flops, and restructurings of the 1980s. It didn't matter whether the conglomerators were business school brains such as Charlie Bluhdorn of Gulf + Western, professional management teams such as that of Consolidated Foods (some sixty businesses sold), or pushy promoters such as J. B. Fuqua of Fuqua Industries (who deliberately shrank $2 billion of sales to $607 million).

Despite the revival of the shares that accompanied Fuqua's contraction, and was its objective, the Atlanta tycoon dropped out of the Forbes 400 in 1985. His slip was caused by the poor growth of his net assets rather than the absolute decline achieved by Victor Posner. The mishmash nature of conglomeration and its multiple possibilities of disaster dropped Posner's worth by an estimated $100 million that year. One company sought protection under Chapter 11. Another had been pushed to the brink by over $200 million of losses. As *Business Week* reported, "Once-profitable conglomerates such as NVF, DWG, and Pennsylvania Engineering—the heart of his empire—have been skidding into red ink and staggering debt since 1982."

DWG has a special place in Posner's pocket. That wasn't because of its performance in the stock market—the shares fell in 1986 to 1⅝; back in 1984 they were 3¾, which was no great shakes, either. DWG came in handy financially by paying Posner more money than any other chief executive in the States for apparently doing least: $12.7 million. Trying to justify what *Forbes* rightly called "grotesque abundance," a spokesman pointed to the dozens of companies held by DWG. "You have all these companies that Posner manages on a daily basis, and they have improved with time and effort."

That failed to explain the poor figures (DWG had just lost $5.9 million in nine months) and the overrich rewards, but it surely did explain the impoverished performance. Nobody, even if younger, more capable, and less selfish than this sixty-seven-year-old Miami Beach millionaire, could manage the morass in any meaningful sense.

The sensible or sharper conglomerators didn't even try. British mutants may be able to claim the credit for pioneering a twist that, from small beginnings in the 1960s, brought large winnings in the 1980s. Under this dispensation, the conglomerator would only manage the assets to the point where, like the bear cub of mythology, they had been licked into shape. The cubs would then be sold off, preferably for cash, while the conglomerate, its coffers replenished, padded off in search of new prey. Where the simple, straight turnaround artists concentrated on one desperate situation at a time, the mutants could handle two, three, four—each time milking or stripping the surplus assets, revamping the businesses, selling them off, then repeating the cycle in other musty, dusty corners of commercial Britain.

The further mutation of this predatory technique removed one whole stage from the process. Suppose you didn't even bother to develop the businesses you bought, saving yourself no end of time and trouble. A different and better set of mathematics could be activated. The arch-exponents of this were two Britons, Lord Hanson and Sir Gordon White of Hanson Trust. They went a couple of bridges further, first by transferring their attentions to the United States and second by seeking far larger targets than the piddling victims of the earlier and less-rewarding phase of conglomeration, in which the Hanson twins had learned their trade.

Now they noted that the share prices of companies that had made a series of overpriced acquisitions, far from achieving the intended growth, languished behind not only the market as a whole (in terms of the price-earnings ratio) but also the value of the underlying assets. What happened next sounds childishly simple. You bid for, say, SCM— a typical example of the conglomerate breed, which had long since run out of rationale and steam. After a tough tussle with Merrill Lynch, you win the prize for the best part of a billion. Within a few months you have disposed of Glidden Paint, Durkee Famous Foods, and a few other jewels for a total of $930 million, or roughly the cost of the entire SCM caboodle. You are left with businesses in titanium dioxide and typewriters that are earning $120 million and are yours virtually for free.

Far from sated, you turn your eyes back across the Atlantic to an even larger British target—Imperial Group. In the manner of its kind, this tobacco giant has diversified not wisely but too unwell, into food, beer, the disastrous Howard Johnson's, and so on. You pay, after an equally tough tussle, $3.9 billion. In a trice, the beer and several other businesses have been sold to eager buyers, leaving you with a munificent cash flow from the cigarettes and with profits that have cost you just five times their annual amount. Even better, your balance sheet has been restored to such lissom shape that you can perform the whole routine all over again.

The only snag, as Hanson and White found, is that what would make a private proprietor (such as Sir James Goldsmith) an immense and immediate fortune can't equally enrich holders of a public company's stock unless other investors are suitably impressed by the virtuosity. Despite these bravura displays, Hanson Trust shares rose by only half from high to low in 1986, leaving Hanson with mere millions to his name in equity.

That growth wasn't how it used to be. Over the decade to 1986, the shares had appreciated by 1,704 percent, outstripping by far a sales increase of 730 percent and topping the rise in pretax profit of 1,217 percent. Even that was small potatoes by the standards of the first conglomerate phase. To give one instance, an Old Etonian practitioner of tender years issued over 17 million pieces of paper as he rounded up terrible, run-down companies in toys, media, advertising, pharmaceuticals, even films. Over his company's four years of life, the shares shot up by 852 percent before the workings of an awful truth made themselves felt.

In hard theory, the higher your shares rise, the less chance the take-your-money-and-run technique has of generating a real profit. Suppose you have a $1 million company with $1 million of assets that issues $1 million of shares to buy another million-dollar business. Suppose that it then performs the standard revamp, cuts the unprofitable products, ceases to serve the unprofitable outlets, sells off the surplus offices, and gets profits back to a respectable height. At that point, a buyer appears ready to pay $6 million in cash for the revamped wonder. (If a buyer is not in evidence when wanted, a handy device is to have a captive customer, a good and true friend, or another company that you control yourself, to take the bargain off your hands.) On the face of it, your firm has a very nice $5 million profit, but that sum depends entirely on what has happened to your shares in the interim.

If they have multiplied tenfold, the effective price paid for the assets now being sold for $6 million is $10 million. Paradoxically, the worse the shares have performed, the better the deal. This basic, uncomfortable formula explains a great deal of what happened to the multimarket, share-sprouting companies as a whole in the up phase. Their share prices ran far ahead of the real value of their wheels and deals. The proprietors could, of course, say the mathematics be damned: if you can cash in on a tenfold share boom, who cares about fundamental realities?

The answer is that the shareholders will, if the value of the equity (as is probable) gets pulled down by the weight of the wheels and deals. The trap doesn't seem to apply to a fast-moving predator such as Hanson Trust, which starts turning acquired assets into cash when the ink is hardly dry on the takeover. Yet the shares still tend to linger. Investors, for some reason, prefer businesses that aren't like the famous Jewish herrings, just for buying and selling, and the reason could be a good one.

The best investments down the years have always been built around a solid core. Businesses whose sole business is making money have not tended to last. What makes pluperfect sense for an individual entrepreneur such as Kirk Kerkorian doesn't translate so well into a corporate balance sheet. When Kerkorian right royally screwed Ted Turner, he netted a $268 million turn on a deal that left him back where he started: owning United Artists. That contributed handsomely to a personal net worth in excess of $600 million. In a corporation such as Hanson Trust, the benefits would have been submerged in the corporate balance sheet.

To put it another way, the corporate wheeler-dealer has to share the proceeds of his brilliance with investors in the mass, who may add insult to injury by refusing to value the brilliance as highly as the genius deserves (or thinks he does). That notion seems to have sunk home with a new generation of can't-get-any-worse practitioners, who have taken the Hanson technique and allied it with the magic of debt finance to produce the amazing phenomenon known as the leveraged buyout (LBO).

The case of John Kluge, and his translation of $1.2 billion of unregarded Metromedia assets into (by the fall of 1986) a $2.5 billion (and still rising) personal fortune, has already been mentioned in Chapter 2. But the case of Donald Kelly and Beatrice is in its way even more amazing. Originally styled Beatrice Foods, the conglomerate had finally overstuffed itself by swallowing Esmark in 1985. That corporation had been run by Kelly and associates, who the next year formed an alliance with Kohlberg Kravis & Roberts, specialists in LBOs, to bite the biter. In a record-breaking LBO, the partnership purchased Beatrice for $6.2 billion and shouldered $6.1 billion of debt, all in junk bonds.

The figures read like lunacy, but the results made magnificent sense. Within eight months, Kelly had sold off enough businesses to retire $5 billion of debt and was all set to refloat Beatrice on the stock market; had the bull market stood firm, his own $5 million investment would have turned into a net of $400 million. Kelly and Kluge were by no means alone in exploiting the leveraged lode. One John Pomerantz, after two LBOs, garnered $60 million in four years, sixty times his initial investment in the dress company, Leslie Fay, founded by his father. *Fortune* also cites Joseph Flannery, chairman of the beat-up tire business, Uniroyal; the $750,000 Flannery down payment on his LBO was apparently worth $20 million a year later.

As the magazine says, tartly enough, "Since 1981, 260 public companies have gone private. Of those, some 30 or so have been taken public again or broken up and the assets sold off. The average increase in value for the 30 between being bought and sold again is about 150 percent. Managers made out like gangbusters." By taking over the company's assets at less than their realizable value and arranging for themselves to receive a large chunk of the dirt-cheap equity, these operators created personal fortunes out of thin air—or, more accurately, from the shareholders' pockets.

There's something strangely unreal about this ultimate form of insider trading. How can a company (Metromedia) be worth $1.1 billion one minute and $6.5 billion the next? Where's the catch? How can great wealth be created, not by building companies up but by tearing them down? The phenomenon even raises a most disturbing thought: managers who devote their best efforts to strengthening the company would be better off, no matter how high their stock options, to run the company into the ground. At that point, when it can't get any worse, they buy the business from shareholders who are only too relieved to pocket a premium; then the insiders can apply turnaround magic to a managerial profit that will easily outdo any stock option.

This highly undesirable prospect has drawn uncomfortably near.

It almost makes the observer hanker for the innocent days that saw the assembly of companies such as the great and mighty International Telephone and Telegraph, once the pride and passion of the archetypal midcentury millionaire manager, Harold S. Geneen. His story, however, truly illustrates the shortcomings of the classic turnaround-cum-conglomerate technique, both in corporate and personal terms.

When Geneen came to ITT it was big, but its bigness was in dreary areas, such as communications utilities, with some illumination from brighter but neglected operations such as manufacturing telecommunications gear in a booming Western Europe. The simple knowledge that Geneen, a man of miraculous reputation, was on the move from Raytheon forced down the price of the latter's stock and boosted that of ITT by several millions—and Geneen, with a single-minded devotion of awesome dimensions, proceeded to prove the stock market right.

In a decade the sales multiplied 6.7 times, the profits 10 times, the assets 6.3 times. Quarter after quarter the wreck that Geneen inherited waxed richer and richer, and Geneen waxed with it in wealth and reputation. The waxing was accomplished primarily through a corporate acquisition program remarkable for its catholic, open-minded nature. If it moved, ITT seemed to buy it; the collection eventually included old ITT items such as Standard Telephones and Cables in Britain, new buys such as Avis Rent-a-Car, a hotel in Hammamet, Gwaltney Smithfield hams—and still the shopping went on. In 1970 alone ITT added $1.5 billion in assets and the next year put on a billion more in weight, as Geneen used what he himself modestly called ITT's "unusual abilities to follow a policy of diversified risks in selected fields of above-average opportunity."

All modesty aside, ITT became the world's all-time champion of the turnaround carried to its logical extreme. Sales in 1972 were $8.5 billion. The original ITT, when Geneen moved in, couldn't have got very much worse without disappearing. The new ITT, so popular belief had it, couldn't get any better; it was the ultimate in modern management, as Geneen himself said. In terms of wealth creation, ITT's progress was broad and strong indeed; at the end of 1972 the former deadbeat was capitalized at a wondrous $9 billion. Probably any ITT fan told that earnings per share in the decade from 1961 to 1971 had grown only by 7.84 percent annually would have refused to believe so blatant an untruth, but that was the fact. What's more, 197 of the biggest American corporations listed by *Fortune* outgrew ITT in that decade (ITT looked better over the period from 1962 to 1972, but only because earnings fell under Geneen between 1961 and 1962). What's still more, the ITT record resulted in part from some elegant cookery of the books.

One year, the gain in earnings was a worthy 10 percent, from $3.14

to $3.45—save for the little matter of losing the Chilean business after a peculiarly inept attempt to overthrow the host government. Adding in (or taking out) this "extraordinary item" reduced the figure to $2.85, a 9.2 percent decline. But the essence of making a bad situation good is that the impression created matters more than the reality, and the impression arises from assiduous public relations and assiduous accountancy. The latter art form is easier to exploit when a company is changing its shape and size almost weekly by merger, spreading itself from microwaves to insurance in the process.

But in that Chilean year, despite all the finagling and fine-tuning, not only was ITT's growth record modest, so was its return on invested capital (194 large companies did better), and so was its industrial performance. In industrial and consumer products, ITT earned hugely less on sales (3.8 percent) than 3M (11.5 percent). In food processing and services ITT could only contrive an abysmal 1.9 percent. The conglomerate's best performance, to nobody's surprise, was in the business in which it started pre-Geneen and which it knew best: 4.5 percent on telecommunications equipment. But behind that higher figure lay a tale of neglected investment and inadequate innovation that, post-Geneen, cost ITT its future. As the diversified businesses foundered, dragging ITT down to a miserable 4.5 percent return on equity and a compound annual decline of 5 percent in earnings per share from 1975 to 1985, so the base business slipped out of its hands.

Forced first to abandon an ambitious assault on the U.S. telecoms market and then to submerge its European empire into a French-controlled merger, ITT had lost any semblance of a raison d'être. Nobody can take away from Geneen his amazing feat in turning a beat-up old telecoms company into the eighth-largest company in the United States. But its retreat to twenty-fifth in the master's absence shows that, although creative accountancy allied to rapid acquisition may appear to equal magnificent performance, the sum won't equal a magnificent company. ITT enriched a lot of people—including Geneen, who collected stock options by the millions of dollars in the much-harder currency of the 1970s. But it was just another turnaround—only a very big one—that turned sour.

Inside every bad business there may be a good one screaming to get out. Every situation, no matter how evil-smelling the egg, contains within it the possibility of a nice, fresh profit. One U.S. operator, Harry Weinberg, once even made $100 million out of the most certain financial death traps in the big cities: bus lines. In his own accurate words, every urban bus company Weinberg bought was "a cow with no milk in." But people still had to get to work; cities were still prepared to subsidize and otherwise assist any big-hearted citizen who would help his fellow citizens on their way; and Weinberg's squeezed-out cattle yielded a surprising flood of cream. As long as the market demand is there, there is some device, some new approach, some scheme of rationalization that will convert the demand into tax-free or tax-paid dollars.

The vital knack for the turnaround artist is to ensure that most of the dollars flow straight into his privy purse. A most useful device in accomplishing this end is the wonderful, the unique, the now-you-see-it, now-you-don't Shell Game—the shell in this instance being a company so burned out that it has almost nothing left except one crucial asset, its stock exchange quotation. Britain has been the richest source of shells, thanks to a colonial past that left relics with names such as Galaha Ceylon Tea Estates or Parit-Bruas (Malay) Rubber Co., companies whose shares sold at infinitesimal prices, when they sold at all.

That was almost never, save for the appearance of a shell gamester. He buys control of the outfit for the laughable going price and, when armed with a suitable stake, passes the word that high-earning interests are about to be injected into the shell. If a company is capitalized at $25,000, with hardly any earnings, the injection of $50,000 of net income must enhance the shares by moonman leaps and bounds, even if the profits are valued conservatively in the market. In fact, a well-massaged market will value the shares on the basis of their inexhaustible capacity for early, spectacular growth.

An American named Roger Felber demonstrated the essential arithmetic with Parkfield Foundries, a company that went public in 1981 at a market capitalization, $600,000, which looked small even then. Two years later, when the foundries were losing $300,000 a year, the $600,000 was a distant dream. Enter Felber, once an executive with Air Florida, in a deal that gave him 22 percent of the equity. He proceeded to use his rapidly rising paper to purchase noncore businesses of large groups and family-owned companies that felt themselves too large to stay private.

Within three years, pretax profits of $12 million were rolling in (three and a half times the previous year's), the shares had risen to $3 from an original price of under twenty cents, and the company was worth $90 million—a goodly chunk of which belonged to Felber. That 153-fold rise in value may look gorgeous enough. But Felber had a long way to go before matching figures such as this: a ten-year return to investors of 55,386 percent, or, to drop to an only slightly more modest level, 42,342 percent.

The latter figure is the capital appreciation over the decade from 1976 to 1986 of a company called Rosehaugh, which was one of those

leftover tea plantations when a tax-avoidance specialist, Geoffrey Bradman, bought control at the typically low-low price of nine cents a share.
The other, even more astronomical gain was recorded over the same
period by Polly Peck International, which was a threadbare textile
company until a Turkish Cypriot, Asil Nadir, moved in and swapped
fashion for overseas trading. Five years later, fruit packaging, mineral
water bottling, electronics, and pharmaceuticals produced over $90
million of profit—and despite the City of London's perennial disbelief
in Nadir's Mediterranean businesses, the valuation of his company was
$300 million in early 1987.

The former tea plantation, though, has concrete evidence of Bradman's brilliance at financing real estate deals, in the shape of residential
and office buildings in London and outlying areas. The ingenuity that
Bradman had previously brought to minimizing his clients' tax bills
produced schemes such as this: unable to finance a development in a
downtrodden area of the City of London in the normal way, Bradman
got large, established investors to subscribe for $51 million of deben-
tures—with no down payment. The money only had to be paid over
later; but meanwhile, Bradman could and did use the stock as security
for the bank finance he vitally needed.

His neat trick contributed powerfully to making Rosehaugh worth
a tidy half a billion dollars. But nothing could have been tidier than the
multiplier effect of injecting a business growing fast in assets and revenues into the tea company shell. In that, Bradman was following in the
footsteps of the two outstanding performers in Britain in the 1970s, Jim
Slater's Slater Walker and Ralli International, run by Slater protégé
Malcolm Horsman. They began life respectively as H. Lotery and
Oriental Carpet Manufacturers—both companies of the obligatory little account.

Their wondrously expanded transformations, though, are now of
no account at all. Despite the previous stock-market spectaculars, both,
by different routes, disappeared from sight. For Slater and his erstwhile
lieutenant, both of whom shared fully in the earlier effulgence, capitalism must have seemed a lovely thing for many years; but in its aftermath, when the Bank of England was left holding the bankruptcy-high
baby, Slater claimed that he was down to a minus million: loveliness
didn't last. The great danger is always that the recovery, the upward
thrust, will run out of acceleration, and even decelerate sharply, in the
same dizzy style, and with the same desolating effect, as the share
plunge in fallen conglomerates such as Litton and Gulf+Western.
Getting back up from poor to moderate is only the first stage of the
battle; the distance from moderate to excellent is far longer, and getting

there can be as arduous as the journey to the moon. Often the astronaut would be best advised to turn for home before the distance and the stock market catch up to him.

The crash of 1987 only reinforced this cautionary tale. Corporate astronauts fell like Icarus all over the stock markets of the world. In London, for instance, Rosehaugh lost 67 percent of its market value. If this seems picayune compared to the previous 42,342 percent gain, consider the numbers involved: Bradman's little real estate business had lost £400 million of market value in a couple of awful weeks. He can only have had one hopeful consolatory thought: "It can't get any worse."

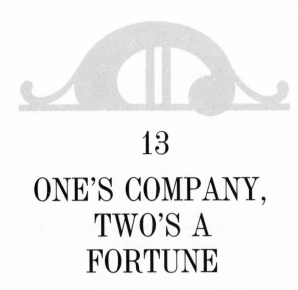

13

ONE'S COMPANY,
TWO'S A
FORTUNE

One of the few unassailable truths to emerge from an age in which nearly every ambitious or half-ambitious corporation has sought to improve its affairs by merger is that merging does not improve corporate affairs. When two Goliaths join in unholy wedlock, the general result is simply to produce a fatter target at which the Davids of business can aim their hard, round stones. When the fat company buys a small outfit, the chances are that the profitability of the buy, and still more the contentment of its people, will be squashed by the fat man's heavy tread.

No matter how the effects are measured—return on capital, growth in earnings per share, movement in the beloved share price, share of new markets—the merging firms seldom outdo the corporate spinsters and bachelors, and often get undone themselves. The unhappy record isn't just the result of an incurable corporate tendency to overpay for company purchases (a habit encouraged by the fact that real money is seldom used), though many a millionaire has capitalized on this generous penchant. Selling out to a fat purchaser, the accepted, easy alternative to selling out to the public, produces generally less-lavish results, but has the advantage that the proprietor can grab his money without delay, and all in the form of cash or negotiable securities.

On his way to becoming America's second-richest man, in the manner described in the previous chapter, John Werner Kluge had no visible trouble in finding buyers for goods as varied as the Ice Capades and Harlem Globetrotters ($30 million), cellular phones ($1.2 billion), outdoor advertising ($300 million), and a clutch of radio stations ($285 million). All these unconsidered trifles came from the $1.4 billion buyout and breakup of Metromedia, in which the biggest morsel was the $2 billion paid for seven TV stations by Rupert Murdoch, the central figure in a whirl of international merger activity that has redistributed media millions in a generous manner which, defying the laws of economics, seems to have made all parties deliriously happy.

In the one month of January 1987, Murdoch's native Australia witnessed the following rich sequence of events: the man himself bid for the newspaper group previously run by his father (see Chapter 3); had to reach an enriching accommodation with and for a rival tycoon, Robert Holmes à Court, before the $1.5 billion bid looked safe; then got topped temporarily by another rival, James Fairfax; and, in the midst of all this excitement, learned that yet another Aussie tycoon, Kerry Packer, had pocketed $750 million by selling his television interests. The purchaser, fresh as a daisy from being knocked out of the America's Cup, was superyachtsman Alan Bond.

"I was presented with an offer too good to refuse," said Packer of his part in a game of musical chairs that dragged in almost every member of the rough and very ready Aussie plutocracy. Now, there are circumstances when an offer too good to refuse is also a purchase too good to miss. But this perfect meshing of interests is far less likely when two rapacious tycoons are exchanging assets for money. When beasts of the jungle fight, there are never two winners. But the Australian media wars, no less than Kluge's sales from his bargain basement, show how, in the global monetary village of the 1980s, awash with funds seeking big borrowers, circles could be squared—at least for a while.

The purchaser of assets gambled on what in Kluge's case was the surest of things—that the asset purchased with borrowed money can be transmuted into cash or equity in time to remove the debt overburden from the buyer's back. This isn't a consideration that bothers the big corporations when they decide to turn a proprietor into a plutocrat. The shares they issue to the latter (or the dollar bills, if the willing victim's persuasion has extended to exacting cash) are a mere drop in the Pacific Ocean of the total equity. When Shell paid over $3 billion for Belridge Oil in 1979, the half dozen heirs of Frank Henry Buck, who made his original pile in fruit, obtained $665 million. Neither sum was significant in relation to a Shell market capitalization in the tens of billions.

The annual return on Frank Buck's original $250,000 investment was 12.5 percent compound, well above the 7 percent par for the course. That poses a very stiff challenge for Frank III, who told *Forbes*: "I don't want banks managing my money. You might as well make your own mistakes." Even if his management of the family money is free from error, Buck won't easily find a situation where an asset (in this case, oil in the ground) is elevated to such high value by passing circumstances (those being the eightfold rise in crude prices) that the family wins a bonanza of the kind that even Santa Claus seldom brings.

The same principle—that a huge personal payoff represents only a manageable fraction of a giant's capitalization—was demonstrated when General Motors bought Electronic Data Systems. H. Ross Perot's second-stage cash liftoff, $700 million, represented less than three days of GM sales, a little over 1 percent of GM assets, and a couple of months' net income. The initial payment in stock and cash had already taken Perot's wealth to a capital appreciation of 149,900 percent on his original $1,000 investment. What's good for General Motors may or may not be good for America. But General Motors has certainly been good for H. Ross Perot.

In recent years, large American corporations on the prowl for privately dominated purchases such as EDS have been joined by Europeans of all shades (such as Shell), bearing gifts across the Atlantic to the proprietors of U.S. businesses. The attractions to most prowlers are the wide open (they hope) spaces of the American market. The attractions to all the vendors are the wide open wallets of the Europeans, who, egged on by Wall Street marriage brokers avid for fat fees, almost by definition paid more than any U.S. national had been prepared to contemplate.

When the two Saatchi brothers, determined to maintain their newly won position as the world's largest advertising group, craved the Ted Bates agency, they quickly paid $450 million for the prize—all in the hardest of cash. The bulk of the booty went to the Bates boss, Neil Jacoby. Within a few months, an uncomfortable Jacoby had decamped with his comforting loot; the market value of Saatchi & Saatchi's shares fell after the Bates deal by no less than 40 percent before they began the long climb back—only to be dashed again by Black October.

The Saatchi payment was exceeded by the $475 million paid by

Bertelsmann of West Germany for the Doubleday publishing house, to the joy of controlling shareholder Nelson, Jr., who had long frustrated his sister's desire to cash in through a public share offer. Britain's Prudential insurance mammoth paid $607 million for a Michigan insurer, Jackson National Life, of which hardly anybody had heard—and these were only three of the deals that cost the British alone $8.7 billion in the first nine months of 1986. The generosity in a sense, though only partially, repaid that of those quintessential expansionists, the Americans, who had gladdened hearts all over Europe as, inspired by the vision of the European Economic Community and its glorious promise, they paraded the pavements of the Continent with their hearts and checkbooks open. On the whole, the wanderers did better in France, where generations of tax-evading capitalists had lived out of the cash box and kept down the apparent value of their family nest eggs, than in Italy, where generations of equally avid tax-evaders had perfected the art of presenting different sets of books that meant all things to all men: no profits to the tax man, huge earnings to prospective purchasers, with the truth (shown only to themselves) somewhere in between.

In one case, the buyer of an Italian business was horrified to get a tax demand for more than the company's entire income. This innocent American had submitted an honest tax return, and the tax man had simply assumed that, like all returns submitted by the previous owner, it had grossly understated the true profits. "Never deal with an Italian" is fairly sound advice to the merging novice. By the same token, "Always deal with an Anglo-Saxon" is the best of counsel to an Italian, many of whom have needed no second bidding.

The British, though nearer in geography and history to the Italians, were no more likely than the Americans to outmatch the local Machiavellis. Vivid proof of this proposition was provided by Leopoldo Pirelli, the lithe, good-looking scion of the second-richest Italian family of industrial aristocrats. The exact nature of the Pirelli riches at the time was hard to establish, thanks to a typically Italian convolution of companies: the original Società Pirelli & Co., founded in 1872 by an inventive genius who simultaneously grasped the potential of rubber and cables, held stakes in two other companies, one Italian, one Swiss (Switzerland is a favorite resort of well-sprung Italians, who have been in the habit of crossing the border with well-filled suitcases of currency whenever the local economic climate gets too hot).

The Swiss company owned part of the Italian, the two shared ownership of the Pirelli interests outside Italy—and there were some other modest investments to be taken into account, such as the second-largest holding in Fiat. This was the financial hornets' nest into which some brave Britons poked.

The Pirelli interests got half of the Dunlop empire, and vice versa: there proved, however, to be more *vice* than *versa*. The Italian business proceeded to lose £18.6 million in the first year of the union and still more in the second, as a wave of labor unrest, managerial arthritis, and technical failure devastated Pirelli's profits. Dunlop's eager Britons were forced to write off their entire £41.5 million investment in Italian bad eggs. The Italian basket, however, still contained half of Dunlop— and those eggs, on a fairly conservative assessment, were then worth £300 million of solid gold, or £150 million to the Pirelli side. By any standards, it was a remarkable exchange.

At the end of a sad day for the Brits, when the Italian connection had been unraveled, the swap looked more remarkable still. Dunlop, already shorn of its European tire interests after a distress sale to the Japanese, had vanished into the local BTR conglomerate for some $150 million, while in mid-1986 Pirelli's equity was worth ten times that amount. Over the previous five years, moreover, Pirelli investors had been rewarded by an 18.5 percent annual return in American dollars, or 26.2 percent in the Swiss francs the family understandably prefers.

The best form of merger for the rich individual is usually that which, like Alan Bond's buy of the Packer television empire, takes the responsibility off the vendor's hands but leaves the riches firmly grasped. When the glove is on the other hand, and the rich individual is merging another business into his own, he runs the same financial and managerial risks as any corporation, whether he is diversifying into some beckoning field of which he is wholly ignorant or merely eliminating some supine or rampant competitor. And it's noteworthy that many of the most brilliant private managements (Mars, Johnson's Wax, Sainsburys, and so forth) have seldom if ever run those risks—despite their own evident operational skills.

All the same, merger magic can be worked. The relevant figure is that 30 percent of $100 million of corporate assets is worth more than 50 percent of $50 million—to be precise, $5 million more—and still gives control. It therefore pays the accumulator to surrender part of his ownership for fresh piles of assets so long as the surrenders are always smaller than the piles—witness the case of Sir Maxwell Joseph.

This former realtor rose so high in the property world that, in his dying days, he presided over a sprawling conglomerate powerful enough to take the Intercontinental hotel chain off a suffering Pan Am. Right up to that last deal, Joseph probably accomplished more by his deals than by any managerial prowess. At one point, his hotel interests, consisting largely of undersize properties around Mayfair, weighed in at a light $15 million of capital employed. Seven years later, after buying up hotels, dairies, dance halls, casinos, and a sizable brewery, all in exchange for a plethora of loan stocks, shares, and other pieces of paper, Grand Metropolitan, the Joseph vehicle, was worth twenty-two times that earlier amount. Immediately after adding an even vaster brewery to the agglomeration, Joseph's personal stake, down to only 18 percent of the equity, was worth almost $30 million—double the value of the entire business at the start of the merger drive.

By 1987, twenty-four years after that $15 million price tag, the Joseph creation, after fighting clear of a takeover threat itself by purchasing Heublein, Smirnoff vodka and all, from RJR Industries, was valued at $6 billion—and 18 percent of that is a clear billion. That number, naturally, depended on the performance of the shares in the stock market, which had produced some unpleasant lurches along the road to $6 billion. But that's a hard-to-avoid penalty of placing too many eggs in the same basket. The alternative is to keep the eggs apart, while still enjoying the fruits of minority ownership.

No family in Europe had a choicer minority than the Flicks. The genius Friedrich Flick, who bridged the Nazi and Adenauer eras, had been deprived of his fortune by the Allies after the war and was in no mood to surrender control of his rebuilt interests in the peace. The rebuilding itself was a miracle within the wonder of German resurgence. At his death in 1972, at the age of eighty-nine, Flick owned $1,700 million of sales in steel, chemicals, paper, and odds and ends such as the Leopard tank; but that bundle excluded the ripest fruit of all, a minority (40 percent) holding in Daimler-Benz, the Continent's outstanding postwar company—seventeenth largest outside the United States in 1986, thirty-first in the entire world, and a perennial joy to its investors: in the five years to 1986, they reaped a total harvest of 49 percent per annum compound.

Small wonder that the old autocrat's death sparked off an unseemly and bitter Flick family squabble. It was only resolved by the final, massive sell-off in 1985, which created a new kind of currency— "Flick money." Whenever rumors ran around markets of vast sums allegedly moving this way or that, "Flick money" proved a handy explanation, which may even occasionally have been true. Yet it can't be said that the Flicks, even the old man himself, had earned their reward by their own efforts. The professional managers at Daimler-Benz had carried most of the burden; the 0.4 percent earned on the other interests (even allowing for the reluctance of German firms, especially family ones, to show more profits than they need) is not the standard preached by the Harvard Business School.

But that is the profound advantage of the personal proprietor in the merger sport: so long as he covers the costs of acquisition, in borrowings or any other out-of-pocket expenses, possession is nine-tenths of the law. Unlike the corporate manager, who is theoretically bent on accumulating higher earnings, which means that the professional corporate merger must be made to work, the millionaire is predominantly interested in assets—which, apart from other blessings, if they carry little in the way of earnings (visible ones, that is) carry no tax, either.

Acquisitions are a challenge to the professional manager's innate sense of order and neatness, his desire to subject the entire corporation to the same systems and discipline. Dorothy Parker had a poem for it: "They hail you as their morning star, / Because you are the way you are. / . . . / And once they have you, safe and sound, / They want to change you all around."

One British entrepreneur, Sir Mack Weinberg, has never forgotten his shock when the full weight of ITT's planning descended on his innocent head. For his proportionately tiny morsel of the corporate feast, some 300 man-days of planning were demanded. (As it happens, the effort turned up a potential seven-figure loss in one product, which was duly corrected; this discovery converted Weinberg to planning, but later, in a very similar business, he found that 3 man-days did the planning trick, with the paperwork the equivalent of *Jonathan Livingston Seagull*, rather than ITT's *War and Peace*.)

Many accumulative individual millionaires are just as incapable psychologically of leaving well enough alone. But, unlike the managers, the rich have the option. If they pile on $10 million of assets earning a beggarly million, it's a matter of some indifference—within reason—whether the earnings rise or fall (a millionaire's reason seldom extends to actual losses). The tycoon, if he wants, can afford to treat his interests, purchased or not, as they really are—a portfolio of investments, no different from a hand dealt in the stock market—except that the holder can call all the plays.

He can put up with large minority holdings that would greatly vex any conventionally managed or mismanaged company: such as the Flick 40 percent of Daimler-Benz. He can run every single company in a different manner, or have it run by somebody else—which is the essence of the rich man's approach. It's uneconomical for somebody whose time equals a fortune to fiddle when perfectly competent hands can be hired to conduct every orchestra in the collection. Far better to sit, as Howard Hughes did, in lofty isolation, surrounded by silent Mormons, communicating with your managers either not at all or by telephone, while they make millions on your behalf.

The Cowdray family, one of the richest in Britain, provides a textbook example of a seemingly haphazard collection of interests; their full complexity was revealed only by the decision to go public. At the start of their consolidation, the Cowdrays owned two public newspaper companies, one of which held the controlling interest in the other; a private newspaper company with no connection with the other two; a book publisher; the obligatory oil and gas; a merchant bank (Lazards); Château Latour and its fine clarets; a sizable share of the potteries around Stoke-on-Trent, including Crown Derby; engineering firms—and so on. Not one of these appeared to be managed by any system common to the rest of the family holdings.

What mattered not at all so long as the fortune was private mattered considerably in its public shape. After the Cowdrays tucked away the best part of $150 million for their interests, efforts to inject professional management were frustrated by the fact that no professional manager would ever have put such disparate twos and twos together—sums that consistently added up to less than four. True, the shares rose by 690 percent in the decade to 1986, taking the capitalization to a figure of $1.5 billion (which cast the original decision to go public for a tenth of that in a distinctly unfavorable light), but the appreciation was due in large measure to precrash hopes of a bid for the family company, S. Pearson.

One of the hired hands remarked of this phenomenon, "The Stock Exchange thought we were dead. But we're not. We're only moribund." In that situation, a business in which the family now held only a minority stake had become a fair mark for sharper operators who reckoned that the whole was worth less than its parts. That is the common fate of multimerger companies, but one that the Cowdrays would have avoided had they stayed private (although the wealth would, of course, have remained only latent unless the family, like the Flicks, had been prepared to sell).

The men who hold the sovereign advantage of personal wealth hate to sell, as a rule. They are acquisitive, and the act of acquisition, like libido in the highly sexed, lasts a lifetime. But, just as they are free to let a valuable investment accumulate more wealth in its own weird way, so they are at liberty to sell without exposing themselves to critics as incompetents, either for buying the thing in the first place or for selling it. In big corporations, disinvestment is usually the pleasurable job left to the next incumbent—pleasurable because the very deed proves him deft and his predecessor dull.

But even the most dexterous accumulator buys the occasional lemon, if only because what makes excellent sense for a free-lance financier may fit uneasily into a corporate blancmange mold; and great free-lance fortunes, if they don't dissipate, mostly become corporate one day. Norton Simon, in the process of extending his tomato-based empire, picked up not only extra tidbits in food but also printing operations, trade books, magazines, and Talent Associates, the film and TV company, all of which his managerial successor refused to have in the shop. (Typically enough, the successor then committed the same folly in his turn. The path to the company's own takeover was paved by the acquisition of too many businesses that made too little money.)

Individual tycoons neither have nor need the professional manager's tidiness. The lucrative lessons of tycoon mergers should not be lost on the professionals (although they usually are). Never buy dear. Manage what you do buy according to its internal logic, not yours. Don't try to manage the new crown jewel at all if some other custodian is already, by your standards, running it successfully. If the selling occasion arises—an offer you can't refuse in good financial conscience, a misfit, a need for resources elsewhere, plain and unadulterated boredom—sell without compunction.

The most unlikely of the conglomerates proved to be the biggest real winner partly because it followed the habits of its rich founder. No sane corporate planner would put his name to a scheme for combining sick textile companies with upholstery cushioning, radar antennas and electronics, all as the base for an "acquisition-of-the-month plan" designed to add forty companies in eight years. This incongruous outfit predictably ended up in a confusion of money spinners ranging from chain saws to upper-class stationery, from watch straps to power lawn mowers.

Yet, in fifteen years sales piled up from $244 million to $1.9 billion; and when Litton was showing a grisly loss and ITT a feeble gain of 1.58 percent, this company, Textron, was still boasting a ten-year total return to investors of an annual 9.84 percent. The founder, Royal Little, "didn't see how the textile business" (in which he had started in 1928) "could ever be good again in my lifetime." He did, however, see acutely how the intelligent use of tax losses for an acquisition program could create the good capitalist life all over again—provided he stuck to good capitalist rules.

Corporate conglomerates, alas, are built on the sands of time, which tends to carry them away. After Little's retirement, to make another fortune in leveraged buyouts, where he was still going strong in his nineties after sixty-seven years in business, Textron grew to $5 billion of sales at the decorous, middle-of-the-road pace of the typical conglomerate. But in other hands the rich-man philosophy has proved even more effective. According to an unidentified source quoted by *Forbes*, the Bass family "have replaced the Morgans and the Rockefellers as America's prime dynasty." Passing over the fact that the Morgans were never much shakes in the dynastic game, the four Bass brothers have taken their millions to billions by more and more worthy ways than just preying on the nerves of big corporate managers.

True, contributions such as Texaco's, which gave the Basses a $400 million profit on buying back their 9.7 percent holding, were gratefully received and used. But the brothers have also prospered by backing winners—"world-class players," in the language of their former aide-de-camp, Richard Rainwater. At one point, the Basses, according to *Business Week*, had over 100 partners striving to make world-class profits out of over 100 different businesses. One of the recipients of Bass investment told a typical tale of this kind of hands-on, hands-off investing: "The first time you meet the Basses, you have some trepidation about a hidden agenda. But there wasn't one. They were there if I needed help, but they never pushed me around."

Equally characteristic was the fact that Fort Worth's City Center (a Bass property) housed only four principals and "a handful of assistants" to oversee the 100. Royal Little would have approved of that. His moral principles included keeping the head office down to a small number of bodies in an unglamorous locale in Providence, Rhode Island; Providence is a long way from rivaling Wilmington, Delaware, let alone Park Avenue, New York, in sophistication. That, by no means incidentally, is another asset of the rich empire builder. His personal and corporate overhead are one and the same thing. While Howard Hughes must have paid a pretty dollar in private air transport and the hire of whole hotel floors, his costs didn't begin to match those of a truly ambitious multinational corporation. To get some idea, one scion of a dollar imperialist, Edgar Kaiser, had $14 million of his money saved in a single year by the head office economies implemented by a newcomer at Kaiser Aluminum, which gives an inkling of the appalling burden that bigger companies still must carry on their backs.

Then, Royal Little would never buy for Textron on less than a seven-year payback of its money, and would throw out with unsentimental dispatch any acquisition that sooner or later failed to come up to corporate snuff. This set of policies by no means implies disinterest in the subsidiaries, their well-being, and their wherewithal. What gives the individual investor and his imitators such abnormal financial potency is the combination of passionate interest in the balance sheet and the bottom line (which is where the earnings are kept) with lack of passionate involvement in the mechanics of each individual enterprise. The large, managed company cannot in the nature of bureaucratic life sustain this potent combination for as long as the individual or the individually dominated company.

Thus, Xerox paid a billion for Scientific Data Systems in 1969—a sum comparing well in real terms with the price paid for H. Ross Perot's EDS by General Motors fifteen years later. The SDS company has long since disappeared totally from sight, taking the billion and a bundle of accumulated losses with it. But founder Max Palevsky, once paid $100 a week as a computer designer, obtained $100 million from the sale, which only went to prove his point, made to *Forbes*: "I have this feel for technology and the market."

You could argue that Xerox, a maker of copying machines, had no business, and no feel for, venturing into computers. But IBM, a computer company, demonstrated much the same syndrome when it spent $1.6 billion on Rolm Corp., whose computerized telephone equipment seemed at least close kin. The purchase had only begun life in 1969, started up by four engineers from Stanford. In 1983 to 1984, riding the crest of the PBX boom in electronic office exchanges, this GPW (Silicon Valley slang for "great place to work") was earning $38 million on $660 million of sales. IBM already owned 15 percent of the company; now, urged on by M. Kenneth Oshman, the president, IBM bought the lot.

To quote *Fortune*: "The timing was great for Rolm shareholders, but not for IBM. Orders for PBXs had slowed dramatically, and the industry had become dangerously overcrowded." The timing was especially great for Oshman, who trousered $41 million for his shares. In this unpromising bind, IBM could fall back on the standard consolations: as a competitor noted, "Say Rolm lost $100 million last year. That comes to four days of profit for IBM. It's like the rounding error for their Rhode Island taxes." No doubt Xerox thought much the same about its losses on Palevsky's baby. So the corpocrats make rich men richer by paying overrich sums for the latter's assets, and then proceed to make their corporations poorer by the awful results.

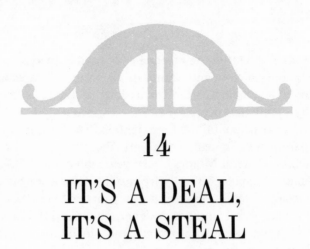

14

IT'S A DEAL,
IT'S A STEAL

"A year later I was offered the Cleaver Lease in Alamitos Heights by a man who had bought it less than a week earlier. I knew the property, and felt certain that there was oil on it." J. P. Getty is describing an incident from his early days as one of his lessons in *How to Be a Successful Executive*. " 'How much do you want for the lease?' I asked. 'I paid four thousand dollars—and I'm satisfied to double my money,' came the reply.

"I didn't argue—not for a single moment. 'You've just made a sale,' I grinned, taking out my personal checkbook and writing a check for $8,000." Then comes the punch line. "The four wells I drilled on the Cleaver Lease property brought in almost $800,000 in clear profit during the next twelve years." This little anecdote tells more about the road to business success than all the rest of Getty's writings put together.

The text reveals, first, knowledge: Getty was aware, not only of the property, but of its oil possibilities. Second is absence of risk, or at least insecurity—he "felt certain." Third is an absence of any awareness of a higher, or different, morality than commercial ethics, even if both Getty's account and his memory are accurate; his attitude would proba- bly have been just the same if the offer had come from his side. *Caveat vendor* is the principle, and if the seller doesn't look out, that's his lookout. Here Getty was showing, as his vendor was not, the single most important quality in getting rich: the ability to sense the difference between a buying price and a selling price.

The vendor had clearly recognized that the lease was cheap at $4,000. His error was to suppose that, because $8,000 would yield 100 percent, a large and satisfying profit, it must be large enough. The correct price—say, $100,000—would still have left Getty with the lion's share. In this way do the successful feed off the mistakes of weaker brethren. Getty could have grinned less and paid more; he could even have offered the vendor a share in the eventual proceeds, although to be truthful, this particular man probably couldn't: the chief characteris- tic of Getty's career has been a passionate drive for total control.

In his dogged pursuit of Tidewater Oil, carried on over several years, Getty never relaxed for a moment in this aim. But it too was a steal of a deal. The first tranche of shares in Tidewater was picked up in the Depression for a song. What cost Getty less than a million dollars became worth billions, which puts the profit on the Cleaver Lease, a mere hundredfold, in its proper perspective.

The Denver billionaire Marvin Davis followed in Getty's dealing footsteps and in his own father's; the latter, a Briton, had flourished reasonably well in the Manhattan women's wear trade before turning to oil postwar. The twenty-year-old Marvin also understandably liked the look of oil, and especially that of cheap leases in the Rockies. The area was then unfashionable, but Davis fashioned his holdings into a bonanza that, while not of Getty proportions, in 1981 took Davis a long way toward his first billion: Hiram Walker paid $630 million for half the Davis oil interests—before the bottom fell out of the market, natu- rally.

Making billions or millions from deals rests on two simple principles. Either you buy a property for much less than its value (the Getty gambit) or you sell a property for far more than it cost, which may also prove to be far more than it is worth (the Davis ploy). The second, obviously, may well be the result of the first. That initial achievement, buying cheap, doesn't necessarily mean paying low. Another Denver tycoon who came into oil through his father, Philip Anschutz, made an equally well timed partial exit in the early 1980s, selling half the fabulous Anschutz Ranch East in Wyoming to Mobil. The price was half a billion, exactly what Anschutz paid for the Rio Grande Railroad two years later. Even at that exalted price, he told *Forbes*, "It was a steal."

The most significant variable in dealing and stealing is time. The quicker the profit is taken, the greater the rate of return—other things, such as the size of the profit, being equal. Getty's vendor, with his 100 percent in seven days, made an annualized return of 5,200 percent. He would without question have preferred the average return of 1,666 percent that Getty made over each of the next dozen years. Yet speed is still of the essence: the vendor had the right idea but the wrong price.

That wasn't true of the profit made by Australian yachtsman Alan Bond on selling a British cinema chain to Israelis Yoram Globus and Menahem Golan of the Cannon Group. The price was certainly meaningful, at $265 million; it left the debt-laden pair scrabbling to find the second $75 million installment. But the price acquired far greater significance from the fact that Bond sold a matter of weeks after lifting the cinemas for $190 million from the conglomerate Thorn-EMI (whose directors were forced into some hasty and unconvincing explanations of just how a property could have risen in value at such wonderful speed).

He who deals with a master of the difference between selling and buying prices usually does end up, like those discomfited directors, by giving him a present. Sometimes the whole business is a gift. That is one interpretation of the deal by which the visionary Canadian Roy Thomson gained control of his English papers, embarking on a road that led to a peerage, hobnobbing with monarchs and presidents of the Presidium, and ownership of the ultimate in media prestige, the *Times*. (That lost him money heavily, but that's the kind of expensive hobby to which a formerly shrewd millionaire is entitled in his seventies.)

In the original deal, the Kemsley family was ready to sell the *Sunday Times* and a powerful chain of provincial papers. Thomson had what he famously described as "a license to print money"—the television franchise in Scotland. His problem was that it didn't print enough cash to purchase the Kemsley control, even at a substantially reduced, bargained-down price. Funnily enough, Kemsley would have faced no problem in buying Thomson. This paradox became the basis of a most ingenious settlement, worked out by Thomson's merchant bankers. In this deal, Kemsley bought Thomson out of Scottish TV for shares; the Canadian was then able to exploit his newly acquired position in Kemsley to complete the transaction, thus regaining the Scottish golden goose. The Kemsleys went comfortably off to green pastures, having, in effect, financed their own takeover.

This is the essence of a good dealer's perfect deal. It should be self-liquidating: in other words, having paid for the property, you should still be richer by at least its full value. There may never be a more perfect, if imperfectly moral, example than John Werner Kluge's ability to repay the $1.2 billion in junk funds required for control of Metromedia and still have billions of assets left at his disposal—and for disposal. Sometimes, the same trick can be achieved without saying good-bye to any of the assets—for instance, when the sitting owners have failed to exploit the borrowing power of the real estate. The pioneers of the technique known as "sale and leaseback" cleared easy millions, selling the undervalued properties they acquired to financial institutions and then renting them back to carry on trading.

Not only do companies sit on unexploited properties, some even have millions sitting equally idly in the bank, waiting for the first predator able to read a balance sheet. Unexploited or underexploited assets are the meat and drink of the corporate raider. The millions prised loose (*liberated* was the elegant euphemism of one generation of raiders) not only pay for the purchase itself, they provide the where-withal to finance a fresh upsurge of assets.

This is how the two most proficient raiders of American assets, Sir Gordon White and Lord Hanson, built a $3,000 nest egg into the $1.3 billion assets of Hanson Industries North American in just thirteen years. To arrive at this destination (and at least a $30 million fortune of his own), the dashing White sharpened his techniques and his teeth on scores of lesser deals. One of his opponents, John B. Fuqua, was fully aware of the part he was playing in White's education. Convinced that he had the better of the Englishman, he told him, "That's what you get for trying to play in the big leagues." By 1986 White had learned his lessons well enough to command double Fuqua Industries' sales—and three times its profits—thanks to self-financing and big-league coups such as the contested takeovers of U.S. Industries and SCM.

All such deals are founded on the ancient tradition exemplified by Getty's $8,000 transaction. Money measures the difference in knowledge between the weak and the strong. A large part of the multidollar fortune amassed by the far right Texas oilman H. L. Hunt measures the distance between his mind and that of C. M. (Dad) Joiner, discoverer of the East Texas oil field that Hunt exploited, who died broke. Alfred Irénée du Pont's fortune measured his ability to see, first, that in 1902 the company was worth far more than the $15.36 million for which his relatives were willing to sell, and second, that they wouldn't be so disobliging as to demand any cash—he paid them $12 million of notes plus shares in the new company.

Any of the new brigade of corporate raiders would have been proud of Alfred I's achievement. Those who deal with hardened, hard-nosed professional deal makers of this variety are well advised to remember the sage Ogden Nash verse: "He who tangles with the cobra is soon a sadder he—and soberer." Another yachtsman, Ted Turner, the cable news king, may not have exuded sadness or sobriety after tangling with the sixty-nine-year-old Kirk Kerkorian; he had every reason, though, to regret and repent the encounter.

First, Kerkorian exacted an enormous price ($1.6 billion) for MGM, part of the MGM/UA entertainment colossus, which had been valued by the stock market, all up, at $826 million only a few weeks earlier. Second, as Turner wriggled on the spit through shortage of cash, Kerkorian agreed to take $477 million of the price in securities instead of cash, making sure that the securities imposed onerous conditions on the other man. Turner was forced, as the screw turned, to give up 35 percent of his company and get the offending securities off his bending back. The 35 percent changed hands for a $550 million price tag. But Kerkorian ended up with everything he had previously owned, plus at least $308 million profit, less an MGM whose performance had meanwhile deteriorated, plus a heavy foothold in Turner's company.

Hollywood in its years of decline has been the happiest of hunting grounds for predatory tycoons—none to greater effect than the previously mentioned Marvin Davis, the prodigious oil wildcatter who, after halving his oil investments in 1981, the next year realized his investment in four Denver office towers for $550 million. That deal, like the oil sale, cleverly preceded nasty, long-lived collapses in the market.

The cobra next struck at Twentieth Century–Fox, working in partnership with Marc Rich, the commodities trader who was understandably persuaded to leave the United States at high speed by sixty-five counts of tax evasion, fraud, and criminality. The Rich-Davis deal was consummated in two hugely expensive gulps by Rupert Murdoch in 1985; Davis emerged with $350 million of profit as well as some real estate—not a bad return for four years as a Hollywood tycoon.

Since Murdoch had himself risen to great fortune and power by deal after deal, the supposition has to be that both cobras knew what they were doing. Murdoch, after all, is the man who took a sick-unto-death paper off the hands of its foolish owners, reduced it in size to tabloid and in tone to what the British call "bums and tits," wrung better terms from the unions than any predecessor—and so found the launching pad for his world ambitions in the resulting profits of *The Sun*. He then proceeded to buy the *Times* and *Sunday Times* off the notably less proficient heirs to Roy Thomson for a price significantly less than the future value of the *Times* holdings in Reuters (his purchase cost £15 million, but was certainly worth half a billion by 1987).

Had Davis charged too little for Fox? Or had Murdoch paid too much? Curiously enough, both apparently irreconcilable positions could be correct. The essence of a mutually satisfactory deal is that the property is worth more in the purchaser's hands than in the vendor's. Murdoch wanted Fox as the cornerstone of his ambition to create a fourth TV network. Davis wanted $350 million of profit. The next year he, too, was network-hungry; Davis preferred to do it the easy way, bidding for CBS, but failing to bear off the booty. Murdoch, in contrast, turns his deals into bargains by working hard and long—often amazingly long—to develop the potential.

The apotheosis of his Thomson purchase came in 1986—five years later. Over those years, Murdoch developed a new printing site in the deserted docklands of London, confidently planning toward the day when, by hook or by crook, he could print his papers there with new, cheap technology. When the moment came, Murdoch struck with devastating speed. A strike by his print workers was the signal for a military-style, overnight move to Wapping: the cost savings were $100 million a year. Shares in Murdoch's master company quadrupled; his own 49 percent interest added $2 billion of value in twelve months (before retreating by $1.5 billion in the crash of 1987).

Whether Murdoch worked out the sums is doubtful. As one admirer says, "Most of us, if we want to cross a river, build a bridge first. Rupert crosses first and then worries about how to build the bridge." The epigram wittily divides the two major classes of dealers: those who look for financial opportunity, and those who look only for opportunity. Murdoch cannot turn down a media buy, whether it's the *South China Morning Post* or Fox. The price is irrelevant: the value that can be created from the opportunity is the only relevance.

Mostly the Murdoch magic works (Thomson); sometimes it doesn't (U.S. newspapers, such as the *New York Post*). So long as the gains outweigh the losses, the bridges go on being built. It doesn't follow, however, that the cautious approach yields lower gains. Few dealers are more cautious than the Pritzkers of Chicago: "The real risk," Jay Pritzker told *Forbes*, "is the embarrassment of a failure." The family can't have been the least embarrassed by the purchase of one asset in Murdoch's media stamping ground—*McCall's* magazine.

191

Bought from Norton Simon in 1973 for $8 million, it was sold thirteen years later for $300 million.

Like Getty's Cleaver Lease, and maybe Anschutz's Rio Grande Railroad, *McCall's* was a bargain. To repeat, that isn't the same as being cheap. Relative cheapness is the criterion—relative, that is, to value. The concept is easiest to understand, and to view in action, when a public company is involved. The most successful school of investors, the followers of Ben Graham, base their approach on the belief that the stock market from time to time grossly undervalues an equity—so grossly that the undervaluation can be proved.

In two celebrated examples, from the days before he made a billion dollars by applying the same technique to Berkshire Hathaway, the demon investor Warren Buffett spotted that Walt Disney was being valued in the market at less than the worth of its feature-length cartoons (*Dumbo*, *Bambi*, and so on), and that American Express in the wake of its salad oil disasters (see Chapter 16) had sunk to less than the value of its beautiful business in traveler's checks (the beauty lying in the fact that the travelers pay Amex for the privilege of giving it free use of their money).

The undervaluation of Disney has been a recurrent theme: Saul Steinberg, two arbitrageurs (Irwin Jacobs and Ivan Boesky), and above all the Basses have drunk deep at the Disney well. Guided to the deal by Richard Rainwater (another devout Grahamite), the Bass family exchanged a Florida real estate company for Disney shares worth $200 million; that brought the first vast Bass profit—more than doubling their money. Next, $330 million bought out the arbs. At the end of 1986, the Bass investors had tripled their money for an $850 million gain—and done so in one of America's most conspicuous companies, proprietor of the world's all-time favorite film stars.

Disney, what's more, was a failing company, if that, not a failed one. Even these can be ripe fruit for the plucking. One Sanford C. Sigoloff built his reputation and fortune on lost causes. "There's a certain creativity in taking something debilitated and increasing its value," he told *Fortune*. Sigoloff climbed on board the sunken Wickes companies immediately after the business had achieved the second-largest American bankruptcy. Within three years, Wickes was solvent and so (very much so) was Sigoloff (known as "Ming the Merciless"—and that is to his friends); the Wickes return to investors in 1985 alone was 65 percent.

Such deals are of the same order as the It-Can't-Get-Any-Worse techniques described in Chapter 12. By combining those with the Company-Way method (Chapter 11), Michael Dingman between May and December of 1986 created a personal stake worth $35 million. The recipe was simple: first, find a mess of companies losing $24.7 million on $3.3 billion in sales; second, make the largest initial public offering in stock-exchange history ($1.2 billion); third, arrange for an executive stock purchase program to provide you with most of your 1.5 million shares; fourth, of course, you have to make the company work. Dingman had done it before—which is why investors were so eager to back the Henley Group companies he spun off from Allied-Signal. But if a business goes bankrupt, or loses money for years, there's usually a good reason, and the explanation may be within that discarded pile of old assets in the bargain basement. The genius of the bargain hunter is to know where the pile of old assets contains gold—what can be successfully mined, either by resale or by the standard technique of slashing costs by firing and forcing; Carl Icahn cut some $400 million out of TWA's bills in turning the airline from $258 million of half-year loss to a $65.2 million profit in the third quarter of 1986. Without that, the raider's $300 million investment in TWA would have ruined him.

Given that the difference between buying and selling levels is critical, how does the dealer work out, for a start, that the price is right? In many cases, perhaps most, he doesn't. The natural man has a feeling in his bones—the Germans locate it in the tips of the fingers and call it *Fingerspitzengefühl*. Just as a knowledgeable musician can recognize an entire symphony from a few stray chords, or a textile expert can identify a cloth by rubbing it between those *Fingerspitzen*, so can a true dealer judge value instinctively from the smell of a proposition.

The dealing instinct was about the only common factor deployed by the real estate millionaires (108 men and two women, according to a careful business historian) created in Britain between 1945 and 1965. By all odds the shrewdest deal in which they collectively engaged was to offload shares in their companies on the public. Starting in 1958 at a value of $150 million, property shares on the London stock market had blossomed into $1.2 billion only four years later as the boys (plus the odd girl) took their top slices out of the action.

The company with which Jack Cotton, co-author of the Pan Am Building and a cheerful, flamboyant bottle-lover who worked in erratic fashion from a Dorchester Hotel suite, started on his way was called Mansion House Chambers. An investment in this receptacle firm, renamed City Centre Properties, multiplied two hundred–fold in only a few years. As Cotton's business methods grew as flamboyant as his manners, his dealing expertise flagged. He made questionable deals for questionable, self-aggrandizing reasons, including the Pan Am Building and the purchase of the real estate interests of a well-known cobra, Sir Charles Clore. The latter, at least, had no doubt where the advantage lay. The delicate question of Clore's corporate title was worrying Cotton and delaying the deal; Clore remarked to the associate who bore these tidings, "Douglas, for seventy shillings, I'll be the office boy," according to writer Oliver Marriott. There spoke a true dealer.

When the Hotel Corporation of America was a willing seller of the Carlton Tower in Knightsbridge (then lumbered with the appalling group name of Sonesta Tower) Sir Charles Forte was willing, nay eager, to buy, but he found his colleagues reluctant. Forte, who had progressed from milk bars to the George V in Paris by watertight deals, simply reckoned that £4 million had to be cheap for an established hotel in a prime site. The managers who opposed the deal were trained in economic and financial analysis. To them, the Americans' price worked out at too much per room, the industry's standard measure; on that irrelevance, the deal was lost to a sharper bunch of traders. In 1981 Hyatt, the Pritzker hotel empire, paid £4 million for the management contract alone; the building had earlier fetched £14 million.

It often doesn't pay to concentrate on the narrower aspects of a deal. When that educational cobra J. B. Fuqua went into television in Augusta, Georgia, his minority partners were the far-richer Martin family. The Martins didn't like the lack of cash dividends, even though they loved the profits, so in 1957 they agreed to take $350,000 for their $130,000 investment of a few years back. Had they not sold, the Martin stake would have had a $10 million paper value in the early 1970s. In hindsight, they had misjudged their partner's potential.

The tips of fingers, or pure hunches, are invaluable. But they need to be supplemented by sound factual assessment—and that can only have one basis: perusal and payback. The perusal is needed to ensure that what you think you are buying is actually there. You can't afford, like one young financier who succumbed to the lure of the dollar, to buy four U.S. furniture plants without visiting a single one. The accounts, the stocks, the snags, all need perusing with a suspicious mind. Remember that, whenever you buy, someone else is selling.

The payback, the simplest financial measure of them all, is your golden guideline. Joseph F. Kennedy, one of the most assiduous dealers ever self-made, was reputed never to enter any transaction if he couldn't see his money coming back home in eighteen months. That represents a 50 percent annual return on capital, the kind of yield big company managers don't even dream of. In a deal, however, it's a perfectly realistic objective: after all, you are never, as purchaser, compelled to complete a deal—the process is entirely optional, and it's nobody's fault but yours if you don't settle at the right price.

A high yield in a continuing business means that once your money has come back you have a valuable stream of free-and-clear income remaining, and it also means that the capital can be turned over at a brisk pace. The faster capital moves, the better; it enables the dealer to make more deals, which (barring accidents) means more profit, which means more deals still. Again, the buying price has to be right. That has nothing to do with the going quotation. If the whole market is grossly overpriced, picking up a deal at 10 percent below the market carries no compensations. Had a bright real estate speculator picked up a Manhattan cooperative at 10 percent below going prices at the creamy top of the market, he would still have been weeping his heart out in 1972, when going prices had dropped by 50 percent. Had he *bought* in 1972, though, he would have been rejoicing in his wealth (as did many New Yorkers) in the mid-1980s.

Those who hung on during the great Manhattan real estate recession likewise have no cause for complaint—none less than Sol Goldman. Two-fifths of the holdings of this former grocer vanished in the storm; among the dear departed assets was the Chrysler Building. In 1977, after the death of his partner, Goldman did a deal with the Di Lorenzo heirs: they divided the properties on the toss of a coin. It was a quarter: Goldman is now worth $750 million, according to *Forbes*. The twenty-five cents did less well for the Di Lorenzos—but their wealth still exceeds half a billion. Goldman has to a marked degree the salient characteristic of many dealers—the conviction that, whatever the price they receive, it isn't enough: "Every time I sell," he says, "I'm sorry."

When there's no public market in the assets concerned, there is bound to be a large element of doubt. Very probably the greatest steals have been purchases of private companies. It's peculiarly difficult to value the latter—even for the owners themselves. Gertrude Ramsay Crain is the matriarch of Crain Communications, founded by her husband in the middle of World War I. *Forbes* estimates the worth of her company, which includes the superprofitable *Advertising Age*, at $200 million. Her son Rance commented: "I really doubt we'd get that much for it, but what do we know?" Them would be fighting words to John R. Simplot, whose fortune is based on 700 million pounds of potatoes sold for French fries to McDonald's and other fast-food joints. *Forbes* also puts the value of his business at $200 million. But Simplot "wouldn't sell for that, that's for sure."

Until the sale is made, of course, Rance Crain is right: the value is putative. Thus, nobody knew that Theodore Cross's purchase of *Investment Dealer's Digest* was a steal at $800,000: on $1 million of turnover, it was losing $150,000. Four years later, however, everybody knew *IDD*'s worth when Cross sold the business for $40 million—a 5,000 percent profit. The difference between the two numbers mostly represents Cross's exploitation of *IDD*'s files on all U.S. security offerings since 1934. Cross certainly got a high price. But was it right? A selling price obviously becomes righter if raised by successful bargaining. But the true dealer won't necessarily haggle.

Getty, when offered an $800,000 potential for $8,000, didn't, according to his account, try to press the vendor down to $7,000, even though $1,000 meant more to Getty than to most. In contrast, one wheeler-dealer still has cause to rue the day when, with terms agreed, he sat down at the conference table to sign the contract for delivery of a whole, beautiful chain of shops. As he raised his pen to sign, he suggested that, as a gesture of goodwill, the price should be reduced by $15,000. His gentlemanly counterpart screwed up his gold fountain pen, gathered his colleagues, and departed for the nearest competitor.

Love of bargaining should never be subordinated to the object of the exercise, which is to make a rich deal. S. N. Behrman told a cautionary tale about one of Duveen's customers, an American multimillionaire, who grew fascinated by the permutations and combinations possible on a load of rugs carried by one of the itinerant Arab peddlers who adorn the Mediterranean spas. After a glorious passage of "How much for these two?" "How much if I also take this?" "What if I don't have the first one?" the disgusted peddler thrust the whole pile into his customer's lap. Buying something you don't want cheaply is almost as bad as buying something you want too expensively.

There's another problem with objects for which the would-be purchaser lusts: their availability. If the owner won't sell, it is axiomatic that nobody else can buy. Lord Thomson, after his Kemsley triumph, was once asked by another company chairman, bred in an older school, how one went about the delicate business of finding out if a property is for sale. The Canadian replied simply, "I ask." It's like the old legend of the direct approach to women: you get a lot of refusals but a surprising amount of sex. By him that seeks, much will often be found.

The great financier William C. Durant, creator of General Motors, once got Henry Ford I to the point of parting with his company for $8 million; the prospect literally gave Ford so bad a stomachache that he writhed on the floor and no deal resulted. But Henry I, of course, was no dealer. He belonged to that class of builders who, if not protected by dyspepsia, native caution, or good advisers, fall into the hands of men with a better eye for the main chance and who appreciate the beautiful finality of a signature on a contract.

There are two classes of dealer, however: those who believe that the other man should always be equally happy when the chips are safely gathered in; and those who argue that, if the other man allows you to take his business, house, wife, and Lincoln for a bag of old peanuts, that's his problem. The first school always leaves something for the other man, the second school is only interested in maximizing the something that the dealer gets for nothing.

If the Metropolitan Museum is willing to de-accession a Rousseau and a Van Gogh that the Marlborough Gallery can promptly sell for a quick double million of profit, one to an art-struck Japanese, the other to a European collection, is it up to the gallery to point out this fact? Those who worry about such problems; those who agonize, on spotting a highly colored harbor scene in a junk shop for $50, about whether to tell the proprietor that it is a Derain that may be worth $3 million; those, alas, may be numbered among the angels in heaven, but they are most unlikely to join the millionaires in the Cloud Club.

This locale, atop the Chrysler building, was where the president of Vick's Vaporub gave a class that included William S. Whyte a lesson in the difference between commerce and ethics. As Whyte described it in *The Organization Man*, the Vick's king asked what the class would do if a long-time supplier, entirely dependent on the company's business, had his price undercut by a new competitor. Did you give him a chance to meet the new price, or what?

The president, in fact, swept aside all such discussion. Either you were a businessman or you weren't, and if you were, there was only one possible course of action: you axed the old supplier and took on the new. Much the same considerations apply to a deal. If the businessman takes his eye off the deal to consider higher things, such as corporate strategy or the effects on the other guy, he won't do as well as the ruthless opportunist to whom weakness equates with loss of money and who can abide neither.

It's this that gives the lone eagle his advantage over the assembled mass of corporate men. His motivation also gains from the fact that the latter can hide their mistakes inside billions or millions of other people's assets, while he must personally and painfully feel the pinch. The lonest eagle in legend or fact, Howard Hughes, demonstrated his skill in May 1966, when he offloaded all his stock in Trans World Airlines, representing three-quarters of the equity, for $546 million, then the largest check ever made out for an individual's sole benefit. Some of the Wall Streeters who bought the Hughes shares were presumably among those who flocked to buy his oil-drilling bit company in December 1972 for $150 million; any of them who still held their former Hughes TWA stock at that date had lost nearly half their money—it stood at $47, against $82 at sale time.

Even when Carl Icahn was trying to buy all the TWA equity, two whole inflationary decades later, the bill was only $770 million—a mere $42 million more than at the time of the Hughes sell-off. Investors in the Hughes oil-drilling business fared no better. In the decade from 1975 to 1985, their total return was a paltry 0.45 percent annually. Whether Hughes foresaw the collapse of the bull market, or that of the transatlantic airfare structure, or sensed that the new-broom management put into TWA by the banks (and busily suing Hughes) had run out of dust, or saw in some crystal ball the boom and slump in oil that lay far ahead, nobody will ever know. Probably, it was a case of *Fingerspitzengefühl*—and even Hughes's fingertips ran out of feel at times. He made a monstrous miscalculation by putting his TWA winnings into Las Vegas, and he also managed, in one deal, to outsmart himself. This was when Hughes, in what looked like a clever tax dodge, put the stock of Hughes Aircraft, then a small company whose title exactly described it, into his own medical foundation. It turned into one of the hotter electronics properties on the West Coast—and was eventually purchased by General Motors for $2.6 billion; Howard Hughes's last steal, and a posthumous one.

But the beauty of deals is the way they change their complexion and their truth. The story goes that long after Andrew Carnegie sold J. P. Morgan his steel interests for $300 million, enough to make all his partners millionaires as well, the two titans met, walking in opposite directions on the promenade deck of an Atlantic liner. "I have been thinking," said Carnegie, "that I should have asked you for $500 million." "I would have paid it," replied Morgan—and passed on down the deck.

15

INSIDE EVERY FAT
COMPANY

The largest source of wealth, the Eldorado, for small men with big ideas is the large corporation. It has many ways to enrich the individual at the corporate cost. It can lapse into a slumber so profound that it presents the newcomer with enough of its market to enrich him enormously (as IBM did with Steve Jobs of Apple). It can spur people forth to turn their own thing into a thorn in the corporate flesh (as IBM did with several of Compaq's shock troops).

It can make deals that self-evidently benefit the smaller partner far more than the large (as IBM did with Robert Noyce of Intel). If all else fails, the fat company can pay the entrepreneur a fat fortune for his business (as IBM did with Rolm and Ken Oshman). This catalogue of fat gifts sounds like an indictment of IBM. But the charge is universal. This is an era when big companies have been exposed—above all, by the leveraged buyout, which is a potent device for transferring assets from fat hands to lean—as indifferent guardians of their entrepreneurial assets (including people).

Outside every fat company there's been a lean raider screaming to get in; and inside every fat company there is a lean entrepreneur screaming to get out. Some of them make their escape, armed with all the experience, contacts, and other equipment a fat company can provide, but free of the main impediment to that company's freedom of movement, which is its lard. The large, unwilling parent may be efficient, like IBM, or merely prolific in hiring, equipping, and losing managers, like Litton Industries in its heyday as a star conglomerate. Whatever the parent's powers, however, baby often outdoes big daddy when it comes to the main point, which is the creation of personal wealth.

No firm has spawned as many profitable breakaways as IBM: it is perhaps the only company that has accidentally created so much of its own competition. That is the inevitable price of being a rich quasi monopoly in a hotly attractive market: anybody who has worked for you literally has a price on his head. Directly or indirectly, IBM has given impetus to the careers of all its successful rivals; it paid An Wang $400,000 for his invention of a magnetic core memory, thus providing ample seed money for Wang Laboratories and a one-time $500 million fortune; even the iconoclastic Ken Olsen of Digital Equipment got the idea that he could beat IBM at its own game during a thirteen-month stint attached to the giant's Poughkeepsie plant. None of the upstarts, true, has come near the awe-inspiring scale of IBM (with over seven times Olsen's sales in 1986). But all have generated wealth surpassing that of the IBM Watson clan.

Since IBM's Tom Watson, Sr., was himself a breakaway from National Cash Register (forced out by a megalomaniac master), there may be rough justice here. All the upstarts, from Max Palevsky of Scientific Data Systems and Ken Norris of Control Data Corporation to Olsen, Gene Amdahl, Steve Jobs of Apple, and Rod Canion of Compaq, have made their marks and their millions by competing in areas where the corporate father of all computer men, for all his big talk, has proved surprisingly ineffective: in very large, complex computers at one end of the scale and small personal ones at the other, with Olsen's minis somewhere not quite in-between.

Even when IBM launched brilliantly successful counterattacks, as in PCs, it only opened the door to new lean men. The IBM product could never have soared past Apple, taking 41 percent of the U.S. market in only four years, if it hadn't become the industry standard. Anybody could write a program for its PC, anybody could add on hardware—and anybody, it turned out, could build a clone. Within a year, the cheaper or better clones had devoured a quarter of IBM's market. Over in Britain, one of the feeders from the rich man's table was a former aerial salesman named Alan Sugar. When his Amstrad company added a clone to its dirt-cheap word processor, its equity value soared to $1.5 billion—of which Sugar owned a sweet half, even after the crash, the value easily topped $1 billion.

Nor was it only making computers that extracted riches from IBM's groaning table. There, fighting equally hard for the meats, were the leanest and hungriest of the salesmen on whom the great company has always depended for its penetration, the assault troops whose dominance largely explained the invincible resistance of IBM to its fat-company foes. The most energetic soldiers in these ranks also spotted chinks in IBM's armor—such as the fact that it overcharged on rentals, if a less conservative view of depreciation was taken, or that the company's customers, while happy to shower millions on the leasing, care, and maintenance of the computer and its servants, had only half an idea of how to use either.

The first vision gave birth to the leasing game, which, for its butterfly time in the sun, spread fortunes like wings and with no more difficulty. The second vision produced the computer service concept, which, while it needed harder work (unlike leasing, which involved no work at all), proved longer lasting in the hands of clever men.

The cleverness of one former salesman, H. Ross Perot, deserves its legend. The computer company thought highly of Perot, as well it might: as the ace of the Texas territory, Perot was chalking up terrific sales for IBM and terrifying amounts of commission for himself—that is, they terrified the bureaucrats at the head office, who couldn't bear the idea of a salesman earning more than the chairman.

The head office, reacting in the way of all fat companies since organizational time began, slammed a ceiling on commissions: nobody could earn more than $250,000 of commission in a year. So Perot walked out onto the streets of Dallas, made his maximum in a couple of weeks—and quit. He put a tiny fraction of his quarter million into Electronic Data Systems, which, by making computers actually work for the people to whom Perot had sold them, enabled him to demonstrate the fat-company syndrome thrice: once, by the billionaire paper fortune he created by the success of his breakaway idea—which his IBM boss, naturally, had turned down; twice, when selling for a real billion to the fattest company of them all, General Motors; and thrice, by so irritating the fat company with his thin-man criticisms that it gave him three-quarters of a billion in cash to be gone—and be quiet.

Attacking the adipose by word and deed has been turned into a career by T. Boone Pickens. His autobiography, *Boone*, takes swing after swing at large corporation CEOs and "the hunting and fishing lodges, the corporate jets, and the yachts, all bought for their exclusive use but paid for by the shareholders." But if it hadn't been so easy to "outthink, outwork, and outfox the big boys," Pickens could never have managed impudent coups such as the $218 million aftertax profit he made when his target, Gulf Oil, merged with Socal in self-defense, or the $120 million profit that flowed from the Phillips and Unocal raids.

The pounce of the corporate raider, armed with his junk bonds and his foxy wit, is easier to envy than to admire. The true leveraged buyout, on the other hand, is wholly admirable. Richard Wesley Snyder, for excellent example, was running Singer's climate-control division in 1982 when the not only fat but often fat-headed corporation sold it to him for $27.5 million. The leverage was colossal: $300,000 of cash changed hands for a business that an independent appraiser promptly valued at $83 million. That was as nothing compared to the worth achieved after four acquisitions and three years of booming sales. *Forbes* in 1986 estimated the well-leveraged Snyder's fortune at over $300 million.

Big corporations are just like big governments in this penchant for accidentally scattering largesse about them. They contrive to share their fat in all manner of ways. Not only do they lend money at low interest, sometimes for nothing at all. Not only do they go into partnership with lean men on terms that give the latter all the butter (if any). Not only do they buy out lean men at gross prices. They also hold up umbrellas that keep off the rain while the leanies, dry and comfortable, dig their gold mines underneath. This is because the fat company, like any bureaucracy, likes to do things in the way in which it has always done them. It objects to changing its fixed practices or its fixed ideas—and if a leanie spots that the rigidity has provided an opportunity to make a killing, the fatty takes an unconscionably long, bureaucratic time about recognizing that it is being taken for a Chicago-style ride.

Saul Steinberg's fat-company formula is a textbook model. He noted that IBM depreciated its computers over a period of between four and five years. The boy wonder observed in his undergraduate thesis at the Wharton Business School that this exceedingly conservative approach made it cheaper to buy an IBM computer than to rent one. If the buyer then took a more-realistic eight- to ten-year depreciation, he could undercut IBM's own leasing terms by 10 percent to 20 percent, while relying on the obliging fat company to go on servicing and supporting the machine free of charge.

If, moreover, this shrewd undercutter borrowed the purchase price of the computer, he had the greatest prize of all: instant money. A million-dollar computer, financed almost entirely by a bank loan, would rent for $225,000, say, against $251,000 from IBM (of which some $200,000 would have been IBM's depreciation). After paying his lower depreciation and his interest charges, the Steinberg-type wizard ended up with $64,000 net profit. Not only would this return his entire equity investment in a year but the stock market was then prepared to value leasing companies at up to thirty-five times earnings.

Now, thirty-five times $64,000 equals $2.2 million. Thus, if the formula worked out perfectly, as it sometimes did, the leasing genius made a clear, untrammeled million the minute the lease was signed. The whistle was eventually blown on leasing by the fat computer companies, which finally got wise to the fortunes being made on their backs and revised their leasing terms. They screwed the leasers so painfully that in 1969 Leasco gave up the activity that had taken Steinberg most of the distance from a borrowed $25,000 and a loft in Brooklyn. A year before that traumatic event, however, Steinberg had ensured Leasco's and his own financial survival by buying an insurance company. In exchange for some paper, Steinberg bought $550 million of real-life assets in the Reliance Insurance Company, dropped the Leasco name in Reliance's favor, and lived, if not happily, at least richly ever after.

Computers, because of the rapid growth of the market in all directions and because the market was dominated by one superlarge firm, with only other fatties competing, was the ideal postwar setup for little outsiders, or for insiders moving outside. But the governing factors are identical in less highly charged and high-flown situations.

These dominants are the sheer size and strength of the giant, which encourage it to believe that small intruders or extruders can be ignored, and that, in any event, the latter are highly unlikely to spot or snatch any opportunity that the big managers have missed, and that, in the final sweet analysis, they can always crush the attacker, or buy him (a device that, once the small company is in the fat one's embrace, often has the same effect as crushing).

Conceit, apathy, and ignorance are not the best ingredients of a commercial brew. The United Fruit octopus, for instance, although its bananalike tentacles reached to every corner of the globe, refused, in its lordly and ignorant way, to believe that bananas could be grown in the Windward Islands. Two brothers named Geest, who knew nothing much about bananas but had deep lore about growing, acquired from early days in the Dutch bulb fields, saw no objection to the islands, duly planted their bananas, and reaped a harvest that gave them half the British market, raising the profits of their entirely private operation to

$3 million a year—at which level the family business was worth a minimum of $75 million. By 1987, the Geests had gone public with a company that the stock market valued at $240 million.

Such companies are the natural fodder, however, for later purchase by some larger entity, operating on the thesis "If you can't beat 'em, buy 'em." The annals of the Common Millionaire are littered with the countless cases where manna has fallen on the entrepreneur from the big-time corporate heavens. Allen Eugene Paulson advanced from self-made thirteen-year-old, via a thirty-cents-an-hour mechanic's job for TWA, to producer of his own successful oil valve—and then to purchaser of Gulfstream Aircraft in 1978. He paid $52 million. Seven years later, Chrysler paid $640 million for the company. Even after using $150 million to clear the debt from his uninspired foray into Wheeling Steel, Paulson had some $300 million, according to *Forbes*— not to mention nine houses and 300 horses, one for every million bucks.

Lately, the pace of fat-company buys has quickened (as has the disposal rate of previous purchases whose charms have withered away). One reason is the restructuring vogue, which has led managements to sell businesses that no longer fit into a sensible corporate strategy—or never did. In a decade, for instance, Guinness had bought 250 firms: one rented yachts, another sold a drug made from snake venom, none was in its core business of beer. The new regime sold off 150 of these treasures in two years—many, no doubt, for a cantata, if not a song.

The study *Fortune* made in April 1987 of seven restructured companies is a litany of buys sold, sales bought (and fat overheads slashed). Ford bought the New Holland agricultural company that Sperry had once proudly purchased; the Ralston Purina pet food firm sold (no joke intended) "a bunch of doggy businesses we had to get rid of" and paid $475 million for Continental Baking, once one of Harold S. Geneen's prize purchases at ITT; Champion International, while buying St. Regis for $1.8 billion, made an exit from (among other unwanteds) envelopes, cardboard boxes, and brown paper packaging.

The latter went to a company called Stone, which promptly showed that, as usual, the larger company had been making a sow's ear out of a brown paper purse; its stock doubled in a year. Champion had sensibly kept a tenth of Stone's stock, which led the vendor's CEO to enthuse: "We've made more money than we ever made when we owned the business," glossing over the question of whose fault that might have been. Often the error is more in the original purchase than the subsequent management; often it's both. Amoco in 1979 paid $669 million for a mining company, Cyprus Minerals, and then proceeded to invest another billion in the buy.

The fat firm was only saved from a $675 million write-down (more than the original purchase price) by spinning off Cyprus to shareholders. It swiftly moved from losing $95 million to $32 million in profit—creating not a few stock-option millionaires en route. As *Fortune* observed, "Amoco executives knew little about mining." So what persuaded them to send $1.7 billion down the mine? To the innocent, it might seem axiomatic that a big company's bosses wouldn't go into an expensive enterprise without careful investigation, without ensuring that they have adequate control, either managerial or financial, and without knowing what they are doing. But Amoco was merely following in many fat footsteps.

When one major publishing corporation decided to back two software pioneers in that insidious computer game, it paid $900,000 for their nascent company and also accepted their dictum that, since publishers knew nothing about computers, they should have no votes on the board, where their ignorance might upset the experts.

At the end of the day, the publishers' losses had come to at least $4.5 million; ignorance is seldom bliss. Nor were they alone. A little later an investment bank led a group of institutions into backing the same entrepreneurial pair with $9 million cash—it wasn't supposed to be that much, but the two got through the original amount so fast that good money began to flow after the bad. Faced with entrepreneurs who use big numbers and make rich forecasts, even financiers, although supposedly able to do sums, lose their senses. Poor, simple managers, who can't add up at all, are utterly lost.

For instance, one modest entrepreneur had fallen into the majority control of a larger company by a series of accidents: the lean man retained an option to buy his big brother out, which proved, in these resolute hands, to be a marvelous asset. The fatty, strapped for cash, decided to sell, and the lean man exercised his option for $2.5 million, financed by a group of banks in a deal raising his stake from 40 percent to 60 percent. A little later, the fat boss inquired after the health of the lean purchaser and was informed that his condition was excellent, as you would expect after receiving a present of nearly $1 million. The fat boss was astonished; it was gently explained to him that, since the deal valued 60 percent at $2.5 million, the extra 20 percent was worth over $800,000. Within a couple of years even that assessment was falsified; the profits having risen in the interim, the entrepreneur's stake was worth $15 million, of which $2.5 million represented the large company's putative loss.

The fact is that corporate managements, unlike lean entrepreneurs, do little figuring when their hearts are set on a strategic purchase. That's why, according to the careful count of a McKinsey consultant, Andrew J. Parsons, the median buying premium in 123 offers was almost 50 percent above market price; 16 of them exceeded the market valuation by more than double. In 1985, for instance, Jack Lupton, the largest Coca-Cola bottler in the United States, believed himself to be worth something over $360 million. A year later *Forbes* valued him at $785 million. The difference was accounted for by Coke's decision to buy up bottlers and never mind the cost.

In the case of Lupton's JTL Corp., that came to $1.4 billion, or double annual sales. Small wonder that Lupton reckoned "the timing was right for this." The bigger the company, the larger the largesse, because big-time managers, like politicians, like to play the paper number game. If the board rejoices in a turnover of $1.5 billion, a million isn't even petty cash—unless one of the submanagers wants to spend it, when the proposal becomes the subject of earnest boardroom deliberations. Even $15 million is only 1 percent of sales; but if you drop three times that much, as ICI's board did in its vain attempt to finance the British textile industry into prosperity, it offsets the value of many minute examinations of managerial spending plans.

The most spectacular of ICI's exertions involved Joe Hyman, whom ICI's grayer managers correctly saw as the strongest individual force in the industry. So they backed him with a vengeance: ICI took a quarter of the Viyella textile shares Hyman had revitalized and provided him with $15 million—most of it in the form of an interest-free loan. Within a week Hyman had spent the boodle on buying another shirt company. "We like to see things happen fast," said an ICI spokesman lamely. Presumably, the ICI directors could see that they were perfectly capable of buying the shirt company themselves; they probably didn't see that their action made automatic millions for Hyman in person, just as surely as if they had pressed the cash into his hand.

If you have the use of a million free of interest (as Hyman did), it will purchase after-tax earnings of at least $100,000; if that is multiplied by a very average stock-exchange multiple of fifteen, the capital value to the equity holders is $1.5 million, half a million of it pure profit. Hyman, as the largest individual shareholder in Viyella, reaped the harvest sown with ICI's seeds. In 1963 alone his shares shot up two and a half times. At least, in this case, the giant, as a shareholder itself, had some compensation for its generosity.

In general, the record of the involvement of giants with entrepreneur-built companies the world over makes sorry reading, partly because the two sides don't speak the same language, let alone work in the same way. The entrepreneur instinctively relates a proposition to his individual well-being; the manager thinks of it strictly in terms of corporate strategy. Take the strange example of Sylvania and Sir Jules Thorn. Sylvania, later absorbed into General Telephone and Electric, was the largest shareholder in Thorn Electrical after its founder, who had made extensive use of Sylvania technology.

The obvious assumption was that the Americans were biding their time until Thorn, who was no chicken in years but not easy to pluck, decided to relinquish control. A plump British affiliate would then fall ready-made into the American lap. While this buildup continued, the U.S. part-owner even increased its shareholding, stirring happy speculation in the City of London. As Thorn grew to a height symbolized by its name in lights high above the West End, the fortune Sir Jules held as closely as he controlled the company grew too.

Thorn's whole career was founded on the lean outsider principle. Coming to Britain as a refugee from Austria and the Nazis, and deciding to sell light bulbs, he found the market encircled by a manufacturers' ring. This broke, not the law of the time, but the Law of Fat Company Preservation; this lays down that every artificial restriction of a market or price level opens up a natural, protected opportunity for any lean man who is not bound by the restriction.

The outsider cracked the ring and drove his company on to a score, at its best levels of 1967, worth some $100 million. He then played his masterstroke by merging, naturally just before Britain's color TV boom, with another TV rental giant. At this one stroke, the American stake was reduced to nonstrategic proportions; it was subsequently offloaded, while the Thorn equity marched on five years later to a best level of over $1 billion, of which the directors' share (meaning mostly Sir Jules) was $75 million.

The fat company's final defense, buying the lean ones out, has the inevitable effect of turning the latter's paper wealth into the real McCoy, and the undesirable side effect that the business is often worth less without its lean progenitor—especially as the latter, by instinct or design, tends to get out when the going is good, or, rather, before it gets bad. In paying its $900 million for Max Palevsky's SDS shortly before the bright lights of the computer market and the SDS profits were abruptly switched off, Xerox was merely both following and setting precedent. IBM did exactly the same with Rolm, Ken Oshman, and its private branch exchanges, where bonanzas refused to come as resolutely as computers resisted Xerox.

Such egregious errors, note, are not rare, but commonplaces of corporate life. Even a case-hardened marketing expert such as Ernest

Saunders of Guinness, advised on all points by ace consultants Bain &
Co. (paid $12 million a year for their services), showed the typical
reaction when simple business sense got in the way of grand strategic
design. The sense went out the window. So Meshulam Riklis of Rapid-
American won ludicrous concessions for Schenley, its liquor subsidiary,
in return for his support of the shares; so another supporter, multimillionaire Gerald Ronson, got paid $7.5 million (returned swiftly, too late
to prevent his arrest, when Saunders was unmasked) for services to
Guinness whose going rate was $75,000, tops.

Ronson himself was fully aware of the fat-company phenomenon.
He built a gas station empire on the basic principle of getting the major
oil companies to pay for the sites, correctly reckoning that in their
determined pursuit of market share they would stop at very little.
Ronson then sold most of the stations for excellent profits—to his fat
financiers, of course. In May 1984, Ronson's company, Heron Corporation, took (that being the operative word) thirty-two stores off the
long-suffering Woolworth. His own publicity called this the High Street
"steal" of the decade. A deal completed in six weeks finally yielded over
$22 million of profit.

You can even go on making money from fat purchasers after
consummating the buyout deal. One entrepreneur made his first fortune
by selling his cosmetics business to a mammoth. He then bought it
back, at a lower price, with one innocent condition lurking in the large
print: the vendor was to take financial responsibility for the old stock.
The purchaser then cruised around his retail outlets, offered to take
back all the stock on hand (which rejoiced the retailers' hearts exceedingly and cemented their affection forevermore), and then passed the
goods back, with his compliments, and in return for a large check, to
the big company. This effectively reduced the purchase price by a third:
there's no fool like a fat fool.

Yet the normal human reaction, when put in a ring with a heavyweight, is to run for the ropes. In making millions this policy is woefully
misguided. The correct course is to search for the weak spot, hit it hard,
and go on hitting until the heavy either surrenders or buys you out,
which comes to the same thing. If the heavy is theoretically on your
side, never make a deal that gives you less than, or only what, you want.
Aim for the moon—the heavy may give you that planet, because it costs
those in charge nothing to give it away; but it costs you plenty to miss
the chance of your private Apollo money mission. If you can squeeze
the fat out of your friend by seemingly modest deals as Gulbenkian did
with his guaranteed 5 percent of Iraq's oil, do so. (They tried to fob him
off with a penny-a-ton royalty, with no success whatsoever.) Above all,

when searching for the opportunity that may make millions, never be put off by the fact that a billionaire company occupies the territory. Rather, take that as a vital sign. It's an old adage, hard for the inexperienced to grasp, that you don't open a fast-food joint as far as possible from McDonald's, but next door, because you will get your share of the heavy traffic—even though this particular competitor is no big-company slouch.

The considerable number of fast-food millionaires who rode on Ray Kroc's apron strings prove the point. No less an authority than Tom Peters, who found so many examples of big company *Excellence* for his all-time business best-seller, now writes that "there are no excellent companies." The large corporation simply presents a bigger target. The intelligent entrepreneur surveys this mass, much of which may be blubber, and finds a different, better way of doing the same thing—like F. Kenneth Iverson, whose Nucor Corporation from 1976 to 1986 grew by 28 percent compound in total return to shareholders, by making steel, the quintessential maxi-industry, in minimills.

If you are luckier than you deserve, the fat company may even force you into enormously profitable competition. That's what happened when the greatest invention in copying was turned down by every giant who was offered the prize. Forced to go it alone, the pioneers created a Xerox empire that, even after fat vicissitudes that included losing half its market to the Japanese, still commanded $9.4 billion of sales in 1986. The figure would have been vastly larger but for one mistake—just one—made early on. Never repeat the error of Haloid, the little company that became large Xerox. In its youth and innocence, Haloid sold the Rank Organization, for $900,000, half the rights to xerography in the whole world outside the United States. On declared profits alone, that giveaway was worth $135 million in a single early decade. Even skinny companies, at times, can have fat heads.

Book IV

THE
PAPER
MILLIONAIRES

16

ALWAYS A LENDER
AND A
BORROWER BE

Many sound rules of management are hollow counsels for would-be millionaires. Those boring words of Polonius to his son Laertes: "neither a lender nor a borrower be," should be engraved on the hearts of the innumerable big-, middle-, and small-time managements that have lumbered their companies with deadweights of debt, thus imposing a high wall of interest payments that must be climbed before the firm can earn a penny for its shareholders.

One of the highest common factors of millionaires, however, *is* their high level of indebtedness. That too sounds like a paradox—if you're as rich as Croesus, how come you need other people's money? But the wealthy use wealth belonging to others—first, because it costs little or nothing to borrow; second, because the borrowing enables them to achieve a far higher equity profit; third, because it enables them to employ their entire capital in the way they like best, which is gainfully; and fourth, because anyway people are dying to lend them money.

In the Age of the Common Millionaire, that readiness has increased by a factor of several powers. One explanation is the pressure of the savings of the Common Man, notably the Common Japanese; these savings have created an insatiable demand for outlets at a time when the traditional customers are less obliging in taking on obligations than they were. The world's great corporations are still its greatest borrowers. But they have discovered the joys, and lower costs, of banking for themselves, issuing their own paper, and cutting out the bankers. The latter, moreover, are now in no hurry to lend to nation-states or Third World companies after the pileup of unserviceable and maybe unrecoverable debt in countries such as Brazil. The junk-bond business has thus been manna from heaven for the banks. But the phenomenon goes deeper than the surface of insolent takeovers and impudent leveraged buyouts. The abundant availability of debt has been the engine powering the rise of the new breed of Common Millionaire—men such as the rapacious Australian trio badly hurt by the crash of 1987: John Elliott, Robert Holmes à Court, and Alan Bond.

Elliott's rise from McKinsey consultant to multimillionaire would have been impossible but for the mighty borrowings that financed his acquisitions, including the $2 billion purchase of the Courage beer business in 1986. Earlier two Australian banks, the Bank of Tokyo, and the august Hong Kong & Shanghai came running to the rescue when Elliott needed a billion in a hurry to secure under a fifth of Broken Hill Proprietary, the largest Australian company. *A billion dollars*—even in the 1970s an operator of Elliott's speed would never have been able to raise that kind of money for solid investment, still less a highly speculative takeover situation.

Nor, once upon a time, would banks have looked kindly on an airline with long-term debt representing 80 percent of its capital, or have aided and abetted its rise through a series of takeovers of troubled operators. Yet, that is precisely how Frank Lorenzo cut a swath through the industry. From 1972 onward, Lorenzo grabbed hold of Texas International, Continental, Eastern, People Express, and Frontier by determined borrowing. While airlines and debt go hand in hand, or hand to mouth, because of the inordinately high capital cost of jet aircraft, Lorenzo ended up with a debt ratio 60 percent above the awesome industry average—and nobody, least of all Lorenzo, turned a hair. As the crash showed, they should have.

There are odd exceptions to the coolness of the rich under a barrage of debts, occasional eccentrics who think that cash is the only reality—for example, the booster of Midland, Texas, who paid for its first hotel with a $1 million check and financed its extension in the same simple way. Another Texas oilman, stating, "I worked for Mr. Interest long enough," displayed an ignorance of financial process that is often no impediment to financial progress. Far more millionaires would subscribe to the sentiments of yet a third Texan, Clint Murchison, who observed succinctly that "cash makes a man careless." Henry Ford, notoriously simple in these matters, thought that you should "get yourself $400 or $500 million in cash, tuck it away and forget about it. It will come in handy some time for a rainy day." Observe, however, that the cash-tucking Ford put not a cent into his own companies: the first three went bankrupt, while the fourth only narrowly avoided the same fate.

Ford thus acquired the benefits of *leverage* (using other people's money to achieve your own purposes) without taking any risk at all: no debt, no personal investment. In modern times, it hasn't been easy to raise money on such terms—and the Common Millionaire seldom tries. On the contrary, debt is second nature to an entrepreneurial soul such as the late Garfield Weston. His Canadian-based food empire, now ranging from Loblaw's supermarkets to Fortnum & Mason, enabled him to tuck away so much that he could actually afford to make the RAF a present of some Spitfire fighters during World War II. Nevertheless, Weston used to claim in later days that he never had any money in the bank, just debts; and, he might have added, a personally controlled empire worth $1.3 billion to leave to his heirs, one of whom in 1985 consequently enjoyed a fortune put by the London *Times* at $400 million.

Yet cases such as Weston's (or Elliott's, or Lorenzo's) raise obvious problems. First, debt is one of the most familiar routes to disaster or distress. Every annual *Forbes* visitation to the super-rich contains some such epitaph as this: "Farley, William F. Chicago 43. Estimated $250 million fortune 1985 (leveraged buyouts). Financial filings . . . indicate that heavy debt has burdened cash flow. Recently liquidating various assets." So what determines when heavy debt ceases to be a propulsion unit and turns into a grinding brake?

Then there's the problem of economic theory. In economics, generally speaking, one man's loss is another man's gain: one nation's balance-of-payments surplus is another's deficit. Financing, or lending, is one of the richest sources of riches, so is borrowing. How can what's sauce for the gander equally be sauce for the goose? Thus, Sam Walton is the richest man in America thanks to Wal-Mart supermarkets; yet the brothers Stephens (Witt and Jack) of Little Rock, Arkansas, as investment bankers to Wal-Mart, became the wealthiest practitioners of their craft outside Wall Street.

Their fortune fell a long way short of Walton's billions, but $800 million was a decent reward for an operation that got properly under way in 1933, when Witt Stephens saw that municipal bonds, buyable at a Great Depression quarter apiece, were salable at a dollar. "If you've got the idea," Witt told *Forbes*, "we've got the money." The money is, of course, unlikely to be theirs—and that is the key to the paradoxes. The borrower and lender are a unit playing on the same side; the loser is the ultimate supplier of the funds, the general public. The ultimate user is the entrepreneur. If he can create values that are sufficiently large (as Weston, Elliott, and Lorenzo planned to do), his lender's charges are no more significant than the minimal return paid to that general public.

Not that the latter can justifiably complain. For the borrowing paradox can be resolved by a truly homely example. In most countries in the postwar world, the shrewdest stratagem open to anybody, rich or relatively humble, was to buy his own house in some established and improving area beloved of the middle to upper classes; then to mortgage that house to the hilt of his financial ability.

The mortgage arithmetic is irresistible. Suppose the family bought a $100,000 house and borrowed $80,000 from a home loans company at x percent (the actual rate of interest doesn't matter, for reasons to be explained). Over twenty years, say, the loan must be repaid, but in steadily depreciating bank notes. For example, in a case where the entire loan is repaid only at the end of the twenty years (which can easily be arranged), a mortgage of $80,000 paid off after 100 percent inflation equals a payment of $40,000 in the original currency.

All this time, the loan has been safely secured by the house—provided that its value has risen, the borrower can always clear his debt and still come out ahead. The post–World War II period has staged few exceptions to the inexorable rise in property prices. After twenty years, if the house has managed to rise by 7 percent per annum (many have far outstripped this pace), it will be worth $400,000.

Remember that only $20,000 of the borrower's own money went into the house. So in twenty years he has made a profit of $380,000, or 16 percent per annum at compound interest. That profit is equal to a simple interest on the $80,000 loan of 24 percent a year—handsomely higher than any rate of interest conceivably charged—and that's the indisputable reason why the actual interest rate doesn't much matter. Another is that the interest is deductible against tax; if the top slice of income was taxable at 50 percent, the net cost of $80,000 for twenty years at 10 percent was not $160,000, but $80,000, on which, remember, the man has made a $300,000 profit.

That's some millstone. The higher the debt, the greater the return on the equity. If every pound or dollar you deploy can be made into ten by borrowing, and you make only one currency unit clear on every tranche of cash, you double your money every time. The trick is either to get the loot advanced on the security of the treasure you want to buy—as in a house purchase—or to manage matters magically so that the money is lent on no security at all. Either way, the borrower can take profitable action that would otherwise have been barred by lack of funds.

Borrowing against existing collateral has the same effect—but with the disadvantage that you need such collateral in the first place. Many real estate millionaires were once in no such happy position, but knew how to make do. One future financier was markedly short of currency when a beautiful vision, a site in a prime position, swam before his eyes. He hastily purchased a month's option, and rushed to his bank to procure a short-term loan secured by the option; he then ran even faster to an insurance company and persuaded the insurers to promise the construction and site purchase money if he could find a tenant; he then sped fastest of all to a company looking for new premises and leased the entire future building to the tenant, who, of course, was impressed by the insurance company's backing.

At this point the developer, who had so far not even paid his architect, had a guaranteed profit, on an outlay of nothing but time and shoe leather, that came to a clear million. Real estate developers the world over have followed the same principles to the best of their ability. They use their talent to extract the maximum finance at the minimum interest rate for the smallest possible loss of equity in the project. During the London office building boom of the late 1960s, the collapse of which came nigh to toppling the entire national monetary system, some developers even found overeager lenders who would cheerfully advance more money than the architectural wonder in question was actually going to cost. Small wonder that these avid fellows were cleaned out as developers. (The American William Stern went down for the third time: his bankruptcy, for £118 million, was the biggest on record.)

The craziest force of nature ever to hit the New York property scene, a stout party named William Zeckendorf, demonstrated the risks of overmighty borrowing with an equally spectacular failure. The amounts he could borrow in orthodox ways failed to satisfy his wayward genius. So he sliced up his buildings, like so much boiled ham, into tiers of convoluted debt. This offended the golden rule of borrowing, which is never to borrow more than you could recover in full by some practicable form of selling up. If this rule is broken, the borrower is in the uncomfortable position known as "overextended"—or, as the unfortunate victims of the Spanish Inquisition knew it, "on the rack." The less you need money, the more easily it can be borrowed; the more urgent your need, the harder it is to borrow—and the higher the interest charges soar.

It isn't merely a question of ensuring that assets cover debts (or, to use the rightly ominous technical word, *liabilities*). The assets must be reasonably quick: that is, you must be able to realize them in an emergency, such as a sudden voracious demand by the lender for his money back. If you can't deliver, he will devour, and you will be dead. In this context, Zeckendorf's words, "I prefer to stay alive at eighteen percent than to be dead at the prime rate," have a ghoulish ring.

The most significant consequence of his passionate borrowing was to launch the Reichmann family on their way toward one of the world's ripest fortunes in real estate; they picked up some bankrupt Zeckendorf acreage for a puny $25 million—it became Canada's largest suburban real estate development. And the Reichmanns, note, did not then believe in heavy long-term debt; only their gigantic, more questionable investments in natural resources later forced them to change their ways, if not their minds.

At less Himalayan levels of commerce, many an overextended entrepreneur has found his fixed-interest lender pocketing the entire business with the same reluctance with which the Walrus and the Carpenter consumed their little oyster associates. In a bankruptcy, the equity even in a flourishing business suddenly becomes so much dross: the first come, the secured lenders, are the first served—and usually the last, since they swallow the lot. That is why the truly clever borrower aims for the perfect situation, where he borrows at nil interest, where the loan is not secured on any of his assets, and where he doesn't even have to repay it.

Who, you may ask, lends at nil interest? Governments habitually do so; major industrial corporations have been known to, in pursuance of what they fondly imagine to be their real interest—the mighty ICI, one of the leading chemical companies in Europe, lent millions for nothing at a time when its own borrowing costs were 8 percent. The secret is to offer the giant the one thing for which, above all others, it slavers: guaranteed sales of its products.

Provided that the supplier avoids getting screwed on price, he puts the giant in a tactically impossible fix. To keep the trade, on which it may be earning miserable profit margins, it must keep the supplier's business alive—even if that means largely financing the operation. The executives concerned seldom reflect, even in this sad event, that they might as well have started the operation themselves and kept the whole bundle in company hands—sales, equity profits, and all. But nothing excites a corporate executive more than an outside entrepreneur.

One failed Seventh Avenue cloth merchant, for example, finally made the big time by driving to his selected fabric supplier in a large blue Cadillac, parking outside the offices, slamming his hand on the horn, and pretending it was stuck. Everybody in the building, including the chief executive, naturally looked out. Equally naturally, the Cadillac owner got the fabric he required for making nylon sheets; the only question asked, without bank references, was whether he wanted thirty days credit or sixty. At a later port of call, visiting the huge AKZO giant of Holland, the now-established sheet tycoon got ninety days and a million-pound loan at an almost invisible rate of interest. At one stage, the borrower was consequently worth some $40 million, or three times the value of the Dutch subsidiary that had advanced the money. That particular enterprise eventually went bankrupt—because of base business errors, but not because of its master's inability to master the constructive use of other people's money.

Few have understood that principle better than the two promoters who spawned Holiday Inns by marvelously constructive use of debt. Kemmons Wilson loved to say that he never wanted to own a million dollars, but to owe it. Significantly enough, both he and his partner, Wallace E. Johnson, started on their milky ways in housebuilding, homes being the easiest security for loans. By 1965 Wilson and Johnson were paying interest on their debts that amounted to $10,000 a day—a comforting situation, if you can meet the interest, but nothing like so comfortable as the formula that founded Holiday Inns.

The first few hotels were built from whatever resources Wilson himself could muster. But once he met Johnson, the pair hit on the wonderful notion of the franchise. They found other men with money or access to money (which comes to the same thing) and generously allowed the latter to build a hotel for the chain, and, what's more, to pay Holiday Inns for the privilege.

The franchisee of a 120-room inn got a 6 to 10 percent return on investment, and supposedly triple that on equity. But he had to find at least $1 million, and pay, among other tolls, a $15,000-a-year license fee and a minimum royalty of fifteen cents a night for each room (at 365 nights a year, that came to $65,700—not a bad return on $1 million of somebody else's money).

Holiday Inns could never have been built to a 400-inn scale, making it the largest hotel chain in the world, without this neat variation of borrowing at no interest, with no security, and without repayment.

The franchisee had to find the borrowed capital, leaving Wilson and Johnson free to pursue the delights of borrowing millions on their own accounts, pocketing the equity profits as they come their way. Those profits came to $65.6 million by 1971; of that golden river, a sizable stream belonged to Wilson and Johnson, whose creation had a stock-market value at the end of the following year of $1,238 million. Fifteen years later, the business they invented had sales of $1.8 billion and profits of $150 million—and without question many franchise millionaires were spawned in the wake of its rise.

Sooner or later, however, mighty franchisers began to become a mite jealous of the profits being retained by the financing franchisees. At that point, the emphasis switches to wholly-owned outlets. In hotels, however, capital costs have risen so high that building a large chain would take far too long, tie up too much capital, and generate too much in interest charges. Even so wealthy a family as the billionaire Pritzkers regarded this as bad business—especially if the finance could be raised free: and it can.

The technique is to persuade some other fellow to pay for the hotel, which you then operate as part of your rich and growing chain. The financier, or "owner," gets an agreed amount of the operating profits, but the lion's share, the cash flow, and the expansion of the business accrue to the hotel company. It thus maximizes its own return on capital and its ability to go on growing. Once again, though, there seem to be no losers—people as far apart as Mortimer Zuckerman, whose $250 million real estate empire includes the Park Hyatt in Washington, and the Choeng family of Singapore have been happy Hyatt customers.

The Choengs were slightly less happy when asked to meet the refurbishing bill for their Hyatt Regency in Hong Kong. It took years to persuade them to part with the $120 million required. The owners in this situation are trapped just as firmly as the supplier who invests in his customer. If they don't invest, the investment won't be protected. If they do, more good money must be sent after good—for the trap is a tender one. Another Far Eastern Hyatt, with an original cost of $113 million, changed hands in 1986 for $250 million.

The value of the 100 percent Pritzker equity in the operations—let alone their own mounting investments in the hotels themselves—can be judged by the sale price of a chain such as Hilton International: sold in 1986 for $900 million. No doubt, the bulk of the capital that has flowed into the enormous global expansion of hotels has ultimately been provided by the lending institutions, to the great satisfaction of all parties. The way in which borrowing, so beautifully beneficial to the borrower, can also be good for the lenders depends partly on the nature of the latter.

Sources of money fall into three groups: the rich, the professional usurers, and the involuntary moneylenders. The accidental ones are those who had no intention of lending anything to anybody, but ended up that way because they weren't paid. Much trade credit falls roughly into this category. One multimillionaire chain store tycoon used to be visited once a month by the chairman of a food firm; after some pleasant chat about business, the weather, and world affairs, the food boss would raise the subject of the bill for fodder supplied three months previously, the store magnate would write a check, and his guest would climb back into his limo for the ride back home. When somebody suggested to the manufacturer that this was a weird way for the chairman of a major company to behave, he agreed; but, he said, "If I didn't do it, I wouldn't get paid for six months."

The greatest coup in the history of involuntary financing was pulled off by history's most inventive engineer, Henry Ford I. Henry had made the cardinal error of allowing his debts to mount far above his quick assets, and the Wall Street wolves were closing for the kill. At this point, Ford I turned on his dealers; he shipped out every car in the inventory and demanded payment on the nose. By this inspired device, Henry routed the bankers and tapped a whole new source of free finance: the money-raising problem was passed on to Ford dealers, whose own survival depended on maintaining a flood of Model Ts. Up to that point, of course, Ford had been involuntarily backing his dealers; he merely reversed the position, thus confirming the law that, like water finding its own level, money always eventually flows from the weak to the strong.

This need not mean from the poor to the rich. It's perfectly possible to be both wealthy and weak, especially if the loot is inherited. Many an heir has been a soft touch for the plausible borrower who has no earthly hope of tapping any harder source. Generally speaking, however, the rich are mean—and if they part with their means, they do so at the highest interest money can fetch and on the most stringent conditions.

One borrower, a millionaire himself, emerged from a borrowing brush with a still-richer man intact but gasping. "The old man does love his rate of interest," he noted—and it is that love that distinguishes the successful lender. In lending, profit equals the margin between the price you pay for money and the price at which you sell it, less the costs of collection, disbursement, and bad debts. Money can be obtained free, by banks accepting ordinary deposits; otherwise, its price of purchase is more or less fixed by circumstances outside the lender's control.

If money is readily available at 12 percent, let alone 8 percent, nobody is going to pay 13—not unless his need is so pressing, and his security so unimpressive, that lenders of first resort love him not. To the usurious at heart, or the bank in a rash hurry for growth, that's less an obstacle than an opportunity. Thus did the so-called secondary banks in the London of the Edward Heath era fall over themselves to advance money to real estate developers; the eager lenders necessarily paid more to attract deposits into their patently unattractive hands and they charged much higher interest to make larded profits. The financial charm swiftly evaporated as the real estate boom, the loans, and the lenders collapsed like a house of cards.

The secondary or second-class bankers mostly clung to enough of their temporary loot to remain millionaires (as did many of their defaulting clients). But it took billions—perhaps three of them—for the Bank of England to prevent the secondary failures from bringing the whole primary banking system down around the heads of the depositors—because the ultimate source of the secondary funds was, as usual, the financial establishment. The domino effect, if it hadn't been arrested by the Bank of England's billions, would have precipitated a world crisis more dangerous than the banking collapse that preceded and accompanied the Great Depression.

For lovers of ominous echoes, the junk-bond explosion in the United States had several of the same elements. For real estate developers, read corporate raiders and empire builders. The essence of the junk bond is to allow those with no security to borrow more than those amply blessed with collateral—and junk borrowers, too, pay dearly for the privilege. The 13 percent on junk, as opposed to 8 percent on normal debt, attracted everybody from mutual fund salesmen via fat cat financiers (such as Saul Steinberg and Carl Lindner) to supposedly staid institutions—not only true-blue investment bankers such as Morgan Stanley and Salomon Brothers, but all the old-line lending institutions, notably the pension funds and insurance companies.

In 1978, when Mike Milken started aggressively marketing junk bonds, only $1.5 billion were sold—if *only* is the right word. Eight years later, the total was a staggering $40 billion, of which an equally amazing half was provided through Milken's firm, Drexel Burnham Lambert. Its rise, one without precedent in the annals of Wall Street, was paralleled by Milken's own. By 1986, his fortune was reckoned at half a billion dollars; his supposed million-a-week income from Drexel was doubled by the yields from his investments. Neatly cutting himself in on the deals that he financed, Milken at the age of forty had not only outstripped every venture capitalist by far, he had moved an equal distance in front of older Wall Street heads.

Were the heads wiser as well as older? Making so fast a fortune from finance without breaking the law is difficult enough; doing so without exceeding the normal bounds of risk is impossible. One of the oldest adages in investment holds that "the higher the interest, the higher the risk." The thought that this applied (as it certainly did) to $150 billion of American debt was not reassuring. The new lending can't escape from the laws that have always governed the old.

Indeed, every now and again one of the new lenders proves the point by getting caught in its own web: Billy Sol Estes trapped Walter E. Heller, the shrewdest finance house to emerge from the Midwest, into lending money on his nonexistent grain silos. But more often than not it's the big, respectable pro lender such as American Express (the principal victim of the salad-oil swindling of Tino de Angelis) that falls for the pro fraud.

Not that Amex had any great need to maximize its loan rates; like insurance companies, deposit banks, and other money engines, Amex contrives to get the use of other people's money for nothing—because of the time lag between selling traveler's checks to the customers and the point when the checks are cashed and Amex must turn over the dough. The size of this "float" in 1985 was a cool billion dollars. That's some flotation; and an essential part of the skillful use of borrowing and lending is to ensure that time is always on your side, that you have the maximum use of the money for the maximum time at the minimum cost.

The best source of usurious rates of return is not the junk-bond borrower but the same pool from which Amex derives its float: the mass market. The $150 billion of junk bonds is as nothing compared to the $2.5 trillion of U.S. consumer debt—a sum actually in excess of federal government borrowings and equivalent to some four-fifths of aftertax incomes. Consumer debt has always had a special attraction for the dishonest. Down the years, crooks have battened on the arithmetic of installment credit (the fact that 1 percent a month on a reducing balance isn't 12 percent a year, but very much more) to such an extent that governments have felt forced to crack down on the sharpest practices—for example, the thief who offers "$1,000 for only $2.30 a week." If the loan lasts for fifteen years, the true interest rate works out at 25 percent. The usurers have secured returns up as high as 280 percent a year—no doubt the kind of return the Mafia finds acceptable on the loan-sharking that is still a major part of its activities.

The sharks batten on need. For most borrowers, the main problem is to find the money at all. They advance on the sources of cash diffidently, expecting to be refused, and they pitch their demands at a modest level. This is not only bad finance, it's poor psychology. In the first place, borrowers should always have access to more than they need—partly because they are likely to need more anyway. In the second place, psychology counts: big men are always impressed by big numbers; nobody gets much charge from lending $5,000. But $5 million is another matter—and anybody who wants to borrow that big must (so the idiot reasoning runs) have big ideas and big capacities.

Try this shrewdity test. Would you place a single dollar of your money in the care of an unproven investor who proposes to secure the loans on privately owned companies whose worth is a matter of either conjecture or the opinion of the genius in question? Would you, moreover, cede him voting control and the bulk of the profits (if any)? The answer is evidently and instantaneously NO. Yet a group of highly respectable institutions lent the venturer concerned, not a single dollar, but 75 million of them. The story illustrates not only the importance of thinking—and borrowing—big, but the gullibility of those who lend other people's money and, in this case (for no profits were ever made), were lucky not to lose the lot.

The bigger the loan, naturally, the more money it mops up. The fact that too much capital has been chasing too few sound investment opportunities reverses the confident predictions of capital shortage expressed as recently as 1975 (when equally misplaced fears of natural resources shortages were also in vogue). Lending standards become lax easily at any time; borrowing standards tend to be lax by definition. The combination of much loose lending with much more aggressive borrowing was a great boon to both new and old millionaires as the bull market rushed toward its fate. It's less clear that the blessings were shared by the economies of nation-states, by the citizens who ultimately supply the loaned and borrowed funds, or by the great commercial banks that in the past two decades have been drawn, as if by an invisible supermagnet, to the least safe large-scale borrowers.

Their massive Third World lending, much of which by 1987 could be neither repaid nor serviced, was merely the largest illustration of a propensity that in recent years has also extended its favors to real estate investment trusts, insecure energy plays, uneconomic farms, and deadbeat corporations such as International Harvester, the pre-Iacocca Chrysler, and Massey-Ferguson. That neither these large corporate borrowers nor the most incompetent lenders (for example, Continental Illinois, Bank of America) have disappeared from the scene owed nothing to the managements concerned; it only reflected the lesson, learned so painfully in the Depression, that nobody, from governments to the banks themselves, can afford a truly large financial failure.

In other words, the larger the loans and the borrower, the more dependent the lender becomes on keeping both alive (if only ostensibly). There couldn't be a better illustration of the result—to him to whom too much is lent, too much more shall be given—than the case of a Hong Kong Chinese named Tung Chee-Hwa. In 1985, this energetic fellow managed to borrow over $850 million. The security? His personal guarantee. The reason for the loans? Money was pouring out of Tung's vast shipping group, the second largest in Hong Kong, and thus among the world giants.

Now, lending money to somebody because he's broke may not sound like the most promising business around. Nor was it. Before the year ended, Tung's creditors made the miserable discovery that, right across the entire $2.6 billion of debts, no possibility existed of anything better than partial repayment. As the *South China Morning Post* reported, the lenders came from all quarters: "Among the creditors are banks, leasing companies, shipyards, and trade creditors holding a wide variety of security or no security at all, and from Phoenix, Arizona, to Oslo, Norway."

Groaning and moaning, the creditors had no option but to accept a massive refinancing plan in which the government of Red China (anxious not to see a major default in its future territory of Hong Kong) and Tung's own fortune (squirreled away in a barely penetrable mesh of mismanaged private companies) also played a part. But what business did a lender in landlocked Phoenix have financing container ships on the South China Sea? Why did the creditors only discover that Tung's empire was a shambles after his debts had curdled, instead of before? What made them ignore the laws of economics and the mutterings of shipping experts, which made it clear that Tung was gambling wildly, and doubling his bets, with their money? Is there really no alternative, in such squeezes, to sending good millions after bad?

These inconvenient questions, however, were safely ignored by those using superabundant debt to convert nothing into plenty. The whole miraculous process was encapsulated in the ceremony that surrounded the delivery of the *Globtik Tokyo*, all 480,000 tons of her, then the biggest in the world. The Kashmiri owner, one Ravi Tikkoo, totally unknown a few years previously, and never heard of a few years later, handed over a check for $25 million when accepting the ship from the Japanese builders. As the *Financial Times* observed at the time, this was "largely a paper transaction." Mitsui and Co. of Japan had lent four-fifths of the money, at the staggeringly low cost of 6 percent. British banks had paid the rest. On delivery day, the gap between cost and insurance value was $7.5 million, every cent of which belonged to Tikkoo's very own Globtik Tankers, a $150 company. That's nice work—and at least up to the day of reckoning, October 19, 1987, you could still get it, if you tried.

17

THE TAX MAN COMETH NOT

The ordinary income earner the wide world over is a complaining taxpayer. Wriggle how the victim may, the tax man always succeeds in extracting the full exaction of the law. Small dodges are practiced by most people, such as taking extra jobs that are not revealed to the official predator. This moonlighting may be the largest single category of employment in the Western world. In the more lax, usually Latin, areas, undercover, under-the-counter, and even under-the-desk payments play the same role.

But when the tax man can't get at your income, he attacks your spending instead, through the more direct method of what are therefore known as indirect taxes. One way or another, like the Mounties, he always gets his man—except, that is, when the man is really flush with taxable money. It's as if the Mounties, while adept at picking off petty thieves, were totally incapable of catching mass murderers.

An axiom of the lawyers who earn exorbitant fees (and thus incur potential tax liabilities of their own) from shielding the rich from the

Internal Revenue is that taxes cannot be avoided forever—only post-poned, if indefinitely. In other words, if the Mounties don't get you, they'll get your heirs, in one generation or another. That should be a prospect that the rich avoider views with equanimity, since whatever life there is after death is presumably free of tax. Most of the wealthy, however, approach the hereafter in the same spirit as the corpse in a famous Charles Addams cartoon; the cortege includes an armored truck that is trying to prove, against all the evidence, that you *can* take it with you.

Certainly the spirit of J. P. Getty must have been revolted by the weight of the tax burden—$1.1 billion—his son Gordon incurred in 1984 on liquidating one family trust. The ghostly revulsion would not have been lessened by relating the tax bill to the billions (four of them) that were realized by the sale of Getty assets to Texaco (in the contested deal that led to the oil giant's filing for protection under the bankruptcy laws). All the same, a 26.8 percent tax charge on the biggest personal bonanza in history wouldn't seem, to your average taxpayer, to be a particularly penal exaction.

But there is nothing average, by definition, about the Common Millionaire. He is driven to exploit to the utmost the strange situation that the more tax you are supposed to pay under the law, the less likely you are to pay it. This is most clearly seen in the careers, not of business moguls, but of movie stars, telegogues, pulp novelists, and the like. Suppose a star earns an income of $1 million; after genuine tax, that should leave a sum that is beyond the spending powers of all but the most determined playboy or playgirl. The residue, after meeting all expenses, would, however, take many years to add up to a seven-figure fortune, even with the aid of shrewd investment. That factor will proba-bly be offset, anyway, by the idiocy to which investing stars are prone (the Beatles' Apple Corps got chewed over by every maggot in town) and by the hugely exorbitant cost of the hangers-on whom show biz personalities accumulate as rocks gather barnacles.

Yet wealth sticks to these creators with a tenacity that any barna-cle would envy. Despite a pronounced lack of interest in business and a penchant for progressive charities, Yoko Ono (on the *Forbes* estimate) still possessed $150 million of the John Lennon fortune in 1984. The far-cuter Beatle, financially speaking, Paul McCartney, was worth a third of a billion in 1985, having continued his career as well as minding his business interests—and a continuing career, of course, makes the performer a moving target for the tax man.

The millions pile up with a profusion that, fiscally speaking, is a profound embarrassment. Between 1968 and 1980, the Led Zeppelin band sold 20 million albums. Within ten years, royalties totaling some $5 million resided in More Luck than Judgment, Ltd., Things That Go Bump in the Night, Ltd., and other exotically named companies that owned the rights to the royalties. The Zeppelin tried equally exotic ways of avoiding tax on this booty—they failed to the extent of a $3 million settlement, which should, however, still have left plenty of loose change.

Many other superstars have equally little trouble in putting together a million in no time at all. Beside the riches of Michael Jackson and Bruce Springsteen, the Zeppelin's take (even before its four-way split) was small potatoes. A high marginal rate of taxation has never stopped superstars from jetting around the world in search of the highest possible marginal income—but nobody in the taxed rabble seems to wonder how these things can be. Sometimes (witness Led Zeppelin) the explanation doesn't work too well, but it is far from complex. The rich pay less tax, sometimes no tax at all, simply because they can afford to employ better accountants, lawyers, and other acolytes and, equally important, can afford to do as the acolytes advise.

As the case of the Zeppelin shows, though, the advice may be addled. They shared their rotten counsel with Beatle George Harrison, Roger Moore, and a host of other business and show business luminaries. All fell into the maw of a tax-dodging outfit called Rossminster, whose doings have been chronicled by Michael Gillard under the title *In the Name of Charity.* Why charity? Take the James Bond star: he bought an Isle of Man bank from the two operators behind Rossminster, thus eliminating their own embarrassing tax liability on its profits, and sold it back to Rossminster at the same price.

The pair then bought Roger Moore's company—thus converting his income into a lower taxed capital gain. Rossminster then sold the Moore company to one of its own creations, which existed for ostensible, untaxed charitable purposes (hence the title of the book), to complete the circle. It was a vicious one in the eyes of the Inland Revenue; under its attack, Roger Moore's plan to get 74 percent of his company's income, instead of 52 percent, collapsed like a pricked Zeppelin.

In 1984 the Rossminster partners were hit with record tax assessments for some $50 million, which disappointed clients such as Moore must have felt served the pair right. They employed a man in Guernsey who was in perpetual motion between that island and the even tinier one of Sark, holding kitchen board meetings with puppet directors drawn from the island's 500 residents—including lady pig farmers and an ornithologist. The whole "Sark lark" was vastly overcomplicated, especially when tax could have been minimized with far greater ease, perfect safety, and the acquiescence of the authorities.

The world is full of remarkable concessions and exemptions. Thus, the ordinary henpecked taxpayer doesn't know that the Republic of Ireland, for some inscrutable Irish reason, levies no tax whatsoever on creative artists. The shrewd creator can find this out, even if his creation is as far, culturally speaking, from *Juno and the Paycock* as Len Deighton's *Ipcress File*; he can also buy a castle in Eire, like Deighton, and take advantage of the benevolent provision.

A swift change of luxury residence is obviously a prerogative of the rich. Best-selling British authors have headed for Malta as earlier generations of American actors and writers sped to Switzerland. That trick isn't open to the average or even above-average income earner. Apart from anything else, your average, even your well above average, man has to live where his work is, whereas the superbly rich can even buy their own island, like the man who was Britain's biggest manufacturer of lipstick cases, or Aristotle Onassis (to go from the financially superior to the sublime). The island proprietor can then, with luck, like the lipstick man, fix his own tax rate. Nor are the exiles condemned to spend the rest of their lives in Malta.

The overrich Briton, for instance, flees to Malta on April 4, just before the new tax year starts. He stays there until April 5, a year thence, at which point he patriotically returns home. Now, all income from self-employment, like all profits from corporations, is taxed one year in arrears. That is, the income of the temporary expatriate for the year of his absence is technically the money earned in the previous year. But since the wandering boy has wandered out of U.K. residence, he has no tax liability for that income in the wandering year—even though he spent every month in which the loot was actually earned living in Esher, Surrey.

That's not all. During his year of absence, the wanderer is not a U.K. resident for tax purposes. Therefore, the money he receives during those absent months, be it never so large, is not eligible for U.K. tax either—even though during the months when, in other circumstances, the loot would have been taxable, he is safely ensconced once more in the splendors of Esher.

The result of this stratagem is that two years' income can be received free of tax; and it takes little further ingenuity to put three years' income, or sometimes even four, into those twelve months by some judicious deferring here and advancing there. Even so, exiles are apt to find the months of exile trying and to skip back to London for a brief taste of something livelier than Malta, all muffled up in false beards.

Another disadvantage is that absence, while it may make the heart grow fonder, doesn't make the control any easier. Humphreys and Glasgow, one of the world's major forces in plant construction, especially in gas, oil, and chemicals, was controlled by a remarkable man called Ambrose Congreve—or, to be more precise, by Congreve and his wife. Mrs. Congreve's family (the Glasgow in the name) had started the business, and the shareholdings in 1970 were as follows: "A. Congreve, 1; Mrs. M. G. Congreve, 119,999; J. F. Burrell, M. Baring, and G. V. C. Davies, 280,000; A. Congreve and Mrs. M. G. Congreve have an interest in the 280,000 shares mentioned above, and the 120,000 18 percent noncumulative preference shares are held by Mrs. Congreve."

This made the Congreves phenomenally wealthy, which had some of the usual advantages—including Mount Congreve, a legendary Irish estate with a fabulous garden; but there were also disadvantages—for tax reasons he could only stay ninety days a year in Britain. In the 1980s and his own seventies, Congreve bought a splendid establishment opposite Lancaster House, at the back of St. James's Palace, and converted it into a most desirable pad for the company. Hardly had it moved in when the Congreves were forced by corporate financial pressures to sell out to an American buyer—absentee landlords in the end make absent-minded managements.

The American tax authorities have the bad habit (mitigated only by the numberless American tax shelters) of regarding an American's income as taxable under U.S. law wherever it is earned or the taxpayer resides. Even here, there are escape routes. The foreign residence loophole has a different shape and mode of access in every country, but there are always potential advantages if the player has foreign income. Generally, money earned abroad can be taxed either where it's earned or where its owner lives—or in some neutral spot on the map selected by the earner for the understandable reason that its government levies little or no tax. The Cayman Islands thus came into unwonted prominence when it was revealed that a former cabinet minister had money, paid him for consultancy services, delivered into a Cayman account, and that the company, Lonrho, habitually rewarded its executives, at least in part, in the same home from home.

The attraction of the Cayman Islands (and other tax havens, on which reams of valuable literature have been written) is that the taxpayer (or nonpayer) can stay put while his money does the traveling. For complete exemption from tax, however, the solution is the other way around. Maintain three homes in three different countries, and travel among the three, never staying more than six months in any of them, and you will very probably pay no tax to any of the three authorities. This nomadic existence is the ultimate form of tax avoidance—not, be it noted, tax evasion, which is strictly illegal.

One who has good cause to appreciate the distinction is Aldo Gucci, who in his eighties received a prison sentence for deliberately overlooking some $11 million of income from his top-of-the-market leather-goods shops. That was Gucci's first mistake. His second, a far worse one, was to engage in a family feud—during which his son Paolo filed documents in court that aroused the passionate interest of the Internal Revenue Service.

At his sentencing, Aldo Gucci observed of his family: "Some of them have done their duty and others have the satisfaction of their revenge." The IRS had the satisfaction of collecting $7 million in back taxes, plus interest. Clearly, Gucci, who only became a permanent resident of the United States in 1976 (keeping homes in Manhattan, Palm Beach, London, and Rome), had lived, fiscally, in New York as the Romans do: a fatal error. In countries such as Italy, tax evasion is almost a second religion. On the assumption that no Italian would ever give an honest account of his income (now that torture is illegal), the authorities were reduced to taxing him on the appearance of wealth. That's why Italians keep private planes at an airfield just inside the Swiss border.

It follows that any foreigner who has income in a land of eager evaders can benefit from the same rules. Being foreign, moreover, he can keep some of his money outside without let or hindrance—and is not reduced, like an Italian who distrusts the lira, the unions, and the government in equal proportions, to humping suitcases full of currency across the frontier that separates Italy from the Swiss paradise.

That's one of the ways in which the one-year exiles can get more than two years of income saved from tax. During the year they finish another masterpiece that collects foreign royalties. If the film script or whatever had been written in Esher, the normal U.K. tax would have applied. As it was compiled in sunnier climes, the proceeds can go straight to an offshore tax haven. Performing artists, of course, never have this problem. Their work takes them legitimately all around the world, and where they choose to be paid (or rather, where their business managers choose for them) is where, if anywhere, their tax is handed over.

Time as well as place is optional. You can defer income over several years, as William Holden deferred his take from *The Bridge on the River Kwai*, or as the original late-night talk show hero, Jack Paar, did with his phenomenal contract. The smaller the annual installments, the lower the tax liability in each year. In fact, the deferred trick can confer more benefit on the employer than the employed. In one case, the interest received by the movie producer on the sum set aside for his deferred star substantially exceeded the payments due each year—so he actually got the superstar's services for less than nothing.

The workings of time can operate the other way around. Sir Charles Clore, knowing his life was drawing to its close, and as reluctant to part involuntarily with his wealth in death as in life, arranged to move ownership of his rich Stype country estate out of the British tax man's reach shortly before its sale. The tax man refused to accept this disposition, pursued Clore's executives through the courts, and finally won a colossal settlement. But the compound interest earned on the funds while the case dragged on turned out, neatly enough, to pay the entire bill.

Media tycoon Samuel I. Newhouse's death in 1979 unveiled another device for disposing of unwanted hundreds of millions without actually doing so. His private publishing empire was valued, by painstaking comparison with public companies in the same line of business, at $1 billion or so. But the heirs held, before the patriarch's death, nonconvertible preferred stock. When a suitable amount of the corporation's worth had been assigned to this stock, the founding father was found to have died with a mere $179 million.

An affronted IRS not only added half a billion to the $1.5 million, but put so low a value on the preferred stock that Newhouse was shown to have died worth $1.2 billion—almost seven times as much. The resulting $609 million tax bill, plus a $306 million fraud penalty, was still in dispute seven years after Newhouse's departure.

Most of the wealthy, and many of the not quite so wealthy, deal with their inheritance problems by the use of trusts. The purpose of most family trusts is to allow father to "make provision" for his children, which sounds no less innocent than popping coins into their piggy bank. The IRS, however, sees this innocence in an altogether darker hue: the greater the protection of the heirs, the less the revenue for the IRS. Hence the constant tightening of the rules. Since 1976, the old-style "generation-skipping" trust, which meant that estate taxes were paid only once, has been taxed. Direct bequests to grandchildren were not brought into the net, however; they are affected by the 1986 tax reform—but only after the total settled passes $2 million per sprig.

In most of the free world, the family trust—the Stranahans of Champion Spark Plugs erected thirty of the things—is probably the most heavily worked device in the whole field of tax avoidance, used even by those families that have graduated to the ultimate in trusts, the charitable foundation. In the American heyday of 1950, foundations were being created at a hundred a month. The donor could give 20 percent of his income to the foundation without paying tax. If he gave it goodies, such as stocks or property, he deducted 20 percent of the value from gross income; yet in seven years the Moody Foundation, set up by a man who owned about half of Galveston, gave away precisely $422,000. The extent of its wealth can be guessed from that of Robert I. Moody, grandson of the great William L. The younger Moody ended bitter family rows over the business by acquiring control of the family bank from the foundation in 1979. A trust under his control enjoys the benefits of American National Insurance and hotels that, *Forbes* estimates, gave grandson Moody a worth of $570 million in 1986.

Even if the donations are of somewhat nobler proportions than William L. Moody's, the charitable founder is enabled to spend tax-free money on some of his own desires—and supporting the Metropolitan Opera is no less a gratification, even if a worthier one, than owning a yacht.

You can, in fact, get the yacht tax-free, too: if not through the trust route, by the company way. Income earned by a company, although the currency is precisely the same color, is different from income earned by an individual. Corporate income, for main example, can have expenses deducted before the taxable amount is computed—so long as the charge is a legitimate business expense. Enter the yacht. Mrs. Bernard Castro, whose fortune was built on convertibles of the sofa rather than the stock-market variety, had a small liner at Fort Lauderdale; scattered around among the convertibles (a sofa converting into a bar at one end and a stereo at the other, a chair becoming a hair-dryer-cum-ironing-board) was Castro sales literature. As Mrs. Castro delicately pointed out, "After all we make this boat tax deductible." Another American taxpayer, a manufacturer of footwear, argued that the entire cost of his oceangoing plaything was legitimately deductible because it afforded the opportunity to study the adhesive performance of various soles on a sloping, slippery surface.

The wealthy taxpayer, indeed, is a sloping and slippery animal. Even two dimensions—place and time—don't exhaust his appetite for avoidance. There is also the third dimension. As opposed to income received by trusts or foundations, which would attract tax if received anywhere else, income of the third degree is income that is identical to every other form of receipt, except for one thing: it pays no tax.

This category, almost exclusively reserved for the exceedingly rich, includes blessings like U.S. tax-exempt bonds, issued by local authorities with the benediction of Washington, which loses heavily on the deal; Eurobonds, the new international medium, also tax-free, from which all governments suffer, without apparently knowing or caring; the oil depletion allowance in the United States, which allows rich men and richer corporations to deduct against tax not only the cost of all holes dry and wet but also 22.5 percent against their gross income; depreciation money all around the globe, which allows those with money to build up still larger investments out of untaxed cash.

The classic depreciation cases are not the Texas oil fortunes. The strongest depreciation cases, because the industry is not inherently lucrative, are the shipping lines. Ships not only attract depreciation charges; in many countries they attract specially generous rates of tax exemption, with subsidies thrown in for sweeteners.

Politicians have a seemingly insatiable desire to foster their merchant marines, lest in some future holocaust their country should get cut off from the high seas (the phobia dates back at least to the days of the Spanish Armada). The net result is that one of Britain's most successful companies, European Ferries, engaged in the vital strategic business of ferrying tourists and their cars to the Continent, earned $30 million and paid not one penny of tax in four years (and then, in the next five, smidgens of 0.2 or 0.3 percent).

This was no mean effort, even by the standards of Dallas—and the extraordinary preponderance of shipping as well as oil magnates among the world's new rich is partly explained by the remarkable freedom from tax they enjoy. Thus Sir Y. K. Pao, when estimated to be worth $700 to $800 million (a mere appetizer for his later accumulation), had two main companies, which one year made profits of $26.8 million— neither paid a penny of tax. Among other fiscal advantages, ships, like pop singers, travel the world about their business, which makes it that much easier for the owner to locate his personal tax base wherever on the surface of the globe he can best ensure that his private income, like his corporate flow, is tax-free.

He can also, which must be a warming consolation for a man such as Pao, whose rich Shanghai interests were expropriated by the Communists, ensure that his assets are moving targets—and thus very hard to hit. What damaged Pao under capitalism, and laid low his two largest Hong Kong maritime rivals, wasn't the Red Peril but the ferocious depression in world shipping. The fiscally innocent always need reminding that tax relief on huge losses is no more use if the losses are genuine than bloodletting is for a case of pernicious anemia.

In one case, the penalties accrued, not to the seekers after tax relief, but to its provider. Tax write-offs were among the incentives that attracted investors to the deals of one Craig Hall. So eager were the players to avoid tax that this thirty-six-year-old had a $3 billion real estate empire under his control, all built, according to *Fortune*, on the following unpromising formula: "Just when inflation was abating, but mortgage rates were still sky-high, Hall paid premium prices for dozens of properties, tacked on fat fees up front, and sold the buildings to thousands of investors seeking deep tax shelter."

The inevitable results moved another Texan to comment, "Nice try, but so long, fella." The hero himself confessed that a claimed $225 million fortune was about to melt by at least $100 million in some six months. The fact that apparently shrewd people are attracted in such great numbers (and sums) to the propositions put forward by operators such as Hall establishes an important truth: impending taxation is so unwelcome to a wealthy man that, like sexual jealousy, it blinds even the shrewdest to reality.

Nobody in America has greater claims to shrewdness than Laurence Tisch and his brother, Preston, who became President Reagan's postmaster-general after helping to build the fraternal fortune to nearly $2 billion. From a dozen hotels in 1955, they advanced to control of Loews movie theaters five years later and then began the spectacular conglomeration that by 1985 had built revenues of $6.7 billion from hotels, Bulova watches, insurance, cigarettes, and so on. By considerable finesse and effective cunning, Larry Tisch ended up in charge of the CBS network, apparently enjoying every minute. By equal care and skill, the brothers had nurtured a second generation of hardworking successes and successors. Yet both these middle-aged financial virtuosi fell (hook, line, and $1.6 million) for the seductions of a mere kid named Charles Atkins.

Still only thirty-two when indicted by a federal grand jury, Atkins was a mere twenty-three-year-old when he proffered a $4 tax-deductible paper loss for every dollar invested in government securities. No less than 400 suckers subscribed no less than $36.8 million. You can easily understand stars such as Sidney Poitier, Lorne Greene, and Michael Landon falling for the spiel. But the Tisches? And Michel David-Weill, owner of one-third of Lazard Frères, which employs some of the sharpest pencils on Wall Street and can command the services of any others it fancies?

According to *Time*, David-Weill stood to lose at least $4.4 million in illegal deductions if the government won its case. These clever, successful, financially wise men (the Tisches, says *Forbes*, are "well respected on Wall Street for fundamental investment skills") were seduced by amounts that could make no material difference to their financial well-being. Against $2 billion of assets, easily $100 million of income, possibly much more in capital gain, what is the point of $1.6

million of questionable deductions? Only that it averts something that, to the Common Millionaire, is even more unpleasant than losing money to a creep in his twenties: paying tax.

This makes it much easier to convince even a Tisch that you have discovered one of the world's tax anomalies and oddities, like the large tax concessions on money paid as compensation to a big British executive who loses his job. Once upon a time, the whole "golden handshake" was free of tax, meaning that it paid a highly paid man hand over fist to engineer his own dismissal.

There was another lost British beauty that allowed retiring barristers to collect tax-free all fees outstanding at the date of their retirement—no matter how often they retired. One or two made almost as many last appearances as Sarah Bernhardt, taking care that, for a year or so before each retirement, no client was encouraged to pay up. Since a goodly proportion of the House of Commons consisted of lawyers, the chances of this loophole being closed were rated about as high as those of a U.S. Congress in which oil interests were the most powerful paymasters doing anything nasty to the depletion allowance. The tax collectors' victory in both cases demonstrates that the life of all loopholes, no matter how gilt-edged, has a limit, But never mind—the ingenuity of moneyed man knows few limits, either, and as soon as one loophole closes, another opens up.

The Middle East of loophole drillers, as rich in cash flow as the oil sands of Arabia, is the differential tax between income and capital gain, which is set to disappear in the United States. But capital in America, as in most countries, is not taxed at all until a gain is realized; so the advantage of conversion of income into capital may still arise.

The simplest and most unstoppable way is to become a genuine incorporated, publicly owned business. In this event, your wealth is no longer your taxable income; it is your income, taxed at the corporation tax rate, and multiplied by the price-earnings ratio: $100,000 a year then becomes, say, $1 million of capital. Enterprising Britons set up two companies whose stock-in-trade was to get stars such as Tom Jones to exchange their future earnings for shares; another company, Booker Brothers McConnell, better known as a West Indian trader, purchased and is still enjoying the future earnings of authors such as Agatha Christie and Ian Fleming.

This loophole was among those gummed up by the Inland Revenue, but the principle can still apply. One neat method is the Bahamas partnership, in which the partner, a local lawyer, is well paid simply to sleep. After suitable passage of time, during which the earnings have poured in at the indulgent local rates of taxation, the partnership is liquidated and the profits are paid over as capital increments, and in the previously determined proportions, to the partners.

This is a relatively new wrinkle on an old device: the Liechtenstein or Luxembourg company in which, again, a local lawyer comes in as the ostensible part (or even majority) owner. Many a rich income finds its way into these safe harbors—but the catch is that a resident in some country with an efficient tax system like Britain's may find it difficult to get his tax-free money back home in the same blissful untaxed condition.

All is less well than it used to be in the grand old sport of tax havenry. Not the least disturbing aspect to the tax evader of the Howard Hughes affair, or rather the non–Howard Hughes affair, was that a Swiss bank dropped the veil of secrecy to the point of total nudity, simply to put Mrs. Edith Irving, the forger's wife, on the spot.

A tenet of the dedicated tax savers who have deposited billions of foreign money held in Switzerland (several billions are said to consist of U.S. tax-evasion money alone) was that Swiss banks, no matter if you opened the account in the name of Mickey Mouse, Scarface Al Capone, or Nikita S. Khrushchev, would protect your secrecy to the death. In this instance, no doubt, the Swiss banks' dislike of helping to perpetrate a particularly blatant fraud, especially on a man with as much money as Hughes, outweighed the racket's traditional respect for the privacy of its numbered accounts.

But however special the circumstances, the Hughes-Irving incident, followed by reforms of the Swiss banking laws and by incidents such as bank cooperation over the Iranian arms scandal, was another example of the steady erosion of what was once the rich man's inalienable right to keep every red cent he earned. In 1969 the U.S. Congress actually decreed that the wealthy had to pay 10 percent of their income in taxes, irrespective of the dodges to which they and their advisers had resorted. A senator later turned up the information that in 1972, no less than 276 Americans with income over $100,000 paid not a bean to the Internal Revenue Service. The minimum tax, it transpired, was to be levied on "adjusted gross income"—and after they had finished adjusting via their favorite deductions, these 276 worthies had an adjusted gross income of nothing.

All the same, one by one, stone by stone, the bastions that protected a millionaire's income in his lifetime are, if not coming down, being chipped away; and it follows that his defenses against depradations after his death are also being gradually eroded.

For instance, the Disappearing Estate Trick, a gambit as satisfying and mysterious as the Indian rope variety, came to the pained attention of the British authorities. It operated on the fact that works of art, instead of being aggregated, were charged after death separately—at the rate that applied to the rest of a man's estate. Suppose a millionaire was suddenly informed by his doctor that he only had a week to live. His correct fiscal response was to rush to the nearest friendly banker and borrow another million, before racing on to Bond Street and the nearest equally friendly art dealer. With the borrowed million, he would buy some assorted masterpieces, and then die as promised.

The following equation then applies, to the great joy of his heirs. The estate consists of a million of assets, less a million of debts, which equals nil. The art must be assessed at the same rate as the rest of the inheritance, which also equals nil. This loophole, created by the general and laudable feeling that artistic patronage is to be encouraged, has been plugged, and the U.S. authorities, too, are getting leery about the tax-avoidance uses of *la belle peinture.*

Time was when a rich man could buy a picture for $100,000, give it after a suitable pause for appreciation to a museum, and deduct the entire appreciated value from his income tax while still enjoying full possession of the painting during his lifetime. Today he must hand it over to the museum within four years, but the provision, again eminently laudable in intent, still has the prime effect of allowing the wealthy to hang on to more of their income than the tax man has a right to expect.

This fact of fiscal life inspired one curator, Dr. Jiri Frel of the Getty Museum, to operate a fraud of dimensions small only by Atkins standards. He persuaded rich Americans to donate, say, a $10,000 sculpture fragment from ancient Greece. Frel then obligingly valued the piece at $20,000. For a taxpayer in the 60 percent bracket, that represented a tax saving of $12,000, or a clear $2,000 profit.

The rake-off probably went much higher. Geraldine Norman reported in the London *Times* that "Frel arranged valuations around three or four times market value." Not surprisingly, he "attracted many donors"—more than a hundred of them. The amount of the donations to the Getty Museum in all came to $14.4 million, according to the Internal Revenue Service, which only started to investigate the offer after the Czech-born curator had departed in April 1984 for a life of some luxury in Europe. It was disturbed only by the breaking of the phony donations story (plus considerable doubts over the authenticity of $12 million of Greek marbles Frel had offloaded on the Getty).

No doubt this story would have caused at least as much pain to the museum's founder as his heirs' billion-dollar tax bill—though in this case the pain was shared by the IRS. The latter's job is like that of Hercules in the Augean stables. The politicians are always creating new ways of keeping fortunes intact—or refusing to repeal old ones, even when the results plainly contradict public policy. One American study, done at a time when estates were supposed to carry duty ranging from 69 percent to 77 percent, showed that those of $20 million or above actually paid 15.7 percent. In Britain, estate duty has long been called an "optional tax," and those who fail to take advantage of such options are often robbed by their own blindness. One was the first Henry Ford. According to an almost certainly accurate estimate, the crisis forced on Ford by his failure to make suitable provision decimated the family fortune; in the emergency, the old man had to give away to his hastily erected foundation the bulk of his interests.

Far lesser men devote far greater time and ingenuity to the blessed trinity of tax avoidance: first, achieving the exemption of income from tax; second, obtaining the conversion of taxable income into capital; and third, accomplishing the preservation of capital for inheritance. One honest scion of a noble house, asked what he proposed to do with himself, now he had come into his fortune, remarked frankly, "Defend it against the Inland Revenue."

The defenders come both low and high. Kathleen Winsor, author of *Forever Amber*, had her income from that work adjudged a capital gain, thus paying a maximum tax of only 25 percent. At the other end of the scale, literary and otherwise, Winston Churchill's proceeds from his war memoirs are supposed to have been treated as a sale of his archives (a capital gain, then tax-free), not as income from writing a book. Since the great old man got $750,000 from *Life* for the serial rights alone, the savings must have been immense.

The sudden enthusiasm of film stars for forming their own production companies, or taking their fees in cuts from the worldwide take, arose because income derived in this way can be treated as corporate rather than individual. Lucille Ball and Desi Arnaz, by forming Desilu, or Frank Sinatra with Reprise Records, exchanged potentially highly taxable income for lower-taxed money; said funds can be retained and invested in a corporation, which then becomes a highly salable capital asset.

The IRS, naturally, is fully alive to these benefits. The taxation of the wealthy is much like a game of pro football, in which, whenever the rich team gains excessive yardage, the IRS forces them right back, only for the Common Millionaires to power upfield again with a new play. For instance, U.S. tax reform was supposed to strip high taxpayers of the exemptions and deductions that gained them most of their yardage in return for lower tax rates.

The latter could be safely banked. But the consequences of other reforms in the package included this: corporations could bring back into their profits huge amounts of tax provision that had been set aside for future payment. The main beneficiaries included companies with substantial oil interests—that is, the very group where millionaire ownership is most conspicuous. For Du Pont, the bounty would amount to over $600 million, a pleasant thought for the du Ponts and the Bronfmans, who share half the equity.

Not that tax has been a painful concern for many U.S. companies; even public ones of great size from time to time contrive to pay no tax at all. That is the precise ambition of private companies far down the economic scale. In theory, the new tax laws made this far tougher. Thus, the former attractions of mergers are crystallized by this neat sum in *Business Week.* You sell a billion-dollar company (book value) for a billion more. On that second billion, under the old regime, the only tax payable is a maximum 20 percent, or $200 million, on the stockholders' profit—which nets out at $800 million.

Under the new rules, the corporation pays 34 percent tax, while the shareholders face a 28 percent maximum. That reduces the profit to $475 million. Before the sackcloth and ashes are taken out of the closet, though, other elements in the law need to be considered. Suppose (which is more than likely) that the company is owned by fewer than thirty-five family members. It might now qualify as an "S" corporation, which has no corporate tax liability at all. And as a securities lawyer told *Time*, "The government will continue to create new loopholes to accomplish economic and social goals."

In this game of fiscal football, in other words, the IRS (or rather its political masters) is always turning the ball over to the other side. In fact, the main wonder, given that so many wonders can be worked by tax advisers, is that anybody should opt for less-favored treatment. But it does happen. Edward Boughton was one of an elderly trio whose Automotive Products, with its chairmanship rotated among the three annually (until one died), made three vast fortunes out of Lockheed brakes, Borg and Beck clutches, and so forth. On his death in 1973, Boughton left £2.8 million. Of that, nearly £2 million went, voluntarily, to the Exchequer, because the ninety-one-year-old Boughton had not availed himself of "ways and means available to reduce death duty," believing that the tax bite was "just and equitable." If Boughton is right, then the rain of tax-avoidance riches has been falling heavily on the unjust and the unfair.

18

THE PAPER
PYRAMIDS

In the Age of the Common Millionaire, the exchange of pieces of paper
for assets has become fundamental. It accelerated in the 1970s and
1980s to a degree, and in a manner, that added a new dimension to the
generation and regeneration of wealth. Quite how large a dimension
emerged before the radical change of scene in October 1987 when the
curtain was drawn aside by that year's Guinness scandal—a scam
pulled apart by the revelations of the disreputable Ivan Boesky.

The king of the crooked arbitrageurs had crookedly helped the
British company to boost the price of its stock (part of the effort needed
to acquire Distillers and its fine Scotch whiskies). In the aftermath of
Boesky's loud singing, the Guinness accountants found over $40 mil-
lion of unexplained invoices. As the explanations came in, one financier
was revealed as the recipient of $7.5 million for his part in the deal;
another was in for $3 million; while an individual stockbroker had $4.5
million—which, he said, wasn't for supporting the stock, but "for key
advice."

The extraordinary size of these payments can be deduced from the fact that the three above (total $15 million) would have serviced for a year a loan of $120 million—and that's *before* tax relief. If $40 million represents, so to speak, the gratuities in a big deal, what's the bill itself? Mind-boggling is the answer, although *Fortune*'s tabulation of the fifty biggest deals of 1986 at first sight shows marked self-restraint by the so-called financial intermediaries—taking from as little as 0.6 percent of the transaction to a high of 5.03 percent.

Those tiny percentages, however, were set against titanic sums. First Boston took its 0.6 percent out of a $2.7 billion buyback of Union Carbide stock: the take came to $1.7 million. That 5.03 percent was shared among a bunch of the boys when Coca-Cola Enterprises sold $1.2 billion of common stock in its bottling companies—and that amounted to a $59.3 million pool. Even this wasn't the biggest bundle: the leveraged buyout that took the Safeway supermarkets private, with a $4.3 billion price tag, generated fees of $81 million.

Now, it's obvious, even to an uneducated glance, that the Wall Streeters' costs for those deals were handily below even the $1.7 million fee, let alone the $81 million blockbuster. Most of what, according to *Fortune*, totaled $615 million in fees will have been clear profit—and that sum, as in the case of Guinness's broker friend, is for "key advice," which doesn't count commissions for arranging the necessary finance. Goldman Sachs alone pulled in over $109 million in fees—which must have guaranteed its partners one last happy Christmas.

It has been a very long time since the Wall Street dealmakers had a dismal Yuletide. The intermediaries are just what the word implies: conduits along which the pieces of paper pass. In the process, however, more and more paper has been sticking inside the conduits, resulting in a thrilling rise (for them, that is) in the pay and capital worth of the Wall Streeters themselves. Some became richer than those they served—nobody in U.S. industry, for instance, began to match the $55 million salary paid to Michael Milken, the genius, of a kind, who developed the junk bond to the greater glory of Drexel Burnham Lambert (which grabbed $143.4 million in just three billion-dollar-fee bonanzas in 1986).

The financing of bids and deals had taken over in the 1980s from where Wall Street left off in the 1920s—stopped cold by the Great Depression to which Wall Street shenanigans had made a handsome contribution. In the 1920s the role of the junk bond in creating fat fees and fatter profits was played by the pyramid. That most elegant of geometrical shapes has twice in history been associated with great wealth. In ancient Egypt the Pharaohs made the elementary error of burying their treasure, the equivalent of Rockefeller- or Rothschild-size fortunes of today, in these imposing structures. There it lay waiting for the next generation of tomb robbers to pocket the proceeds: as neat a demonstration of the passage of wealth from weak hands to strong as history can offer.

Pyramids did not reappear until the halcyon days of free and untrammeled capitalism, in the hell-bent-for-leather run-up to the great slump. But in this reincarnation the pyramids were made not of stone but of paper, and their construction served the opposite purpose—the transfer of money was still from the weak to the strong, but this time the weak were many and the strong were few. No device conceived in the great boom and destroyed in the slump provided a more geometric multiplier of money.

If a roaring promoter had a business in the 1920s that the stock market, roaring away, valued at $100 million, that sum rapidly ceased to seem adequate in the light of the still more rapturous paper values being created on all sides. But what if a second company were created whose principal asset was a major holding in the first? Bonanza number one was still worth $100 million; bonanza number two could rapidly be run up to the same comforting figure. A third company could then be formed whose prime holding was a major share in bonanza number two. If that, in turn, could be rushed up to $100 million, the entire paper fortune had been tripled without any commensurate improvement in the underlying assets.

The practitioners of the 1920s carried the device of the holding company to undreamed-of extremes: in his supreme deployment of the pyramid art form, Samuel Insull constructed an edifice in which, on one estimate, $1 invested in a company called Middle West Utilities controlled $1,750 held by the public in the operating companies that actually produced the nation's electricity, or at least 12 percent of it.

But pyramids, for all their seeming solidity, have a basic weakness. If one lower layer starts to crumble, all those above must fall in on top. Insull's frantic efforts to protect part of his unimaginably complex pyramid from the imagined depredations of a rival financier deposited a $20 million profit in the latter's lap and eventually, after a terrible collapse in his shares, deposited Insull in court, accused of using shareholders' funds for his own pyramidic ends. (Despite having fled before the law to Greece, the old boy, pleading an "honest" accounting error of $10 million, got off scot-free.)

The wily outwitter of Insull was none other than Cyrus S. Eaton, who a later generation knew only as the capitalist friend of Khrushchev, the founder of the East-West Pugwash conferences on nuclear science, and the author, among other tomes, of a work titled *Is the Globe Big Enough for Capitalism and Communism?* Eaton used his investment bank, Otis and Company of Cleveland, and his holding company with skill and daring—muscling in on Insull and on the territory of mightier forces still, the Mellons and the House of Morgan.

Eaton later memorialized his own exploits under the simple description of "Organizer, Republic Steel Corporation and United Light and Power Company." His was an extraordinary survival into the Age of the Common Millionaire of a man who wrestled with the giants of the silver age on their own terms and with their own philosophy. As somebody remarked when Eaton was building up his huge holdings in Insull stocks, "Eaton wasn't really interested in running things. All he wanted was the money."

For Insull, it was the other way around, even when in fifty days of the fatal summer of 1929 his securities were appreciating at $7,000 a minute, day in, day out—which must be some kind of record. He fell two years later for a very simple reason, as his market operator explained: "You can't go on buying your own stocks forever. Sooner or later you run out of money."

That observation isn't quite as true today as it was, though the restriction certainly still applies. When Union Carbide, struggling out of the attempted bearhug of GAF, bought 55 percent of its own shares, the cost was $3.3 billion—more than half the cost to General Electric of buying RCA in the biggest deal of 1986. Normally, large companies and their proprietors have therefore contented themselves with buying back marginal amounts of the equity—just enough to bolster the share price and the value of their stock options: Pennzoil's Hugh Liedtke (as described in Chapter 10) has been a shrewd practitioner and beneficiary of this gambit.

Even shrewder performers have spotted that, if you purchase all the equity, the money restriction need not apply: the junk bond came riding to the rescue as the company in effect devoured itself, only to spit itself out again in a form bringing far more profit to the management. The bills for the leveraged buyouts of Beatrice Foods and Safeway Stores were, respectively, $6.2 billion and $4.3 billion, dwarfing the Union Carbide buyback operation—and enriching the Wall Street wizards by $56 million in the first case and, as noted, $81 million in the second.

The deals, and the fat capital gains that resulted for the buyers-out, were perfectly legal, which wasn't the case when Guinness committed perhaps $300 million to the support of its own shares through various intermediaries. Getting rid of an illegally purchased tenth of the entire equity before the sheriff arrived was the problem: Guinness was in a fix no less painful than that of Insull, stuck with stock for which he couldn't pay.

Insull's monument was only the most conspicuous of the structures erected by the latter-day pharaohs. As for others, John Kenneth Galbraith has described the furious progress of outfits such as the American Founders Group. It started in 1922 with two investment trusts, which shared a capital of $500 between them. By 1927 the two companies had become three, which among them had sold $70 to $80 million of securities to the thirsty public of the day. In 1928 and 1929 the sale of stock, in a group swollen to thirteen companies, reached epidemic proportions: its total resources had enlarged gigantically to a clear billion. A third of that, however, was accounted for by shares in the American Founders Group itself.

The terrible result when the steps of the pyramid crumbled away and the laws of geometric progression worked in reverse, are demonstrated by the performance of Goldman Sachs. This began its rake's career by organizing the Goldman Sachs Trading Company as the base of its pyramid. The public was let in on this ground floor at $104 a throw. After the debacle, in 1932, the ground-floor entrants were deep in the basement: their shares were worth less than $2.

Small wonder that Insull or Goldman Sachs pyramids have not been allowed to reappear. But the holding company is, as we noted earlier, alive, kicking, and capable of generating profit at a most becoming rate. Indeed, holding companies are still the prime medium for organizing corporations. Every big company has a pyramidic legal structure, the critical difference being that, with insignificant exceptions, the apex of the pyramid holds 100 percent of each layer, a percentage that serves as an effective enough cement.

Dynasties also have holding companies. But lurking behind most of them is a private company or trust in which the personal holdings are located. This is a handy device, used by many millionaires to provide more strings to their bows and to place a decent distance between their income and the tax man. A typical dynastic pyramid— typical in all respects save its size, which *Fortune* estimated at $3.5 billion—is the one that brings financial balm to the hearts of eighty-three Rockefellers. The so-called 1934 Trusts owns 94 percent of the equity of Rockefeller Group, Inc.

This outfit, with an equity value to the Rockefellers of $800 million, owns outright two partnerships with a dozen buildings in Rockefeller Center, an investment fund that no doubt deserves its "dedicated" description in more than the technical sense, real estate in New York and New Jersey (including more of Rockefeller Center), and a bundle of businesses that manage real estate and operate in the entertainment and telecommunications industries. The pyramid culminates in a real estate investment trust, set up by RGI to wring the maximum worth from the Rockefellers' purchase, for $400 million ($34 million an acre), of the land under their beloved Rockefeller Center. This deal with the previous owners, Columbia University, generated $1.2 billion for the dynasty—and that loot accounted for much of the $2.3 billion in the 1934 Trusts.

On top of that, the 1952 Trusts held a mere $300 million in stocks and bonds, while in "Room 5600," actually three floors in the RCA Building, 175 people (over two per heir) ran individual accounts worth $900 million and also supervised Venrock, the family venture-capital partnership. With all this going for them, the younger Rockefellers could afford the luxury of turning their well-clad backs on business: "In spirit," writes Carol J. Loomis in *Fortune*, "this family is down to the Cash-Out Generation." Even the philanthropic urge has dwindled, along with the assets needed to gratify it: the Rockefeller Brothers Fund is down to its last $235 million.

The fraternal generosity in fact totaled some $400 million, a great sum, though handsomely exceeded by the $550 million of the founding dynast and the $552 million of John D. Rockefeller II. The third generation has also tried to mix business with the pleasure of bringing benefit to mankind. The International Basic Economy Corporation, for instance, was founded back in 1947 by Nelson Rockefeller. It threw itself into worthy activities such as food distribution, housing, marketing, and manufacture in various deserving geographical spots, all in an attempt to stimulate the local economies.

But in 1971, when Rodman C. (Nelson's boy) took over the helm, IBEC had succeeded in making only $796,000 nine months' profit on sales of $213.1 million—which practically classified it as an outright charity. Nine years later, the business was sold and Rodman went into what Loomis describes as a kind of rich limbo: "More absorbed in business than any other member of his generation but never accepted as a leader by the family, he is today a developer of commercial real estate around the country." Today, Rockefeller charity mostly begins at home.

Nor is charity the word that would instinctively be applied to the pyramid put together by Frank Lloyd, the past master at separating artists from their paintings and, in exchange for the same, millionaires and museums from their cash. The difference in cost between the two processes got Lloyd enough millions (reputedly then twenty-five, calculated in dollars) to buy a French holiday home from uranium king Joseph Hirshhorn and to finance a convoluted legal and fiscal structure. At its head sat the Lloyd family trust, based in Liechtenstein; that useful principality was also conveniently the home of the master company, Marlborough AG, and of two associated firms, Art Finance and Kunst und Finanz (which means "Art Finance" in German).

Art Finance owned the two New York galleries, while the master company held directly the four businesses in Zurich and London, not to mention the four partnerships in Rome, Toronto, Montreal, and Tokyo. According to his partner in the latter business, quoted in *Time* magazine, "Lloyd-san almost seems to understand Zen." Be that as it may, the case of Frank Lloyd (now resident in the Bahamas) shows to a fine degree the natural understanding of the process of financial self-preservation—which, in a sense, is why the pharaohs built their pyramids, too.

Liechtenstein also apparently came in useful for Robert Maxwell, who became one of Europe's richest men, thanks to his ownership of Pergamon Press, a publisher of scientific periodicals, the Mirror Group of newspapers, and the lion's share of the British Printing and Communications Corporation. The latter is a spectacular case of the It-Can't-Get-Any-Worse technique. Maxwell picked up control of this hulk, with $300 million of turnover, for $18 million. Within a few years it was worth a precrash $2 billion—no sow's ear has ever been turned into a larger silk purse.

The financing of Maxwell's forays had always excited curiosity. The curious, though, found out something even curiouser. It turned out that Maxwell didn't really own these blessings at all. During one of the tycoon's numerous takeover attacks, the victim (who eluded the predator's grasp) elucidated the information that ownership rested with a Liechtenstein trust—one of a very special variety that is not obliged to reveal anything about itself save that it exists (and hardly that). The most that Maxwell's lawyers would divulge was that the trust existed for the benefit of relatives of the Maxwells' grandparents living overseas.

Presumably that definition was meant to exclude Maxwell himself—but presumably he had the best of fiscal reasons for placing the fruits of his genius in this eminently rich apex company. No apex to a family pyramid entombs more wealth, however, than Christiana Securities, 75 percent owned by the du Ponts, who deposited therein the lion's share of their interest in the family gunpowder store. Paradoxically, as the clan's numbers have increased, so the usefulness of the structure has declined. The du Ponts, eager to exchange Christiana for straight holdings in the family store, ran into legal obstacles. Their motive was to make it easier to sell the shares; the usual reason for family pyramids, however, is to hang on to the contents. These family holding companies consequently rarely live and breathe—they are receptacles, legal conveniences, paper pigeonholes.

Nobody could say that of James P. Ling's Ling-Temco-Vought, which reinvented the pyramid in a most ingenious way and became the ultimate in holding companies. All conglomerates, partly because of their bad habit of buying companies too expensively, suffer through most of their lives from relatively low price-earnings ratios. This irritates their masters beyond reason; anybody who wanted to excite a flow of logical passion from second founding father Harold Geneen of ITT merely had to ask his opinion of the company's P/E.

Anthony Sampson found the perfect description for both ITT and this type of construction. "The whole massive conglomerate, from Tokyo to Chile, from smoked hams to telephones, rested like a vast upside-down pyramid on a pinpoint—the share price on the New York Stock Exchange." If the price on the NYSE rocked, or rocks, the pyramid sways to the same rhythm; and if the bough breaks, the cradle may fall. . . .

Ling was virtually alone among conglomerators in deciding to take this cradle by the rockers. If the NYSE price stuck at a point where the parts were worth more than the whole, he reasoned, float off part of the parts and you would, by establishing a stock market value, simultaneously despatch some needed public cash to the L-T-V coffers and enhance the balance sheet.

One of the newsmagazines published an endearing map, rather like a game of snakes and ladders, that showed how Ling, through an intricate series of deals ending with the flotation of the Wilson companies (nicknamed on Wall Street "meatball, golf ball, and goof ball"), paid for the original acquisition and was still left holding control of Wilson's meat-packing, sports, and chemical businesses—all for free.

But Ling's empire always sounded too good to be true—and indeed it was. The poor boy from Oklahoma had built up the fourteenth-largest company in the United States by initially developing an electronics and aerospace business; he shot himself down with a sequence of careless and costly purchases.

The sad truth pyramid builders overlook is that the underlying value of the business, which resides in its operating and earning assets, is not changed one iota by all their financial architecture. The separate market quotations for meatball, golf ball, and goof ball couldn't increase either their intrinsic value (whatever that was) or L-T-V's, and on the latter score, the market was perfectly right—the sprawling, bloated body of L-T-V was worth less than the parts, which had simply cost too much money, even if the money was funny.

That's where the deadly serious Wall Street dealmakers came in. The pyramid was a means of making the whole worth more than its parts; the junk bond has helped to make parts worth more than their contribution to the whole. The Revco drugstores were bought out for 355 percent of the value at which they stood on the books. Ted Turner's huge price for MGM/UA was 563 percent of book value. Given that the average stock on Wall Street, after a long bull market, stood at three times book (200 percent), something very odd must have been going on.

To keep the merger pot boiling, to a total of $92.6 billion in 1986 (not far short of the 1985 record), the financiers had encouraged their clients into riskier and riskier deals at higher and higher prices (and fees). The junk bond, like the issue of pyramid paper in the 1920s, created value where none had existed before. The danger was much the same—that, if the paper lost its putative worth, real values would collapse, setting up a chain reaction as investors in junk bonds either lost their money or, seeking to limit the damage, sold, driving them down further still.

But that was an irrelevant consideration for Wall Streeters waxing rich as never before on the merger magic. Their vast pay packets were only for starters; three men from Phibro-Salomon shared nearly $9 million, while Shearson Lehman similarly put some $3 million the way of its chairman. The president of First Boston contented himself with a mere $2.5 million. None of this largesse, however, counts the doubtless far greater value of cuts, not only of the equity (not counting the stock options) but also from lucrative individual deals.

One of the mysteries of dishonest takes such as Roger Siegel's $700,000 swag (delivered in cash in suitcases) from Ivan Boesky is that Wall Streeters with $2 million salaries such as Siegel's were in a position to reap rich rewards in considerable safety by investing honestly (more or less) in the transactions passing through their hands. Mike Milken's half-a-billion-dollar fortune may have been the summit of this particular iceberg—though who knows? The financier clever enough to maximize his opportunities is equally clever enough to minimize the exposure of his interests—and his liability to taxation.

Take Sir James Goldsmith. As *Business Week* observed, he "operates through a bewildering maze of offshore companies that allow him, among other things, to escape capital gains taxes." Goldsmith himself, it may be presumed, is among those not bewildered by the maze. He is an old hand at mazing. In his European days, when his main interests were a French holding company, General Occidentale (or GO), and a British food firm, Cavenham, a French cousin, Baron Alexis de Gunzberg, was his partner in interlocking enterprises of formidable complexity. For instance, in March 1968 the pair took control of a former Algerian tramway company and pumped various interests, ranging from a chunk of Cavenham to banking, into the shell. They also bought, quite separately, another bank, which controlled another group of firms under the abbreviated name of FIPP. By the time FIPP had taken over slimming foods from UTP, and had then been merged with Cavenham, and had agreed to merge with a French food group, GASA, and UTP had been merged with SGF to form GO, almost nobody could keep pace with the initials, let alone the interlocking and unlocking—except presumably Goldsmith and Gunzberg.

At the end of the day the formula FIPP + UTP + GASA + SGF added up to around two-thirds of GO, half in Goldsmith hands; its one-third of Cavenham alone was worth $90 million at the 1972 peak, the share price having soared eightfold in a year.

These European complexities baffled local interpreters, who were left still more uninformed when Goldsmith, peeved with Europe, moved control to Hong Kong, dismantled his interests, and prepared for the American invasion that eventually gave him control of some $2 billion of assets. FIPP + UTP + GASA + SGF was a mere hors d'oeuvre compared to the structure erected for that latter empire.

Goldsmith, too, has a financial liking for Liechtenstein, where the Brunneria Foundation resides (whether it was formed for the benefit of relatives of Sir James's grandparents isn't known). That foundation owns a Panamanian company, which in turn owns another Panamanian company, which in turn owns a Cayman Islands company, which in turn used to own both *vieux ami* GO (Generale Occidentale) and Cavenham Forest Industries. At that point, the visible assets came into sight—Grand Union supermarkets, 3.4 million acres of timberland, the French publishing business, all manner of interests large and small whose success bore witness (in 1987, neatly forestalling the crash he saw coming, he started liquidating them for much cash) to Goldsmith's mastery of business from a career that in its ups and downs, its twists and turns, has demonstrated the basic pyramid principles both positively and negatively.

Negatively, never buy from strong hands; positively, always buy from the weak, which means, generally speaking, large corporations. Positively, coalesce diverse interests to extract their maximum value; negatively, don't diffuse your activities over too many unrelated fields.

Negatively, avoid backing the wrong business horse; positively, capital-ize on your mistakes by learning from them. Positively, remember that the ultimate gain from the ultimate holding company resides in keeping its control in your hands; negatively, don't allow your operating base to become so weak that it won't support the holding structure above.

The essence of the modern pyramid can be seen, as through an X ray, by examining its opposite—the public company in which the ultimate holder personally owns most of the shares. He is limited to the latter and to their possibilities. The law doesn't allow him to build vertically much beyond one layer. So he turns to horizontalism. The holding company owns the master stakes in all the subsidiary or associated companies, but the latter can own useful holdings in each other and can deal and wheel incestuously as much as the master likes. This is not only a convenient way of realizing investment profits but also of burying mistakes or the so-so performers with which all holding operators are afflicted.

This utility was well demonstrated by George Weston Holdings, the master company of Garfield Weston's empire. For a group so little known, Weston's pyramid was of stupefying spread, with powerful companies in Britain, Canada (Weston's home country), South Africa (a regime to which Weston was partial), and the United States. In the United States, when National Tea lost money and omitted a dividend, the first such omission by a Weston company for half a century, the late patriarch, then aged seventy-five, whipped in one of his sons to repair the damage.

But terrible troubles in finding a solution to a self-created British problem were less easily dealt with; he had attempted to build the mammoth Fine Fare supermarket chain without adequate manage-ment. First he imported a flock of Canadian managers who flopped; then he put the whole collection in the care of an allegedly ace Canadian whose supervision was decidedly hampered by his refusal to cross the Atlantic in airplanes. So Weston neatly transferred ownership of the Fine Fare supermarkets (and their losses) to the Canadian wing of George Weston Holdings until such time as the losses had turned to sufficiently respectable profits.

That day duly arrived, thanks to the discovery of James Gulliver, a consultant who had unearthed and cleaned up a mess in a small part of the Fine Fare stables. At which point Weston had a business well on its way to a worth of something like $200 million, a wonderful profit on his original investment. Fine Fare's ownership was then repatriated across the Atlantic, where it became once again an ornament of Weston's British empire, a company capitalized in early 1987 at over $2 billion. What an astute millionaire holds, he has: none more demonstrably than the aforementioned Jimmy Goldsmith, whose liquidations before the crash left him $400 million ahead of the game—and something like $1.6 billion ahead of formerly ace investor George Soros, whose Quantum Fund lost 37 percent of its previous $2.5 billion value. Soros had told *Fortune*, only weeks before, "Just because the market is overvalued does not mean that it is not sustainable." Oh, yeah?

19

TOO MANY
BROTHS DON'T
SPOIL THE COOK

The fortunate few who climb step by ambitious step to the summit of large corporations are subject to the understandable vice of behaving like grand tycoons when they are nothing of the sort. Lack of tycoonery, with all its aggression, egotism, and passion for chopping pieces out of corners, is almost an essential qualification for the long haul up to the top. Once installed on the peak of their local Popocatepetl, however, the corpocrats begin behaving in what they imagine to be tycoon style.

In particular, they become magnetically attracted to the sight of other baskets into which they can deposit their (or rather, the shareholders') eggs. Although the results usually range from ghastly to middling, the proposition on which the mistaken policy is based is substantially correct. A high proportion of the world's rich have variegated interests here, there, and everywhere—and go on accumulating more like so many thieving magpies.

The proposition, however, isn't matched by sufficiently careful analysis. Corporations are best advised to keep as many eggs as possible in one basket, otherwise the outfit itself becomes too diffuse, and its senior men—the very same survivors of the long race up the bureaucratic ladder—are forced to dissipate their talents and experience over fields where neither apply. Worse still, the parts become worth less than the whole—often much less, as in the bizarre case of Beatrice Corp., taken private in a leveraged buyout for $6.2 billion in April 1986 and, after selling Avis, Coke bottling, four-fifths of International Playtex, and a $2.15 billion clutch of assorted businesses, valued at around $10 billion before the coming of the crash.

The multiple millionaire, however, is interested only in the parts and is happy to let the whole look after itself. The list of sidelines is amazing in its diversity and its dollar values. Thomas S. Monaghan is "a pizza man. I'm proud of that"—so he should be, since Domino's Pizza, with its 3,300-plus outlets, delivers pizzas to clientele in four countries. The 95 percent ownership of Domino's is what mostly made this ardent self-helper worth *Forbes*'s estimate of $250 million (a suitable advance on the borrowed $900 that started a small pizzeria in 1960). But Monaghan also owns a baseball team, the Detroit Tigers—sports teams being a pet millionaire method of combining business with pleasure.

A media king, Robert Staples Howard, has nineteen newspapers—but also just one "small oil and gas exploration company." A real estate tycoon, Mortimer Zuckerman, returning the compliment, is also in publishing, owning *Atlantic* and *U.S. News & World Report*, which cost him $163 million (a pretty penny in relation to a total worth put at $250 million). The *Penthouse* plutocrat, Bob Guccione, is deep into powdered milk for the Arabs.

And so it goes. Like the above examples, the rich entrepreneur usually has his base load, just as the big company does. But his accretions are less in the nature of a corporate policy than of a once-yearly bet on the Superbowl. Unlike the corpocrat, the entrepreneur has both flair and personal resources. Consequently, he is betting on himself; and, if the bet fails, he bears any loss or (more accurately) offsets it against his taxes. The corpocrat is betting on other people, the underlings who formed or will execute the plan; the loss, in the event of failure, will hurt his profits, balance sheet, or both, but the gain of a million in a $300 million company won't even be noticed.

That same capital profit, however, will look clean and sweet to any individual; and the rich, after all, have to do something more constructive with their money than burying it in the ground. That, however, is precisely what one multimillionaire did, and to his great profit—Kemmons Wilson, who made most of his money by housing the quick at

Holiday Inns, but turned a considerable number of extra bucks out of the dead.

Wilson bought into the cemetery plot business, but was put off by the low density of corpses. He applied to the question the same ingenuity that evolved his franchise system for hotel multiplication. Stiffs occupied so much ground, he observed, because they were stored horizontally; insert them vertically, and the entire dimensions of the problem would be changed. Wilson then adapted an oil field machine to bore the vertical holes, and made a special cylindrical coffin designed to fit the slots. His new basket was then ready to receive its golden, if macabre, eggs.

That combination of opportunism and technical innovation is not easily reproduced. But expert entrepreneurs down the ages never seem to have hesitated before a new possibility; they needed only to see that, if the barriers between hope and realization could be removed, a rich margin would result. The rewards don't even have to be realized fast— again, the individual investor, as opposed to the corporate one, has the inside track.

Since income is a potential embarrassment to the individual, he can be wholeheartedly content with an unrealized gain, so long as it is sufficiently gainful. Virtually all grades of the well-to-do have these sidelines, extramural activities that are bred by the very existence of their wealth. It acts as both magnet and propulsion unit. Propositions are irresistibly attracted to the point of the compass where possible finance sits, and the financing possibilities irresistibly urge their possessor to diversify—often in nutritious fields unrelated to the sources of their seven-digit or eight-digit bread and butter.

Kemmons Wilson's corpses were no further from his Holiday Inns than Norton Simon's art collecting was from his erstwhile tomato ketchup. In that case, the sideline became the mainline activity, and a rich dish on its own. The $100 million with which Simon departed from the commercial market had probably doubled within sixteen years largely devoted to the art bazaar. An inescapable truth is that, for those who could afford them, Old Masters of the Simon quality or Impressionists of the foremost rank have been among the most purse-warming, as well as culturally rewarding, investments of the postwar period. Take the £798,000 price Simon paid for Rembrandt's *Titus* (after the auctioneer got tangled up in Simon's tortuous instructions to the effect that when he was standing he wasn't bidding, when he was sitting he was, and so forth); it had already begun to look like a bargain within a couple of years.

In a sense, Simon, like Duveen in the age of the supreme dealer, created his own market: his prices were a major force propelling his own art values upward. Simon, however, had prodigious help from other purchasers, above all the Getty Foundation. Its unimaginably vast income makes Simon's resources seem like petty cash. The Getty gold flows in such embarrassing daily profusion that, in a sense, the higher Old Master prices rise, the better for this dominant buyer— better because more of its own embarrassing purchasing power is mopped up.

The boom in museums, mostly endowed by wealthy individuals, has spread the wealth wide and far—and deep. The $10 million fetched for a Manet of no surpassing wonder in late 1986 marked the new leap forward in Impressionists that culminated in a $40 million record for any work of art for a Van Gogh sunflower. The Manet came from the great collection assembled by Samuel Courtauld, whose other holdings, including many masterpieces far beyond the Manet in importance, must constitute a fortune to compare with the textile wealth that financed the purchases; just as J. P. Getty, shrewd beyond the tomb, by moving assets from oil to fine art, must have poised his portfolio perfectly to take advantage of an era of slumping prices for crude oil and soaring ones for oil paint.

The soaring has by no means been confined to Old Masters, Impressionists, or even modern masters such as Picasso and Braque, whose important works are now seven-figure phenomena. Dominique de Menil, as a Houston heiress whose father's pile came from the oil field services of Schlumberger, has made a heap of her own in modern art, with over 10,000 examples that must account for a major proportion of her $200 million.

Robert Scull, the New York cab king, achieved more than social prominence when he became the biggest buyer of pop art with his wife, Edith—although subsequent legal disputes took the bloom off the rosy fortune that resulted. The price appreciation on the new has handily outstripped that on the old. For only one example, the collector Sydney Lewis in 1986 paid $380,000 for a work painted thirty years earlier by Cy Twombley. Lewis had refused to buy the same picture back in 1964, when the price was just $1,000. That gives some indication of the phenomenal gains that must have been recorded by heroic, pioneering buyers such as Joe Hirshhorn, the uranium king.

His philanthropy ensured that the benefits would go to the public, rather than his pocket or that of his heirs; governments vied heatedly for the prize before President Johnson clinched the collection by offering the present site in Washington's magnificent Mall. Similarly, Dr. Peter Ludwig, made super-rich by his chocolate interests, has liberally endowed superb collections in West Germany with the results of his great sideline in modern art. Determined not to be outdone, the British advertising *wunderkind*, Charles Saatchi, has been spending a reputed $3 million a year in wholesale purchases of the avant-garde art of the 1970s and 1980s, buying so much of the output of artists such as Julian Schnabel as to affect the market materially.

Quite inevitably, the activities of a vigorous collector, public or private, do have much the same effect at the top end of the art market as a corner in commodities—when one determined buyer goes on buying until he possesses so much of the available supply that the price is at his mercy. This privilege of the wealthy diversifier, though, must be used with extreme care. He can, in theory, move sufficient resources to the chosen area to make his dreams come true. But the area of choice is the key. Many markets are too big even for Croesus to corner— although that may not stop him from trying.

It only briefly looked to be a good idea when the two Hunt offspring, super-rich both from Dad's oil and their own endeavors, in 1973's silver rush cornered enough of the world's supply to make their hoard worth a quarter of a billion dollars. Close to half of that early 1974 figure was the paper profit of Nelson Bunker Hunt and his brother Herbert. They should have taken it. The 6 percent of the world supply represented wasn't enough to swing the deal; subsequent efforts to save the day only bogged the Hunts deeper in a mire of losses and debts. The subsequent fall from $16 billion of wealth to perhaps $400 million must give Bunky Hunt the record for fast dissipation of fortune—and for one simple reason.

The Hunt boys didn't know what they were doing. The nature and range of a man's understanding determine how far he can diversify, and in what ways. Many men of surpassing wealth feel uncomfortable more than a stone's throw away from their business hearths and think little of happier, luckier spirits who fool around with coffins and casinos. There's a line in a Frank Sinatra film, uttered by Keenan Wynn as a rich promoter offered a Sinatra proposition for a Florida Disneyland, that sums up the attitude. "Disneylands," said the Wynn character brutally, "are for Disney." (Whose company proceeded some years later to build one, to its great profit, in Florida.)

The choice is truly a matter of temperament as much as ability. The diversifier has to regard himself as an investor, which is an utterly different role from that of the entrepreneur. Those who are content to sit back in their leather-padded swivel chairs and collect the money, however, have made some extraordinary extra piles. The oil-rich Texan Amon G. Carter, for instance, bankrolled American Airlines. That older generation of oil fortunes generally had less impact outside Texas and the other oil states than might have been expected from the venturesome nature and vast resources of their owners. Part of the reason was that oilmen habitually (and very sensibly, given the then-prevailing economics) put their profits right back into oil. Another factor is that states such as Texas contain a great deal of land; those oilmen who invested in these enormous tracts have done nearly as nicely as those Texas land barons who went into oil.

At that, Texas contains few if any oilmen with richer fortunes under their control than William Walter Caruth, Jr., who stuck to the land habit his grandfather and father had never kicked. By making North Dallas his backyard, Caruth built a worth estimated by *Forbes* at $600 million. That calls to mind a rueful story about Albert D. Lasker, the Lord & Thomas advertising genius whose $115 million packet is still one of the greatest yields anybody has had from Madison Avenue. Lasker offloaded the Texas land bequeathed by his father. Had he merely kept that rich soil, let alone cultivated its profits in Caruth style, Lasker would have died half a billion better off.

The new generation of oilmen, with the Basses the most conspicuous example, have diversified more potently than their predecessors—because they had a more potent reason for doing so: their oil, while still a handy asset, is not the cornucopia of old. The roller-coaster set going by OPEC, culminating in the shock price slide of the mid-1980s, made it imperative for oil money to seek other outlets, and, responding to that necessity, the oilmen were quick to develop the requisite skills. Billionaire Marvin Davis has thus assuaged the pain of falling values in the oil fields (which he wisely began selling at the start of the decade) by the profits on sweet deals such as selling Twentieth Century–Fox to Rupert Murdoch (a $575 million touch).

Another Denver tycoon, Philip F. Anschutz, pocketed half a billion from Mobil in 1982 for only half his interest in Anschutz Ranch East. In 1985, *Forbes* found it difficult to make up its mind whether Anschutz was or wasn't a billionaire (by 1986, he had the benefit of the doubt), but with his remaining oil, his other minerals, his 11 million acres of ranchland, the Rio Grande Railroad, and the Anaconda Tower in Denver, among other glories, Anschutz has plenty of insulation against the cold wind blowing across the oil lands, just like Davis—$20 million of whose comfort represents his Beverly Hills home, previously owned by Kenny Rogers.

As in Davis's case, much wealth has been automatically created from the fact that even a footloose millionaire must live somewhere, and while buying two or three houses, he might as well have a small patch of land to call his own in their vicinity. If that patch contains a farm, or trees, or various other conveniences, moreover, its acquisition will reduce his estate duties, his taxation, or both, and while performing its good deed of reduction, it will appreciate mightily. In 1961 Sir Charles Clore, seeking a suitable home for a couple of million pounds, bought 16,000 acres near Hereford from a London hospital. A dozen years later Clore's country pied-à-terre was worth, on a conservative estimate, £14 million.

In fact, this profit, gathered from imitating the lilies of the field and neither toiling nor spinning, outdid some of Clore's more spectacular achievements founded on real entrepreneurial effort. When he paid £550,000 for the site of the London Hilton, the first building to upstage Buckingham Palace, he was widely thought to be pulling off a masterly coup. But the site vendor invested Clore's thousands in land about as far from the metropolis as Britain can provide, up in Scotland, where his capital multiplied five and a half times in a decade—handsomely beating the profit on the Hilton for much less trouble.

That kind of appreciation has been recorded by almost every member of the well-endowed classes who put money into real estate—and in the United States, where the investor can charge depreciation on the purchase price even of old buildings, this type of diversification is practically obligatory. There is no doubt some screwy logic in allowing a millionaire to deduct from his taxes the notional annual fall in the value of a building that, as everyone knows (even in the Internal Revenue Service), is actually appreciating in worth.

You could indeed argue that America's rich and would-be rich would have been best advised to forget all about their mainline interests and come to the same conclusion as John Jacob Astor in 1848: "Could I begin again," he mused, "knowing what I now know, and had the money to invest, I would buy every square foot of land on the island of Manhattan." Astor certainly did his best to achieve that end. Not that Manhattan real estate has been an infallible source of real wealth. The abovementioned Clore, for instance, emerged from his purchase of 40 Wall Street, seventy stories high and, at the time, forty-one years old, with a feeble profit (feeble, that is, by Clore's standards) and that much only because of a technicality in the foreign exchange transactions.

Clore was trying to add Manhattan clam chowder, so to speak, to a collection of broths that included shoes, department stores, shipbuilding, textile machinery, and jewelry. In buying his Wall Street status symbol, however, he broke one cardinal rule of self-preservation: he bought from another tycoon, William Zeckendorf. Every British tycoon who brushed up against Zeckendorf got crushed in his embrace. Those who emerged with profit needed all the strength and skill of Davy Crockett wrestling with a bear, and presumably got small comfort from the fact that the bearlike Mr. Zee eventually crushed himself under a great load of unserviceable debt.

Millionaire investors are no more likely to avoid bear hugs than anybody else. Their double-barreled safety valve, however, is that, first, they can afford the inconvenience of an error. Looked at in the worst light, "Charlie's bad egg," as 40 Wall Street was known, tied up some $5.5 million of his capital in a sterile manner for half a dozen years; that might have broken a lesser fortune, but didn't even cause Clore to break stride. And second is the fact that the more pressing considerations drive the tycoon to pastures where the diversifying is likely to be greenest—not only into property, but into U.S. oil, where the tax breaks are worth having even if the drilled hole isn't.

Bing Crosby and Bob Hope had ample reason to sing about the day when a Fort Worth friend put them into 16 percent of an especially sumptuous deal; after one dry hole, fifty-eight came good and wet in succession. If other Hollywood wallets have been emptied by less-benevolent Texans, that's only fair recompense for the terrible damage done to those brave Texas millionaires who have put their silver dollars into Broadway plays and ended up with dirty faces. (The angel, however, isn't truly buying a stream of future income. Like the millionaire customers for Duveen art in the silver age, he is buying cultural respectability, and the prestige is presumably worth the fee.)

There are, however, other soups that confer both kudos and riches: for instance, owning your own *grande luxe* restaurant. In New York, the great Henri Soulé, who became a millionaire himself as a result, was set up in Le Pavillon by rich men who had enjoyed his cooking at the 1939 World's Fair. It's the most charming of diversifications, quite literally having your food and eating it. Almost certainly, however, the patrons have fared far better, financially speaking, than their backers. High cooking of the Soulé, Bocuse, or Troisgros variety is an intensely personal business, in which the profits are plowed back into either the restaurant or the pockets of the master chef on whom all depends and around whom all revolves.

Better by far to drink your bottle and keep it. When Lord Cowdray, heir to the great Pearson fortune, which had its roots in the railroads of Latin America, was persuaded to take control of Château Latour, it was a run-down vineyard that only clung to its precious First Growth status by continuing to make great wine—even though the vines and winery were dilapidated. One of the richest private purses in England repaired the dilapidations with expert local help; by 1970 the stocks held at the château were said in Bordeaux to be worth more than the entire Cowdray outlay, on purchase, maintenance, and repair. That was before the atomic price explosion from 1971 onward. With 1972 first-growth clarets selling at £8,750 a barrel, a rise of 50 percent over 1970, Latour would rank as one of the happier investments of all time even if the wine were less than marvelous and the multiplication had stopped. But it went on apace. The rival Lafite up the road, which had doubled between 1962 and 1968, did so again by 1984, and then took a mere two years for its next doubling.

C. Douglas Dillon, investment banker and former secretary of the U.S. Treasury, can't be any less happy with his possession of Château Haut-Brion; as for Baron Philippe de Rothschild, the 100,000 bottles of rare vintages in his private cellar at Château Mouton must be worth well over $1 million in their own right—a five-bottle jeroboam of the 1929, after all, fetched $9,200 at an auction in the 1970s. By the standards of later sales of rare wines, that was a snip. In 1980, a bottle of Lafite, cultivated 158 years before its sale, fetched $31,000 in San Francisco. Three years later an imperial of Mouton Rothschild of relatively tender years (1924, the first successful vintage of Baron Philippe) went for $60 a mouthful—over $12,000 at 1986 exchange rates. The next year, a jeroboam of the 1870 Mouton cost a Texan some $40,000.

Viticulture is too technical a game for the armchair investing in which most of the rich prefer to indulge. Thus, Dillon's Haut-Brion bottles, part of a $180 million fortune, are presided over by his daughter, the Duchesse de Mouchy. It's not uncommon, however, for the diversifier to throw him or herself into the outside activity with as much energy and passion as were devoted to the prime source of the wealth. James Binger, for instance, used to run Honeywell but now has theater interests on Broadway, plus the Tartan horse farms, shared with his wife, Virginia, a 3M heiress. Their steed Dr. Fager broke the record for the mile—and it is characteristic of the rich to want to excel even in their sidelines.

The sidelines, though, have one advantage over a million shares in 3M. The investor has far more control over the fate of his funds. That doesn't mean the entire bowl of soup has to be in private possession—that may be not only impossible but illogical. The lesson is rather to avoid, in financing, anything that will prevent the maximum benefit from accruing to the most important person in the operation—yourself. In a mainline operation, this, while still commendable, may be impracticable. Acquisitions may necessitate cashing in some of your own chips, turning them over to others, and so on.

But since the sideline is on the side, you can afford to wait until the manna is ready to drop from Heaven. And very handy it can be, too, as Spyros Skouras no doubt found when, in the wake of the $30 million *Cleopatra* disaster, Darryl Zanuck ousted him from Twentieth Century–Fox. At that point Skouras must have been glad that he had succumbed to the ancient Greek temptation of the sea, building up substantial shipping interests on which, presumably, he could continue to float.

If off-the-cuff successes suggest that casualness is the path to extramural pelf, they are dangerously misleading. Let the case of Dan Lufkin, who made most of a $35 million fortune from the Wall Street broking house of Donaldson, Lufkin and Jenrette, stand as a warning. Lufkin made "spur-of-the-moment, almost impetuous commitments . . . on the spot to people he had never met or knew only casually." The trouble with this method is that it tends to balance every hit with a miss; to match Pan Ocean, a North Sea oil strike, with the Ontario Motor Speedway, a $27 million flop; to offset the hit show *Oh! Calcutta* with the *Saturday Review*, a perfectly good magazine massacred by a pair of assiduous promoters with their marvelous ideas for renovation.

Sidelines should never commit more than sidestakes. It defeats the definition if an extramural activity begins to eat up resources. History does, of course, record cases of spin-offs that have either outgrown the original activity or become great economic empires themselves. Thus, two founders of American Express, Mr. Wells and Mr. Fargo, set up what became the West's fourth-largest bank when their Amex partners turned down their proposal to extend the service to the gold of California. In the same state, the Safeway supermarket chain was promoted by Merrill Lynch Pierce Fenner & Smith (né Bean), the world's largest stockbrokers (and very possibly its most prolific spawner of millionaires—when Merrill Lynch went public in 1971, 175 employees reached that financial status overnight).

The many-soups technique isn't confined to those whose bowls are already brimming over. It can be used in reverse, adding together many mites to make a nice, fat mint. Owning several small businesses is one route, but tends to be hard on the arteries—the scurrying about required is out of proportion to the payoff, while the chances of one egg in the basket turning horribly bad are just as great when the eggs are small as with the dinosaur-size dollops of the conglomerates.

Far more promising is to fit in between these two extremes: to buy in a high, wide, and handsome style—making the mainline, in effect, from a series of sidelines. The distinction between the dabbler and the financier (or somebody who makes investments) isn't easy to make; a dabble such as that of Manhattan real estate tycoon Samuel LeFrak in music (Barbra Streisand, Diana Ross) may in fact be a larger personal commitment than that of the Bass brothers to Americana Hotels, of which they hold a goodly portion.

But holding such hands is the name of the financier's game. He doesn't hold them for love, which is usually the motivation of angels such as LeFrak (though since his motives led him to *Cats* and the "Fame" series on TV, they could just as well have been thoroughly mercenary). The financier, in contrast, holds only to let go. Sooner or later he expects to take his profit; meanwhile, the untaken capital gain builds up in his portfolio.

It's a game that has become the biggest in town. Of the *Forbes* list of 1986, the main or secondary activities of 26 out of 400 multimillionaires were described as "investments." That doesn't include most of the 180 inheritors, who also invest. Some of their accretions of wealth are passive, such as those of the du Ponts or the Phipps heirs mentioned in Chapter 1, with their steady 7 percent appreciation year-in, year-out, managed by investment professionals and compounding effortlessly but unexcitingly. The lack of excitement was immediately remarked by Sid Bass and his sidekick Richard Rainwater. To quote *Business Week*,

> The running of family fortunes has always been a backwater—albeit a lucrative one—of the investment management business. Traditional family managers are notoriously risk-averse investors whose main function is to decide how much money to allocate to bonds and how much to blue-chip stocks. They then select portfolio managers to handle the task if actually investing the money. To two hotshot MBAs, this seemed like a glorified exercise in coupon clipping. Rainwater and Bass were drawn to more daring investments, and they wanted to make them themselves.

That sums up the mentality of the true multiple investor; what is called "the Midas touch" actually means not that the rich man only lays his finger on a project for it to mint money but that he instinctively and daringly orients even his sidelines in that direction. That can happen even with a relatively absentminded millionaire such as Nelson Doubleday, whose family publishing business did not enthrall him—a detachment that showed. When he turned his reluctant mind to refurbishing the family assets, he still only cranked up its profits to $7 million, of which all but $2 million came from the New York Mets.

Nevertheless, that was good enough to attract a phenomenal half billion from its German purchasers. Buying back the Mets cost Doubleday and a partner $100 million, a 400 percent increase over the price paid in 1980. The family thus got back its Mets investment, plus $17.5 million—but Nelson still owned half the Mets. That sweet deal demonstrates just why sports franchises are such hot favorites with tycoons. Quite apart from the fact that only multimillionaires can afford the current prices, the capital appreciation as the rich pass these sporting baubles from hand to hand produces suitably high scores.

It helps greatly, of course, if, like the Mets, the team manages, however narrowly, to win the World Series on the way. But the general point is that major franchises in the major sports are more or less finite in number. There is no corresponding limit in the number of millionaires who are keen enough on sports (and money) to want all or part of a franchise. Even the super-rich Crowns—as strictly business as any family—own over a quarter of the basketball Bulls in their hometown of Chicago, plus a tenth of the New York Yankees. This interest (plus four ski resorts in Aspen, Colorado) evidently owes more to son Lester Crown than to the legendary Colonel Henry.

The latter, however, has shown your true many-broths man's knack for turning side dishes into what for nearly everybody else would be most filling main courses. The Crown stake in Hilton Hotels, for instance, came about through the colonel's friendship with Conrad Hilton. The paybacks have continued long after the latter's death: when TWA was taken over by Carl Icahn, the Crowns, shareholders in the airline thanks to its purchase of Hilton Hotels International, duly got their piece. It's sound advice to base sidelines on personal taste, to put wealth in a side enterprise partly for friendship or for a kind of loving. The pleasure derived from, say, owning Château Latour enhances the chances that, even though you have only a fraction of your mind to devote to the property, you will tend it well.

The pleasure, moreover, is a useful antidote when soups curdle— as they often will, even for more careful investors than Dan Lufkin. Take Henry Crown again. His involvement with General Dynamics, whose bad habits included losing $450 million on the Convair jetliner, screwing the Pentagon and getting caught, and running through presidents like a paper shredder, has been an ups-and-downs affair. The pains must have been soothed by other, more hospitable interests, such as the Hiltons, and, still more, the Empire State Building. Owning that landmark should have been a matter of pride as much as property—like a Parisian buying the Eiffel Tower or a Londoner landing the Tower. Whether or not his ego was well massaged, the colonel eventually sold his sideline in the sky to the Prudential insurance company—and massaged his wallet with a profit of $50 million.

His technique has in general been to use his profits to trade up (though you can't go much higher than the Empire State), buying bigger and better properties and exchanging his own businesses for shares in much larger ones. The $850 million stake in General Dynamics, for example, arose from its acquisition of Crown's Material Services Corporation, which cleaned up big from supplying the construction industry where the colonel had his Chicago beginnings. In the widely held modern corporation, 29 percent is control—and the Crowns have used theirs to exert a decisive influence over the company's affairs.

This is where the many-broths phenomenon has implications going beyond the extra wealth generated for the wealthy. Thanks to the proliferation of equity ownership, even smaller stakes than that of the Crowns in General Dynamics can give highly effective control, or at least a highly persuasive voice. In consequence, the retreat of the rich from the visible peaks of the economy has not been accompanied by commensurate loss of economic and social clout. On the contrary, many broths mean many levers of power.

The same family or the same man may be instrumental in determining the fate (to take the Crowns) of a key defense industry, midwest banking, whole chunks of the most valuable midtown territory, a piece of baseball, a scattering of textiles—and much else, perhaps, of which the public knows nothing. Maybe this pervasive influence is used benevolently, on the whole; maybe the ability of the Basses, say, to call the shots (or some of them) across the spread from manufacturing to media, from fried chicken to high tech, does nobody any harm (but their own privy purses a power of good).

The fact remains that no more than 100 rich dynasties or personal proprietors reign over most of the broad range of the American economic society. The exercise of power is not the only point. Its existence matters in and of itself. In the Age of the Common Millionaire, the reality is that, work and travel and buy and play wherever you will, there in the background or the foreground is the might of personal wealth.

20

YOU CAN
COUNT ON ME

Once upon a time, in a real-life fairy story, there was a wise old general and business school professor who spotted a bright little computer engineer and gave him both blessing and backing. Within eleven years, that good old military man had seen his investment multiply to a quarter of a billion dollars. Compared to that golden windfall, the general's initial backing was no more expensive than the winning ticket in a national lottery. It cost just $70,000 to obtain control of the computer prodigy's shares, which then proceeded to multiply down the years like a family of particularly sexy minks.

The investor was the late General Georges F. Doriot, whose American Research and Development (ARD) became an international byword for the astute backing of advanced technology. Backing successful outsiders is as rare in business as on the track, but picking so big a winner in advanced scientific wonders is approximately as easy as drawing a straight flush at poker. Doriot's record in this esoteric field was exceptionally good, even without his wonder hand in Ken Olsen's

Digital Equipment. But exceptional achievement in this mine field often means very little more than avoiding detonation. While ARD made some other pricks with the general's educated pin, none compared with the DEC gold mine. And the net result, when ARD was finally sold out to the Textron conglomerate, was not the kind of capital gain to make a mutual-fund manager cry with jealous shame.

ARD was a forerunner in what became known as *venture capital* and dignified as an industry. In its earliest days, venture capital lacked the glamour of its "industrial" future. In the early 1970s, *Time* magazine estimated that some 600 firms already existed solely to pump money into other people's ventures. They deployed around $3 billion of assets, according to *Time*, and pumped in annually as much as $700 million. That would have exhausted the kitty in a little over four years if nothing had come up trumps—and often it didn't.

Some of the backers, in any event, had little faith in their essential judgment of the venturer. Take a scion of the Phipps steel line, Paul Bancroft III, who said, "I do not want the president to have control. If his management isn't going to make it, you have to be prepared to remove him." But if his management isn't going to make it, very probably neither is the business, no matter who runs the shop.

As the game grew more and more sophisticated, so the venture capitalists grew more secure in their judgment of entrepreneurs and their enterprises (many highly technical in nature) and much cannier in their final demands. The best defense against a low strike rate is a massive reward when you do hit. The capitalists duly structured their deals so that their money would multiply, say, tenfold in five years if their targets were met—and they used extremely conservative numbers in working out these sums.

For example, a venturer comes hat in hand for a million bucks, for which he's prepared to surrender a quarter of the equity. You point out that he's implicitly valuing said equity at $4 million. So in five years time it must be worth $40 million to interest you. Using a lowly price-earnings ratio of 10, he's got to make $400,000 of profits after taxes before the five years are up. If you believe that to be feasible, he gets his money—and you get a potential gain that is far greater than tenfold.

The reason is that a business that climbs from losses or small profits to that degree of success within five years, going public en route, will command a price-earnings ratio far higher than 10. The process is more complex than the basic principle described above, because the entrepreneur typically comes back to the venture-capital trough once or twice more. But the basic arithmetic stays just as simple and just as simply gratifying—ask Ben Rosen and his partner, L. J. Sevin.

Better still, study their sums. When General Parametrix made its debut in the over-the-counter market, the original $2.5 million supplied by Sevin Rosen had already appreciated fourfold in four years. In a much shorter period, $2.5 million placed in Compaq Computer turned magically into $39 million. Lotus Development, whose 1-2-3 spreadsheet became the best-seller in personal computer software, took $2.1 million of Rosen's money—that investment was worth $63.8 million when Lotus's shares were sold to an avid public. Rosen expressed the principle vividly: "If you want to get home runs, you've got to take a big swing with the baseball bat."

With all these enormous swings, you might expect to find the Rosens of America up there in the monetary Hall of Fame. They are, indeed, multimillionaires, but their known fortunes are restrained by several factors. First, the essence of venture capitalism is to spread the risk—the funds typically draw their money from the super-rich, sometimes from people who (such as Intel's chip genius Robert Noyce) have themselves waxed rich on venture finance. Thus, the venture capitalists avoid having all their eggs in one basket but miss the full benefits if any of the eggs are golden. The second brake on the venture capitalist's riches is that he tends to take his profit—when all history shows that staying for the long haul pays best for those who back a wonder company. Third, the strikeouts have to be set against the home runs—and that may mean big money. Trilogy, intended to produce a superchip to match the transcendent reputation of its founder, Gene Amdahl, was the largest venture-capital financing ever—and by definition the largest loss, to the tune of $200 million, when Amdahl's plans ran into the ultimate technical hitch.

Venture capitalists would—to state the obvious—be best advised only to choose the surest winners and stick with them, steadily upping the stakes, until the ultimate payoff. The technical hitch here, though, is equally obvious. Sure, Doriot would have done better to place every egg in the basket that paid off best—if only, that is, he could have foreseen the future. This is one variety of foresight not given to man, even to a man of such surpassing shrewdness as the general. A possibly apocryphal story tells of the general's being offered an ingenious plan for selling hardwood trees and bringing the valuable timber downriver to the sawmills below. The general listened carefully to the details, the extrapolations of hardwood demand, the behavior of prices in the key markets, the increasing proportion of expensive veneers in furniture, and what not. He then killed the project stone-dead with one simple question: Will the logs float?

If Harold S. Geneen of ITT had known this story, it might have saved the colossus from a loss of $600 million. That followed from a forestry project for the Rayonier division. Geneen's approval, taken for granted by his executives after a discussion lasting no more than five or ten minutes, was made in ignorance of a crucial fact. The maximum diameter to which these Canadian trees would grow was too small for the purposes of the project.

Successful backers need to ask log-floating questions. This demands some instinct about where the project is most liable to sink. The instincts of laymen confronted with technologists, especially technologists of advanced breed, are unreliable and tend to be suppressed by false (or risky) modesty. Backers of technological wonders usually come unstuck, not because of failure to understand quantum theory or the significance of the Second Law of Thermodynamics, but because, hornswoggled by the bewildering magic of the unknown, they ignore the simple rules that they should know by heart and by common sense.

If an inventor fails to keep a watchful eye on how his money is being spent, or to force his pet technologists to give him meaningful progress reports on the latest wonder of the world, he only has himself to blame when the logs sink (as, in such circumstances, they always do). One set of bemused bankers allowed their technical playboys to pile up monstrous extravagances on complex equipment such as Rolls-Royce cars and interior decoration, completely ignoring the fact, which the simplest of checks would have unveiled, that there were hardly any customers in the whole wide world (only one finally turned up) for the particular magic being peddled.

In contrast, the potential clients for an instant camera were numbered in the multimillions, and it is a law of wealth that the bigger the market, the greater the chances of achieving financial greatness. The early backers of Dr. Edwin Land can congratulate themselves on following this elementary rule with conspicuous reward; they were, as it happens, a conspicuous group, financially and socially. Averell Harriman, James P. Warburg, and Lewis Strauss put up $375,000: family wealth never sowed more fertile seed.

The small sum of $1,000 invested in Polaroid in 1938 would have been worth $4 million within a quarter of a century. Plainly, backing will more often than not come from the rich—after all, they have the money. But it does not follow that rich killings, the creation of the new fortunes of Polaroid dimensions, will inevitably also fall to the wealthy. If you have twice as many shots as the next man, you have twice the chance of hitting the target and striking in the center (or the gold, as archers appropriately call it). But the man with fewer shots may still strike gold with his first aim, and the annals of golden backing contain many proofs of this satisfying truth.

One shrewd backer had built up a chain of 300 radio and TV stores over fourteen years (after starting with the small amount of cash he had taken out of the service after World War II). He had trouble getting supplies from the established manufacturers, when his gaze lighted on a small rival maker whose fortunes were in the tight grip of a young unknown named Arnold Weinstock. The retailer, John James, became the largest nonfamily investor in Weinstock's company, and thus later in its giant purchaser, the General Electric Company. As Weinstock led GEC into Valhalla, and himself to a peerage, James cashed in painlessly on the richest transformation ever wrought on a major European company to that date. By 1986, his investments in GEC and elsewhere, plus the £6 million received for his store chain, allowed James to promise a bequest to his fellow citizens of Bristol that would yield them spending money of $1.5 million a week.

How can talent like Weinstock's be spotted? One clue is that he was a "lean and hungry man." Such men, as Julius Caesar noted, are dangerous—in this case to business opponents; for off-track bettors, they are generally safer choices than those who are heavy on the hoof. There are exceptions, of course, in both directions. But men who are big, fat, and sleep o'nights seem in general to lack the well-placed energy, insatiable drive, and self-made success of the true tycoon. The latter class tends rather to run to short, thickset, small men such as General David Sarnoff, the genius of RCA, or Lord Marks, the creator of the modern Marks & Spencer retailing wonder. Samuel I. Newhouse checked out at five feet three inches, at least $300 million, twenty-two newspapers, seven TV stations, twenty magazines; Meyer Lansky, the Jewish Mafioso, at five feet one inch. Many other millionaire magnificos wouldn't be much use, physically speaking, as part of a basketball team.

In contrast, the truly disastrous receptacles for other people's cash often float high in water—like the salad-oil swindler, Tino de Angelis, who, while only five feet five inches, weighed in at 240 pounds; or John King, the would-be ruler of IOS; or William Zeckendorf, Sr., the real estate tycoon who took several of Britain's overambitious property men for a ride around the city centers of the Americas before going bust himself; or Marion Harper, the advertising man who created both the biggest and the brokest group of advertising agencies in the world.

Most such men are terrific talkers, which is another uneasy augury. One clearly identifiable characteristic of many super-rich men is that they talk as little as possible, especially in public. This is partly because words waste time, and most men of true action are deeply, instinctively conscious of the way in which time, which is also money, runs through the fingers. They are also acutely aware that the more you say, the more you are apt to commit yourself—and commitment, unless you are exceedingly careful, also costs money. As in poker, so in business; part of the art is to keep the opposition guessing, because, like everybody else in the world, they will more often guess wrong than right.

Preference for the short, strong, and silent is a good start along the critical road to making a personal assessment. In the end this is the nature of the backing decision. No matter how developed the nose for a good idea, no matter how careful the checking to ensure that the logs will float, no matter how quick and comprehensive the financial controls over the loved one, in the end everything comes down to the man himself.

There is no such thing, however, as the right man in the wrong opportunity; if you are backing somebody in ventures such as deveined shrimp (to name one of General Doriot's failed brain waves) you by definition have the wrong man. The right one, such as Ken Olsen, at DEC, does the right thing, and usually, like Olsen, has eccentric characteristics that stamp him as an unusual creature, a man unlikely to get diverted from the important business of making your money grow at the most urgent possible speed.

In 1987, when worth some $300 million, Olsen still worked out of a converted woolen mill in Maynard, Massachusetts. He has always kept a paramount interest in the pure, unadulterated beauty of computer circuits. "I still keep my hand in at engineering," he once said, "for fear that I might one day be out of a job. I do it some Saturday mornings." Between 1968 and 1972 the sales presided over by this curiously indifferent, deeply religious capitalist shot up from $15 million to $180 million as Olsen survived a ghastly catalogue of errors in shipping out the PDP-6 minicomputer. It was by no means the last of Olsen's calamities—in 1983, profits plunged 72 percent in a quarter when no change had been forecast. Accountancy failures had compounded yet another product crisis—the embarrassing inability of DEC to achieve any impact, let alone the triumph it expected, in selling personal computers to business.

What seemed to be the beginning of DEC's end as a wonder company, however, was turned by Olsen into its golden age. That, maybe, is the hardest thing to predict about an entrepreneur: how he will react in the all but inevitable crisis. Toughness alone won't see the man through; he requires, over and above courage, the ability to stick like a leech to the essentials of his job—which in Olsen's first crisis was

271

to produce ingenious small computers that actually worked, such as the PDP-8, which promptly sold over 10,000 units.

In 1983, Olsen embarked with equal success on dismantling the famous decentralized system that had worked like a charm since 1964, when individual managers were made responsible for whole product lines. Now, to place the entire weight of DEC behind the new VAX range of minicomputers, Olsen wanted to create a unified sales and marketing organization. It worked as well as the VAX technology, which leapfrogged a potentially lethal minichallenge from IBM.

Profiting from painful truths is the ultimate test of the entrepreneur. Among several moments of such pain, the most agonizing for Henry Ford I was the year the Model T, thrashed by the ritzier models of Chevrolet, ran out of road. Ford closed the plants for a year, came out with the Model A, and drove on to a greater fortune than ever. This, admittedly, was an eccentric procedure. But Ford conformed so perfectly to the entrepreneurial stereotype as to define it: secretive, taciturn, passionate about engineering, eccentric to the point of lunacy, but crazy (most of the time) like a fox.

No backers of talent in history ever reaped what they sowed more richly than the few who climbed onto Ford's running board. When Ford bought them out there was one little old lady whose $100 had come back to her 3,550-fold: $95,000 in dividends and $260,000 in the final payoff. Another, bigger Ford backer cleaned up $17.4 million tax free on an initial stake of $5,000. The surpassing loveliness of such returns is that they involve little or no effort on the part of the backer, while the backed one works himself to somewhere near the bone—a fact, no doubt, that inspired Ford's burning desire to regain all of the equity.

General Doriot, in fact, got the lion's share of Ken Olsen's equity for his $70,000, and although the general's firm provided a lesser amount in loan capital, along with doubtless excellent advice on money matters, there is a certain disproportion in the rewards of the backer (whose bundle was worth $350 million at the apogee) and the backed (even though $90 million, the Olsen stake at that point, was enough to keep a Siberia full of wolves from the door for several generations).

In most cases it is dangerous policy for the backer to control the stock—otherwise he may get to think of it as a subsidiary and interfere with the management; or for the backed entrepreneur to hold the thin end—otherwise he may get miffed and move to plusher pastures. When a South African, Mark Weinberg, spotted that the British life insurance industry was stuck in its selling methods at around the year 1817, he also saw with perfect clarity how to exploit the delicious opportunity they had left wide open. Weinberg got backing from two American combines, Georgia-Pacific and the ubiquitous ITT, selling his own stake for what proved, in hindsight, to be peanuts. When ITT bought out its partner, the deal cost $38 million; Weinberg's take had been in the thousands, and it surprised nobody when he promptly stepped off to open a rival shop dealing in much the same line of goods. This time, Weinberg was careful to ensure that he and his colleagues obtained a fair share of the loot. The billion-dollar price paid for Hambro Life, Weinberg's second coming, by the cash-rich tobacco leviathan, BAT, was widely shared, but this time Weinberg pocketed millions.

The odds are heavily stacked against finding a trusty who is vigorous and self-assertive enough to deliver a big bundle of goods, sufficiently mild to tolerate interference from on high, and unworldly enough not to demand a deep slice of the pie. Preferably, high partners should sleep; and the entrepreneur should let sleeping partners lie, unless, that is, he needs their help. Rich, well-connected, and self-interested men make excellent advisers; what's more, their counsel comes free.

The disadvantages of the partner who is awake, or thinks he is, can be seen in the saga of Fairchild Camera. Sherman M. Fairchild's inheritance of several noggins of IBM stock, and his enjoyment of the good things of life thereby financed, did not stop him from showing a marvelous eye for an opportunity. The discovery of a semiconductor group working out of a garage in Palo Alto was perfectly handled. (Another demonstration of the fact that truly rewarding enterprises have an affinity for beginning life in garages, lofts, and workshops in the garden.) Fairchild financed the electronic pioneers, led by William Noyce, to the modest extent they required, taking an option on their locks, stocks, and barrels. When Noyce's team delivered the semiconducting goods, Fairchild took up its option for $3.5 million—one of the decade's most outright bargains. In just the first of the good, soft years, Fairchild earned as much as $8.4 million from Noyce's inventions.

But under Fairchild in person, as chairman of the board, the growing pains of the semiconductor market were compounded by the upheavals in Fairchild management. The stock gyrated, the managerial wonder boys came and went. Although Texas Instruments had its full share of the market troubles, its rise in the same fiendishly clever trade worked out far more impressively. The Texans whose little instrument company found itself sitting on a fortune in silicon chips allowed it to develop its own life. The net result was that every worthy connected with TI, the two original partners, the executive who ran their show, and the Texas watchers who spotted the electronic oil well, eventually sported fortunes worthy of the Spindletop gusher.

As for Fairchild, it passed into the unhappy hands of Schlumberger, a company that knew far more about oil well drilling techniques than microelectronics, and which the purchaser was avid to sell in 1987 after long and hard lessons, costing $1.5 billion in losses over the years, in its new subject. Noyce, unlike his company, showed total sureness of touch. At Intel, backed by venture capital, the pioneer outdid even his own earlier technological achievements. The microprocessor, the device that made the personal computer possible, may well be ranked as the most potent and far-reaching invention of the century's last quarter.

What Noyce and Co. achieved under no control but their own, with the typically arm's-length involvement of the venture capitalists, says a mouthful for the wisdom of proprietorial restraint. The Intel backers reaped an enormous reward for their essentially passive participation in a company that by 1985 had $1.4 billion of sales and had rewarded its investors with 16.33 percent compound growth over a decade. The hyperactive partner, along with getting in the way, is prone to the most debilitating disease of the off-track bettor: impatience. The full, fair, and fine reward takes time to mature, like a benign Burgundy. If you try to uncork your Romanée-Conti 1961 too soon, you will miss the ultimate splendor of its bouquet and body. The Ford beneficiaries had to wait sixteen years before the last roundup. Even the great General Doriot's company hung fire for three years at its start, pottered along on a higher plateau for seven more years, spent another decade on a more elevated plateau still, and only then achieved its summit (with a jump from $93 million of net asset value in 1966 to $349 million the next year), as DEC delivered the goods.

Backing isn't subject to the same laws as stock exchange investment: on the market, one share is never unique; there is always an alternative. The backer, in contrast, is on the hunt for a Unique Buying Proposition (UBP), and if a return of DEC proportions (360,000 percent, no less) is the object of the chase, the hunter can afford time. What he can seldom afford is to raise his stake continually when the hopeful provider returns for more. All good development projects cost more than their developers estimate. But the UBP must not run up so steep a bill as to remove its own ripest attraction—which is the modest size of stake in relation to potential.

The well-and-truly-chosen human receptacle of your cash will detest overspending no less than you. The spendthrift, whose initial request is in the millions and who spends all seven figures in the first few months, is like the locusts of Africa: let him thrive, and he will strip you bare. The backer is in two hazardous activities simultaneously: deciding on the merits and staying power of a business he doesn't understand, and judging the ability of a particular individual, almost certainly with no achievement behind him, to develop that business into a screaming success.

He needs the combined genius of a brilliant investment banker (a rare animal in investment banking itself) and a selection consultant of trenchant insight (equally rarely found in selection consultancy). There are men with a Midas touch who instinctively back only winners, but in most cases the ratio of failure to success is as low as must be expected when playing against the odds. That's why the response of the venture capitalists is to spread the risk, even though this dilutes the profit, and to apply rigorous rules to both the backer's functions.

The most successful of the venturers, for instance, may not be a Valley-wise veteran of the silicon chips such as Ben Rosen, but a Bostonian banker named Peter Brooke. Not that Brooke has missed out on the high-tech explosion that, more than anything else, explains the late-century efflorescence of venture capital. His company, TA Associates, popped $1.7 million into Tandon, the microcomputer company, over a few years ending in 1980. Starting in 1982—five years after the first investment, note—Brooke sold out for $77 million. That's a gain of forty-five times (handily outstripping the standard tenfold).

Switching technologies, Brooke did even better with Biogen in genetic engineering: $171,000 became $10.5 million when TA cashed in its chips. The early sellout that limited the gains (however marvelous) had to be shared with the backers—people who placed, according to *Fortune*, $1.3 billion in the two funds headed by Brooke. By the time the investors had taken their due share, Brooke was left with personal wealth that, after nineteen years and over 200 deals, is estimated at between $10 million and $20 million—or at most $100,000 a throw.

Compare that with the fortunes and the fortune of a man backed by Brooke in his Bostonian banking days: Dr. An Wang. The banker gave the Chinese-American computer genius twice the $25,000 loan he sought. In 1986, despite his company's costly failure to sustain, in the personal computer age, its word-processing preeminence, the doctor's family stake in Wang Laboratories (with Brooke as a director) was worth $550 million—a sum that might be worth more than most of the venture capitalists put together.

Exactly the same could be said of Ken Olsen's pile at Digital Equipment—though, even by the greedy standards of venture capital,

Olsen and his partner, Harlan Anderson, signed a bad deal. General Doriot's firm, in return for its $70,000, pocketed 77 percent of the infant company's stock. Olsen's share was 13 percent. You could argue that, even so, this homespun, eccentric business genius came out well ahead. In 1987, his fortune was much greater than the wealth amassed by Doriot (who, despite the 77 percent, was still a close Olsen friend and adviser to his death at the age of eighty-seven).

Given that DEC became a $7.6 billion company with $617.4 million of profit, breathing as hotly as possible down IBM's neck, the venture capitalists could claim much credit for their work—and their worry. Nobody worries more than Brooke as he inquires into the basic issues: the quality of the entrepreneur, the amount of money to be invested (not too little, not too much, but just right), the strength of the business idea. To make up his own mind, Brooke uses other people's; he telephones incessantly—one Brooke trainee learned that fifty to a hundred calls a day often made the difference between success and failure. Above all, though, Brooke only backs entrepreneurs strong enough in their technological prowess and business know-how to manage by themselves. His philosophy is markedly different from the interfering distrust of Paul Bancroft III, the Phipps heir quoted earlier in this chapter.

"The money man doesn't control nothin'. That guy going home every night with the technology in his head is the asset, and if he sits down on you, you're dead," Brooke told *Fortune*. Curiously enough, the Phipps family venture-capital fund is where Brooke started his own venturing in 1961—it's clear who has best mastered the game, and it isn't the Phipps heir, Bancroft III, with his highly provisional faith in the men he backed. Still, at least Bancroft III had a rule to go by—even if it's a bad one. For the backer's best overriding guide is to stick to his own rules.

The correct lodestar is what, in the past, has worked well for you. If you invariably select men with deep anatomical snuffboxes (there are truly people who believe this wrist formation has some psychological significance), or shun those whose gaze is shifty, or insist on getting a graphologist to give your selection's fine Italian handwriting a going-over, don't break the habit—not because your method means a thing (it doesn't), but because it means something to you, and you are the man whose money is going to have to live with the fellow and his faith.

Unless you as backer share this faith, you shouldn't be backing. Half hearts lead to full ulcers. But faith must have foundations in fact, not fantasy—and if you can't get the facts you need (and intelligent backing needs plenty), you have the wrong fellow. Not that the business protégé can ever be expected to conform, either to his backer's demands or to convention. But even an eccentric must comply, within reason, with the necessities of economics.

Every backer of another's business needs to keep a Brooke-like eye on the balance sheets, the market reports, the cash flow, the budgets, and all other information that should be gratefully received. Yet, while the need to know of a Peter Brooke is a safer approach than the impulsive backing of a rich man's fancy, impulse buying may well produce more glorious returns than compulsive care. The venture-capital industry has to be placed in proportion. It handles vast sums of cash, but the $3 billion of new money supplied in 1986—a figure sharply down from the previous year's $44.5 billion—is a mere drop in the ocean of total American investment. The 3 billion is obviously out-weighed, too, by the unventuresome bankrolling provided by rich families such as the Basses for stock-market deals.

The wheels and deals of such clans may do far less to develop the productive advances on which the American future depends, true. The microprocessor, the personal computer, the memory chip—these and other wonders were spawned by venture capital and brought to market, as Ben Rosen loves to point out, in far shorter time than any large corporation could have envisaged. There's been a real element of inspiration involved, too, along with the perspiration.

Indeed, the bright backing of bright ideas is perhaps the most virtuous use of the millions of the plutocracy. If, inevitably, it makes its members more millions still, it also creates new wealth, not only for individuals such as An Wang or Apple's Steve Jobs, but for the United States and world economies. More often than not, the motivation of the miracles may come down to mundane matters such as tax breaks; indeed, doubts over the changes in American law helped explain that one-third drop in the venture-capital flow in 1986. That doesn't affect the issue. Venture miracles do happen, and it is of fundamental importance to America that they should never cease.

Book V

THE
MONEY
MAGICIANS

21

LIES,
DAMNED LIES, AND
NUMBERS

The economic world is full of engaging, exploded ideas in which every-body believes: none more engaging or detonated than the notion that only governments can print money. Ever since the invention of the banking system by the Italians, banks have been creating paper gold, and ever since some genius stumbled across the joint stock company, individuals have been free to engage in the same profoundly rewarding activity.

Printing money means producing a piece of your own paper that others will accept in exchange for the pieces of paper put out officially by the government. Just as the government's paper no longer has to be backed by solid gold, the paper spawned in streams by individuals and corporations need have no foundation either. That is why the old, simple tests of millionairedom no longer apply—even though so sea-soned and flush a hand as J. P. Getty used to believe that a millionaire was still someone whose assets are worth $1 million.

That depends on what you mean by worth. It can't mean that the man should be able to produce $1 million of his own cash, since a large proportion of the assets won't be readily negotiable and many of them may be covered by debt. Even if he can write a million-dollar check, all that proves is that somebody will honor the paper. Getting the paper honored is the real necessity, and getting the maximum amount of honor is the real trick. It may have nothing to do with the underlying economic assets the paper pusher possesses, but everything to do with clever mathematical games.

Another of the obsolete, absurd ideas in which all men believe is that figures mean what they say, which is even less true than the idiotic notion that the camera cannot lie. Since the world of paper money is founded on figures, if you can fiddle around with the numbers you can also manipulate the money to your great and gratifying advantage. The multibillionaire H. L. Hunt once remarked (he could afford to) that "money is nothing. It is just something to make bookkeeping more convenient." He had it the wrong way around. It's bookkeeping that's nothing—only something to make money more convenient.

For instance, a man purchases twenty garages for $50,000 apiece, a price that represents five years' purchase of aftertax profits; he has profits of $200,000 a year, and he is presumably worth neither more nor less than the million with which he started. That presumption, however, is demonstrably false. Suppose he takes the company to the stock market as Auto-Electronic Developments; he sells a quarter of the shares for $250,000, and the market thereupon values the firm, modestly enough, at seven times earnings. So his smaller stake is *still* worth a million, and he has $250,000 in cash to be getting on with.

Still not satisfied, however, he borrows $1 million at 10 percent, buys another twenty exactly similar garages, thus raising earnings by the $100,000 that represents the difference between $200,000 of profits and his interest costs. Beyond doubt, the stock market will be vastly impressed by this powerful growth rate: 50 percent per annum is the stuff that analysts' dreams are made of. So Auto-Electronic gets revalued to ten times earnings, at which point our hero is worth $2.5 million—representing his $250,000 in cash, plus three-quarters of the pile of Auto-Electronic paper, which is now valued at $3 million.

The uninitiated may marvel how a property with a market value of $2 million can suddenly, with no material change, generate a million of new wealth. Equally, just how has the hero deserved or managed to multiply his original million two and a half times? There is no good answer to these questions, merely an incontestable observation: on this simple statistical foundation have been erected most new fortunes of our time.

That applies in spades to the empire of Robert Edward Turner III, another obvious example of son striving to expunge the memory of a failed father. Like the first Gallo, the senior Turner killed himself, leaving not a vineyard, but a near-bankrupt billboard company. The former scapegrace Ted Turner threw himself into the business with all the energy of a risk-taking sportsman and went public in 1969 on the acquisition of what *Fortune* calls "a ratty little Atlanta TV station."

Ratty or not, seven years later WTBS pioneered the cable network, not so much the jewel in Turner Broadcasting's crown as the gold itself; with the news operations, cable was bringing in some $100 million of operating cash flow a year in the mid-1980s. That might seem more than enough to explain Turner's wealth, save for the fact that after losing money for half the years in the previous decade, and making a pretax operating profit of only $17 million in 1985, the next year the company dropped the mind-blowing sum of $200 million. Given that the debts, after the apparently disastrous deal that bought Turner the Metro-Goldwyn-Mayer studio, rose to over $2 billion at one point, the business wouldn't seem to be worth many lights.

Yet Turner's personal fortune in mid-1986 reached nearly half a billion. The explanation lay in that public quotation: Turner had clung on to 81 percent of the Turner stock, which the investing public then valued at *500 times* the previous year's exiguous earnings. Even after the shares retreated, Turner's paper was still worth enough to place him well up the Forbes 400 with a wealth of $280 million. The magazine quoted him as saying, "The game I'm in is building assets"; the previous year's snappy quote was, "Crash along at full speed until you hit something."

Investors were plainly betting that Turner would have built enough assets to survive the crash. It was a bet of stupefying size. The aforementioned garage proprietor had $1 million of debt, $1 million of equity, and earnings of $300,000 a year; a Turner-size price-earnings ratio of 500 would value his business at $150 million. That's obviously pure fantasy, yet the financial health of that little mythical business compares most favorably with Turner's real-life loss of $200 million, debt of $1.6 billion, and equity of a tiny $21 million.

The stock market, used with enough daring, is a machine for turning fantasy into fact—passing fact, maybe, but real enough while it lasts to make a promoter's pieces of paper worth many times more than Treasury bills. The promoter can intensify the process of converting hope into cash, too, and not only by big talk (Turner even boasted to *Fortune*: "I've got more debt than anyone in the world. That's something, isn't it?"). Note that the figures in the garage fable were all uncooked. But suppose that the proprietor's expenses included a major Christmas promotion that cost $50,000 just before the year's end, and suppose that his accountants were persuaded that this bundle should be treated as deferred expenditure. The logic is unassailable, if you're not too keen on assailing; after all, the bulk of the sales will occur in the next financial year, so shouldn't the cost more properly be apportioned to the year in which the sales will fall?

This change will have the not-so-incidental effect of producing $50,000 of extra profits. Instead of the 50 percent profits jump achieved by the merger, the proprietors can now boast a 75 percent advance. Even if the stock market sticks to the same price-earnings ratio (P/E ratio) of ten times pretax earnings, the company will magically become worth $3.5 million, and the delirious owner now weighs in at $2.9 million, stark naked.

The beautiful truth is that, if a company boasts a P/E ratio of 40 (after tax), each extra dollar in aftertax profits equals $40 in capital value. It follows that any device that maintains or enlarges the P/E ratio, or that inflates the earnings per share, is worth more, by virtue of the multiplier effect, than any amount of honest toil. That is why profits are so rarely undercooked. The bias in accountancy is always toward producing the highest figure possible, and the possibility of bias exists, first, because accountancy is as imprecise as the music of the spheres, and second, because accountants know on which side their bread is buttered. If there are few millionaire accountants, it is partly because they expend so much nervous energy and time in making millionaires of their clients.

The deferring of the garage promotion, for example, is no far-fetched joke. One year a London evening newspaper actually commended a paint company for the *conservative* practice of costing its advertising expenditure in the year when it was incurred. That same year, American oil and gas men waxed indignant because the SEC turned thumbs down on an accounting method that allowed them to spread the cost of dry wells across several years instead of taking it in the actual year of the expense; in one of the charming euphemisms that litter accountancy, the smellier, *partial* method was called "*full-costing*."

Equally partial were the habits of two very different but equally bankrupt British companies, both prefixed with Rolls: Razor and Royce; one deferred the commissions it paid to door-to-door salesmen of its appliances, the other put off the costs of its massive research-and-development spending. In every such case, a respectable—nay, an eminent—auditor was prepared to approve the approach, and if by any chance the auditor wouldn't approve, the correct response was obvious—get another one.

Precisely that course was adopted by one U.S. computer-leasing outfit, whose profitability hinged on renting out its machines for seventy-eight months. Unfortunately, its customers obliged only to the extent of leases that averaged forty-eight months. If the outfit managed to lease the machines for the missing thirty months or more at roughly the same terms and without much extra marketing cost, all would be well. If it didn't, however, heavy losses would stare it in the face.

When its auditors couldn't be convinced that the re-leasing would duly occur, the company found a more trusting set of accountants. In such circumstances, the offended company usually takes the precaution of asking its prospective auditors their views on any contentious points. Surprisingly often, total harmony results. Maybe that divine music is connected with the fact that auditors' fees provide so much flavorsome food for thought.

Quite how much nourishment can be guessed from the combined revenues of Peat, Marwick, Mitchell and KMG, which announced merger plans in September 1986. The very grand total was $2.7 billion. That was not only double the figure for the runner-up, Arthur Andersen, but equal in size to the twentieth ranking diversified service company in America (that firm being the accountants' friend, Dun & Bradstreet) or the eightieth-largest industrial company. Even runner-up Andersen ranks alongside prime client fodder of the order of Intel, the microprocessor leader, or *The New York Times*.

The Andersen practice earned two-thirds of its stupendous income from audits in the days when one famous client, International Telephone & Telegraph, was accumulating the largest conglomerate collection on earth. You don't pay the kind of money that changes hands in major audits to get your profits carved away. ITT is a case in much point. Originally its accountants wanted to include the paper profits made on unrealized capital gains in a newly acquired insurance company's investment portfolio. When this ingenious step was barred, ITT simply sold off enough of the portfolio to equal the unrealized gain and took that into the profit instead. The object of this strange exercise, which had nothing to do with the trading of either ITT or the insurance managers, was "to maintain the continuous rise in earnings per share."

Now just why would Harold S. Geneen, the millionaire boss of ITT, have wanted to achieve that objective? Through a passionate desire for symmetry? Or had it any connection with the fact that Geneen and his managerial cohorts were all, thanks to the wonders of the stock option, heavy holders of ITT stock? Remember that the rise in earnings was purest bunkum. The true, underlying earnings of the arch-conglomerate had not altered in any degree. All that had changed was their presentation—as approved by the distinguished auditors.

As a shrewdity test, ask yourself if, should the value of the insurance portfolio drop, ITT would have deducted an equivalent amount from its profits. You can bet *The Godfather*'s profits against the proceeds of a piggy bank that few boards of directors would do any such thing. By an agreeable irony, ITT's auditors were advocates of a brave new accounting world in which accountants might "discard their exaggerated concern for conservatism and objectivity, which have too often resulted in irrelevant, unfair, and imprudent information."

This statement can be tested against the case of Four Seasons Nursing Centers, where, by disagreeable irony, Arthur Andersen was again the auditor—and where a couple of its own partners were indicted by the U.S. government for their part in the affair. In their search for millions, the Four Seasons founders had correctly diagnosed that untold wealth lay in wait on Wall Street if the nursing home idea could be successfully marketed. That in turn meant showing a suitably rich and fast-rising profit record. This was duly produced by devices that, so the accusation ran, included sales of nursing homes that never took place, and, still more imaginative, sales of the dud, money-losing homes to a buyer secretly owned by Four Seasons itself. Since figures, not facts, sway markets, the multiplier took immediate and telling effect. The shares zoomed up from $11 in 1968 to $181, before plunging all the way back to the nothing from whence they came.

In fairness to auditors, presenting a true and fair picture of a company's finances is by no means as simple as it sounds. There is, for example, a rule of thumb in the movie business that film costs should be written off over three years. The high-flying Israelis, Yoram Globus and Menahem Golan, appear to have followed this rule as they built their millions through low-budget movies and high-cost purchases of theaters and screen rights. But were the costs of duds (of which their Cannon Group made plenty) written off with sufficient speed? How did a company that made $15 million of declared profit one year end up owing $430 million the next, while short of some $122 million in working capital?

As the investigators and the lawsuits closed around Cannon, with Warner Corp. riding profitably to its immediate rescue, its accountants, Arthur Young, were detailed to conduct a special audit that, the company told *Business Week*, could lead to a "material change" in its declared results—even though Globus claimed that charges of accountancy deviations were "a lot of baloney." One of the attorneys attacking the company described the accounting used before as "part of a scheme to inflate Cannon's earnings and the price of its securities." Millionaires are, however, much like managements in this respect—not in the habit of using accounts and accountants to deflate their profits and the price of the stock.

That was certainly true of Charles W. Knapp, whose inspired creation, Financial Corp. of America, soared so high that it became the largest savings institution in the United States, but whose financial performance fell so low (to a 1984 loss of $15.53 a share) that the Wall Street nickname, Financial Corpse of America, rang true. Knapp's notion was to borrow short and lend long, doing the former at the highest going rates and the latter at fixed interest. This self-destructing device brought him a mass of customers on both sides of the equation, but even in March 1986, when Knapp had been off the premises for a year and a half, the problem loans resulting from his hell-for-leather expansion totaled $1.7 billion.

If the accountants had blown the whistle earlier, they would have been judging, not so much the truth and fairness of the corporation's accounting as the very principles of its business. And it's much harder to usurp the directors' role in this way when a stock is riding as high as FCA's. (Even in 1985, after the fall, investors were still showing a 37.4 percent average annual gain for the previous decade, so high had been the orbit.)

Four Seasons and FCA were not isolated cases of their times. National Student, a totally busted flush, was a wild wow. This operation, headed by a hyper-salesman named Cort Randell, was allegedly founded on marketing techniques developed by young marvels selling to the explosive young growth market on campus. As an alumnus of NSMC, Andrew Tobias, has revealed, this company too was a free-running machine for generating reported or projected rises in earnings per share.

One November Randell dangled before the New York Society of Security Analysts a forecast that earnings would all but triple in the current fiscal year, and even broke down the rise into 78 percent from internal operations, 5 percent from recent acquisitions, 7 percent from an extraordinary item, 10 percent from acquisitions under consideration. According to Tobias, the paper value of Randell's own stock jumped $6.5 million on such good news, backed by such precise—and utterly meaningless—figures.

More meaningful information would have included the fact, for example, that NSMC had reported perhaps $1.4 million of sales that were never actually made as "unbilled receivables"—in a year when its earnings came to $700,000. Another half million of expenses was deferred to the next fiscal year (there's that deferral trick again). For an extra twist, NSMC had to count in $3.8 million of earnings from companies actually acquired after the end of its financial year—simply to show any profit at all.

When the spiraling corporate overhead, the heavy lossmakers, and the past accountancy stratagems caught up with NSMC, it had to report a first-quarter loss, and the shares promptly and properly collapsed. But in the long dizzy ride up from $6 to a peak of $143, how many nests had been feathered? When a twenty-point rise in the stock is worth over $6.5 million, you have a license to print money—and too many accountants will happily provide the rubber stamp.

Don't suppose that the reporting of unmade sales or the disposal of money-losers to corporate insiders (both used by NSMC) are rarities. Not only did Four Seasons use the same devices, so did a company selling houses, which counted in its turnover figures (approved by its accountants) letters of intent to purchase homes for which no sites existed. The key to many of these larks was the Material (or Immaterial) Gambit. If the accountants were satisfied that a proposed distortion of the corporate earnings wouldn't affect them as much as 10 percent, many let it through as not "material."

In the case of the crashed Penn Central, use of the most liberal accounting interpretations (all properly detailed in five pages of footnotes) generated a profit of $0.18 per share, before extraordinary items when—according to analyst S. Scott Nicholls, Jr.—the same figures, on conservative principles, added up to $1.18 of loss. Now, it's easy to understand why corporate managers, backs to the wall, would settle for a piece of fast accounting. But what drives a multimillionaire in the same direction?

The question could well be asked of Dr. Armand Hammer. After he took control of little Occidental Petroleum in 1957, the company grew at a miraculous rate. Between 1963 and 1972, sales multiplied eighty-three times, one of the most explosive rises even in the oil industry's history. Yet in one of those magic years, so the SEC declared, $14 million of the $49 million profit reported for the first three quarters resulted from unrevealed changes in accounting methods. Behind the facade lay an unwelcome fact—Oxy's trend had become negative. Two years after the well-timed accountancy change, it had to report a $67 million loss; the next year was no great shakes, either.

Hammer had loaded $900 million of long-term debt on the corporation's back, a larger sum, in real terms, than even Ted Turner contrived to borrow. And the doctor's wish to protect and preserve the company's surge—which did indeed carry on all the way to 1985 sales of $14.5 billion—is wholly understandable. The urge was no weaker in early 1986, when yet another of Hammer's incessant deals had elevated sales to $24 billion, making Oxy the thirteenth-largest industrial company in the United States. The eighty-seven-year-old corporate patriarch told *Business Week* that he had only two goals left in life: "I want to get Oxy stock to $100 a share, and I want to bring peace to the world."

Neither task looked like being particularly easy—not with the stock standing at $31 at the time. Its tripling, however, would have an extremely beneficial effect on Hammer's own estate, just as Wall Street's relative disdain acted as a drag on his net worth. Any wealth that rests on publicly quoted stock is, so to speak, a hostage to fortune. When his company was valued at $345 million in the market, owning four-fifths of the stock meant that Turner's wealth rose—or fell—by $17 million with every 5 percent shift in the share price. Half the fortunes that fell out of the Forbes 400 in 1985 did so because of declining stock prices; by the same token, major accretions, such as Sam Walton's rise from a humble $2.8 billion to $4.5 billion in 1986, or Leslie Wexner's advance to $1.4 billion, came from the stock-market bubble (Wal-Mart rose 60 percent; Wexner's The Limited doubled), whose burst in a week cost Walton $300 million in 1987.

That being so, it must pay the private fortunes of public millionaires to elevate the stock price by all legal means, including fancy figuring. The problem is that the larger the corporation, the harder it becomes to move the stock. Occidental Petroleum, for example, may have had a break-up value of double the market price when Hammer was talking hopefully of $100 a share. That is the exact reverse of the situation with smaller companies on a growth track—like the fictitious garage mentioned earlier, they can use the magic of accountancy to make their company worth more, not less, than its parts.

The beauty of the doing-it-with-figures approach is that it has infinite variations and can be repeated ad infinitum—not to say ad nauseam. The garage proprietor who miraculously turned $1 million into $2.5 million can carry on buying businesses on the same mathematical basis; each new business acquired, moreover, stands to offer new chances for rearranging its figures in a more profitable light. And if he gets tired of borrowing money to finance acquisitions, the figure man can always use his licensed paper money.

One conglomerator, Meshulam Riklis of Rapid American, while on his way to accumulating a rapid fortune large enough to spend on constructivist art and other worthy diversions, observed of the handy pieces of paper he was employing that "by the time the debentures (Russian rubles) or warrants (Castro pesos) become due, the company you acquire can generate more cash than they are worth." Yet, for all his Russo-Cuban ruses, Riklis could not sustain his momentum. By 1985 he had dropped out of the Forbes 400, while still a powerful enough wheeler-dealer to intervene in the scandalous takeover of Distillers by Guinness. After a timely (and illegally undeclared) purchase of just over 5 percent of the former company, Riklis emerged with a renewed contract for his Schenley Industries to handle Dewar's in the United States, the American rights to the brand, and a brand-new contract to market Gordon's Gin. The ill-gotten boost (resulting in Schenley's sale to the Brits) was badly needed.

Riklis owned Rapid American lock, stock, and barrel, a holding theoretically worth $150 million in the fall of 1985; but *Forbes* observed tartly that the "company's high debt renders estimates shaky." So much for Russo-Cuban theory. In fact, there are built-in obstacles to multiplication by mirrors. Thus, assume that you really do have a great $1 million business, growing at 50 percent per annum and commanding a P/E of 40. You have a million shares in issue, so the firm is worth $40 million, of which you own half. You buy a few siblings for half a million shares, which produce profits, at a twenty times P/E, of another $1 million. This raises your earnings per share to $1.33, boosting the capitalization to $80 million, of which you now own a third—or nearly $27 million.

So far, so marvelous. The next year, however, your original activity produces its 50 percent but your acquisitions stay put. The earnings per share rise again to $1.66, and the capitalization rises by another $20 million. A third of that, however, goes to the new shareholders whom you unhesitatingly brought in, and the lost $7 million or so is really a delayed cost of the original purchase.

The situation can get even worse. A progression from $1 to $1.33 to $1.66 looks like a slowdown, and that high P/E may wobble. So the temptation is to make another set of acquisitions and buy another $1 million of earnings for half a million shares. But that isn't enough—earnings per share will only rise to $1.75. Try $2 million for $1 million instead—now you're really cooking with gas. That's $1.80 a share, representing another increase of a third in earnings and pushing the capitalization to $180 million.

Your stake has now, after much huffing and puffing, risen from $20 million to $36 million—but so has that of the new shareholders, who brought in only $1 million of profits. And what will you do for an encore? Another 50 percent rise in the original business is now utterly swamped. Even an acquisition program twice as large—$4 million of earnings for 2 million shares—won't do. You either have to engage in supercolossal buying or somehow get your 33.33 percent growth rate from the existing businesses.

That is precisely why figure specialists (of whom the conglomerators were the prize breed) so often fell into ludicrous overstretching (like James P. Ling's purchase of the Jones & Laughlin steel company, which culminated in the inevitable Chapter 11 bankruptcy in 1986). Accountancy games, either controversial (like ITT's) or downright illegal (like NSMC's), only put off the evil hour. If that black moment doesn't bring disgrace, it may simply dole out disappointment—and dismemberment (like the huge sell-off at Gulf + Western after Charles H. Bluhdorn's death in a plane crash).

Very fast foot and figure work was needed to keep the conglomerates ahead of a losing game. The fastest feet (and feat) belonged to Saul Steinberg. In 1985 he was a *Forbes* dropout: an estimated $400 million fortune had been called into question by positive debts, negative cash flow, and goodwill items that exceeded the shareholders' equity. Since Steinberg had sensibly taken his empire private in 1982, however, he was spared, unlike other wheeler-dealers of his day, from the public embarrassment of a falling share price.

From his private seclusion, Steinberg made some very public forays, including a raid on Walt Disney that was a conspicuous, notorious piece of greenmailing. How much stuck to Steinberg's fingers was indeed unclear—but the picture became notably less foggy when the young (forty-seven-year-old) master took Reliance, after only four private years, public once more. Little had changed in its financial situation since *Forbes* had turned thumbs down a year before: the company, after removing Steinberg's beloved intangibles, had a negative net worth of $200 million. The offering raised $140 million and left the Steinberg family sitting on stock that, at the offer price, was valued at some $650 million—or $100 million more than the entire company had fetched on privatization four years before. As in the case of Ted Turner, a lion's share of a messy meal became worth far more than the meal itself—thanks to the numerical magic of the price-earnings ratio. What's more, since share prices are determined by supply and demand, if you restrict the supply (by keeping four-fifths or whatever of the equity as your own), you must swing the demand/supply equation in your favor.

The multiplier's effect is multiplied. But there's a catch. . . . That multiplier has a nasty knack of working in reverse. If the P/E is 40, if the profits are $10 million, and if you own half the shares, each $1 million of extra profit is worth $2 million in your safe-deposit box. Suppose, however, that the profits fall by $1 million in one dull year, and that a disillusioned stock market consequently pushes down the P/E to 20. That one slight slip will cost your kitty no less than $110 million.

Now, being able to lose a fortune of that size may be gratifying in its way—Ross Perot, king of the computer gee-whiz experts, lost almost half a billion on paper in a single day as his 85 percent of Electronic Data Systems zoomed down from its high; but that is not how most millionaires like to be titillated. Indeed, the awful prospect of that slide is what keeps the millionaires and their ever-loving accountants on the hunt, not for bigger and better profits, but for something that looks just as good and even works as well, if only for a time: bigger and better figures.

22

YOU *CAN* FOOL ALL THE PEOPLE

You can fool all the people—not all the time, but for enough of it to steal their money. The definitions of theft range from criminal dishonesty to false bills of goods, and the penalties range from mere business failure to moderate prison terms. But the punishment seldom fits the crime—somehow or other, the thief nearly always ends up in possession of enough loot to line a gilded cage for his retirement or future activities, even if he is caught.

Mythologists of crime dream of a Mr. Big, the Mephistophelean brain behind the £2 million Great Train Robbery in Britain, the $2.75 million Brinks caper in the United States, the removal of the Nazi gold reserves at the end of World War II, the wave of art robberies that have run curators and collectors ragged all over Europe. But only a pervert would suffer the possible prison penalties, the logistic difficulties, the dangerous and incompetent colleagues, and the other risks attendant on robbing even a small bank—when he can start his own bank and rob the depositors in comfort.

Simple thieving is no longer followed by real bankers, on the whole, because they are too tightly policed and regulated (politicians and cops, after all, need somewhere safe to put their own cash). That observation, though, needs to be heavily qualified by two facts: first, a good (or bad) many banks have been managed with an incompetence tantamount to theft; second, not a few bankers actually have embezzled their customers' money in the past two decades (including one sly Italian who siphoned the depositors' funds into an account in the name of his favorite racehorse).

Yet it's not only the fuzz that keeps the good banks straight. It's also the fact that their money is, relatively speaking, easy to earn. People deposit their hard-earned dollars, pounds, marks, lire, francs, yen, or zloty; the bank pays them either no interest at all or as little as possible. There was even a time when Swiss banks, the world's stingiest, made their depositors pay for the privilege—and so profoundly did the rich foreigners trust the Swiss that they accepted the imposition. When lending the same money, though, banks in theory insist on cast-iron collateral to protect the loans on which they charge the highest rates that the traffic will bear.

If you are borrowing $1,000 or $1 million or $1 billion and lending it for interest rates yielding $160 or $160,000 or $160 million, you need little else to wax rich; even after paying for the marble halls and marble-headed managers with which banks are traditionally supplied. The heads, though, are the source of the recent trouble. Faced with increasing difficulty in generating growth from their corporate customers, who were inconveniently raising more and more of their money direct, the banks, virtually as one misguided man, rushed for the nearest fashion in the effort to fill the lending gap.

In this pursuit of still more wealth for its owner, the Penn Square bank in Oklahoma City lost so much good money on the security of bad energy plays and on the say-so of a single walking financial disaster that it contributed powerfully to the near busting of the eighth-largest bank in the United States. The downfall of Continental Illinois, in turn, was founded on the foolish notion, to which bankers are occasionally prone, that you can buy growth by taking on lower-quality business (such as the Penn Square loans) or by accepting lower margins.

Cut-price trading is especially foolish, because it undermines the basic economics of banking. However, the banks' understandable insistence, when thinking straight, on borrowing cheap and lending dear is what opens the door to a whole school of would-be millionaire frauds. The gambit is to persuade people to give their money to you, rather than the bank, by the simple expedient of offering them a much higher but impossible return.

The recorded annals of such deceptions (probably there were variations in ancient Egypt) include the Apple Miracle, the Pig Payoff, the Casino Caper, the Pyramid Ploy, and many, many others; as soon as one con is destroyed, another (often the same one) rears its head. With apples, the idea was that the city dweller should buy himself a piece of the action in an orchard, because (as everybody knows) one little seed will grow into a big tree, showering apples and wealth on its owners forevermore. Pigs were another form of armchair farming; those noble animals have enormous litters, at great speed, so that possession of just one sow, cared for for you by the promoter, would confer the benefits of compound breeding and interest for all eternity.

Casinos were for armchair gamblers. You turned over your money to a wizard who had an infallible system for winning at the tables; he creamed off a commission for his pains and paid all the rest, at stupendous rates of interest, to his happy backers. One such scheme offered the suckers a 360 percent return in theory; in practice, none of the 20,000 of them got more than a fifth of their money back.

These frauds have one thing in common: the name Ponzi, after the Italian-American who practiced the art with notable success in Boston. (Italians have a long record of financial innovation, from double-entry bookkeeping onward—and downward.) Some of the brightest luminaries in business and show business were caught by a particularly pretty Ponzi in the early 1980s. It spiced the normal cupidity of the Ponzi victim with the zest of tax avoidance: the rich subscribers, knowing that oil wells were among the country's most prolific sources of tax dodges, happily fell for the fabulous, fictitious returns offered on syndicated oil investments.

The essence of all such schemes is first come, first served, or last come, not served at all—otherwise known as devil take the hindmost. The few who receive the promised reward from the apples, pigs, oil wells, casinos, or whatever are paid out of the subscriptions of the majority. Simple arithmetic shows that the latter are bound to find, one day, that the well has run dry—and even that the promoter has run off with the loot, like a 280-pound commodities wizard who parted several suckers from some $18 million of savings in the Britain of 1985.

The oldest ploy, possibly older even than apples, is the pyramid, adopted with unstoppable enthusiasm by U.S. promoters such as Glenn Turner of Dare-to-Be-Great, a motivational marvel, and Koscot Interplanetary cosmetics, if you please, or the late, unlamented William Penn Patrick, under whom Turner learned the trade, and who the Securities and Exchange Commission accused of taking 80,000 investors for more than $250 million of Holiday Magic—which sold soap as well as cosmetics.

295

In its origins the pyramid possessed perfect simplicity—best shown by the chain letter idea. Each participant is supposed to find a fixed number of other kindred spirits, who in turn each find the same number, until by the laws of geometrical progression a sum of money vastly greater than the original small amount comes in turn to each link in the chain. The logical defect is that no money is coming into the scheme from outside. Even if the chain doesn't break, the first come are again the first served—but break it must. The mathematical fact is that with each person recruiting four people, it takes only a relatively few stages before the entire population of the country—men, women, children, and possibly even a few dogs—will be in the pyramid.

Precisely the same objection applied to schemes such as Koscot. The gimmick of the Koscot-style pyramid is that its structure is linked to the sale of the wonder product: cosmetics, or liquid cleaner, or whatever. Each link in the pyramid recruits other links to sell the goodies in a carefully constructed hierarchy of regional bosses, distributors, and salesmen.

The subscription is a purchase of the wonder inventory, offset by bonuses for each new link recruited into the chain. It looks absolutely safe; the money hasn't gone for nothing, but for goods you can see, feel, count—and sell at a satisfyingly high profit margin. The mathematics are magical; according to the SEC, if each Holiday Magic distributor had signed up as many others as he was supposed to, 305,175,780 people would have been flogging the junk (presumably to each other) within twelve months. The existence of the stuff, however, appears to make the pyramid more plausible; in actuality, it makes the whole scheme utterly incredible.

The combined profit margins add up to several times the ex-factory cost at the start of the chain—a price that presumably includes a profit. What the pyramided suckers should have wondered was why, if the product were truly salable at such gigantic markups, its proprietor would want to let so many others into so lucrative an act. This is the selfsame question that should be, but isn't, asked by those tempted by piggies, apples, casinos, and so on: If the profits are truly so great, why does the man need my money?

Even when the promised returns work out at an annual rate of over 300 percent, the victims still wonder not. Their own urge to get rich quick blinds them. Actually, if you could invest £250 at 300 percent, you would be a millionaire in six years—nice work if you could get it. What is more pathetic, however, is that millions of people down the years have been tempted to part with their cash by quite small rates of interest, or (which comes to the same thing) small savings of money.

Two firms that crashed in Britain, for instance, regularly offered interest on deposits 2 percent or 3 percent above the going rate. There was no obvious way in which they could earn enough on the deposits to cover the interest; actually, there was no way. One firm, called Pinnock Finance, was Australian-based and was vaguely supposed to be in sewing machines. After its presiding genius had vanished with the boodle, it appeared that Pinnock too had worked that oldest trick in the con game, paying off the first suckers from the money generously provided by the next set, and so on not quite ad infinitum. Just as the pig scheme only contained a third of the happily breeding pigs promised to investors, so much of the Pinnock money went nowhere except into the Pinnock money. The crunch comes when the flow of new money dries up and the owners of the old money start wanting it back.

This painful conjunction caught a slippery specialist named Dr. Emil Savundra in its icy grip. Savundra's specialty was to offer motorists insurance on their cars at premiums well below the going rate. Note that phrase again: if a rate is going, there's a prima facie case that it's the correct rate. Unable to resist the bargain, drivers earnestly loaded their cash into the hands of Savundra's Fire and Auto and Marine, where the proprietor, with even greater earnestness, off-loaded as much of the proceeds as possible into his own pockets (located mostly in overseas bank accounts). When the inevitable collapse came, as accident claims by motorists exceeded the amount of money left in Savundra's kitty, the cops followed fast—and so did his imprisonment.

Savundra's fraud thus had a serious defect, shared with the devices of even greater removal experts, Tino de Angelis, the salad oil magician, and Billy Sol Estes, the silo wizard. All three men made, or conjured up, personal profits running into several millions. Both de Angelis and Sol Estes preyed on the Achilles heel of the modern economy, which is its total dependence on bits of paper. If a man waves a document that says there is grain in a silo, or oil in a storage tank, banks are wont to lend money on that security just as readily as a Savundra customer, having purchased a policy, believed that his car was safely insured.

If bankers checked every individual paper transaction for its underlying reality, the logjam would reach intolerable proportions by noon on the first day. De Angelis fastened on this fact (just as, in an earlier era, Ivar Kreuger issued $500 million in fictitious bonds). Nobody knows how much of the resulting sums—$167 million zoomed out of the de Angelis company in its last six months of life—was stashed away awaiting his exit from jail. But there's the catch: the convicted con has to face the inconvenience of a spell behind bars before he can enjoy his proceeds.

De Angelis caught a ten-year sentence, meaning seven years with parole. If the estimates of his take were correct and he hung on to half, that works out at $100 per hour of maximum captivity. In fact, that's not a great rate of return. However you look at it, going to prison is a bad technical lapse, a blotch on the escutcheon of an alleged expert in the business of persuading the customers to part with their money.

It took another American to elevate this craft to the status of a higher art: Bernie Cornfeld, caliph of Investors Overseas Services. At its peak this megamishmash contained $2.5 billion of the people's money. How much of it ended in the maw of the IOS mob will never be known. But the public flotation of IOS Ltd. alone, the final act in its *Götterdämmerung*, made the Cornfeld and Co. stake worth $52 million.

Cornfeld's advantage over other practitioners was that, while holding out the selfsame bait of riches, he actually offered *less* than the going rate. His idea, a stroke of pure genius, was to sell people dollar bills for more than a dollar. Any IOS customer in the U.S. armed forces, where the business started, could have bought mutual funds direct. The disadvantage of these investments, especially those of the so-called front-end-load genus, is that a major part of the investors' money goes straight to the salesman and the management, not into the investment.

With front-end load, the investor may lose half of his initial outlay in this wildly unproductive way. On one calculation, the load and the continuing management charges meant that if an investment doubled in ten years, the investor would have had to wait for six of them to get back on speaking terms with his own money. In Cornfeld's case, the customers paid his Fund of Funds to put their money into the same mutual funds the overseas Americans whom he first tapped could easily have bought for themselves; the funds also paid IOS and exacted their own toll, before finally depositing the cash into some kind of investment.

The setup was so glorious that eventually IOS couldn't stand seeing any of the public's money going into somebody else's wallet. So it set up its own internal mutual funds. The customer still paid twice for the same service, but (which was a great improvement) he now paid IOS twice. What's more, the internal funds were not confined to staid, quoted investments whose market value could be ascertained in a trice by reading *The Wall Street Journal.*

This unconfined joy in turn made it easier to deliver what the customers thought they were buying—which was capital gain on (it was implied, advertised, and blazoned forth) a phenomenal scale. With funds as large as those of IOS, however, it was impossible to generate this kind of performance. The sheer weight of so much money was bound to bring down the funds if world stock markets fell. Cornfeld could not suspend this law of financial gravity. That law applies so efficiently to all mass money that in 1986, a miracle year for stock markets, America's mutual funds collectively contrived a feeble 13 percent return to their investors—only *half* the rise in the Dow Jones index.

For all that, and maybe as its cause, the amount of cash pouring into mutual funds *doubled* during the year. When the citizens connive so eagerly at their own financial maltreatment, the need to cheat is negligible: the $200 billion of mutual fund sales in 1986 provided an avalanche of commissions, management fees (probably around $2 billion), and loadings. Indeed, the success of legal rackets has been so great that it may explain the relative absence of big-time public cons in recent years. Crooks there have been aplenty, but they have been preying directly on their own kind.

The victims of scams such as insider trading or the multiple shenanigans at E. F. Hutton are internal to the financial industry: check-kiting cost the venerable Wall Street firm a $2 million fine and $4 million repayment to the banks it had cheated of interest due; the fall of a mortgage company forced Hutton, alleging fraud, to set aside $16 million; and the stumbling investment bank next ran into a $48 million loss, blamed on bad checks and duff collateral allegedly supplied by a Houston hustler.

Indirectly, of course, the cost of all successful scams filters back to the general public in lost taxes, collapsed shares, and higher charges. But the impact of the robbers is greatly diluted by the time it reaches home; anyway, with thieves such as Dennis Levine, the first insider trader to be nailed by the Feds, who was robbed? His employer, Drexel Burnham Lambert, was certainly betrayed. But the $12.6 million profit Levine made in five years (from fifty-four deals based on inside information) didn't come from Drexel.

Even the inside tip-offs weren't actually stolen; rather, criminally misused, just like the information about pending *Wall Street Journal* stories released by reporter R. Foster Winans to the renegade top broker, Peter Brant of Kidder Peabody. The real losers were the people who sold the shares bought by the insider traders—holders who, had they held on, would have pocketed the profits garnered by Levine, Boesky, and others.

Yet the problem of distributing the damage doesn't lessen the crookedness. Ivan F. Boesky actually raised almost $1 billion, a substantial sum even by Cornfeld standards, to invest in what he dignified, in his book *Merger Mania*, as a higher investment art form. The book, now a literary curiosity, was a lie. It's hard to disagree with the securities lawyer who told *Business Week*, "He beguiled everybody about his exhaustive research and canny stock analysis when he really made money the old-fashioned way. He stole it."

Just as clumsy heirs can be protected from maladroit management by diversified holdings and legal devices, though, so Wall Street crooks can line their nests comfortably enough to survive disgrace in style. *Forbes* put Boesky's wealth at over $200 million before the fall (and before the $50 million fine and $50 million of repayments). But nobody expected the proceeds of the 200-acre Westchester estate, the Impressionist paintings, or the $136 million sale of the Beverly Hills Hotel (half owned by his wife) to disappear in the same direction as his $100 million. The wife's assets are the last protection of the scoundrel.

Boesky's problem had some similarity to Cornfeld's—as the scale of his activities, and the success of his fund-raising, grew, so it became more difficult to achieve the results on which the reputation and fund-raising rested. "Investing almost $1 billion with a strategy probably based largely on inside information exponentially increased Boesky's chances of getting nabbed," wrote *Business Week*. As one quoted arbitrageur said, "Ivan was playing Russian roulette."

In Cornfeld's case, the performance need drove him into dubious areas such as the oil land operations of another master of the people's money, John M. King.

King's bait was oil for the masses. Working on the mutual fund principle, including that of deducting heavy compensation for his pains, King was supposed to invest the money in oil wells drilled by his own corporation—which provided all other services required, at a price. The beauty of this scheme defied imitation; investors naturally had to accept that some oil wells came up dry. If King failed to deliver the bounty, it was an act of God rather than man, deductible (what was more) as a tax loss.

The King of Denver truly delivered for his friend Cornfeld. IOS invested in some territory found by King; a sale of a fraction of the tract was arranged at a staggering price that, when applied to all of the IOS holding, amounted to a $145 million capital gain. Since that tasted too rich even for Cornfeld's and King's palates, the mythical gain was whittled down to a mere $91 million. In a weird twist of fate, later on, long after IOS had crashed, the land actually did turn out to bear oil and to be truly valuable. For all anybody knew at the time, though, the IOS profit was the purest fairy gold.

But in practical terms, it hardly matters whether a value is fictitious or real, so long as the fiction is believed. This lovable fact spawned an entire new branch of the money-lifting industry. Devoted students of Cornfeld's success plugged the main weakness in his operation: its ultimate dependence on stock markets, which by their very nature fluctuate. Real estate, on the other hand, is popularly supposed to go up and up as it goes up. A real estate mutual fund could therefore offer an investment paradise on earth—absolute security with everlasting growth, and good income to boot.

The investors (milked from the front end as usual) were therefore offered little pieces of large buildings in the lush United States. Gramco, the most successful of these operations, would run the properties (at a substantial fee) and would periodically announce how much they had increased in value. In fact, the real value of this real estate was purely putative: you can sell shares at any time, but offloading a portfolio of up-valued skyscrapers is no easier than selling your house at your own top price.

In other words, the investors who flocked to Gramco (and to even more obviously fraudulent imitators such as Jerome Hoffman of the very unreal Real Estate Fund of America) were unwittingly burying their money in the most illiquid form of investment possible. The whole credibility of the edifice depended on the suckers continuing to believe it. If too many of them simultaneously wanted their money back, even in a completely honest operation, their Comstock Lode would have to sell its fairy gold—and if the fairy gold failed to fetch fairy prices, down would come the entire estate, buildings and all.

To illustrate this truth, say that the suckers have paid $1 billion for their stake; you decide, after a time, that the buildings are worth $1.5 billion, when actually their realizable value is $1.2 billion. Any not-such-a-sucker who thereupon takes his money out gets 50 percent more than he put in; it follows that if half the clients ask for the loot, you must pay out $750 million, leaving only $450 million to satisfy $750 million of claims. Actually, crisis would be reached well before that point. As soon as schemes of this kind start, for whatever reason, to experience a net outflow of investors' funds, the jig is up, their days are numbered, and the vultures gather.

The Gramco fund, USIF, was eventually stuck with $1 billion in property, 20,000 anguished stockholders, and 1,700 salesmen running to keep a step ahead of the aforesaid investors. John Thackray reports that the El Salvador representative, on learning of the disaster, checked with an atlas to find the furthest spot on the globe from El Salvador and took a plane there forthwith. Many Gramco and IOS customers were Latin Americans bent on sending untaxed money to safer, less-inflationary climes. It served them right. Gramco was caught in the IOS backwash—but it would have fallen anyway.

The Cornfeld Gambit and its variations not only proved unprecedentedly efficient at putting greedy hands in investors' pockets, they generated so rich a cash flow that, preceding the vultures, other and fatter fowls of the air came clustering—the brokers, the fund managers, the bankers, the underwriters—all clamoring for a piece of the action. Drexel Harriman & Ripley in the United States, Hill Samuel in Britain, and the French Rothschilds (the English ones asked to be excused) were intimate actors in the final stages of building Bernie's Valhalla, and in the twilight of the gods that ensued, many and white were the respectable hands being washed.

Respectable front, back, or side names are no protection for the investor. His true defense is simple refusal to believe that money is subject to miracles. His true weakness is envy. Armchair farming, gambling in plush casinos for high stakes, wheeling and dealing on world stock markets, owning oil wells and skyscrapers—all these are hobbies for those who are already rich. Would-be millionaires fall for their own envy, and the Cornfelds of this world shrewdly exploit that temptation—so shrewdly, in fact, that there is no reason why, given self-restraint, they could not have lasted far longer. So much money was flowing into IOS at its peak that merely lending out the cash before it was invested produced a torrent of wealth, all of which would have belonged to the gang if they had known how to stop it from streaming right out again.

But the expenses of running a worldwide door-to-door selling operation are also wondrous: the instincts for mob psychology of these entrepreneurs arise from their own weakness, which rules out any chance of retrenchment or caution, and, anyway, they are terrified of any fall-off in the money flow.

The writing on the wall for Gramco, in fact, appeared even before the IOS blackout: the Gramco proprietors, Keith Barish and Rafael Navarro, as unlikely a pair of boy wonder financiers as ever flashed across the sky, took over two dozen pages in a newsmagazine to discuss their financial and philanthropic virtues, in full color. Those sufficiently unenthralled with these gods among men to seek details of the company's system for paying commission (a highly material subject) were cross-referenced to number eighteen of the unnumbered pages; the eighteenth page contained no reference whatsoever to the commission system. But the customers of such leeches don't really want to know anything, except that they are getting richer. And they do not share the instinctive feeling of the experienced hand that if somebody has to buy two dozen pages of advertising to say how wonderful he is, he can't be.

There was, truth to tell, something terribly, appallingly wrong with all the great con artists of our time, something so abominably amiss that any reasonably shrewd child off the Brooklyn streets (where Cornfeld grew up) could be expected to spot the defect at once. They are not the obvious philanthropic types, these gentry. They are flashy, showy, greedy, conceited; they give themselves away by hiring expensive political names as window dressing; they act like exactly the kind of used-car salesman from whom you shouldn't buy, the type that only has to accomplish one trick to sell the jalopy—which is to sell you themselves. If you can believe them, you can believe anything, including their unbelievable propositions.

Inevitably, in a suspicious world, on the theory that kills always attract buzzards, large-scale public rip-offs attract rumors of involvement by the real mob—the Mafia. The stories are not encouraged by *Fortune*'s 1986 ranking of the fifty top capos, which mentions, among the illicit pastimes, narcotics, loan-sharking, illegal gambling, and prostitution, and, among the more agreeable activities, entertainment, construction, and the wholesaling of food and liquor.

Fraud, as opposed to extortion, doesn't appear to be a favorite activity of organized crime. Maybe it is too subtle an activity for operators who eliminate competition simply by eliminating it. But the mobsters may be right to eschew the more complex forms of fraud on strictly economic grounds. The President's Commission on Organized Crime believes that the mobs retain an income of $30 billion a year after expenses, taken from a $50 billion gross; that appalling sum far exceeds the take of known defrauders. Once upon a time, moreover, the latter were also more likely than mobsters to land in jail. This is no longer true—and, then, the cons face far less chance of assassination.

They sleep no easier at night, though, to judge by Robert Vesco and the entourage of armed guards required to protect him in his latest, Cuban exile. Vesco first came to ill fame with the collapse of IOS. As Cornfeld's sun sank painfully slowly in the west, his associate John M. King made the early running at rescue. As King's empire in turn melted in the glare of publicity, Robert M. Vesco appeared from nowhere like a Jack-in-the-box. Within a remarkably short time, Vesco had disappeared with equal rapidity in his private Boeing 707, into the welcoming arms of President José Figueres of Costa Rica, while the SEC sought, in high dudgeon, to discover the exact whereabouts of $224 million in IOS funds.

"We brought down our families," said Vesco, "enrolled our children in excellent schools, and started our new life in this American Arcadia." There was no Arcadian resting place for either Vesco, caught up in the Watergate disaster and hounded by the authorities, or for Cornfeld, arrested by the aggrieved Swiss authorities on a visit to his aged mother and popped into a Swiss jail where he could ponder over the dwindling of his IOS fortune from $150 million to $5 million.

Vesco's ill-gotten gains took longer to dwindle. He was still among the Forbes 400 as late as 1984. After his Watergate brush (he made an illegal $200,000 contribution to the notorious Nixon reelection committee), Vesco upped the ante: he offered a $10 million bribe to Carter administration officials in 1977. That didn't help, either; a year later, his American Arcadia showed Vesco the door. Next, escape from the CIA and deportation terminated his Bahamian residence—and according to a book by Arthur Herzog, Vesco's latter-day sojourn in Cuba was no more idyllic.

Yet, if Vesco had stuck to his original conglomerate guns, his grandly named International Controls Corp. might be keeping him in corporate jets to this day. Of course, ICC wasn't what it seemed, either. To the crooked, all things are crooked. These Joe McCarthys of the business world live off the Big Lie, off the law that the more outrageous a proposition, the more likely its hearers are to suspend their critical faculties altogether. In this the ungodly are aided and abetted by the virtuous—not merely in the way the latter, too, fall both for the Big Lie and the easy commissions it generates, but because the godly also make such hay out of the savings of the small.

Take the most popular form of investment, the thoroughly respectable industry of life insurance. The insurers take people's money year after year, with no firm undertaking to pay back more than the face value on expiry—if the investor wants his money back in midterm, he has to take a loss; he has no information about what investments, in turn, the company is making on his behalf, or how well they have done, and by and large, the results are no better than could have been achieved by investing in a mutual fund (a fact that spawned a whole new industry, and crop of millionaires, who simply threw in life cover with their mutual fund sales). The profits to the orthodox insurance company are so large that it can afford to pay very handsome commissions to the agent who merely books the business.

In the United States, by this happy conjunction of circumstances, the men who sell insurance have profited so mightily that they account for a significant crop in the harvest of postwar millionaires. These are

men such as the tub-thumping supersalesman W. Clement Stone, practitioner of success through a positive mental attitude, open-handed
distributor of largess to Richard M. Nixon and other positive political
thinkers, and author of the ripe remark: "If a family has wealth in the
neighborhood of $400 million, what's a million in gifts?"

At least, you could assume that regular insurance companies were
honest—until Stanley Goldblum came along, that is. Ex-butcher Goldblum was the genius behind Equity Funding, the "blue-suede shoes,
hipster type of outfit," in the posthumous words of one Wall Street
observer, that made the immortal discovery that you don't actually
need to sell people insurance policies to achieve $2 billion a year of
sales. Far easier to invent the people—then you can invent the policies,
too.

At the first count, Equity had 50,000 phantom policies, and had
sold the premiums to other insurance companies (so-called reinsurance)
to create $25 million of far from phantom income. Not only were the
purchasers fooled, so were the investment experts, which, as a matter
of unpalatable fact, is their normal form. Equity's dishonesty was bred
from the need to feed a stock price that had soared from $6 to $80 in
five years, and then had dribbled down to $13 a year later. Yet a group
of analysts specializing in this area chose Equity Funding as their pet
stock among all the finance and financial services bundles on the market. That was at the beginning of 1972—about a year before the whistle
blew on this people-fooler. The whistle always does blow, in the end,
but too late to save the people's pelf.

Sooner or later, another large-scale fraud on the public is bound
to develop. It will always be necessary to remind people that financial
miracles can never be worked for the masses. That being so, any offer
that purports to generate the miraculous is certain to be yet another
modern, inverted version of the philosopher's stone, turning gold back
into base metal. That will never deter the unwary, and around that
stone, coming out from under it if necessary, will cluster all those with
a highly developed nose for the scent of other people's money.

The money can be tempted from its owners' pockets with surprising ease. Try this for a proposition. You pay $42,000 for a commercial
film-processing machine, which is in effect costing you $60 a week in
lost interest; you are assured that if you only process three rolls of film
a day, you will, even after paying for paper and chemicals, break even.
True or false? Develop ten rolls a day, and you'll make $23,000 on your
$42,000 investment. Do twenty, and you've paid for the machine in a
year. How about that?

All three propositions look unlikely, especially when you know that the machine, supplied by a French firm named KIS, costs only some $1,500 to make. If a profit of $42,000 is available year after year, why would the supplier take his return up front? That sort of question suddenly lowered the reputation of Serge Crasnianski, formerly re-garded as one of the best and brightest businessmen in France. One of his erstwhile journalistic boosters, *Business Week*, after a praiseworthy investigation, challenged the entire basis of the KIS operation, report-ing that clients and employees were disgruntled, and official investiga-tors offended, all around the world.

The KIS caper is a variation of the franchise device, which is a well-known mine field for the life savings of investors who stray from such world-renowned names as Holiday Inns, Kentucky Fried Chicken, and Benetton. Even in impeccable cases, where franchisees have risen to the wealth they were promised, there's no doubt who makes the most: the franchisor. In the real world, the exchange of something for nothing seldom takes place between the strong and the weak. It's the weak who, unless protected, feed the strong. They will always need all the defense the law can provide; for their own common sense, alas, is a feeble shield against financial folly and the buzzards who would dine at their expense.

23

THIS MESS
IN WASHINGTON

Corruption in government excites almost as much scorn in the ranks of business as bureaucratic proliferation and constipation. Yet big business can teach even the civil service a knot or three when it comes to red tape, protocol, and waste of money—the main difference being that the shareholders, unlike the taxpayers, don't have fairly incorruptible watchdogs who will, from time to time, expose the stupidity, greed, and inefficiency of officials who destroy other people's substance.

The executives at Allegheny International, mentioned in Chapter 2, would no doubt still be enjoying the fruits of the company's fantastic $50 million corporate overhead if the corporation's results hadn't moved in the opposite direction to the lavish boardroom spending. There's no reason to suppose, though, that former chairman Robert J. Buckley was alone in corporate America in lavish tastes such as the "Allegheny Air Force" of no less than five executive jets.

On the contrary, the pattern of executive compensation suggests that Buckley (with a salary of $537,000) was merely conforming to the norms. According to the compensation consultants, Hewitt Associates, Buckley's contemporaries in the chief executive ranks of the 200 largest companies listed by *Fortune* averaged $700,000 in salary and bonuses. As the magazine says, that's enough to finance a $750,000 house, a $200,000 vacation home, and a yacht—without having the company provide them for you.

Many executives don't look at matters that way. The more the firm provides, the less they need dip into their income, or into the various capital transfers that, Hewitt reckons, will bring the *average* CEO over $15 million in ten years. There's nothing in Washington to match this *average* velvet lining of nests. As for the exceptional, even a Tammany Hall politico would have blanched at the money Steven Ross proposed to suck out of Warner Communications. Not content with a company helicopter, company bodyguard, and company villa at Acapulco, Ross stands to make not $15 million, but $142.6 million over ten years—and some $90 million, if, perchance, the movie corporation gets taken over before Ross can dip fully into the cookie jar.

Big business evidently has nothing to learn from politics when it comes to parting the people from their pelf. It also knows no peers when it comes to exploiting for its unique benefit the mess in Washington, London, Paris, Bonn, Caracas—or wherever in the world some unstable mixture of politicians and career officials tries ineptly to manage an economy that is swimming with financial sharks.

Straight corruption, of course, exists, and flourishes like a dirty green bay tree. The bulk of the bezzle (bribery offered and taken is nothing but an indirect embezzlement of the public's hard-earned bread) lies in bribes. An unpleasant odor was exuded, even before Watergate, by U.S. campaign contributions. (The Nixonian acceptance of $200,000 in bills from Robert Vesco, the alleged picker-over of the IOS carcass, was no nastier than the unpunished and much larger amounts with which the U.S. dairy lobby greased its way to higher price supports.)

In the same category lie, or lurk, the fat jobs offered to former officials; the largesse scattered around useful contacts, as by the bribers of Spiro Agnew; the jobs, loans, and holidays offered to those with contracts in their influence; the obligatory payment concealed in tenders submitted to Latin American bureaucracies.

In the latter method, at its most methodical, bank notes of ascending denomination are interleaved in the tender, enabling each succeeding official in the hierarchy to take his appropriate cut as the contract wends its way to the top. It's the same principle that governed between-wars tipping in restaurants in gay Vienna: customers left piles of coins for each rank of waiter spaced around the edge of the table, the principle being that whatever the horny hand of the head waiter could span was his alone.

But the criminal bezzle is as nothing compared to the legitimate take. Even if you throw in the depredations of dictatorships such as the Trujillos, the Marcos duo, the Shah of Iran, the Duvaliers, or Perez Jimenez (who is supposed to have taken the Venezuelans for $250 million, or more than Meyer Lansky, father of the modern Mafia, purportedly put in his poke), the grand total is still only a drop in the ocean of legislated transfer of funds from the taxpayer to the pockets of the rich.

The largest, most splendiferous flow of money in the world is tax: no other industry comes near tax-collecting in efficacy or profitability, millions of money pouring in daily for negligible costs of collection. If predatory pairs of hands can seize a modest smidgen of one day's flow, all financial problems evaporate with sublime ease. The funny fact is that other, perfectly clean hands will be equally eager to give it to them.

The natural law of taxation is that spending rises to surpass the revenue earned, from which the corollary is that those in charge of the public purse must always be searching for outlets for its contents. Businessmen therefore do their utmost to encourage the politician's natural desire to live well and die (or lose office) in dignified economic circumstances.

In the United States, because of the spiraling cost of elections and the clear relation of expenditure to electoral chances, the tendency is for politicos to make their moolah before plunging into the fray: the 1960 election was a forerunner of what became a convention—out of all the candidates for nomination, only Hubert Humphrey and Richard Nixon were not millionaires, and Nixon before long corrected that deficiency. Any candidates who are not provided for previous to their election have a strong chance of being well looked after subsequently. Wealthy to start with, George Washington died worth $530,000 in 1799; Dwight Eisenhower benefited from special tax legislation that made him a million. While "resting" (as actors put it), Richard Nixon was converted from a poor boy to a well-heeled former corporation lawyer with real estate in choice locations on both sides of the United States.

Similarly, Edward Heath's time in the City, where he was employed as a merchant banker, while being the leading light of Her Majesty's Opposition, presumably helped him to enter 10 Downing Street better than empty-handed. Indeed, Heath could by then afford costly racing yachts and private madrigal concerts. He is unlikely to have been a banker of brilliant success, given the small amount of time that politics can have left for banking; presumably fortune favored the politically brave, as does literature.

In an age when a madam, Sydney Biddle Barrows, can earn the equivalent of ten years of her escort service income by $525,000 of book income, politicians have been able to accomplish more by their memoirs than by honest (or dishonest) graft. It's this fact, even more than the powerful urges for self-vindication and the swift rewriting of history, that explains why Nixon exposed himself to the Frost interviews and why, like him and the other Watergate villains, politicians on both sides of the Atlantic have rushed into print as soon as they are rushed out of office.

In an earlier generation, Lord Beaverbrook made it his business to see that ill luck never ran the way of his political friends. He would buy choice investments on their behalf and present them with the profits when he sold. (If, by some strange quirk of fate, the investment fell, there are no prizes for guessing who stood the loss.) But nothing that Beaverbrook contrived for his favorite prime minister, Bonar Law, can match the accumulative feats of the poor young congressman from Texas, Lyndon Baines Johnson, who ended up, not only as the most powerful senator in Washington, and the most arm-twisting president, but as the owner of broadcasting stations, land, securities, and other odds and ends that *The Wall Street Journal*, back in 1964, assessed at $9 million to $14 million.

Yet this is picayune compared to the amounts accrued by LBJ cronies such as oil tycoon Sid Richardson, and it doesn't rank particularly high in relation to the estate of a relatively minor state official, the former speaker of the Illinois House of Representatives. He died in 1970 worth $3 million, of which $175,000 was found in notes in a shoe box in his hotel room. The accidental revelation of the Powell hoard, a consequence of sudden, ill-planned death, coincidentally reveals just how much swan's down must have stuck to the nests of politicians at all levels of the U.S. system.

The really large, billion-dollar burglary of the public purse arises, not from such mutual back scratching, but from the ineluctable nature of economic forces. These can be visualized as a mighty torrent, fed by innumerable tributaries. As it surges down the riverbed, events threaten—a village swept away here, a cornfield ruined there—that no responsible government can allow.

So the torrent is blocked in one place, diverted in another, by measures that are economic in effect but political in motivation. So long as their interference meets the political requirements (or appears to), the politicos are indifferent to the economic effects. These, however, are gigantic—not only directly, but indirectly. For the force of the torrent is in no way lessened by a blockage or diversion. Narrow the stream in one place, and you must enormously increase the force of the flow somewhere else: and someone will be waiting there to drink.

Thus, at first sight, the beneficiaries of a historic decision by President Reagan in March 1987 were to be the U.S. manufacturers of semiconductors. After all, they were the very people who had been pressing the president, against his free trade instincts, to smack huge tariffs on Japanese products that, the Americans claimed and complained, were damaging their livelihoods, threatening the national security, and (no doubt) posing an affront to American motherhood. When the 100 percent tariffs duly arrived, though, who stood to benefit?

The intended effect was to double or triple the prices on Japanese chips. Once upon a time, manufacturers used to wax rich by forming cartels to maintain prices at an artificially high level. Executives hankering after a golden past have, in modern times, been imprisoned for the same practices. The reason why they were prepared to risk jail is that higher prices mean (other things being equal) higher profits. According to VLSI Research, other things would be so equal that the Japanese victims of U.S. protectionism would garner $3.5 billion of additional profits over four years.

If so, Japan's electronics millionaires, as they plowed the proceeds into still more efficient plants and still more powerful technology, would be joining a long roll of the similarly blessed. The U.S. farm-price supports once even made rich men richer still for agreeing not to farm their land (under Ike they got $100 an acre). Agriculture the world over has been a perennial beneficiary of this bounty for troubled industries— of which none has been more troubled, or more bounteously treated, than shipbuilding. In Britain at one point the Labour government was innocently offering cash grants to non-British shipowners who were building ships in foreign yards for operation by non-British crews under non-British flags of convenience (the convenience in the case being no tax).

All that the lucky Greeks needed was a plaque on the door of a London office. Some £60 million is supposed to have plopped into Greek and other foreign pockets before the civil servants of Whitehall, as ever reluctant to spoil the perfect symmetry of a scheme by correcting a ludicrous error (it never occurred to them that London shipping firms weren't necessarily British), were persuaded to block the drain. The Labour minister, a businessman himself, who spotted and ultimately scotched this boondoggle, was convinced that the drain only failed to gurgle more because most of the Greeks simply didn't believe that even in bureaucratic Britain, Santa Claus had been so miraculously reborn.

The old gentleman was back at work in the 1980s, this time under a Conservative government—and with the difference that everybody believed him. Margaret Thatcher was so eager to pursue the cause of denationalizing British industry that she created the biggest mass speculation since the South Sea Bubble; the distinction being that, this time, the punters were betting, not on the most unlikely speculative venture in history, but on the safest investment imaginable—the national telephone monopoly. The government should have been forewarned by earlier forays into privatization. A high-tech company called Amersham International, offered at 142 pence, shot up by 35 percent in seven days. That, however, was a relatively minor gift: even after the price had gone on to quadruple, Amersham was only valued at $450 million.

The City experts, however, unanimously advised that investors in Wall Street and London would never cough up the required $11 billion for British Telecom unless the shares were most attractively priced. Millions were promptly poured, with the full blessing of the government that ultimately provided them, into a share-pushing campaign such as the world had neither seen nor imagined. Sold at 130 pence, of which only half had to be subscribed at once, the shares in days were offering a 100 percent profit. The deal represented a transfer of some $3 billion from the weak government to the strong financiers (who, of course, received suitably great fees and commissions for their services—including the advice that had cost, or lost, the government so much money).

The American government, which, Conrail apart, is sadly short of nationalized industries to privatize, has contributed its full share to the greatest floating crap game of all time: floating exchange rates. When the dollar was a perennially strong currency, in effect tied to gold, speculators were limited to chips of lesser magnitude—such as the pound sterling—and to anticipating major, rare devaluations. And even before the free-for-all created by floating rates, British politicians' addiction to defending the pound sterling at all costs (the latter being paid by the taxpayer) created wonderful openings for international speculators.

At one point, on a careful estimate, the official regulations had created eighty-nine varieties of sterling, a profusion that offered endless opportunities for switching profitably from one to another. What the politicians damned as speculation and attributed to people unpleasantly nicknamed "gnomes of Zurich," was actually intelligent action on reasoned anticipation of inevitable events. The pound's devaluation was made certain by the incompetent financial policies of Her Majesty's ministers, not by the machinations of astute men playing the international money market.

Premier Harold Wilson was constantly boasting how these fiends would get their fingers burned. In truth, their fingers were tastefully licked as the speculators cashed in on the fact that sterling's ability to rise (its upside risk) was limited by international agreement to a small percentage shift, while the downside potential was of mouth-watering size. The killings in sterling were only matched by the later slaughter of the even longer American defense of the dollar.

In the one month of February 1973 at least $600 million was cleaned up entirely by those who bet on deutsche marks in two weeks' heavy speculation on the fact that the dollar had nowhere to go except down. Probably the majority of this take was cleared by corporations, but a goodly number of clever individuals went along for a free ride, which was financed by others and entailed (like all good speculation) a minimal degree of risk.

After revival under Ronald Reagan, the dollar became overvalued for much the same reason as before: the gigantic balance-of-payments deficit, the mirror image of the equally vast deficit on the federal budget. As the flow of Arab money into the United States dwindled with the oil price, the dollar could only be sustained by faith, hope, and charity. The Reagan administration thereupon proceeded, as a matter of policy, to "talk the dollar down." The speculators took their cue, plunged into the yen and the deutsche mark, devalued the dollar mightily, and reveled in a completely safe profit that ran into billions.

The carelessness of governments with money when their minds are on higher things was amply demonstrated by the Iranian arms scandal. To quote Senator John Tower, millions upon millions in profits from the deals "sort of disappeared into a black hole." It's a safe bet that many of the missing millions (not counting those paid into the wrong Swiss bank account) vanished in the general direction of the multimillionaire arms dealers—including, maybe, those who protested that they lost loot on the transactions. If so, it must have been the first failure in their shadowy lives to part their clients from the taxpayers' wealth.

Nor are arms dealers, speculators, shipbuilders, and shipowners the only beneficiaries of the insatiable desire of governments to make millionaires, or to make millionaires richer still. Economic development, in much of its operation, represents less a boon to backward masses in the neglected corners of the world than a means of creating instant private fortunes out of public funds. In country after country, the government will lend (cheaply) or give you the capital to build a factory, charge you no tax whatsoever (or very little tax) for several years, and impose no restriction on your right to divert the profits to anywhere you have in mind.

Cement plants in Trinidad, engineering or textile factories in Northern Ireland, electronics plants in Scotland, all will do nicely. As for the *Mezzogiorno* of Southern Italy, the beneficence exceeded even the famous generosity of Italian politicians and tax collectors to businessmen all over the country.

Any entrepreneurs who start their enterprises in a British development area (a euphemism that means that the district suffers from above-average unemployment) can spell out some seductive arithmetic. The capitalist is eligible for grants; the local authorities may even provide the site at no rent, or rent a previously built factory to the entrepreneur, who can write off all plant and machinery costs against the first year's profits. One local authority advertised its charms under the headline HOW TO MAKE £378,000; that was the whopping total value of "Tax Benefits and Grants" on a £1 million investment "in Year One Alone."

Many men of absorbing wealth have been made wholly or partly by the government's desire for their technological hauteur. Georges Dassault became one of the richest men in Europe thanks to the Mirage and Mystère fighters whose development was allegedly 60 percent financed by the French government. In this case, it could be argued that defense capability had to be preserved; its preservation, however, also ensures the safekeeping of the riches of its owners.

If a company such as Lockheed heads into bankruptcy as a result of egregious management errors (mainly on a civil project at that), the politicians will always bail it out, not only because of its vital defense capacities and powerful political pull, but also because of the jobs at stake. The curious, or not-so-curious, fact, however, is that (with exceptions such as James H. McDonnell) the defense fortunes enshrined within big corporations have tended to suffer severely from the effects of monstrous mismanagement.

Periodically, the major U.S. defense contractors produce awful financial results, which takes some achieving, given that the government, first, provides plant and factories for them, gratis; second, advances working capital; and third, often ends up by paying vastly more than the originally agreed price. Any civilian in the same happy fix—a building contractor, say—would clean up millions in a trice. Yet defense contractors such as Lockheed or General Dynamics have sometimes had the utmost difficulty in keeping their shareholders' bodies and souls together.

What an efficient contractor can manage was shown by two British cases. In that of Bristol-Siddeley, the company was found to have made an excess profit of many millions on merely repairing aircraft engines. In the even more celebrated Ferranti affair, the profits from making the Bloodhound missile came to so much more than the government was prepared to stomach that, even though this profit would have been pleasant for the Ferranti family, who owned all the shares, the political recoil forced a hefty refund.

Many a pile of similarly shining profit must be concealed beneath contractors' bushels. But true lack of profit reflects in part the tendency of main contractors to share the mindless extravagance of government. Take Concorde: as that misbegotten project moved inexorably toward £1 billion of spending, many hands must have plunged into the till, if not for negotiable cash, at least for costly facilities, all wholly paid for by the taxpayer.

At all times the makers were reluctant to explain, even to interested politicians, exactly how it was possible to spend £1 million a day on a single project, even a supersonic one. The case of the pilot's chair explained how easily the spending materialized. Seats for Concorde's crew were originally ordered at a development cost of £54,000. Dissatisfied with the results, the prime contractor upped the ante first to £216,000 and then to £409,000. At this point even the civil servants in the act grew queasy. After a probe they finally approved £351,000—still over six times the original estimate. If the wizards can achieve such marvels with mere seats, it's no wonder that they can provide such bottomless pits for tax money with entire aircraft. Bottomless pit is hardly the right phrase for a celebrated piece of Lockheed overcharging: $640 for U.S. Navy toilet seats (eventually reduced to $100).

To get rich from public contracts, the privateer has to tread a narrow tightrope between being efficient and being too efficient—that is, becoming careless enough to let the profitable results of superefficiency show. The other guideline is the same as for borrowing: aim high, think extravagantly, and press the moneybags on whatever is currently their most sensitive point.

The aluminum companies, when being pressed to erect smelters in Britain to save foreign exchange, played this game to perfection. They got multimillion loans at favorable rates of interest, cheap electricity (a subsidy that had the extra convenience of being incalculable), plus all the normal investment grants (that is, cash presents) and tax breaks.

The beneficiaries of this bounty included such poverty-stricken companies as Alcoa, embodying the aluminum interest of the omnipresent Mellon family.

Politicians, like big company managers themselves, are victims of the paper number game. Harold Macmillan (a publishing millionaire by inheritance) airily observed that alerting the forces early in the Suez crisis cost "only £10 million." Now, the professional millionaire knows to the depths of his being that £10 million, or £1 million, or even £1,000 is never "only." But paper number players simply forget that the game isn't Monopoly: the resources are for real.

Governments are equally benign in circumstances in which they are not actually called upon to disburse coin. The flood principle of economic affairs also applies with physical controls, such as licenses and quotas; hence the huge fees commanded by the lobbyists who cluster around the regulatory agencies of Washington. That city, in the shape of the oil import quota, produced the perfect pork barrel of its day, which lasted for a whole decade—at one and the same time protecting domestic prices and profits, and presenting oilmen with valuable, completely free, marketable assets, salable at $1.25 a barrel.

British governments, not to be outdone, produced the triumph of television licensing (which generated profits so embarrassing that special levies had to be clamped on). Gambling provides another instance. The right side of the tables has always been where they keep the money. But the casinos of England received a rich extra lining of plush from the unwitting munificence of the government. After gaming was legalized, clubs proliferated to an extent that bothered the puritans and affronted the police, not least because the Mafia regarded it as only proper that its members should take their share of this expanding market. Movie star George Raft, hired as host by one casino, was among those sent packing by the authorities as they insisted that British gaming should, so far as possible, stay in spotlessly clean hands.

No doubt, no person in the entire apparatus of British government foresaw that strict gaming controls would inevitably create gold mines for those to whose ownership the casinos were restricted. Among those able to count his blessings several million times over is Sir James Goldsmith, himself a noted player of the tables. The British gaming joint Aspinalls had a spectacularly successful public flotation: in early 1987, it was sold for over $100 million—of which a goodly number of millions belonged to Sir James.

Often politicians would be best advised to let things be and to stop monkeying about with economic tides neither they nor anybody else truly understands. The praiseworthy idea of redistributing wealth by taxing high incomes to the hilt, for instance, has had the paradoxical effect of making the rich still more wealthy. It has very possibly increased, rather than diminished, the inequalities of wealth.

The main explanations are twofold: first, the high-tax principle has put a premium on converting income into capital at all times and in all possible ways; second, the use of the devices by which capital is created (borrowing and investment) has been made wondrously cheap, and the higher the tax rate rises, the cheaper it becomes. If a man is taxed at a marginal rate of 90 percent, an interest charge of 10 percent comes down to 1 percent; where a completely untaxed pauper would over twenty years pay 200 percent of the capital in interest, the millionaire coughs up only 20 percent.

As for investment, any plunge that is tax-deductible is subject to the same painkilling effect. It cost the 90 percent millionaire only $100,000 to make a million-dollar investment, and that investment would be subject to all the delectable, automatic rewards by which governments seek to conjure up the genie of economic expansion. If the million of investment yields a modest 10 percent, that profit will be offset for ten years by tax allowances, including depreciation; in a decade, the already rich investor thus makes a further clear million on, effectively, a risk of only $100,000.

It's very hard, and possibly very wrong, to keep a rich man down. But governments generally don't try too hard, anyway. The danger against which Eisenhower warned the United States in his valedictory address was the military-industrial complex. But there is a far more insidious conspiracy of which the Pentagon capers form only a part: the old boy net of rich men who finance and flatter the would-be statesmen, batten off their economic ignorance, and work their way into political favors by natural and unnatural means.

The American habit of blatantly selling embassies in return for campaign contributions has long been a source of wonderment to more sophisticated machinists in this shady area where politics and plutocracy overlap. A little embassy like Luxembourg, purchased by Mrs. Ruth L. Farkas in the Watergate election, fetched $300,000. *The New York Times* suggested that the $254,000 Nixon contribution advanced by Walter H. Annenberg (who could afford it, having sold the family newspapers for $55 million) could be regarded as the renewal of the lease on the London embassy—the plum in Nixon's ambassadorial pudding.

As Watergate revealed so horrendously, however, the exchange of American plums is private as well as public. Richard Nixon expressed no qualms in reporting, although under intense pressure, that the aerosol king, Robert Abplanalp, had helpfully lent him $625,000 to finance the purchase of San Clemente, and, even more kindly, had relieved the president of his surplus Californian acreage for a nice price. It must help a millionaire to have an indebted friend wearing the crown. But there is more to the courtship of the rich by the powerful (and vice versa) than sheer greed for possessions and their enjoyment.

It's no accident that plebeian politicians—Eisenhower, Johnson, Nixon, Wilson, Heath—have chosen favored sidekicks who are among the self-made rich. Those who don't have big money are fascinated by those who do. But there is one ever-present danger in rich sidekicks: the threat of rich kickbacks, if not at the top, somewhere down the receiving line. And that's quite apart from the difficulty of making any change in the system that won't benefit the rich disproportionately. For instance, exemptions and tax relief at high rates are greatly to their advantage.

Looked at from this angle, the worldwide trend toward lower taxes for the rich, led by the United States, and accompanied by removal of many deductions, is an attack on their fortunes. But it doesn't work out that way. Take a man who sells a business for $10 million. He invests it to return $1 million a year. On a 50 percent tax rate, he would lose $500,000 to the government. But if he invests $500,000 in a manner that shelters that income from tax, his tax bill drops to $250,000.

How will he fare if his tax rate drops to 25 percent? Remember that he made $1 million in gross income and paid only $250,000 in income tax under the previous dispensation for a net (before any return on his half-million investment) of $750,000. Now what happens? His potential tax liability is $250,000. He again invests $500,000, which cuts his tax bill by $125,000: he again has his $500,000 investment with prospect of capital gains; deduct $125,000 of tax, and he now clears $875,000 in net income. Heads he wins, in other words; tails, he wins even more.

Soaking the rich, or "squeezing them until the pips squeak," as British Labour politician Denis Healey once charmingly put it, is exceedingly tricky, and self-defeating anyway, in any system that maintains capitalistic institutions and personal liberty. Both can be abused. But the greatest cynicism, and the greatest insult to the intelligence of the citizens, is to argue that capitalism and liberty cannot both be preserved without the abuse.

Book VI

FORTUNE STILL FAVORS THE RICH

24
SOMEONE
UP THERE
LOVES ME

If the good fairy ever offers an aspiring businessman one wish, there's no question what he should ask for: luck. Good fortune is the essence of all fortunes, and it is the common factor that all the rich, *nouveaux* or otherwise, should be honest enough to acknowledge. Maybe Julius Rosenwald of Sears Roebuck was exaggerating when he attributed as much as 95 percent of business success to luck, leaving only a twentieth to aptitude and application. Indeed, the history of his own heirs hardly supports the theory: born with golden spoons in their mouths, they needed only reasonable aptitude and application to enhance the 12.5 percent family stake left by the mail-order maestro. Kept intact, that would have been worth $2.5 billion early in 1987. Yet *Forbes* assessed the family fortune at only "$300 million or more"—shared among 100 heirs, at that (a proliferation which you could describe as collective misfortune).

Even after making allowance for the many philanthropies of Julius Rosenwald's son Lessing, and for the impact of so many births, the

Rosenwald fortune must, in shrewder hands, have yielded far more in the third generation. The Rosenwald ratio is certainly wrong. It is still no exaggeration to say that, without luck, all the other virtues are only slightly more useful than a bridge player who consistently draws bad cards. Fortune presents the opportunity at the time when the opportunist can exploit it: cometh the man, cometh the moment. And fortune has to attend most subsequent actions if the man and the moment are to combine in satisfactory monetary terms.

Winning a couple of million on a $1 lottery ticket, as did the California furniture deliveryman José Caballero, is sheer luck, true. Keeping it, after being shipped back to Mexico as an illegal alien, was even luckier—the California state lottery had somehow forgotten to exclude unauthorized immigrants from its loot. If Caballero's papaya ranch, purchased through his lucky break, bears financial fruit in due season, though, that will be fortunate—but not lucky.

Every boom, from papayas to property, is in theory available to all. The great real estate bonanzas since World War II, in urban areas from the mighty Manhattan downward, were all obvious and irresistible, in hindsight. For instance, anybody who was in, or even near, the London real estate business when a new, Conservative government, scything away at every socialist control in sight, removed building restrictions, should have become a millionaire. Many were called, but few chose this route to instant riches.

Those blessed included lawyers, realtors in fair number, surveyors, the odd architect, established real estate developers who fell upon this manna from heaven, and several businessmen who merely happened to own a piece of London when the action started. One such was Max Rayne, who was to become Lord Rayne, developer of what is now the General Motors Building in Manhattan and chairman of Britain's National Theatre (artistic, social, and financial prestige have an engaging habit of marching hand in hand). Rayne only got interested in the real estate deals that created this golden future when, finding that his father's business didn't need all its modest premises, he arranged a sublease and discovered that renting was far more profitable than making clothes.

Encouraged by this tiny start, Max Rayne moved on to mightier things. A fat and none-too-bright company, which owned Selfridges in Oxford Street, allowed him to develop the priceless site at the rear of the store. At this point, Rayne owed thanks to fortune twice: for the initial discovery of property and for the folly of Selfridges' owners. His third stroke of luck must have seemed heaven's tastiest manna: Marks & Spencer, the bluest chain store chip in the land, intimated that it would lease Rayne's new building.

Enter calamity: Lord Marks decided on another site to the north, leaving Rayne apparently stranded like Sailor Kelly up his flagpole. Rayne scurried about, obtained additional backing, and went ahead. By the time of his building's delayed completion, rents and hence its value had soared far beyond the terms abandoned by Marks & Spencer; Rayne was most of the way to his first million—and he had as tenants IBM and 3M, which must have eased any lingering pain from the loss of Marks.

Everywhere in the world, the real estate sagas are the same: the future hero spots one opportunity and, emboldened by initial success, moves on to finer things. Gerald D. Hines was a building systems engineer—luckily enough, in the soon-to-boom Houston—when he converted a frame house into offices: by 1966, nine years after he plunged permanently into real estate building and development, his fortune totaled $6 million. Twenty-one years and a Texas real estate slump later, Hines still weighed in at a heavy $200 million on the Forbes estimate.

The Durst brothers, Seymour, Roy, and David, had the luck to possess a father in the business who passed on his wisdom: "Never buy anything farther than you can walk." The boys have done "all our walking between 42nd and 50th streets," which converted father's simple axiom into a $30 million cash flow and a $600 million fortune. Such stories, with variations of time and place, will be repeated again and again as the upgrading of property proceeds to widen relentlessly from the already fashionable to the adjacent (the Dursts colonized Third Avenue). The people who made the most of such chances had to display acumen, persistence, and initiative, but fortune kept on dealing the right cards.

Sometimes the cards are so apposite, with a royal flush appearing at the very moment of truth, that the less God-given factors are blotted out from sight. The late Charles W. Bluhdorn, the founder of Gulf + Western, was once a Wall Street wonder boy. He was then infected by the bubonic plague that hit nearly all conglomerates. Behind Bluhdorn's share slump lay the usual conglomerate hang-up. As sales continued to pile up, operating income first took a sharp tumble and then resolutely refused to grow. Among his acquisitions was Paramount Studios, picked up, so report had it, as much for its real estate potential as for any money in the allegedly moribund movie game. Yet Hollywood, old-style, came to the rescue of the new-style front office. When the shares plunged to just 9½, compared to 64¼ at their brightest and best, Bluhdorn had to be grateful for the $80 million of mush-money from *Love Story*, one of the hot properties in Paramount's can.

However, this success didn't generate great front-office fervor at Paramount for another best-seller—who was interested in a gangster movie these days? The disappointing returns from another gangland epic supported the point; yet *The Godfather* was allowed, not only to proceed, but to devour a $6 million budget. The results, a gross of $120 million, gladdened Gulf + Western's lucky balance sheet for years.

In fact, everybody is lucky in some degree or dosage. The luck may not be readily translatable into capital: the lucky one may studiously or stupidly fail to recognize his good fortune, or he may make the elementary error of thinking that luck is the sole ingredient of success, whereas in truth nobody, apart from the winner of a lottery or a surprise inheritance, ever has wealth poured on his head without the need for effort.

Consider the case of Zographas, one of the two Greeks who gave their national name to the Greek five-man syndicate. Nobody can survive in big-time professional gambling without being luckier than average, even with the mathematical advantages of baccarat, the Greek pastime. For all that, one disastrous week in 1926 Zographas lost the equivalent of $672,000 in play at Cannes. On the last night he risked a further million francs and won everything back. The romantic would call this pure chance. The realist, the Greek himself, knew the odds exactly, knew that their failure to work in his favor before was unlikely to be repeated, knew himself, knew the game, and judged his decision accordingly.

The pure gambler, unless the table or cards are impure, loses a great deal of the time. Nicholas Andrea Dandolos, alias Nick the Greek, is said to have seen $500 million move through his hands (including $6.4 million of winnings at stud poker) as he passed between the opposite poles of wealth and penury seventy-three times. This is because ultimately the run of the cards is something the gambler cannot influence. This fact, paradoxically, makes it bad luck that gaming should be their profession.

There are those who, with similar varieties of flair and equal application, stumble into fields where the cards are more closely under their own control—and that fluke start, part of the perennial mythology of capitalism, is where luck truly comes into its own. Starts don't come much flukier than in the case of Dr. Osman Khalil Osman, who became a Sudanese of many millions after originally setting up shop in Kuwait as a veterinary surgeon. In this capacity, Osman treated and cured a cow that was the prize milk producer of the then crown prince.

In his gratitude, Sheik Saba al Salem, the next ruler of the then richest country on earth, helped to set Osman up in a business career that was a combination of textiles and courtship of the appropriate rulers. Being called to that particular cow's bedside was (if the story hasn't been embroidered over the years) pure luck: curing it was skill;

gaining the sheik's business confidence required visible talent; capitalizing on that confidence, and recognizing that in the underdeveloped world politics is where the payoff is, demanded lesser assistance from fortune; but by far the greatest contribution came from the talents of the world's most moneyed cow doctor himself.

Like the real estate tycoons of Manhattan, London, or Houston, Osman and the subsequent platoons of Middle East fixers such as Adnan Khashoggi had the inestimable fortune to be in the right place at the right time—the rightest moment of all being when quadrupled and octupled oil prices generated a tidal wave of wealth for the oil potentates. For one of the richest beneficiaries, Mohamed Al-Fayed, as for Lord Rayne, it was an ill wind that first blew him good. A dozen years before the oil price explosion, Al-Fayed's shipping business in his native Egypt was nationalized (like the Suez Canal) by Colonel Nasser. An alternative version says that Al-Fayed was not a shipping scion, but the son of a customs officer. There is, however, no argument about the way a ferry service taking pilgrims to Mecca had by 1966 developed, no doubt valuably, into advising the Dubai regime on constructing a port. Nor is there any question that twenty years later the Al-Fayeds were close advisers to the Sultan of Brunei, who as the world's richest man is indubitably the right person to advise.

Al-Fayed's own family wealth is adequate enough, at an alleged $4.5 billion. It has purchased, among other trinkets, the Ritz in Paris (renovated at a cost of $45 million), the Bois de Boulogne former residence of the Duke and Duchess of Windsor, a Scottish castle plus 33,000 acres, and a British retail fiefdom whose crown jewel is the Harrods department store. The Harrods deal was both lucky and unlucky: lucky because a rival tycoon sold Al-Fayed his own 30 percent interest, thinking he could repossess the shares at his pleasure—only to find, in Al-Fayed's own words, that "he gave me the chance on a golden tray."

The ill luck was that the mortified loser pursued Al-Fayed ever after, accusing him, among other crimes, of concealing the origins of the near-billion-dollar purchase price. To defend himself against the accusation that the Sultan's Brunei billions had financed the deal, Al-Fayed gave a rare interview to the London *Times*, which (with equal rarity) showed how bounteous the fortunes of the oil state fixers had been. Letters from three leading construction companies put the value of Middle East contracts secured for them by the Al-Fayeds at a stunning $3 billion.

From that, the fixers obtained at least 15 percent, or $450 million. "A fraction of our international business," claimed Mohamed. "Does that make it seem that the Fayed family are poor? Paupers? Unable to buy Harrods even for £615 million with their own money?" The questions were interesting, but not so interesting as some others: such as how the lucky intermediaries achieved their positions of influence, and how profitable the contracts must have been to provide them with such juicy shares. The multiplication of the Fayed wealth thereafter is no mystery. Once people like the Al-Fayed brothers and Osman the vet become rich, the odds of fortune that favor the well stacked can come freely into play. But the dividing line between the luck and the hard work of the wealthy is a fine one. For instance, it was a misfortune for the McAlpine family, though a common enough catastrophe in the building trade, that the clients for whom they were putting up the Dorchester Hotel in Park Lane ran out of ready cash in the Depression. But the McAlpines owed their own financial security, which enabled them to take over the hotel, to their own Scots diligence and prudence: Sir Robert had begun as a Glaswegian bricklayer—there are few starts more basic or less blessed. In 1962, the family was offered $9 million for the hotel, which they very properly refused: at its last change of hands, to the Al-Fayeds' friendly Sultan of Brunei, the price tag was $75 million.

The McAlpines can't originally have known much about hotels, except how to stay in them. But knowledge can be bought. The courage to seize an opportunity can't be acquired. Like sex appeal, either you have it or you don't. Without question, Jack C. Massey has opportunity appeal. After retiring from wholesaling surgical supplies at fifty-seven, with a clear $1 million in the purchasing company's stock, the bored Massey, according to a quote in *Fortune*, "went back to Nashville and started looking for a business to buy."

An introduction to the ancient Colonel Sanders was Massey's first lucky strike; the second was that Sanders liked him well enough to offer a $100,000 salary and half the profits if he would manage Kentucky Fried Chicken. The third lucky break, though, was that Massey turned the colonel down, saying that he would find another buyer if the old boy wanted. The latter promptly replied, "I want *you* to buy it." The fact that Sanders consulted a horoscope to back up his hunch wasn't nearly as endearing as the low, low price: $2 million.

Ten years later, Massey sold the by then public company for $239 million. But for all the strokes of fortune from an elderly, oddball millionaire, KFC was no lottery win. Massey and his sidekick, John Y. Brown, brilliantly developed the business concept and the international currency of the colonel's goateed image beyond the latter's most eccentric imaginings. Just as Sanders and his horoscope had correctly assessed, Massey was the perfect choice for the job—and that has nothing to do with luck.

Indeed, Massey has been one of America's canniest and most assiduous users of the Common Millionaire's most common gambit: the multiplication of wealth by the sale of stock to the public. Among the dozen-plus public companies that owe their flotation to Massey, three are quoted on the New York Stock Exchange—a record no other man has matched. One of these, another restaurant chain named Winners, was admittedly and perversely doing its best to lose when Massey, early in 1987, was nominated to *Fortune*'s Business Hall of Fame, but you truly can't win 'em all.

Like billionaire Carl Lindner, who wrote off his whole $123 million investment in Mission Insurance Group, everybody gets unlucky once in a while—except that luck may have little to do with it. Lindner simply made a bad mistake. So did the numerous banks that invested heavily in the duff oil and gas loans of the Penn Square banking disaster. One Wall Street banker refused to join this party, but only because he happened to be in a restaurant when Penn Square's energy loan genius was drinking champagne out of a Nazi helmet and wearing jackboots.

That understandably caused the putative lender considerable anxiety. The revelation was lucky for his bank: its good fortune wasn't shared by Continental Illinois, the largest banking victim, or by Penn Square's own insiders. (One of them did, however, contrive to look on the bright side; as he told his wife, "Well, honey, there's one good thing. We don't have an estate planning problem anymore").

The price of folly can't be described as misfortune, so the reward of shrewdness cannot be accurately described as luck. Take the case of Colin Forsyth, an Oxford man who was learning the investment trade on Wall Street, when, with time hanging on his hands, he found Hampton Gold Mining Areas in a London stock exchange reference book. The shares, 4 million in all, were selling at 1½ pence apiece. But this unconsidered trifle owned freehold land in Australia: dividing the market value by the acreage, Forsyth worked out that land anywhere in the whole wide world, the Sahara and odd tundra excepted, must be worth more. He told his broker to buy any shares that came up at 1½ pence to 3 pence and, from 1962 to 1964, collected a bundle thereof.

Forsyth went out to Australia for a general look, which confirmed his particular view on Hampton. He formed a noble scheme to sell land to Americans as an investment for their grandchildren—the Trans-Australian Highway was due to pass by Hampton's land, and the Hampton board, which big shareholder Forsyth had now joined, didn't mind. But the land scheme ran into political difficulties, and Hampton was still hanging fire when, around 1966, Western Mining found nickel on adjoining land. Those once-unconsidered Hampton shares burst into flame after the Western miners negotiated an excellent deal with the company to allow drilling, and hence discovery, on its land. At the peak this ardent enthusiasm took the Hampton shares to £6: representing, on an investment of 1½ pence, a profit of 95,900 percent; and on 3 pence, a gain of 47,900 percent.

You could, if you wished, attribute this to the purest fortune. But Forsyth was looking for his luck, by studying the form, in the first place; he followed not hunch but judgment in working out that the company must be worth more than its market value, even though he had no idea how much; he took the trouble to inspect what he had bought; and he was conveniently placed, by his own initiative, in the cockpit when the Hampton jet took off into the blue skies beyond. The luck, a colossal stroke of the stuff, came in the unsuspected presence of nickel. But chance, as Pasteur once said, favors the prepared mind.

Commander Eugene McDonald, the quality fanatic of Zenith, lost the hearing in one ear as the result of a car crash in 1940. Forced to buy a hearing aid, he was so shocked by its price that he ordered his designers to come up with a cheaper model. They succeeded, and Zenith went on to become the biggest force in the market. The bash from fate was converted into a touch from Midas not by luck alone but by McDonald's habit of acting on observation and by his possession of a competent design team and of the finance to underwrite both the designers' work and the production.

A somewhat different illustration of the conversion of ill luck into good cash appeared during the awful moment between the wars when salt water appeared in the oil being extracted from the Mexican Eagles concession originally discovered by the first Lord Cowdray (and exploited by him in partnership with the most forceful man in world oil, Sir Henri Deterding of Royal Dutch, and the wiliest, Calouste Gulbenkian).

The initial find had been a matter of fortune, like so many in oil. One of the fattest Texas cats, Sid Richardson, liked to tell the tale of how his takeoff depended on a choice between two drilling sites: the one he chose, at random, was a fabulous West Texas pool; the other, when he got around to it later, proved dry. The luckiest break, however, might not have been Richardson's, but that of the Bass family, whose mother lent the oilman $40 to get started, and which received a bequest that multiplied the loan 1.25 million times. Cowdray's good fortune with oil, when he was plain Weetman Pearson, arose from his main and highly lucrative activity of building railways all over Latin America. His Mexican oil rights were a by-product, discovered while laying track. The misfortune of the salt water that ruined the oil find for keeps was mitigated by the fact that many millions of shares had been sold most profitably to the public before the bad news became known.

As some counterblow from fate, Cowdray's heirs, many decades later, decided to dispose of a little-loved painting that had long hung in their Whitehall offices. It fetched a few thousand pounds and was promptly resold by a deliriously happy purchaser as a Rubens for the best part of a quarter of a million. The common truth, that bad luck is often poor judgment, affects rich and poor alike—the difference being that the rich can afford it; like Carl Lindner with his nine-figure bath in Mission Insurance.

For making a few millions, the lucky combination of being alive and well in the right place at the right time in the right business will do. The difference between entrepreneurs who stick at this point (or, far worse, undo themselves in the mistaken conviction that they are men of genius) and those who advance to mightier things lies not in luck but in other qualities. Jim Powell, in *Risk, Ruin and Riches*, has written eloquently of the pains taken by the Reichmanns to speed construction on First Canadian Place: "We built elevators for forklifts," explained Albert Reichmann, "so they could unload materials from trucks, then go direct to the floor where the materials were needed. We devised a conveyor belt which delivered concrete to the floors much faster than conventional buckets. As a result of these various measures [which cost over $3 million] we saved over a million man-hours and cut our construction time 40 percent." The savings were a highly material factor in stopping this huge 5-million-square-foot building from draining the Reichmanns' financial lifeblood when recession unluckily hit Canada as it was opened: the first year cash outflow alone was $20 million.

Absorbing misfortune on that scale, no less than building fortunes far smaller than the Reichmanns', requires some kind of infinite capacity—very possibly that for taking pains. But constructing a lasting empire requires other forms of genius. For instance, the Vestey meat-packing empire would be lucrative, but less all-embracing, save for the mishap of its founder in meeting shipping difficulties out of the Argentine. Reacting to misfortune in the born manner of the entrepreneur, he built his own shipping line.

That decision amply cushioned his major mishap—failure over eight long years of hard trying to establish a meat-packing industry in Australia. The net result of the founder's luck and labor (he started as a stripling of seventeen) was that his descendants in the 1980s presided over what was probably the biggest private empire based on Britain, according to the London *Times*, with a value of $2 billion (which must have been considerably enhanced by the success of the Vesteys and their

329

financial and legal advisers in weaving a network of trusts that conveniently kept their tax bills down to a mere nubbin).

Chance, just as mythology says, can play a critical role in establishing a major business. It was chance that led Lord Rank, as an ardent Methodist, to make his religious film *The Rising of the Sun* and, on being unable to secure distribution, to buy into movies, which took him into the optical industry, which led to a tie-up with the U.S. camera firm Bell and Howell, which culminated in the epic saga of Rank Xerox.

It was chance, you could say, that forced so many émigrés out of Hitler's Europe, including the Reichmanns. Had they stayed in Europe, where the future real estate wizard Paul was content to work in Jewish education, North America's largest single fortune would have been made by somebody else. But here again, as with the cost-cutting that helped the family survive Canadian recession, the Reichmanns met both fortune and misfortune more than halfway. They had prudently placed assets in England long before Hitler came to power; they quit Vienna as soon as Hitler arrived; they walked out of Paris thirty-six hours before the Germans marched in; and for the $3,000 cost of a truck drove briskly into Spain and thence to Morocco. They duly arrived in Canada with much of their wealth and, more important, all of themselves intact.

The similarly farsighted and fast-moving immigrants who arrived in an industrially backward Britain found that their talents, especially in modern industries such as chemicals and plastics, were at a premium. They virtually created whole galaxies of growth industries as a result. One, Sir Frank Schon, began unpromisingly by making firelighters out of sawdust. When he moved on to the indispensable ingredient for the new synthetic wonder detergents, Schon happened to build his factory on top of a thick seam of the essential anhydrite rock. This golden stroke was like building a steelworks and finding that the thing is sitting on a solid deposit of iron ore.

Schon sold out his $1,500 company for $3 million and stayed aboard to manage it for the purchasing chemical conglomerate. He quit in a considerable huff years later when the chemical colleagues, against his advice, insisted on putting up a giant phosphorous plant in Newfoundland. It proved to be an unmitigated disaster, haunted by what the uninitiated call bad luck, like a leakage that poisoned the local aquatic fauna, but that the cognoscenti recognize as the invariable price of bad decisions—and that led, as bad leadership will, to failure (the firm ended up inside Tenneco).

Much the same line of thought—that the follow-up matters more than the fortunate landfall—applies to the lucky men who catch a tycoon's eyes early in their careers. The cow-curing Osman isn't the only multimillionaire who can thank an encounter with the superlatively rich. Cyrus Eaton was a seventeen-year-old office boy when he came to the attention of John D. Rockefeller I. That Rockefeller background taught him how to tackle the Morgan interests in head-on conflict, and to beat them. But mutual admiration was not the only characteristic Eaton and John D. shared. They had the greatest good fortune of all—living to a great age.

Those whom the gods love don't die young; they die old and rich, and the older they are, the richer they get. The magic of compound growth, on which all great accumulations of wealth depend, works under their control, saved from the depredations of inept heirs and unwise stewards. The man who dies at seventy loses two and a half decades of compounding, compared to a John D. Rockefeller I, who died at ninety-four; and Rockefeller II proceeded to live to eighty-six.

Survival to these heights of antiquity is not altogether chance. The ability to purchase the finest and most concentrated medical attention available (although it killed off several rulers and rich men in an earlier stage of medical ignorance) has preserved many tycoons beyond what nature intended to be their natural span. One American insurance millionaire was kept walking and working for over fifteen years with an interior constructed mostly of plastic tubes. The exceedingly rich, like all potentates, can take their personal physicians with them on trips: President Nixon even took his osteopath to Russia.

Armand Hammer, a physician and son of a physician, took himself to Russia—many times. His work to relieve Russian suffering in 1921 turned into gold, or to be more accurate, furs, jewels, and pencils; the Soviets granted the young Hammer a monopoly on the latter in exchange for grain. The lucky chance of making friends with Lenin started Hammer on a lifelong career of cultivating potentates as assiduously as any Arab fixer ("Knowing top leaders," he told *Forbes*, "pays off if you have problems with bureaucrats") and of exploiting his sanctified Russian connections.

This flying start, and the fortune in fine art that accompanied Hammer back from his first foray into Russia, were only foundation stones for a career that, with only one break for a swiftly regretted and reversed retirement, was still going strong two-thirds of a century after Hammer first saw Moscow. If long life is a business boon, it follows that a long career also helps. Many rich men of the past, such as Eaton or Rockefeller himself, started at an early hour of life because no other option was available. Fate decreed a start that today might be delayed by school, college, possibly even business school.

This wasn't what John D. I meant when he uttered the sanctimonious judgment: "The poor boy is in a position of impregnable advantage.

331

He is better off than the son of the rich man," but it is possibly the only sense in which that persuasive phrase is actually true. What Rockefeller meant is that the poor boy has the sovereign impetus of wishing to escape from his poverty, which is true. But the exercise of that magic motivation, the unsparing expenditure of that abundant talent and effort, merely lands the former pauper in the same situation the rich boy achieved painlessly by the mere accident of birth.

Some of the once-poor rich have arrived in that category by the mere accident not only of time and place but of money. The last-mentioned chance is often crucial: the accidental availability of cash when needed has made many careers. Money does tend, in a mysterious manner, to stick to the fingers of certain men in the same way that certain baseball greats need only stick out a hand for a ball to fly into it and stay there.

The general reaction to money catchers, to men with a modernized Midas touch, is to attribute their acquisition to luck. In the sense that all natural talent is God-given, they are lucky. The curious fact is that the very rich often do talk of their success in terms of acts of God rather than acts of themselves—Julius Rosenwald's attribution of success to 95 percent good fortune is echoed by Big Al Abplanalp, Nixon's pal, who believed that genius is "2 percent inspiration, 8 percent work, and 90 percent luck"—and leading luminaries in oil's hall of fame seem to think likewise.

H. L. Hunt declared: "You have to be lucky"; Sid Richardson that "luck has helped me every day of my life, and I'd rather be lucky than smart, because a lot of smart people ain't eatin' regular"; R. E. (Bob) Smith that "my West Texas oilfield was solely luck. It has thirty-eight million barrels in reserve and cost me five dollars an acre. The lesson you learn as you get older is that it's luck." In oil, no doubt, the good luck story is truer than in most contexts—although the fact that the great discoveries were made by men who died broke demands some explanation. In truth, the emphasis on luck is a variation on the theme of false modesty, the opposite of whistling to keep your spirits up—moaning, so to speak, to keep your guilt down.

The self-deprecation of the rich should never be taken at face value. Claude ("Doc") Pennington says he "thought I was getting a bad deal" when he founded his oil empire by paying $400,000 to get into the Port Hudson property in Louisiana. The former optometrist almost certainly had 20-20 financial vision from the start. In my book *The Supermanagers*, I looked at two men credited by *Fortune* magazine with much more luck than long sight—Charles Lachman of Revlon and William Fox of Twentieth Century–Fox—and the magazine's argument didn't carry great weight.

True, Lachman invested $300 in Charles B. Revson, for which he got 30 percent of the stock, and devoted himself from 1932 onward, as he told Andrew Tobias, to gardening, financially speaking: "I've got a rake, and I rake it in!" But entering the ground floor of the cosmetics boom, in company with the man best equipped to exploit it, was as long-sighted in its way as Fox's persistence, after being conned into buying a no-good prototype cinema, in sticking with the nascent movie industry for a couple of decades. As the book noted, Fox "truly earned his millions, not by luck, but by persistence, talent and performance—the usual trio."

Close analysis of a brilliant player of any game, including the oil and money ones, always shows that behind the success lie application, method, and motivation that anybody can imitate: the difference being that mastering the mechanics of Arnold Palmer's swing won't turn anybody into Arnold Palmer. The distinction is exemplified by the bad, black day of one publisher who turned down Joseph Heller's *Catch-22* in the morning and Joy Adamson's lioness saga, *Born Free*, in the afternoon—the latter being on the grounds that he didn't publish animal books. Bad luck, you might say, thus unwittingly condoning what was truly poor professional judgment.

Not that making million-dollar mistakes is in itself a condemnation of the professional concerned: being wrong, sometimes, is a corollary of often being right. The Midas millionaire simply has a surer instinct for when to be right, when to be wrong, and when to get out before a mistake exacts its penalty. Luck has merely an ancillary role in this connection. Three quotations from three very different men put fortune in perfect perspective. One, Thomas Stanley, is a Georgia academic who has made a specialty of studying millionaires: "The real way people make money is hard work for thirty years, six days a week." The second is from Jack Parker, another of the briefly retired whose second careers proved far more glorious than the first: after Stanley's requisite thirty years of hard work, and after putting $300 million in his heirs' names, real estate developer Parker told *Forbes*: "You bet your money on the future and hope your vision of it is correct. That's the crapshoot."

It's the only game in town. The third quote comes from a composer musician, and a rich one: George Gershwin. It's said that the great composer, traveling across the United States in a luxury train, looked down from his upper berth at his wonderful pianist, Oscar Levant, and said, "You know what this represents, Oscar? The difference between talent and genius." Rightly Gershwin didn't mention luck: the would-be millionaire who blames his failures on bad luck deserves his unlucky fate.

25

THE
ONE-HORSE
RACE

The man who hasn't got everything suffers a fatal disadvantage in the effort to get rich the easiest way, which is in return for virtually nothing, otherwise known as gambling. Apart from the British football pools or national and other lotteries, there are hardly any opportunities for sudden, lightning conversion of the poor.

The sad truth is that, if a thousand-to-one shot comes home with $10 on its nose, you only pocket $10,000; whereas if you can afford $1,000, the proceeds are a whole, round million. It is even sadder that thousand-to-one shots rarely return to the fireside, a fact of which those who can afford $1,000 bets are fully aware. Which is why the rich prefer to speculate only on stonecold certs: this has the advantage that they can never lose.

The richer you are, the easier it becomes to arrange the necessary degree of certainty. At the extreme, the best way of profiting from gambling is to run it, as the Mafia long ago discovered. However, the techniques that piled up an alleged $150 million for the pursued waif

Meyer Lansky have as much to do with banking as with gaming. Like banks, the Mafia parts the masses from their cash and makes sure that, before any of the loot is actually paid out, the mob collects its unfair share. It's the latter-day version of Robin Hood: taking from the poor in order to give to the rich. (The gambit is far safer than fixing fights or horse races, where the fixed contestant can always defraud you by having a heart attack.)

Behind every mass gamble there stands a proprietor with a large fortune—even if he does no more than allow the odds to work in his favor. The essence of any book or gaming table is that, no matter what combination of winners comes in, the house comes out ahead. The take has always been terrific. William Crockford, whose gaming club was the birthplace of London's postwar gambling renaissance, died in 1844 worth the equivalent of £5 million—or $750 million in 1987 money. By 1961, on the *Saturday Evening Post*'s figures, profits from gambling in the Las Vegas area had topped $150 million. The mob's payoffs—$2 million a year in police protection from one Philadelphia ring—give some indication of the profit margins being protected.

The total loss suffered in 1986 by the U.S. public to one form of gambling alone—the casino—was $5.8 billion, or $1,000 per player. *Fortune* expressed the equations succinctly: a slot machine in the Golden Nugget in Atlantic City cost perhaps $5,000; the average profits per machine in 1986 were $100,698—a return of over 1,900 percent. It follows that, if a millionaire is defined as the owner of an asset yielding $100,000 clear, a couple of slot machines will do the trick.

Labor costs are also low (croupiers got only $4 for the $2,000 they collect per hour, but tripled their income from tips). And the odds are always weighted in favor of the house: 89 percent in roulette, a maximum 98.5 percent on baccarat, 98.6 percent, mostly, in craps, 99.4 percent in blackjack. Translate these odds into the experience of a gambler playing over and over again (as most do), and the house keeps between 15 and 25 percent of the wagers laid.

Yet casinos, like their unlucky clients, have played themselves into financial trouble. It sounds impossible, yet the *Las Vegas Review Journal* reported nearly a third of the Nevada casinos as losing money in the 1986 fiscal year. As famous a joint as the Dunes went into Chapter 11 protection against bankruptcy. The money left behind by the paying customers, unfortunately for the casinos, is revenue, not profit. Deduct the everyday operating costs, the mountainous interest payments to bankers, the sky-high promotional expenditures, the fulsome fees to entertainers, the expensively free travel, bed and board for high-rollers, and the inevitably substantial bad debts, and you end up with a business that—to take the well-managed Caesar's Palace—earns a hard 22.7 percent of operating profit on its easy revenues.

No tears need be shed over Caesar's palatial plight, or over the $600,000 a day that real estate *wunder* tycoon Donald Trump must win to cover costs (mostly debt) at the Castle (one of his first two Atlantic City casinos). Casino properties sell at high-rolling prices—$725 million for Caesar's World's $41 million of earnings, for example—that certainly yield enormous capital profits, despite the overbuilding of the 1980s and the expense thereof: the unfinished Taj Mahal in Atlantic City, picked up in early 1987 by Trump, will cost $600 million.

The high costs and surplus capacity largely explain why casinos have stopped being licenses to milk operating money. Get the dairy right, though, and the milk can still become cream: witness the case of William Gordon Bennett and William Norman Pennington. They acquired Circus Circus from a less-astute entrepreneur who thought you could attract big spenders with circus acts. You can't. The partners were then forty-nine and fifty-one years old, respectively; they cleverly lowered their sights from upper rollers to middle-class families. Low-cost, high-turnover, clown-aided Nevada casinos (now five) have been packing 'em in ever since, making the partners' two-thirds of the company, plus receipts from its public offering, in excess of $200 million apiece. Bennett summed it all up by telling *Forbes*: "This isn't gambling at all." He went on to say, "It's hands-on retailing." The first half of the quote, though, can stand by itself: it's a one-horse race.

True, the customer sometimes wins. Caesar's Palace loses, according to one executive, on fifty days in the year. But the losses, however huge, are paradoxically a measure of the mighty sums made. One successful bookmaker illustrated this point neatly enough after paying out $1.2 million in winning bets one week. "That's not what we call a bad week," he said. "It only worked out at 9:8 against us on the stake." What this philosopher called a good week must have been really something.

On the other side of the odds the bettor, too, can turn speculation into certainty if his stakes are high enough. Exact calculation of the odds, plus a deep bank, enabled the so-called Greek syndicate (actually three Greeks, one Frenchman, and one Armenian) to win consistent fortunes from baccarat over many decades of parting stupid American tycoons from their teeth. They chose baccarat because the bank has a slight mathematical advantage and can stop play whenever it fancies.

An even more enterprising Frenchman succeeded in rigging the national, state-backed betting game in his certain favor by careful and massive placing of bets around the country. All these operations appear to be perfectly within the law, which cannot be said for the gang of Britons who substituted a horse in a minor race, suddenly inundated off-course bookmakers with bets on this "ringer," and defeated the anguished bookies' efforts to lay off their bets on the course by cutting the telephone wires. But even here an element of chance existed. The substituted horse, the "ringer," might have fallen over its own feet.

Pure business offers the perfect solid state, the only sporting contest in which you can back all the horses and still win. As with most millionaire ploys, the mysterious absurdity of the stock market contains the formula; witness the Company Raid Gambit Declined, and its variation, the Company Raid Accepted, otherwise known as greenmail, arbitrage, insider trading, or raiding, depending on circumstances.

As everybody knows, especially after the Blackest October, Wall Street, London, and similar emporia of shares are risky casinos: what goes up always comes down, and you never know in advance when or by how much a share will rise or fall. But everybody is wrong. In this stratagem, the player knows when the share will rise and himself determines how far—and when the rise will stop. The first move is to assemble a suitable quantity of shares in the selected company. In halcyon days, before the spoilsport law deemed otherwise, the amasser could build up a stake of any size in sublime secrecy. But that now-forbidden ploy has proved to be superfluous. The player can announce his intentions, or speculate about them to well-placed cronies in the media, long before launching his next, decisive move. That is to make a bid for more of the victim's shares—pitched well above the current market price and even further above the average cost of his own collection.

On the "heads I win, tails you lose" principle, the bid must be realistic (that is, cheap), so that, if by chance it succeeds, the gambit player has a bargain on his hands. But since it is cheap, the odds are that the attacked directors, reeling from one hastily arranged meeting to another, will fight to the death (or at least to the opening of their golden parachutes) in defense of their company's beloved freedom (not to mention their own interests). This fight for liberty may take the form of finding some other bidder to deprive them of the same priceless possession: the so-called white knight.

The gambit player doesn't mind; he welcomes the appearance of anything—a rival bidder, a scrumptious profit forecast, a swift revaluation of properties, the sale of underexploited assets—that forces up the victim's shares. True, he may have to raise his own bid, but that may cost nothing. In contrast, the market rise in his previously purchased

337

shares is money in the bank, all the way to which he is going to laugh. If the bid succeeds, he pockets the company; if it fails, he pockets the capital gain.

The bigger the company, the better. For large companies are the ones most likely to stuff their cupboards with underrealized assets and their executive suites with managerial dodos; there will also be enormous numbers of shares around the place, held mostly by financial institutions that can rarely resist a certain profit—remember, the bid is well above the original market price—and which may, of which more anon, exist solely to make such profits.

Such practices had been in play for decades before terms such as *greenmail* or *arbitrageurs* were invented for the processes and players involved. The new vocabulary had become necessary simply because the scale of exploitation had expanded so enormously, both in numbers and sheer size. Previous forays had been somewhat limited by the need for the bidder to be credible, which limited the available targets to companies that were smaller than the predator; that restricted the spoils still more, since large companies of earlier days didn't like to look too predatory—even giants controlled by multimillionaires.

But a full fifteen years before the Boesky scandals, a typical gambit profit was turned by a raider attacking one of the most famous firms in America—the once-great A & P supermarket chain. It was a sitting duck for the gambit, as essayed by the late Charles Bluhdorn of Gulf + Western. After a blistering attack on A & P's grocery price tactics (in truth, inane enough) by a Bluhdorn pal, Bluhdorn steadily bought shares in the sagging supermarket chain. It had fallen to a $50 million loss in nine months, on rising sales, by the infallible expedient of giving away its goods to customers at less than true cost.

Market purchases of a million-odd shares by G + W were followed by a tender offer to buy another 3.75 million at $20—a price usefully higher than the $16 at which they stood at the start of Bluhdorn's gambit. The existence of his interest in itself supported the A & P price, and Bluhdorn duly cleaned up in the manner men such as T. Boone Pickens, Saul Steinberg, and Sir James Goldsmith made famous—or infamous, according to taste—in the 1980s.

The ultimate beauty of such gambits has always been that the purchase money can easily be borrowed from some friendly neighborhood bank. The dealing creates automatic collateral for the loan, in the shape of the shares to be bought, and the bank gets what bankers love best of all: fast turnover of their money and, if they are investment bankers, a nice slice of the action.

All was wondrously improved by junk bonds. Now anybody,

within, or even without, very much reason, could bid for anything. Undermanaged companies of any size, if overstuffed with undervalued assets, could be attacked by any operator capable of mustering the support of Drexel Burnham Lambert or some other investment banker trying to muscle in on Drexel's racket. You weren't obliged to use junk bonds. But the new financing and the new easygoing Reagan climate opened the floodgates to bids and counterbids that would previously have been unthinkable—and to machinations that should have been.

In the classic theory of such operations, only the prime predator would be baring his teeth. *Arbitrage,* in the days of Bluhdorn's raid, usually meant taking advantage of discrepancies in stock prices or currencies between different centers. The new "arbs" (the unaffectionate shorthand for arbitrageurs) lived only to make takeover profits. They cleaned up (again in theory) by spotting one of the vulnerable corporate hulks in which the 1980s abounded, taking a position in the shares and offloading at the most beneficial point after the predator pounced.

It was easy to believe that a renowned arbitrageur such as Ivan Boesky got his financial kicks by shrewdness—building strategic blocks of shares in the trembling targets and then swiftly disposing of them to the highest bidder. Honestly applied, it was, or should have been, a painless way of winning one-horse races. But the vultures faced an inescapable element of risk. The bid might (1) not arrive; (2) not drive the shares high enough to yield a profit; (3) take so long to succeed that the interest rates on the arb's borrowing became insupportable; or (4) fail before the arb could escape with the loot.

The risk, however, could be almost entirely eliminated if the arb knew about the bid in advance. There were two ways of achieving this highly desirable technical improvement. The arb could persuade another party to make the necessary bid, with the arb's own holding dangled as a carrot. Or a third or a fourth party could obligingly (and illegally) tell the arb where to strike and when the iron was hot. The attraction of this improved method must have been especially manifest to Boesky, who collected some whopping losses along with his loot.

For instance, T. Boone Pickens had literally bid for fame with his Gulf Oil coup: the petroleum giant, fleeing from Pickens's impudent embrace, ran into the arms of Socal at a fat price—and a famous profit for Pickens and his Mesa Petroleum. Pickens made another $41 million out of a failed bid for Phillips Petroleum, whose workers and townsfolk sprang to its defense, but Boesky dropped a supposed $70 million. The agonizing size of that loss can be seen by comparison with the $150 million he is thought to have made on just three other bid situations where he guessed right—or was told right. The inside information of Martin C. Siegel, then with investment bankers Kidder Peabody, netted Boesky $28.3 million in one blow, when Carnation agreed to a bid from the Swiss Nestlé.

Making money in this manner was like shooting fish in a barrel. That raises an interesting variation on the old question: "If you're so clever, why aren't you rich?" In Boesky's case, the question is: "If you're so crooked, why weren't you even richer?" The floor value *Forbes* put on Boesky's fortune before he was exposed as the King of the Insider Traders was high enough, at $150 million, but with easy profits such as the Carnation deal available, the sky should have been the limit—in theory. In practice, the mergers and acquisitions game is full of uncertainties.

For instance, that same year the magazine didn't put any value on Saul Steinberg's loot, even though the latter controlled such riches as a major insurance company and—for example, by greenmailing Walt Disney—had cleaned up spectacularly with the Company Raid Gambit Declined. *Forbes* baldly commented that the $400 million of 1984 had become "uncertain" a year later. The fact is that players in the takeover game spend so much time juggling with debt and equity that apparently large fortunes can be shaky, and vice versa. The most successful contestants are those who play the game with the minimum commitment of capital, the maximum deployment of cunning—and the greatest degree of honesty.

In theory, playing the market this way has the possibility of being completely honest, or (to be more accurate) entirely legal. However, the players are in a mine field of rules and temptations, any of which can blow up in their faces. The first of the United States' postwar company raiders, Louis E. Wolfson, who assaulted the heaving mail-order bulk of Montgomery Ward, had some $210 million of assets under his control at one point, but ended up in prison uniform. Such retribution has been too rare. In practice, insiders have been fixing themselves with illegally informative dope, and sharing it with their financial cronies, since the beginning of stock market time—but their crime, being difficult to detect, has seldom been punished with anything save money.

The fatal error is greed. The more shares insiders buy in a stock that is heading for Cloud Nine, the more likely it is that some interfering busybody will notice. The more shares insiders offload in a company that is heading for the tomb, the higher the chance that somebody will compare before-and-after holdings in the shares. The crookedness is more difficult to spot in takeover situations, because their very essence is that a knowing person (that is, the bidder) is building up positions in the shares. Inevitably, too many other people become knowing—the advisers and the associates, the bankers and the brokers. Despite engaging fictions such as "the Chinese wall" (which is supposed to prevent secrets leaking from the part of the bank that knows them to the sector that can profit by the knowledge), Wall Street is a sieve of valuable, leaking information.

When a man such as Siegel, capable of earning $2 million a year, sells his soul and endangers his career for $700,000 of Boesky's tainted money, the wonder (as over Boesky's wealth) is that insider trading isn't even more rife and the killings even larger. True, the tip of the iceberg may be all that the Wall Street investigators had uncovered by the fall of 1987. But one restraining factor, other than honesty and good supervision, is that the leverage of money is needed to make really big money. The insider may know precisely when a bid is coming at double the market price, but to reap a million from his coup, he may need to lay his hands on a million—and raising that kind of loot renders the necessary concealment even harder.

This could explain why crooks such as Siegel and Dennis Levine took such small profits from feeding Boesky—which gravely increased their own risks, though Levine had gone to great lengths to hide the one-horse transactions that netted him $12.6 million and two years in jail. Greed undid them all. For when the stakes are warming enough, caution always gives way to avarice. Back in the early 1960s, an observant Canadian living in a hick town called Timmins in Ontario noticed that a certain aircraft used by a U.S. company was flying the same route every day to a prospecting site. Being shrewd as well as long-sighted, he bought any land he could find in the area, which proved to bear silver, zinc, lead, and other gewgaws in delectable quantities.

Back at the ranch, however, the Americans who controlled the exploration, executives of Texas Gulf Sulphur, had far more precise information than the plane-spotter, and far earlier. Their public statements played down the value of the finds while their private dealings built up their stakes in a stock that was bound to multiply gloriously. When the true glory was finally unveiled, Timmins was swamped by a minor gold rush—and the Texas Gulf Sulphur insiders reached for their piggy banks. After due delay, alas, the sheriffs of the Securities and Exchange Commission reached for their guns and hauled the insiders off to the courts. They had offended, not simply by getting caught, but by being too obvious.

The essence of the Company Raid Gambit Declined, though, is to be obvious—blatantly so. The existence of Saul Steinberg's stake in Mercury International, for example, was no secret: it was large enough to upset the directors' digestion (their prime asset being London's top-ranking S. G. Warburg merchant bank); with equal publicity, he faithfully promised not to buy any more of their lovely shares (he then did precisely that, to their still further abdominal distress). At which point, with remarkable providence, a Canadian pension fund popped up and bought Steinberg's shares at a premium over a market price that had already been inflated by his appearance.

That left everybody living happily ever after—especially Steinberg, who had spared himself the necessity of actually fighting a contested bid, which is one of the major and expensive inconveniences of the gambit. Despite that, the ploy should still, in the hands of the expert, have every virtue of the one-horse race. All the bidding gambit player need do is let the embattled board work away, forcing up the share price by every device that an overpaid investment banker can concoct, before the player finally collects his just or unjust reward.

His major risk is that of being lumbered with a target company he may not really want. Much was the rejoicing when Carl Icahn apparently overplayed his hand and ended up controlling TWA. That was supposed to be the raider's comeuppance. Much was the disappointment when Icahn the manager proved sure and ruthless enough (especially with the unions and their members' pay) to free Icahn the raider from the trap to reappear, still firing with both guns, to bid for and buy heavily into USX, another corporate hulk.

That seemed a less marvelous idea when the shares fell, in the Boesky aftermath, to below Icahn's buying price—thus defeating the whole object of the raider's exercise, which is to get more than he paid, possibly from the corporate target itself, if it buys off the bidder for a pretty price. These greenmail numbers have become gargantuan. Sir James Goldsmith's take when Goodyear parted with $621 million to be rid of him was over $90 million. Ronald Perelman, the man who raided and won Revlon, engulfed $39 million from the $558 million paid by Gillette for his shares—to the fury of Wall Street.

One Street analyst fumed to *Business Week*: "Look at Perelman. We've created a monster. Who was he three years ago?" The monster had been created by the junk bond and its ability to bring almost any deal within the web of almost any financial spider. Even after the busting of Boesky, Perelman could probably have financed his bid (and through the beleaguered junk champions, Drexel Burnham Lambert), and Goldsmith, too, had $1.9 billion in short-term finance standing by.

The financiers, of course, swallow their superlative fees come what may. Yet greenmail is a peculiarly indefensible form of one-horse racing. The greenmailer makes no economic contribution for his reward.

At least, the raiders can argue, as Icahn would at TWA, that their Company Raid Gambits Accepted remove assets from weak managements to stronger. But the greenmailer merely removes cash from the shareholders pockets and places it into his own pockets, leaving behind the very directors whose weak management made the company vulnerable—and who may be running a weaker company still as a result of their sell-offs and other defensive maneuvers. A David who tackles Goliath always attracts sympathy. But a fat-cat David who breaks off the engagement on being bribed by the Philistines with the shareholders' money, and leaves them with an enfeebled giant, is no hero.

In the Age of the Common Millionaire, the latter can be a villain without necessarily being a crook. There's no ducking Peter Drucker's conclusion, in his book *The Frontiers of Management*, that the takeover free-for-all, which launched the crooks, villains, and neovillains alike, was economically and socially harmful. It is harder to accept Drucker's belief that the abuses will surely be stopped by public intervention— that is, unless, the Boesky scandals having failed to be the enabling catastrophe, the Great Crash of 1987 precipitates the necessary corrective laws and action.

No less than the rise in American gambling, the surge in bids and deals and in the number of bidders and dealers (double-dealers and otherwise) is a response to the powerful worldwide forces that made money and credit too freely available and that thus weakened the defenses of the once high, mighty, and invulnerable managements of large corporations. If Mike Milken of Drexel Burnham hadn't existed, somebody else would have invented him—and his junk bonds.

Those economic forces turned the Wall Street of the 1980s into the greatest one-horse race in history, but, as the October massacre proved, there can be no such thing as a race that everybody wins. The shrewd economic suspicion is that the ultimate loser is the American productive apparatus, that the constant shuffling and reshuffling of corporate assets and the Wall Street rake-offs that resulted did nothing to strengthen, and plenty to weaken, American strength in world competition. Nobody can now have any illusion about the consequences if that becomes a one-horse race for the Japanese.

There's nothing wrong, and everything right, in the individual Common Millionaire seeking a "heads I win, tails I win" outcome—provided that the rules are rigorous and that he obeys them. The astute man will always seek the sure thing—like the British multimillionaire, Sir Maxwell Joseph, a grand master in the art of sure things, at the time of the 1964 election. He put a massive bet on a Labour victory, not because of any loyalty to the party, but on grounds of impeccable logic. If the Conservatives won, all his shareholdings would soar. If Labour won (as it did), he stood to collect a tax-free fortune on the bet.

It's only in mythology that risk is the way to millions, on the general assumption that "the higher the risk, the higher the potential reward." This is an inaccurate analogy from what is a true statement about investment: "The higher the interest, the higher the risk." Between interest (which is income) and a dealing profit (which is a capital gain) there is a great canyon fixed. Where the odds are a hundred to one, it's because the chances of the bet succeeding are small.

The true speculator, however, is concerned not with the percentage of his payoff, but with its degree of certainty. The surer the thing, the more heavily he invests. True and high risks are for those from whom the true speculator makes his true rewards. The trouble—the very big trouble—in the mid-1980s was that the truth became lies, the rewards grew far too high, and the risks thus too great for the ultimate financier of the Common Millionaire and of the bull market that exploded on October 19, 1987: the common man.

26
GLUTTONS
FOR
PUNISHMENT

Minginess is an occupational disease of the millionaire. Money in the global sense has long ceased to have any meaning. Figures are simply statistics with the zeros left off the big sums in conversation: thus does familiarity breed respect. But the man to whom "two fifty" means a quarter of a million dollars is likely to be obsessional about $2.50 or even a quarter, as if those twenty-five cents were all that stood between him and the workhouse door.

Psychoanalysts have speculated about the infantile origins of this miserliness. If some of the theorists are to be believed, the best course for any poor mother who wants to have a rich old age is to give her little boy hell on the potty. Unfortunately, cause and effect don't work out so obligingly. Even if all or most millionaires did acquire their retentive habits at stool, it by no means follows that all men with anal problems are worth a million dollars.

A more confident assertion, however, is that the more retentive the Midas is, the more canny, suspicious, supercautious, and self-centered, the more likely he is to last out the long run and to bequeath an intact and inviolate fortune. The historian of wealth must be impressed by the similarities among Gulbenkian, Rockefeller, Getty, Ford, and Hughes: secretive, taciturn men whose grip on their businesses was only matched by a firm hold on their privy purses.

The tight way of the wealthy with their own young is another strange expression of this psychological compulsion. The eldest Rockefeller's heir wanted just over $1 million to snatch J. Pierpont Morgan's Chinese porcelains from the hands of Frick and Widener; Rockefeller didn't happen to have $1 million in cash handy (the very rich often get into such scrapes), applied to his father for a loan, and was turned down. Rather than lose the beautiful objects, Rockefeller, a man of forty-one, wrote a begging letter to his father that, even after the passage of half a century, has a pathetic ring.

He told his father: "I have never squandered money on horses, yachts, automobiles or other foolish extravagances." Collecting porcelains ("the only thing on which I care to spend money") was a costly hobby but "quiet and unostentatious and not sensational." Having softened up the old buzzard, John D. II then delivered the knockout punch. "The money put into these porcelains . . . is all there, and while not income producing, I have every reason to believe that . . . a sale under ordinary circumstances would certainly realize their full cost value, and, as the years go by, more. . . ." He got his million—as a gift, not a loan.

A public relations genius, Ivy Lee, converted this vice of Rockefeller's into a virtue by instituting the giving away of dimes by his narrow-fisted employer. Whatever John D. thought about this prodigality, stories about Getty (with his pay telephone kiosk installed at Sutton Place for the benefit of his visitors) and of the first Ford, show them adhering to the same sound maxim: "Don't look after the pennies, and the pounds won't look after themselves."

Another art story, told by S. N. Behrman, recounts the rare collaboration of the leading New York art dealers, including Duveen, to offer Henry Ford I, the last untapped billionaire in the world (it was during the Depression, and they were desperate), the choicest items from their combined stock. They produced a sumptuous catalogue, which the grand duke of Dearborn received with much gratitude. They then tentatively suggested that Ford might like to purchase the items he was admiring. "But, gentlemen," asked Ford, "what would I want with the original pictures when the ones right here in these books are so beautiful?"

Men with deep collective experience of the excessively rich should perhaps have known better. Their success, especially Duveen's, in persuading equally close men, such as Frick and Andrew Mellon, to pay astronomical sums for the priceless and for its housing (Frick's palazzo on Fifth Avenue and Mellon's National Gallery in Washington, thanks to Duveen, are the costliest monuments of the epoch) blinded them to the equal tendency of the rich to grasp free handouts with the avidity of a drowning man hunting straws.

One transatlantic emigrant to Britain, although rich enough to eat a hundred dinners a day at the Mirabelle or Savoy Grill, was constitutionally incapable of refusing an invitation to a free meal. Nubar Gulbenkian, the free-spending, chatty son of the tightfisted, closemouthed Calouste, was another one who found free food all but irresistible—even though he could and did afford to have Lucullan repasts delivered from his favorite Caprice during the intervals of a particularly enjoyable legal action in London. Nubar was the author of the perceptive remark that "not knowing how to spend a lot of money is the least of life's problems"; although, since his father, Calouste, kept Nubar on a tight financial rein, getting a lot of money to spend was Nubar's own major anxiety.

To be fair, and generous, possibly the rich feel easier about accepting gifts because there is little prospect of their being bribed. But whatever the cause, they can never resist the lure of something for nothing, any more than, when offered a deal, they can spurn a profit of several hundred percent. The liking for free samples and free dinners is part and parcel of the acquisitive urge, a lust they conceal behind standard non sequiturs, such as the immortal line that millions mean nothing to them, because they can only eat three meals a day. Or, as one Francis Leo Cappaert put it, "I don't care how big you are. You can only drive a Cadillac, you can only drink champagne."

To that, the discourteous retort is that, if nature would allow, many millionaires would eat many times more, drive many Cadillacs, and corner the entire supply of Bollinger '75. As it is, they indulge other appetites where satiation point is further removed. Even the Rockefeller-type recluse always has some diversion on which he spends inordinately.

But the *i*-dotting, *t*-crossing, punctilious, meticulous, introverted recluse even spends—like John D. II—in an organized, controlled manner. In business, if not in enjoyment of life, he has a clear edge over the extravagant extrovert who uses his money and the company's with merry abandon. One giveaway of the con company, in fact, is the giveaway itself. The firm that lavishes free liquor, free flights to faraway places, and free entertainment on journalists and other contacts, or whose executive living standards are lush beyond reason is rightly suspect on those counts alone. There was no greater cornucopia of goodies for all than Bernie Cornfeld's IOS, just as Mr. Nixon's CREEP election committee had many a lavish creep on its secret books.

At IOS, the $52 million raised in a public offering dwindled to a mere million before the check even arrived. Of the drain, $29 million went on loans to assorted insiders, including $4.9 million for the purchase of Cornfeld's very own BAC-1-11 jet. At the crashed National Student Marketing Corporation, the supremo, Cortes Wesley Randell, at the height of its ill-found fortunes, possessed $60 million of stock, a $600,000 castle in Virginia, a 55-foot yacht, a company Lear jet, and overheads that were rising even faster than the fictitious profits.

The pattern was just the same at one company in the Midlands of Britain, whose chairman achieved highs in conspicuous spending that contrasted starkly with the grubby products of the family business— such as machine tools and motorbikes. His own tastes ran to a great white yacht; a zebra-cushioned, gold-plated Daimler (his company made them, too); and a diamond-studded, talkative wife. As she described the personal disaster that followed: "They denounced us and sacked my husband because we had dared to bring some glamour to selling nuts and bolts." "They" were the gray men among the institutional shareholders, who were offended, not by the indifferent company results but by the blatant extravagance, refusing to accept the lady's argument that her special Daimlers were no more than good advertising: "I got a million pounds of free publicity, and we always managed to promote the company." Despite this assistance, the Daimler name, once to be mentioned in the same breath as Rolls-Royce, slipped out of public regard and ended as a badge on the Jaguar; the motorbikes were mauled to death by the Japanese; and the family businesses followed the bikes into oblivion.

Despite such earnest efforts, the truly lavish life in the late twentieth century is no longer found in the West on the scale of the robber barons; in the Age of the Common Millionaire, when even the super-rich merely indulge middle-class tastes to the extreme, the big spending action has moved east. Above all, it's the Arabian oil potentates (and the Sultan of Brunei farther east) who have untold hundreds of millions to spend, no work to divert them from the expenditure, and no compunction about its scale, objects, or mindlessness.

These are not strictly business fortunes, however, but feudal inheritances. The hangers-on of the potentates are the true gluttons, the real heirs to the likes of William Randolph Hearst, whose extravagance in buying and building castles, and filling them with expensive guests and even costlier art, came near to finishing off one of the greatest fortunes ever created in America. Hearst's only real equivalent in the Age of the Common Millionaire is the Saudi arms dealer Adnan Khashoggi—and in the latter's case, too, Nemesis has always lurked around the corner of the big spender.

At his peak, this fattest of the Arab go-betweens could afford to spend a quarter of a million dollars a day to support himself and his entourage in a style to which even Saudi princes of the blood were not accustomed. Or could Khashoggi afford it? In contrast to Hearst and the robber barons, the little arms dealer didn't have an identifiable business that could pay him the necessary $85 million a year.

His palmiest days were in the 1970s, when the Arab states were rushing to exploit the quadrupling of oil prices by stocking up on the necessities of the princely life, including arms. According to *Time* magazine, Khashoggi's take in commissions totaled hundreds of millions in 1970 to 1975; the $106 million paid out by Lockheed was only one payment in the crowd. Khashoggi must previously have earned vast sums as the Saudi sales agent for the likes of Chrysler, Fiat, Westland Helicopters, and Rolls-Royce. In striking these home runs, Khashoggi principally used two bats: intimacy with the Saudi royal family and that hyper-extravagant standard of living: as he told *Time*, "My life-style was my only way of making important contacts. . . . In a few years, everybody wanted to be on *my* guest list."

The 400 everybodies who made it for Khashoggi's 1985 celebration of his sixtieth birthday had three days of lush entertainment and pieces of cake cut from a model of Louis XIV's coronation crown. The latter-day Sun King, at his apogee, owned a dozen pieces of real estate around the world, including two entire apartment floors of Olympic Towers in Manhattan and a 5,000-acre estate in Marbella, Spain; three commercial jets, one a $40 million DC-9; a 282-foot yacht and a piggyback helicopter (both up for sale by 1986); and 100 vehicles, including a dozen stretch limousines from Mercedes.

This early 1987 list of assets, though, had begun to look as evanescent as the palatial Moorish party decor that Khashoggi had just used for his Christmas festivities. Disgruntled creditors ranged from a British tycoon (who had the Manhattan pad and the DC-9 seized) to contractors and investors in a suspended, billion-dollar real estate development in Salt Lake City. That venture, like many of Khashoggi's deals outside arms and the Middle East, was deeply flawed, and even in his special field, Khashoggi made an apparent mess of Colonel North's fateful Iranian arms-for-hostages deal. Nobody would have been surprised by further, even ultimate Khashoggi disasters.

Using life-style extravagance to buy business is a game that easily gets out of hand, until, like Khashoggi with his spurious wheels and deals in North America, the Midas seeks business—any business—to support the very life-style whose raison d'être is allegedly to bring business in.

By the opposite token, stinginess with money is an encouraging sign, and for good reason. The excellent businessman knows in his finger bones that a pound, dollar, mark, franc, lira, or yen spent represents, not only an outflow of the aforenamed currencies, but the disbursement of the yield, profit, or return from several pounds, dollars, marks, francs, and lire of hard-won business. To the professional miser the ideal situation is one in which he spends nothing at all. That being impossible, he concentrates ferociously on spending only when it's inevitable—which to him means when there is some measurable return from the expenditure.

Among the West's richest private accumulators was an eccentric whose septuagenarian hand would not allow executives to travel abroad unless they could prove that their journey was of direct financial value to the company. Such nit-picking is silly, and possibly self-defeating; executives quickly become adept at shifting spending from a banned area to an allowable zone, for one thing, and, for another, nobody ever measures the loss a company may have suffered from hoarding its money unwisely.

But certain benefits flow from the nit-picking mentality. He who stamps on all unnecessary spending must have some system of identifying and measuring what is necessary. He who forbids spending on this, that, or the other frivolity must have some system of checking what is actually spent, by whom, and on what. In other words, he must have control; and effective control, especially of the purse, is the heartbeat of all sustained business successes.

A would-be last of the big spenders, in contrast, has very little idea of who is spending what, when, and why—sometimes even how. This lack of control is a concomitant of the big spending. If somebody is actually counting the outflow of cash, somebody else is liable to break out in a nervous rash at the sums. If nobody is counting, nobody cares. True, few businesses, even small firms, have perfect systems of control: they have systems that are adequate (or inadequate) for their present purposes and present manipulators. While a business pours forth cash, whatever system its creator uses is safely hidden under the Niagara Falls of wealth. But if a dry period comes, and the creator is as slapdash as most big spenders, an awful sequence of events automatically follows.

First, he (like the world) finds out about the horror too late. Second, because of the lack of system, he doesn't find out its full extent. Third, the lack of control that allowed the catastrophe to start also means that there's no mechanism to stop the disaster from developing: the vehicle lacks brakes as well as steering.

The du Pont family, which should have picked up a thing or two about business methods over the years, provides a case in sharp point: an unusual diversification, started in 1931, a brokerage firm called F. I. Du Pont. The second generation nurtured this house into a position of high respect on Wall Street. When Wall Street as a whole stumbled and bumbled into the most appalling debacle since the Great Crash, a crazy pavement of paperwork and bookkeeping failures, the du Ponts were in the van. They had to be bailed out, of all indignities, by the Johnny-come-lately Texas computer billionaire, H. Ross Perot (who failed no less miserably himself, so great was the shambles).

The initial bail was set at $70 million. The Texas rangers discovered, among other mind-boggling facts, that this vulnerable house settled its books not every day, not every week, not even every month—but once a year. Small wonder that staggering sums were missing and couldn't be traced. Before its collapse, Du Pont had hastily merged with Glore Forgan, whose Russell Forgan once observed sagely that "Wall Street firms pay a lot of attention to how companies run their businesses. But we don't pay enough attention to managing our own firms." The catch is that Forgan said this, not after the event, but in 1963, long before first his firm and then the merged operation with Du Pont went down the mismanagement drain.

Wall Street has continued to demonstrate this built-in tendency to lax control: at times, it has seen bizarre lapses—such as at least half a billion dollars in customers' securities disappearing by simple theft and another half billion lost by rotten bookkeeping. The chain of mishaps at E. F. Hutton is as much of a piece with this incompetence as the spider's web of insider trading scandals elsewhere. The bosses of firms such as Kidder Peabody and Drexel Burnham Lambert are deeply culpable for their failure to detect the illegalities and cheating going on right under what should have been highly sensitive noses.

The lost sense of smell, and the laxity of control, plainly came from the easy money sloshing around Wall Street—the financial inducements and extravagant salaries paid to very young people (reflected, of course, in still larger amounts paid to their seniors) and the enormous fees earned from deals whose promoters dared not count the cost—for fear of losing the prize. It's not surprising if mundane matters of financial and management control dwindle into the background for men who deal with the kings of commerce, possess millions themselves, and are adding to said fortunes at the rate of $1 million a week (Milken of Drexel Burnham) or $4 million in six months—simply as a bonus (Alan "Ace" Greenberg of Bear Stearns).

It doesn't follow that gluttonous incomes must lead to gluttonous spending and sparse controls, though the temptation is always there. In particular, if you're employing an ace with a multimillion-dollar income and a reputation for fixing billion-dollar deals, you can't expect much from any efforts to control the beast. When the British merchant bank Morgan Grenfell got deeply snared in the Guinness scandal, the blame was initially heaped on the head of its merger wizard—a man nicknamed "Roger the Dodger" because nobody in the bank, including his superiors, knew where he was, or, apparently, what he was doing. Wealth and success, in other words, are no excuse for neglecting the more fundamental functions of being wealthy; and, if they are being neglected, spending will prove deadly, to corpocrats as well as plutocrats. When John I. Snyder, the builder of U.S. Industries, died of a stroke in 1965, "we were just ahead of the sheriff," said his successor, who had the job of selling off a few of Snyder's purchases: seven aircraft, a 110-foot yacht, a fleet of limousines, and a hunting lodge in England.

The expenditure tends to have a certain repetitive pattern—gracious living, big game, and yachts, for instance, were blamed for the reduction of the third Duke of Sutherland's estates from over a million acres to a mere hundred thousand. Gambling has also exacted a heavy toll in its day. Gordon Selfridge, the American who brought the department store to London, went bankrupt at the noble age of eighty-three through a passion for the tables that, in his case, was coupled with a taste for terribly expensive women. While his beloved Dolly Sisters were in the process of gambling away $8 million over a quarter of a century, Selfridge would console them for their losses, paid by him, by sending them diamonds. He thus compounded his own misfortunes.

The reason the Michelin tire family, as frugal a bunch of multimillionaires as France has to offer, own Citröen cars is partly because of André Citröen's insatiable enthusiasm for, and execrable skill at, the game of baccarat. After Citröen lost a record $550,000 in one session, he also lost control of the car firm, which he had built up by his genius, to the banks. By 1935, after another crash, the business had passed into Michelin ownership. The second time around, Citröen was accused of gambling foolishly on front-wheel drive, the innovation that, as it proved, sustained the company for the next four decades: his gambling errors were committed strictly at the tables.

An addiction to gaming need not be gruesome in its effects. John W. "Bet-a-Million" Gates, who could afford to lose $1 million in a single year of poker after starting as a barbed wire salesman in Texas, lived and died a millionaire. Even for gluttons, easy come doesn't easily go unless there is a deathwish present, a destructive urge for which the wild gambling, like that of Selfridge and Citröen, is only a means of expression.

Gluttony takes other forms: the gluttony for power, for instance. The power glutton surrounds himself with secretaries, official flunkies (such as chauffeurs), unofficial flunkies in the form of yes-men managers, and is abominably rude to all of them. His greed does no harm to his fortune until that avarice starts to grow; then, like a gambler feverishly raising the stakes to counteract a losing streak, he starts to exaggerate the unpleasant and noxious characteristics that, up to now, have been tolerated by his victims. In these circumstances, victims will put up with anything short of physical torture, and sometimes even with that, only so long as some pretense of normality is maintained.

In one case, the last camel which broke the back of the managerial straws concerned stemmed from the tycoon's discovery that one of his far-flung subsidiaries had dared to raise a price without his permission. He summoned all the offending executives from afar for a breakfast-time meeting. They dutifully arrived—to be kept outside the tycoon's office for an entire day before being ushered into the presence. Not long afterward the tyrant was unceremoniously deposed.

Faced with such eccentricities, the beleaguered underlings assume that the overlord is mad, and so, using the word loosely, he is. The megalomania can assume certifiable proportions. The behavior of William Randolph Hearst became intolerable enough; that of his nearest British equivalent, Lord Northcliffe, passed the point of no return. As increasingly incoherent messages arrived from the demented Nero (for example, "fire all redheaded men"), his staff had to ignore them and rely on the restraining influence of his medical attendants and family. Yet this power-besotted plutocrat was the self-made genius who invented the popular press and demonstrated an uncanny instinct for the motivation of the masses. The power glutton, more often than not, does possess genius. It's almost as if the extra dimension to his mind, which produces intuitive flashes of which other men are incapable, is acquired at the expense of the more humdrum dimension that keeps other, more ordinary human beings stable.

If you start living like a latter-day Roman emperor, however, you begin to imagine that you really are Julius Caesar, Augustus, and Diocletian rolled into one; you forget that you are just as likely to be Nero with a dash of Caligula. Absolute monarchs get brought down by the corruption of their absolutism. Tycoons who persuade others that they can do no wrong are corrupted by the absolutism of a wealth that they can deploy to satisfy their whims at both work and play (20 of the Forbes 400 own 30 percent or more of leading baseball, football, or basketball teams). The deep purse is equally attracted to the expensive mass franchise and the esoteric sport, where shoulders need only be rubbed with those who are similarly well accoutred. There are certain enterprises that regularly attract wasteful diversions of funds—such as attempts to wrest the America's Cup from the Americans.

In this game, the prime disadvantage was that the world's best designers of yachts and sails happened to be Americans, on whom any non-American challenger perforce had to depend. Sir Thomas Lipton, the tea and grocery tycoon, spent a clear million prewar pounds in five tries at lifting the cup from the United States. The first Australian to try, newspaper magnate, Sir Frank Packer, had no better luck in modern times. Nor did the Bic ballpoint baron, Marcel Bich: he charged his forlorn attempt to the publicity account. But in Lipton's day this kind of expenditure was pure pocket money, which meant that, if the pocket turned shallow, the player was out of chips.

In times of low taxation, that's how the game was played. But with taxes high, the burden of spending, even on some activities that might be considered pure sport, has been shifted onto the corporation, à la Bich. The box at the racecourse, the subscription to the opera, the shooting lodge in Scotland, the racehorses, the ski lodge in Aspen; with luck, good management, and an understanding tax man, all these can be financed by the Inland Revenue. Hence the successors to Lipton are wheeling and dealing Australians such as Alan Bond. He would unquestionably argue that his rise to still greater riches was helped along powerfully by the campaign that, defying history, took away the America's Cup from the Americans and thus paved the way for the donnybrook at Perth in 1987—in which commercial sponsorship and commercial motives played a dominant role.

If the beneficiary is spending only corporate money on each pound or dollar of pleasure, it's far harder to spend himself into bankruptcy than in the good old days, when every cent was actually his own, instead of money that would otherwise go in tax. In the Age of the Common Millionaire, efforts to soak up the resources of the rich have thus enabled them to finance their gluttony at the public expense. A latter-day Gordon Selfridge would probably have had the Dolly Sisters on the books as publicity consultants.

The glutton with truly well-bred financial tastes can have it both ways: tax reliefs and capital gains. If the lavish hobby has a direct financial benefit built in, it can cost less than nothing. Buying fine art, especially in the United States, is a notorious example; the purchaser can either choose to reduce his tax liability and build up credit in heaven by giving his art purchases away, while retaining them on his walls, or he can hang on to the pictures for his private enjoyment and watch the capital gains build up in an effortless manner.

Stocking a large cellar with fine wines, a game with similar advantages, was among the most lucrative activities recent decades have had to offer. Collecting of any kind, apart from its aesthetic joys, offers constant prospects for this kind of double pleasure. You can control it by buying your own art gallery (Armand Hammer of Occidental Petroleum financed Knoedlers), but unless your appetite for bad art and high prices is insatiable, spending yourself into bankruptcy by way of the auction rooms or the dealers is a difficult feat.

If spending has become less reckless than in the times of the Whitneys, of Jay Gould, or Diamond Jim Brady, and of the various British and French noblemen who set themselves seriously to the task of destroying their patrimonies, the reasons are in part obvious. First, the necessity to ensure that the spending is in fact going to meet the tax man's approval, or at least not excite his displeasure; second, the fast fading of royalty, which, in its heyday of spending, inherited both wealth and the taxpayers' money with equal abandon and set lofty standards for the proletarian nobility of wealth; third, the fact that in the days of high taxation on income, the rich developed the habit of turning income into capital—and all rich men with any sort of instinct for survival are reluctant to dig into capital.

Fourth is the change in tastes generally with democratization. Parties or estates on the Edwardian scale have fallen out of favor: one peer had his footmen clad in gold livery for a visit by Edward VII. Today, if you want a private railroad coach, you can again have one. But no longer are these playthings the toys of the indecently rich. Indeed, J. P. Morgan's private *Erie 400* is now part-owned by an attorney from West Virginia, one of a whole community of private-car buffs. Their association had 157 full and 240 associate members in 1986, when the 230 cars registered with Amtrak compared with just one in the 1950s. (That little luxury item, then owned by socialite Lucius Beebe, is still in service.)

One Denver physicist, according to *Time*, spent $280,000 on his 1948 Pullman, and the president of a Milwaukee electrical supplies firm ran to half a million for his car. But in the Age of the Common Millionaire, there are abundant middle-class, moderately rich people who can afford $40,000 to $100,000 to get a car (known as a "private varnish" to the buffs) into prime condition, and even to pay $14,500 to have Amtrak haul it from Milwaukee to California and back. The private rail car today is in much the same category as the luxury auto or the good-size boat, but in terms of truly devouring wealth, this type of minority transport is a nonstarter—a million dollars will buy too many Rolls-Royces and Ferraris for anybody's comfort.

True, the private jet comes much more expensively, at prices of up to $18 million for a Grumman Gulfstream IV, or over $3 million for a Learjet 35A, and $7 million for a HS 125. The truly ambitious giant of commerce can take to the air in a DC-9 with walnut paneling (Kirk Kerkorian), for which he could buy several of the above. But it won't be the tycoon who does the shelling—it will be a company plane, tax deductible, and depreciation attracting all the way along the air corridors of the world.

As the emphasis in status symbols has swung to the air, yachts have slipped down the scale of desirability. President William Tolbert of Liberia moved into the same $15 million mansion his predecessor, William Vacanarat Shadrach Tubman, built during a twenty-seven-year demonstration of the political route to riches; but Tolbert sold Tubman's $2 million yacht. Very few of today's oceangoing spenders, including men such as Stavros Niarchos, who are not apt to worry about being in when the tax collector calls, are up to the spending standards of real yacht owners such as J. Pierpont Morgan, whose *Corsair* has few rivals today. The British royal family's *Britannia* is one: her seven-figure annual cost is paid for by the taxpayer; the ship officially belongs to the Royal Navy, and will presumably come in useful one day if the British Isles are ever attacked by a fleet of sampans.

For all these reasons, sheer gluttony, or eyes bigger than the purse, is unlikely to decimate more than a modest fortune these days. Gluttony must be accompanied by some attendant vice, such as egregious folly or paranoia, before full punishment is meted out. It used to be thought that, even if most of the rich run to expensive trappings, only the weaker vessels reveal their frailty by talking about it. "I have a taste for gracious living," confessed one well-heeled crook who was about to part some fat companies from a silk purse containing £1 million in exchange for a sow's ear of a business. But today the self-made tycoon who spends $14,000 on one bathtub is merely maintaining current standards, which are far behind those of the golden age.

Eugene Klein of National General planted his Beverly Hills mansion, according to John Brooks, with modern pictures and antique furniture worth millions and bought his Rolls-Royce secondhand (at some removes, be it said) from the Queen of England. But all this spending is still a pale imitation of the devotion decades before of a Henry Clay Frick to the disbursement of his cash. The Frick palazzo on New York's Fifth Avenue cost $17 million—and that was without its indescribably beautiful and precious contents, for which any museum board in the world would give its collective soul.

For every hot, now passé conglomerator who made a poor shot at becoming a latter-day Frick (and Frick, although addicted to unpleasant habits such as machine-gunning his workers, was a tight and tightfisted businessman), there were plenty of others whose life-styles, if not Puritanical, certainly showed no trace of Texan or Californian flimflam and flamboyance. Maybe Toots Shor, the Broadway restaurateur, had the right idea: "I don't want to be a millionaire," he said, "I just want to live like one"—and in recent times, that hasn't been too difficult.

The taste for gracious living has spread inexorably. Financial writers in New York knowledgeably sip their Clos Vougeot. Managers from Hamburg cavort in Adriatic resorts where once only yachts carrying the like of Edward, Prince of Wales, could penetrate. Japanese businessmen easily find the millions to buy at auction the jewels the latter gave to his beloved Duchess. Expense account executives monopolize the most expensive tables of Paris. Some 2,850 people every year take delivery of a new Rolls-Royce (or mostly, their companies do). In such sad times for the exclusivity of exclusive spending, it may not only be safer to be like the Norwegian shipowner (with fifty vessels) and industrialist, who drove to work in a battered station wagon, and the small number of other truly frugal millionaires—in this age of lesser gluttons, such frugality may even be the new smartness.

27

IF YOU CAN'T
BE CAREFUL,
BE GOOD

At the start of this book, a mighty socioeconomic question was raised. Has private property changed, as Adolf Berle believed, until it is not truly private anymore? Has the diffusion of ownership through the spread of equity (the very system that has so encouraged the proliferation of Common Millionaires) altered the nature of private wealth until Common Millionaires present no social problem, give rise to no troubling queries?

The Berle analysis founders on several points, not least that sharing the wealth is uncharacteristic of today's rich; the majority of private wealth remains in private hands, to be diminished, not by generosity or taxation, but by the passing of the generations. One conclusion is manifest: the focus of private wealth has shifted, probably forever, from the old commanding heights of the economy, partly because, in an economy moving inexorably toward services, the heights no longer command as once they did. Equally important, the great factories, the vast energy supplies, the major chains of distribution, the storehouses of finance, the arsenals of democracy—by and large, these are owned by the mass of shareholders, including the wealthy, and managed by professional managements.

For all the dint of greedy option schemes, overgolden parachutes, and unprincipled buyouts, these pros do not become so wealthy that they greatly affect the balance of social and economic power. The wealth within the too-easy reach of the commanding-height executives may have a harmful effect on their stewardship. But proving cause and effect between the stock options at General Motors and the gross mismanagement of its affairs in the 1980s isn't easy. The connection between Henry Ford's senility and his company's near collapse in the 1940s, however, is plainly demonstrable—and the fact that there are few Ford equivalents in the *Fortune* list of leading corporations in the United States, and in the world, is a profound change.

Most thinkers would call it a change for the better. The diffusion of economic power is certainly more democratic, and probably more efficient, than its concentration in overmighty trusts controlled by family dynasties. To put it simply, the West's economic eggs have been placed in infinitely more baskets—and if that system is not working well (as it isn't), then wider explanations must be sought than the malefaction of great wealth.

The verdict could be nothing more profound than the difficulty of managing any large (or small) economy, given the fallibility of human beings and the large number of unknowns. But before other anxieties about the role of wealth can be put aside, one question must be asked: just where below those commanding heights have the super-rich settled?

Settled is the right word. What the rich have abandoned in the industrial heartlands, they have occupied in the cities and the more fertile land tracts (monetarily speaking) that lie between the cities. Nobody may suffer much, if any, harm from the fact that the Reichmanns, like the Rockefellers before them and the Astors before them, have acquired so much of Manhattan's prime real estate. But it must be true that the competition of the wealthy for the choicest acres has raised the prices.

The many Common Millionaires with big holdings in real estate amassed them from that conviction, expressed so succinctly by billionaire Harry Helmsley to *Forbes*, that "the values go up." It is, of course, a self-fulfilling prophecy. Because they paid enormous prices for the real estate, and then locked it away, so reducing the supply, the continuing demand (again, from the rich) pushed the prices higher still. Yet it is impossible to argue that the economic contribution of a skyscraper in Manhattan—or Montreal or Montparnasse—has risen during the process.

That is one glaring example of the inherent defect in the Age of the Common Millionaire: the entirely random, and often grotesquely skewed, relationship between economic contribution and financial return. The idle heir is the most common case, but by no means the most conspicuous. What did John Werner Kluge, for instance, do for his billions other than execute one deal of dubious propriety? Hasn't his prime fortune really come from the pockets of those holders, owning 74 percent of Metromedia, who sold out to Kluge at far too low a price?

That particular demonstration of wealth passing from the weak to the strong is one of the many paths to wealth charted in this book in all their astounding variety (not to say, richness). The evidence of its chapters is that the chosen path matters less in determining the ultimate reward than the chosen means. Manipulating money is the fastest way of multiplying it—and this is the key to that uneasily disproportionate relation between achievement and riches. Observing this morally not-so-golden rule—that the means multiplies the mass, the Law of Leverage—comes more easily to some rich men than others, more readily to a Kluge than to a Ken Olsen, whose Digital Equipment Corporation is a creation of genuine genius and economic benefit.

Kluge's Law of Leverage is, perhaps, the only reliable rule for maximizing millions. There are none, however, for achieving the seven-digit nirvana; there are only guiding principles, for use on the way up, while on top, and, if the best comes to the worst, on the way down. As in every set of rules compiled since the Ten Commandments, every item isn't relevant on every occasion or to every worshiper; the man or woman who covets his neighbor's ox (or Boeing 727) may have no use whatsoever for adultery.

But the charm of rules is that they can be broken, every single one of them, and the breaker can still win. Making money, after all, is a competitive sport, and success in competition doesn't depend on your observation of precept; it depends on whether you outscore the competition.

It may help to achieve this result by sandbagging the poor fellow, putting downers in his tea, taking uppers yourself, lining his track shoes with lead, tripping him, and so forth. But cheating isn't necessary, even if many millions have been made by cheats. The rich, in fact, divide into three categories: those who would trample over their grandmothers on any pretext, because that is their horrible nature; those who, faced with the choice of losing money or grandma, would kiss the old lady a tender good-bye; and those who would honor their grandmother in any circumstances, no matter what the cost.

The general view of economic history is that most millionaires fit into the middle category; they behave decently, or no more indecently than the mass of mortals, unless pushed, when no holds are barred. A small but significant number are natural grandma tramplers; and a tiny minority are upright, benevolent, and honorable at all times.

Virtue in this sense has nothing to do with good works; all the Rockefeller benefactions can no more wash away the memory of the old boy's sins than the perfume of Araby could cleanse the hands of Lady Macbeth. Many godly religious sects have been handsomely financed by royal flushes of fortune—notably in Texas—but the common assumption is that these benefactions are more often expiations for past offenses committed in the service of Mammon than expressions of great goodness.

It's the same with noble motives: they do not invariably express noble natures. John Spedan Lewis, a second-generation genius who transformed his family department store inheritance, handed over control of his business to all the employees under a unique partnership scheme. True, the Lewis family was inordinately rich by this time—but Lewis also gave the staff his Longstock Park mansion, complete with contents, plus a handsome riverside estate for their partnerly recreation.

Those bald facts might imply that Lewis was a saint among men, let alone millionaires. In truth, however, for all his partnership ideals, Lewis was a highly autocratic, high-handed ruler who, after surrendering control, tended to regret the surrender. Admonitions to his successors would appear embarrassingly in the partnership magazine, despatched from his self-styled "burrow in Longstock Park"—and in Lewis's version of partnership it has always been clear that, to paraphrase Orwell, some partners are very much more equal than others. Generosity with material goods is not the same as a generous attitude to power.

Much the same tale can be told of another great social reformer, who was indifferent to personal wealth: Gottlieb Duttweiler, the brave Swiss who spotted that big companies were ganging up on the customer by charging unnecessarily high prices; Dutti undercut the overchargers by selling first from vans, then from his chain of Migros outlets. Migros was a cooperative, owned by its grateful customers in Switzerland, or so it was supposed by those who had not studied the Migros constitution. The setup left Dutti and his family a controlling interest, special rights, and effective power for as long as they cared to exercise it— which in Dutti's case was until death did him part.

There is the case of the greatest banker ever to bounce a check, A. P. Giannini, who steadfastly refused to make his family super-rich from his building of the Bank of America; and there is that of the Tatas in

India, whose former wealth was vested in charitable foundations, but who continued to rule the East's biggest private industrial empire with iron rods.

The cynical view (and cynics have a saving habit of being right) is that capital accumulation in the private sector plays the same role as tax in the public sector—it provides the means by which the mighty and their minions exercise their power. Indeed, the millionaire's millions, no less than the IRS's riches, represent a tax levied involuntarily from the citizenry.

The citizen contemplating a war in Vietnam, or a strike against Libya, or the backing of the contras in Nicaragua, knows that the finance came from him and his fellows; contemplating the Bar Harbor estate of the Rockefellers, the sizable choice acreages of Europe owned by the Rothschilds, or the whopping incomes of the Japanese industrialists, the citizen never thinks that this money came from exactly the same source as the tax dollar: from a percentage of the earnings of the masses. (Not to dwell on the fact that sometimes the private dollars and the tax dollars are one and the same, transferred to the private sector from the public by the beneficence or corruption of the politicians.)

In public life, it was long ago recognized that politicians have to be kept under constant scrutiny and ultimate control if they are not to abuse their power. That process works imperfectly; but the devices for controlling malefactors of great wealth, in Teddy Roosevelt's phrase, are less powerful to start with, are less numerous than the political restraints, and work no more effectively.

This fact should intensify the pressure on the financially potent to exercise restraint on themselves—although nobody can expect them to behave in those ways considered normal by people who think themselves normal. The rich begin by being exceptional, original, unusual, eccentric in varying degrees and styles. Their differences start them on their way, and the rush of power to their purses accentuates their differentiated traits. But to all the rich one law applies: if they have to count the money, pound by pound, dollar by dollar, something is wrong, somewhere—a clerk in the counting house is running away with the loot, or an investment is hemorrhaging, or Midas himself has mislaid his touch. And the sensation that something somewhere is awry must never be ignored—like a pain in the abdomen, it's nature's warning, not to be ignored.

The messages of nature are a millionaire's most valuable communications. Few fortunes could have been created without a successful hunch, a display of divine intuition. Hunch is not luck, however lucky a hunch may seem. Instead, the computer in the skull has run through a whole series of complicated routines, operations research sums, market research equations, multiple regression analyses, discounted cash flow calculations, opportunity costings, and decision trees complete with probability factors. All these mathematical marvels have flashed through the brain's maze of electrochemical circuits with speed so dazzling that the computer's owner himself is unaware of the brilliant series of algebraic assessments that led him to express a hunch or "gut feeling."

To ignore this highly sophisticated machine is a folly—akin to that of the owners of a computer, programmed to play the stock market, who refused to believe the thing when it resolutely refused to buy a single stock. "Computer," they said to it, "there must be something you want to buy." It thought again, and still said no. "Computer," they sadly observed, "you must have made a mistake somewhere. We're going to have to override you." The market promptly went into a flat spin, vindicating the computer and mortifying its masters.

The lesson, which applies to millionaires and nonmillionaires alike, is to heed your computer; it will even obligingly provide extra warnings—not flashing lights, but physical symptoms (a tightening sensation in the stomach, tingling of the scalp, pulsations in the stomach, commotions in the bowels). These messages from inner space mean that your computer has evaluated whatever asininity you propose to undertake and found it bad.

The warnings seldom come from the conscience. Only the moral have moral qualms—the immoral or amoral, such as the denizens of Richard Nixon's White House, believed self-righteously that their ends (self-evidently right) justified their means. There's no argument on this point: the virtuous course (such as not stabbing some unsuspecting partner between the clavicles) is always clear, and virtue should always be pursued, even if it costs money. After all, few sensations are more pleasant or enduring than the odor of true sanctity: it's worth every penny. As a bonus, bear in mind that although virtue is not its own reward, the wages of sin are sometimes death. Grave misdemeanors frequently have grave consequences. For every Rockefeller I who escapes scot-free with his moral crimes, there is a Krupp III who reaps the harvest of his ancestor's misdeeds. Admittedly, finding a fault-free tycoon appears to be only slightly easier than hunting through a haystack for that recalcitrant needle.

Two separate inquiries into the iniquities of wealth (*The Rich and the Super-Rich* and *America, Inc.*) each came up with only one candidate for goodness and pelf combined: the same man, T. R. Danforth of Ralston Purina. All that this paucity of saintly candidates implies is that, in making money, as in most areas of achievement, idols have not feet, but entire lower limbs, of clay.

Goodness is a private matter. What is known about Danforth is not the whole picture; maybe the entirety would reinforce the good image, maybe not. The good that men do lives after them; the evil is oft interred with their bones. If evil, or quasi evil, does litter your path, however, the same rule applies as to any other vice: don't carry it to excess. If you must cheat somebody, for instance, don't try to cheat the same man or men again; next time around, they may be ready.

It pays, in any event, to be careful whom you pick to cheat, outbargain, or battle with. Remember the natural law that money flows upward from the weak to the strong, from the many to the few, from the poor to the rich. It is flying in the face of nature to tangle with a richer tycoon. (A contest with a corporation, as noted in this book time and time again, is a different matter. The odds are on David's side because, in all probability, he is both richer and craftier than the paid servants of Goliath.) The plain millionaire who seeks advantage from dealing with a fancy multimillionaire needs a large insurance policy.

Not only does the richer man have more resources; the chances are that he arrived at his higher status by deploying greater wiliness and garnering greater bargaining skills along his path. Anyway, he has an inherent advantage. By definition, the sum at stake is more important to the smaller man, which makes him more eager to consummate the deal. In that overeagerness, he is apt to overpay. Far better to stay on the top side.

Keeping the top slice is also highly advisable. Common Millionaires derive their wealth from equity interests. Dilution of that equity—that is, reducing the proportion of profits or assets to which it is entitled—is only justified if compensated for by a nourishing increase in capital worth. But the most tempting form of dilution is rarely justified, and that's the ancient game of sending bad money after good. If a venture blasts off rapidly and then requires further infusion of capital, the sound course is to raise the money from some friendly neighborhood banker. The return on equity must fall sharply if the millionaire dips into his own resources. Cutting others in on the game is always to be encouraged so long as that first or top slice grows thicker and fatter as a result.

If you are predominantly interested in the money rather than the business, moreover, it makes no sense to maintain any stake higher than respectability demands. You can reduce a controlling interest to 20 percent before anybody smells either a rat or a sinking ship. A high stock rating should always be cashed in by a cash addict, for the simple reason that what goes soaring up must come crashing down, and always does: witness the awful October of 1987.

Recognition of that law of financial gravity demands the virtue of humility, which is the essential element in goodness—and one that goes against the driving urge. So the driven man should propel himself to as lofty a height as possible while the propulsion works; he can then more easily withstand a terrible fall. The megalomaniac John H. Patterson of National Cash Register was a loony who insisted on his minions chewing each mouthful thirty-two times, who closed down his Dayton plants entirely to teach the city fathers a lesson, and who absented himself for two years in Europe—all without destroying the cash-generating power of a mighty business. His successors, with not a smidgen of mania between them, did more harm by the mistakes in computery and product development that wiped out NCR's profits in 1972: the moral is that mad inspiration beats dull honesty every time.

For Patterson was also a notable breaker of laws. It's easier for the rich and powerful to offend against statute, not only because the legal authorities are more reluctant to proceed against plutocrats than pickpockets, but also because the rich, and the rich company, can afford rich lawyers, and because the laws the wealthy break are often so complex that it takes squads of lawyers several years to work their way through the maze (a tangle made more impenetrable still by the tendency of the rich and their legal eagles to complicate the simplest transactions).

After Calouste Gulbenkian's 5 percent deal with his partners in Iraq's oil fields had been rewritten, one of the lawyers remarked that these contracts could never be the subject of litigation, because nobody would ever be able to understand them. The labyrinth in which financial minotaurs lie in wait for their prey similarly appeals to the labyrinthine mind and is the final defense of the ungodly. But some brave Theseus will wend his way through in the end, and it is a matter of historical fact that, by and large, the criminal millionaire (or, for that matter, the millionaire criminal), although he may die in luxury and honors, often does suffer some blow of fate that punishes his sins, like a Capone imprisoned for tax evasion and dying of syphilis, or a Buggsy Siegel bullet-holed by his pals.

This Calvinist-sounding truth has morals as well as morality on its side. He who already has millions no longer has any excuse for immorality: even the usual badness. He can afford to be good, which doesn't only mean donating wealth to charity, still less to tax-dodging charitable foundations. It means following strict standards of decency—and often that demands the hardest self-sacrifice of all, which is for the human leopard to change his spots.

One tycoon, caught in a mess of deceitful accounting by his bright young men, was bewailing his bad luck to a business associate—such a mess had entangled him before, he moaned, referring to a well-known incident a few years back in which he had been widely castigated as a crook. His version of the old story utterly convinced his hearer; as the tycoon reasonably argued, he was now over sixty and very rich—why on earth would he have engaged in any personal skulduggery?

The true answer was simple: he did, just because he didn't need to. The honest crook, so to speak, lies and cheats because he must, and at the time (let alone in hindsight) can't tell the difference between fact and fiction. In this case, not only had the tycoon in the first place been guilty as charged (or not charged—the police stayed clear) but was reenacting a very similar scenario at the time of his apologia.

Many leopards need a professional spot changer or watcher in their employ. As a generalization, a master is only as good as his best servant; the quality of a man's nearest and dearest associate is an excellent guide to his own true stature. If the deputy, partner, or sidekick is made of clay, so, more often than not, are the master's feet.

This is an uncommonly useful fact; so long as the master can maintain objectivity about those around him, he can, by applying this test, derive an objective judgment about himself. Unfortunately, the self-deceptive mechanism comes into play. Surrounded by ninnies, the maestro convinces himself that his staff is made up of every genius known to the business world. They naturally demonstrate that true and fine talent by hanging on to his every word and behest.

The ultra-rich can be excused for living in a dream world, since so much of their life story is in itself of dreamlike quality. The billionaire H. L. Hunt once said, "There are times when I wish I would wake up stone broke. It would be a great adventure to see how good I was, to see if I could create lots of wealth again." This, of course, was wishful thinking of the wooliest kind; the process that took him from fifty bucks in 1921 to a couple of billion three decades later proved nothing about his "goodness" in any context other than oil.

But the story, like all get-rich tales, is a true adventure, and a true-life one. You could excuse the old cuss for saying, in effect, that he wanted to live so rewarding a life all over again. And, in his use of the word *good*, he put his oil-stained finger on a vital clue: that, in addition to human decency, the rich can afford high professional standards.

By and large, the millionaire has some professional talent that is incomparably superior to those of his fellows. This talent is the horse he rides to the winning post. To develop this star talent fully, and surround it with the most able supporting cast money can buy, is a relatively dignified pastime, and one that has the concomitant virtue of defending a man's fortune. It's not asking much to demand that the man be good at his job and insist that others be equally proficient at theirs.

In this he will differ from one not untypical monster who, in addition to forcing an audience of 140 to listen to a two-day masterly monologue, would sabotage anybody else's ideas as soon as he heard about them—in order to prove that he was indispensable. Very few fortune makers are, but even those who are possessed of rare genius must recognize that, if man doesn't dispense with them, God certainly will—at least from this earth.

Until that event, certain moral precepts will guide the feet more safely to their destination, material as well as spiritual. If you are happy being private, count your blessings, not your hypothetical unmade public millions. If you can't manage by yourself, buy somebody who can. If you've made money by fooling all of the people, stop it before some of them find out. If you're telling lies to others, tell the truth to yourself. If you succeed by doing less badly than others, don't kid yourself that you've triumphed by doing much better. If you must buy other businesses, run the many as carefully as the few or the one. If you maintain a complex structure for tax, divorce, or other reasons, make sure that at least you understand it. If you diversify, keep your eye on the real ball and the main chance. If you must bet, pick certainties. If you back others, don't pick a simulacrum of your younger self, or anybody else, if your choice is not governed by expertise and experience.

If you borrow, borrow big—and with security. If you lend, lend proportionately small—and with double security. If you work for a company, remember that feathering the corporate nest is the honest way of feathering your own. If dealing, don't steal. If you start small, preserve your little virtues. If you put your hand in the public purse, do so legitimately; graft is criminal. If you are lucky, light a candle. If you are dealing with a fat corporation, light two candles.

If you are paying too much tax, change your tax adviser. If you have an invention, sell it reluctantly—and dearly. If you are selling, don't cheat. If you can make things better, go on doing it. If you know what people want, give it to them. If your personal life is complex, put plenty in the piggy bank: two Humble Oil beneficiaries, Mrs. Cecil Blaffer Hudson and Bobo Rockefeller, collected nearly $13 million between them as they competed for the then world-record divorce settlement.

All these are laws of the obvious. But making gigantic fortunes is mostly nothing but the exploitation of the obvious—an obvious so glaring that nobody else has noticed, or known how to exploit. The discovery must be obvious because, unless the truth is large, it will never yield the gains that will add up to a net worth of suitable size. Countless big fortunes have arisen through standing self-evident propositions, received truths, on their heads—including the ancient saw "If your idea's so good, why isn't anybody else doing it?"

The answer is that one reason why the idea is so good is exactly because nobody else has caught on. What the financially blind use as an excuse for their lack of vision, the long-sighted employ as a radio telescope. There are, true, examples of fortunes made by indulging in some general, obvious passion. All that proves is that making money proves nothing.

That fact adds to the questions asked down the centuries by religious leaders and philosophers, by political thinkers such as Veblen and Marx, questions that will never go away, because they have no answer. To put them at their simplest, these permanent doubts, partly moral, partly rational, partly egalitarian, can be expressed in one huge query: Why does one man possess so much, while another has so little?

In a world where the inequalities of wealth are increasing, not only between North and South, but among the citizens of the prosperous industrialized countries north of the equator, it's strange to find concern over these inequalities lessening. More extraordinary still, the drift of politics toward conservatism in the Reagan era brought with it the interesting theory that, for the general good, and not just for their own, the rich should be made richer still.

The Reagan tax reforms, applauded by both parties in Congress, turned America's back on the long-standing tradition that from him to whom much is given, more should be taken. True, millionaires have been adept at avoiding taxation in life and death. True, the reforms remove or reduce a few of the devices that have helped the rich in their self-appointed task. But every economical means will be used to defer and deter a maximum 28 percent tax bite—and with just as much enthusiasm as when the rate was 60 percent.

Anybody who doesn't believe that doesn't know his millionaires. It must follow that, as the unstoppable engine of the consumer economy continues to expand the number of millionaires, the new methods of multiplication will increase the level of absolute wealth and new generations of heirs will come into possession of more money than they can conveniently spend. The wide and far-reaching acceptance of this modified plutocracy is evident: thus the American citizen has apparently consented to an electoral system that, because of the high cost and crucial impact of television time, has made political office available mostly to the rich and those backed by the rich.

The acquiescence could be involuntary, but equally the democratization of wealth could have encouraged a wide belief in its availability to all—and with some reason. Thus, the way in which real estate prices have been forced up by big money seeking a safe and growing home has inevitably raised the value of properties owned by small money. People who bought their own apartments in Manhattan many years ago at what seemed reasonable prices have become millionaires by virtue of that one purchase alone—and that story has been repeated over and over in every capital city where people own the roofs over their heads.

There are countless other ways in which the millions of the few spill over and trickle down into the pockets of the many. Yet trickling down will never accomplish enough to reduce the enormous overhang of private riches. Those new fortunes are less likely than those of Ford, the sugar king Havemeyer, the railroad magnates, the Morgans, and the tribe of the robber barons to be whittled away by time and error—and by the large-scale philanthropy to which many of the conspicuous rich were driven by the temper of the times. The prospect looms of endless family trusts, innumerable offshore companies in tax havens, countless piles of sterile wealth remorselessly compounding.

Philanthropy should be some of the answer, although a proliferation of foundations, each pursuing some different hobbyhorse of the founder, isn't especially attractive. How the wealth is used is not an issue that can safely be left only to the wealthy. Any sensible person would, of course, want to do more with his possessions than create rich heirs, but, as this book has shown, that kind of sense has very little to do with making or keeping millions.

The specter of private affluence and public squalor was raised most eloquently by John Kenneth Galbraith in *The Affluent Society* in 1958. The ghost still rides. The dozen years to 1987 were wonderful for the affluent but not for the public services of those who were in squalor in 1974, when I first studied the Common Millionaire. The level of what is thought of as squalor has risen, but that of affluence has risen more. The widening of the gap between the rich and the poor is worrying, not solely on moral grounds, but because of its implications for the stability and cohesion of society.

The concrete expression of the consequences is the protected compound behind whose walls, uniformed guards, and electronic security devices the rich shelter from their fellow citizens like so many besieged tyrants of Renaissance Italy. There is indeed a parallel between the situation of the modern rich and that of their Renaissance predecessors. Like the latter, the Common Millionaires can accumulate grand houses, patronize art, give lavish entertainments, build empires; but like

369

the palazzi of the Renaissance princes, the Common Millionaires' houses are built on the sands of the society in which they live.

Will the sands shift? The fallacy of redistribution has long been exposed. Taking from the rich to give to the poor has been a popular legend ever since Robin Hood. But if all the assets in the possession of the Forbes 400 could be realized and divided (which they could not), the redistribution wouldn't amount to $1,000 per head of the U.S. population. True, for the families at the bottom of the economic pile, $1,000 a head would spell the difference between despair and hope, but that raises a quite different issue.

Undernourished children, unemployed parents, untreated disease, uninhabitable housing, and the other social wrongs are as evil in a poor society as in a rich. The possessors of riches, however, have self-interest at stake. The better the condition of society at large, the more likely they are to continue enjoying the fruits of their wealth. They stand to gain most from insisting that society give priority, not to the interests of the few, but to the needs of the many. The few, after all, can look after themselves; and this book has shown conclusively that they do.

The social sands probably will shift back toward the side of the underprivileged; they always do. Whether the wealthy will assist the shift, though, is more doubtful. It shouldn't be, of course. But there are few social or economic pressures on the rich to conform to the social and economic truth that the American fabric is indivisible. These last twenty years have been palmy days for the rich, the palmiest since before the Great Depression, the time when the social fabric tore apart, when many of the rich fell through the rents, and when society turned against the well-to-do.

The wheel has turned again. But because the unanswerable questions of ownership, inheritance, control, and accountability have never been answered (and by definition never can be), society has stayed uneasily divided between fascination by fortunes and guilty resentment of the rich. In the 1980s, without question, the balance of that division swung still further toward the fortunate. But any student of the wealthy, and of the means by which they acquired their wealth, must return to that lack of rational relationship between the riches of the Common Millionaires and their actual achievements.

Whichever way the question is viewed, the one is wildly disproportionate to the other. This statement of fact carries inevitable connotations of disapproval. It is also the reason (as a few of the rich have had the grace to recognize) behind the powerful truth that "From him to whom much is given, much shall be required." For it is equally true that, to him to whom much is given, too much is given.

370

This partly answers Adolf Berle's rhetorical question: What part of the "quality of wealth" can be called private? As the preceding chapters have shown, the forces of the modern economy, far from institutionalizing great wealth, have been an engine for multiplying the quantities in private hands and the number of those hands. One statistic raises a corner of the curtain behind which most private wealth is cloaked by its very privacy. In spring 1987, before the crash, the public flotation of a small, obscure company created the *six-hundredth* British millionaire to arise through the Unlisted Securities Market.

The market, a branch of the main London stock exchange, had been created only a few years back to ease the passage of private companies into semipublic ownership. *Semi* is *le mot juste*. In many cases, the public subscribed for only a fifth or less of the stock. The multiplying magic described earlier in these pages then set to work to make the proprietors' holdings worth, on paper, at least seven figures— and repeated the trick 600 times.

Set that number in the context of the far more fertile economies of the United States, Japan, West Germany, and so on, and you catch a glimpse of the probable size of this army of the new rich, the Common Millionaires. There's no doubt here of the answer to Berle's question. This is private wealth, privately created, privately multiplied, privately controlled, to be privately disbursed and disposed as the private owners decide. In the terms in which he posed the question, which were those of economic power, this wealth is trivial. But that relative triviality is also, perhaps surprisingly, true of the billionaires and the other super-rich who have been featured in this book.

Even Sam Walton's $4.5 billion represented only an infinitesimal percentage of the American domestic product and far less of total American wealth. Neither he, nor John Kluge, nor H. Ross Perot, nor anybody else discussed in this book—not even Rupert Murdoch, with his media interests circling the globe—can make or break industries and governments in Rockefeller or Morgan style. The Common Billionaires and Millionaires can, however, make or break *companies*—including businesses of international spread, on which whole communities and hundreds of thousands of individuals may depend for their livings and futures. The malefactors of great wealth have resurfaced on this smaller, but still politically and economically vital stage of the corporate economy.

The issue of how merger and acquisition activity can be controlled and contained (which was raised in virulent form by the Boesky scandals) is also an issue of private wealth. Rich families and rich individuals were the powerhouses behind the corporate raiding and the spectacular megadeals that destabilized the American corporate economy—and eventually Wall Street—in the mid-1980s. No less than the Boesky scandals and the megapay of corporate executives, they were symptoms of a system running to excess. Left to themselves, the holders of private wealth are no more likely to correct the excesses than big-time corporate managers are to crack down on their own excessive salaries, ludicrously risk-free capital gains, and unearned payoffs.

Modern American democracy is founded on the principle that what the private sector cannot or will not do for itself, the public, as represented through the government, must do instead. The problem is that, in the Age of the Common Millionaire, the common politician is cut from the same cloth. The interests of the legislator and the wealthy individual may well start near to each other, if not wholly intertwined. They are cemented by the politician's need for the campaign contributions and continuing support of the rich. When the tribunes of the poor speak with the same tongue as the defenders of wealth and privilege, whose interests will receive priority?

For a long time, blind eyes have been turned to latent problems— such as the domination of the media in the United States by a few wealthy families, many ruling over local monopolies—that threaten abuse. If the media abuses have mostly been mild by Hearst standards (a loss in quality, lack of variety, political uniformity), that could be the result less of proprietorial integrity and more of circumspection. The specter of public control always hangs over industries as public as newspapers and broadcasting, and the editorial staff within the empires represent some kind of protection (if inadequate) for the rights of free and fair opinion and information.

The need for public control of private business excess, for effective rules governing corporate self-enrichment and the fate of companies, is no less important. A great and greater good stands to be preserved. The Common Millionaires have sprung from a richness in society itself, in its profusion of new tastes, new technologies, and new opportunities, that has given men and women a potential, at work and at leisure, to improve their own fortunes and the lot of humankind to an extent that was once the stuff of dreams. On balance, the gains far outweigh any inherent disadvantages in the accompanying profusion of private fortunes. The series of stock-market earthquakes that shook the world in the fall of 1987, coming so soon after the second great crash of the 1970s, may be the last warning—and stopping that balance between the advantages and drawbacks of great personal riches from tipping too far must be still more desirable for the wealthy than for the common man, who is both the ultimate beneficiary and the ultimate source of the Age of the Common Millionaire.

ACKNOWLEDGMENTS

Every writer on the rich rests on the researches and writings of others, and with this book I rest in part on my own previous labors. Those who assisted me so nobly when I first tackled the subject in the early 1970s still have my gratitude—and my hope that they have enriched themselves as much propr·tionately in the intervening period as the heroes (or villains) of these pages.

Today the seam of information about millionaires and billionaires is much thicker, as well as more golden. For that, one contribution stands out above all others: the Forbes 400. It is more than an extraordinary exercise in reporting. Its pithy writing and vivid use of quotes make the 400 the most enjoyable work of reference I know. I am very grateful to the publishers for its existence and for their kindness in allowing me to make such liberal use of the 400.

Business Week, Fortune, and *Time,* although not dedicated to chronicling the rich, do so with their characteristic skill and vitality. To them, too, I owe a debt of gratitude, especially to *Business Week* for its annual survey of executive reward (fair and, all too often, awfully unfair, except to the executives themselves). The standard of reporting on the American rich leaves the European press shamefully far behind—and the European rich happily concealed in their much greater privacy.

My greatest debt, however, is owed to the friends and colleagues who have helped me through the writing of my own book: my publisher, Truman Talley, has made his invariably courtly but decisive contribution; and I must mention in particular June Barber for her unfailing help in many ways. My sister Jacqueline Edelman helped with the typing, as did Francesca Flowers: to them my gratitude. I am less grateful to the foreign exchanges whose movements kept on upsetting the money translations in these pages. The dollar-pound conversion used—£1 equals $1.50—now looks positively antediluvian, but who knows?

My final vote of thanks, however, must go to those without whom this book could certainly not have been written: the rich themselves.

INDEX

375

INDEX

Learning Resource Center
Santa Fe Community College
Santa Fe, New Mexico
(505) 471-8200